Daily Modernism

Daily Modernism

The Literary Diaries of Virginia Woolf, Antonia White, Elizabeth Smart, and Anaïs Nin

ELIZABETH PODNIEKS

McGill-Queen's University Press
Montreal & Kingston · London · Ithaca

© McGill-Queen's University Press 2000
ISBN 0-7735-2021-X

Legal deposit second quarter 2000
Bibliothèque nationale du Québec

Printed in Canada on acid-free paper

This book has been published with the help of a grant
from the Humanities and Social Sciences Federation of
Canada, using funds provided by the Social Sciences
and Humanities Research Council of Canada.

McGill-Queen's University Press acknowledges the
financial support of the Government of Canada through
the Book Publishing Industry Development Program
(BPIDP) for our publishing activities. We also acknowledge the support of the Canada Council for the Arts for
our publishing program.

Canadian Cataloguing in Publication Data

Podnieks, Elizabeth, 1964–
    Daily modernism: the literary diaries of Virginia Woolf,
    Antonia White, Elizabeth Smart, and Anaïs Nin

    Includes bibliographical references and index.
    ISBN 0-7735-2021-X

    1. Women authors, English—20th century—Diaries.
    2. Women authors, American—20th century—Diaries.
    3. Women authors, Canadian—20th century—Diaries.
    1. Title.

PR908.P58 2000   828'.91203   C99-900977-X

This book was typeset by True to Type in 10/12 Sabon.

Some of the material included in this book has been
drawn from previously published articles, and the
author would like to thank the publishers for permis-
sion to use it here: "The Theatre of *Incest* – Enacting
Artaud, Mirbeau, and Rimbaud in the *Diary* of Anaïs
Nin," *Anaïs: An International Journal* 13 (1995):
39–51; "'Keep out / Keep out / Your snooting snout':
The Irresistible Diaries of Elizabeth Smart," *A / B: Auto
/ Biography Studies* 11, no. 1 (spring 1996): 58–81;
"Five Days in L.A.: Searching for Nin; (Re-)searching
Her Diary," in *Anaïs Nin: A Book of Mirrors*, ed. Paul
Herron (Huntington Woods, Mich.: Sky Blue Press,
1996), 199–216; "'OO – I have been well loved': Eliza-
beth Smart and the Three Musketeers," *Deus Loci: The
Lawrence Durrell Journal*, no. 4 (1995–96): 41–61.

For my mother,
Elizabeth Macdonald Podnieks,

and my grandmother,
Emily Podnieks

Contents

Acknowledgments

Although much of this work draws on the published diaries of Virginia Woolf, Antonia White, Elizabeth Smart, and Anaïs Nin, a crucial part of it was dependent on my being able to examine the original manuscripts. I funded my own trips to Woolf's archive, but I would like to thank the University of Toronto for a grant which made possible my travels to the archives of White, Smart, and Nin.

The Woolf diaries are in the Henry W. and Albert A. Berg Collection at the New York Public Library. The collection has been preserved on microfilm, but I am grateful to Lisa Browar, acting curator of the Berg Collection, for giving me the special permission necessary to see the holograph diaries. I also thank the librarians at the British Library for their assistance

The White diaries are in the possession of White's elder daughter, Susan Chitty and her husband, Thomas Chitty, at their home in Sussex, England. They generously invited me to their home so that I could examine the diary manuscripts, and I thank them for their hospitality, as well as for their openness in talking about and sharing the work of Antonia White.

The Smart diaries are housed in the Elizabeth Smart Fonds at the National Library of Canada in Ottawa. I would like to thank Lorna Knight, the curator of the collection, for her assistance, not only in having the materials waiting for me upon my arrival at the library but also for her knowledge of the collection, her constant readiness to help me find particular volumes, and her incredibly fast photocopying of selected items.

Nin's diaries are in the Anaïs Nin Special Collection at the University of California at Los Angeles. I am grateful to the curator, Anne Caiger, for accommodating my visit to the library, as well as to librarian Octavio Olivera. And I would like to thank Rupert Pole, the executor of Nin's estate, for giving me permission to use the collection. During my time in Los Angeles, Mr Pole was most kind in providing a tour of the home that he had had built for Nin. He readily answered all of my questions about her, and his reminiscences about their life together were a pleasure to listen to.

Thanks are also due to David and Judy Gascoyne. Their hospitality at their home on the Isle of Wight was most appreciated, as were the many biographical connections and stories which they provided about White, Smart, and Nin.

Closer to home, I am in debt to Crystal Verduyn, professor of English at Trent University, and Heather Murray, Mark Levene, and Michael Sidnell, professors of English at the University of Toronto. They read the manuscript in its earlier stages as a doctoral dissertation and offered valuable criticisms which I took into account during my revisions. Most significantly, I would like to thank Professor Rosemary Sullivan, who served as my doctoral supervisor at the University of Toronto. This work could not have been completed were it not for the attention she paid to it. I am privileged to have been able to work with such an inspiring, insightful, and generous writer.

Thanks are also due to both the internal and the external readers for McGill-Queen's University Press, as well as to the readers for the Humanities and Social Sciences Federation of Canada. I found their comments crucial as I made the final revisions to the manuscript. My editors at McGill-Queen's deserve my greatest thanks, especially Peter Blaney for his initial encouragement; Philip J. Cercone, who oversaw the manuscript in its middle stages; and Aurèle Parisien, whose unfailing support and guidance led to the finished product. Elizabeth Hulse, my copy editor, has my gratitude for her thorough and painstaking efforts in shaping the book into its present form.

Finally, I would like to thank my mother, Elizabeth Podnieks, and my husband, Ian Smith, for everything.

Abbreviations

A	Smart, *Autobiographies*
D	Nin, *The Diary of Anaïs Nin*
	White, *Antonia White Diaries*
	Woolf, *The Diary of Virginia Woolf*
ED	Nin, *The Early Diary of Anaïs Nin*
ESF	Elizabeth Smart Fonds, National Library of Canada
F	Nin, *Fire*
HF	White, *The Hound and the Falcon*
HJ	Nin, *Henry and June*
I	Nin, *Incest*
ITM	Smart, *In the Meantime*
NS	Smart, *Necessary Secrets*
PA	Woolf, *A Passionate Apprentice*
VWC	Alice Van Wart Collection of Elizabeth Smart Papers, National Library of Canada

Daily Modernism
The Literary Diaries of Virginia Woolf, Antonia White,
Elizabeth Smart, and Anaïs Nin

Introduction

As a teenager I often wore a perfume called "Anaïs Anaïs." I was intrigued by the name on the bottle as much as by the scent inside. I had no idea what the words meant, and it was only years later that I discovered the perfume had been named after a woman, Anaïs Nin. I was first introduced to her and her diaries in the mid-1980s, in an undergraduate course on twentieth-century American literature. I had been keeping a diary of my own for over a decade and treasured it as a manuscript of sorts, for I was writing it with a certain amount of literary intention. I had never, however, seen a diary on a course syllabus – that is, one that would be studied as a literary text in itself rather than as a source of biographical information about a famous author, or as the raw material from which a writer's "real" art had sprung. The effect of analyzing Nin's use of images, symbols, allusions, and recurring themes to deliver her supposedly private thoughts and experiences was that I realized I was reading something new, and reading in a new way.

My excitement at discovering this text was dampened by some classroom discussion which castigated Nin for being a confessional poseur, for giving us a diary which was, after all, a fake – crafted, revised, and edited for the benefit of her audience. By virtue of being examined as literature, the diary could not also, or still, be a genuine diary. I determined to address the issue of what makes a diary authentic and, in the face of such criticisms, to find a way to recoup a respectable position for Nin as a life writer. This mission was inspired by the fact that I considered myself a real diarist although I too had all along been crafting my journal as a "work."

Until recently, the diary genre has received limited critical attention. As will be shown in chapter 1, studies of life writing have tended to focus on autobiography, and those that mention the diary often cursorily dismiss it, or marginalize it as a "sub" or "lesser" form of autobiography "proper." Felicity A. Nussbaum explains this historical neglect: "Diaries often remain unpublished documents; their length may make reading tedious and difficult; they lack the formal cohesiveness that lends itself to New Critical readings; and, despite their articulation of human chronology, diaries are not classic realist texts."[1] Judy Nolte Lensink points out that diaries have traditionally been considered valuable only for their content: for what they reveal about the character of the diarist, and the social and historical period in which she or he lived. Lensink observes that interest obtains only when the diarist is "extraordinarily established in literature."[2]

Though there are studies specifically of the diary, they have been historically few and far between. Many of these – beginning with Arthur Ponsonby's *English Diaries* (1923) and *More English Diaries* (1927) – tend to discriminate between "pure" and "false" diaries and to privilege those written by men. Tracing a diaristic tradition through its paternal lineage, they largely ignore the copious numbers of diaries written by women. But beginning in the nineteen seventies and eighties and flourishing in the nineties, feminist revisionism of literary history has produced a plethora of texts devoted to establishing, retracing, or resurrecting a female tradition of diary writing.

The many studies that apply traditional theoretical distinctions which value "pure" diaries against consciously – and thus "insincerely" – produced ones are inappropriate and are based on reductive assumptions about what a diary *should* be, rather than on what it more often *is*. The debate over the status of the diary is polarized by scholars such as Arthur Ponsonby, who stresses that it has nothing to do with art,[3] and those such as Lawrence Rosenwald, who contends that it has everything to with art.[4] The diary is either a spontaneously uncrafted document or a carefully crafted text. The crisis that obtains is this: a definition of the diary as literature necessarily hinges on its conception as an aesthetic work; but if the diary in question is artistically motivated, it cannot be a diary per se.

Entering the debate, Robert A. Fothergill observes: "To endeavour to write well, to consider the formal structure of the book one is writing, to address oneself to a putative reader or think of publication, to edit or rewrite one's own entries – all these practices must appear to corrupt the pure spontaneity of utterance that should mark the 'true' diary."[5] In an attempt to reconcile this dichotomy, he contends that "the major achievements in diary-writing ... have been produced out of a conscious respect for the diary as a literary form."[6] It is precisely this assertion that informs my work here.

My focus on literary diarists stems from the belief that writers, with their heightened consciousness of literary form, are more aware of the aesthetic possibilities of the diary. Like Lynn Z. Bloom, I believe that "for a professional writer there are no private writings ... [O]nce a writer, like an actor, is audience-oriented, such considerations as telling a good story, getting the sounds and the rhythm right, supplying sufficient detail for another's understanding, can never be excluded. All writers know this; they attend to such matters through design and habit. A professional writer is never off duty."[7] Moreover, even non-literary diarists practise similar controlling strategies, and it is this characteristic that makes it necessary for us to reconsider the existence of a "true" diary in the first place.

The issue of genre authenticity is linked to the question of whether the self can ever be known and whether it can be rendered accurately, if at all, in words. Defining the self is one of the most problematic tasks facing theorists of life writing, one that today remains unresolved. Shirley Neuman lists four contradictory assumptions posited about the autobiographical self, assumptions that can equally be posited about the diaristic one: it is variously regarded "as individual and unified, as split, as textually produced, and as impossible of production."[8] These versions of selfhood reflect historical changes in critical thinking, from the individualism arising out of Renaissance humanism to current post-structural, linguistic, and psychoanalytic modes of analysis. How we interpret the self impacts on how we read a diary. Though definitions of selfhood remain problematic, theorists of life writing generally acknowledge that the self is always to some degree invented; the diary that contains this self is thus at least partially fictive.

The particular selves in which I am interested here are women's. The undergraduate course referred to earlier offered about ten authors, but Nin was the only woman. Whereas the class was reading novels by the men, it was reading her diary, not her novels. I gleaned from this fact that women might be especially associated with the diary form, a notion that I kept in mind as I approached my later investigations of the diary as a significant literary space for women authors. The ideological motivation driving my work is the one that informs Harriet Blodgett's *Centuries of Female Days: Englishwomen's Private Diaries*, in which she states: "I do not make a case for the diary as an inherently female form, but rather as a characteristic one."[9] Blodgett admits that, although "The serial form women use may parallel that of men's diaries; the topics, attitudes, and self-concepts expressed within the form and their manner of expression differ from men's because the interests, status, and lives of the diarists have done so."[10] These differences have rendered the diary not a more female than male space, but a more necessary and meaningful site for women than for men. The diary is a place where women can express themselves through narratives which conform to culturally scripted life stories, while at the same time they can rewrite them to reflect their subversive desires and experiences.

Having recorded my interest in literary diaries, I must explain my focus on the diary as a subversive literary space for women. While women writing in the early twentieth century certainly had access to the literary marketplace, it was restrictive in terms of accepting radical or taboo subject matter, especially that which was sexual. Consider the fate of Jean Rhys's novel *Voyage in the Dark*. One of the few modernist novels to depict an abortion, the work was rejected three times and published in 1934 only after Rhys agreed to change the ending. Whereas in the original version, protagonist Anna Morgan died from a botched abortion, in the sanitized reworking she survived. Despite this revision, the novel, like all of Rhys's work about the crude underside of women's urban lives, was not a success. By 1939 all her books had gone out of print, and Rhys was relegated to obscurity.

Further examples support the idea that the marketplace was a fairly conservative one. Shari Benstock discusses how Gertrude Stein created a secret language in order to inscribe lesbian experience in her public texts. Benstock explains: "The question of audience suggests again the problem of style, which may act as a protective covering for that which might otherwise be censored."[11] Bonnie Kime Scott shows how Djuna Barnes threw a similar kind of "protective covering" over her lesbian novel *Ladies Almanack* (1928): "Privately published, and sold largely by her friends in the streets of Paris, this work escaped the censors by its very mode of production."[12] Like Stein's coded language and Barnes's private press, women's diaries offer "protective" modes and sites of production: the supposedly private nature of the form allows writers to express themselves freely without the immediate fear of censorship.

One of the most famous cases of modern censorship was the banning in 1928 of Radclyffe Hall's lesbian novel *The Well of Loneliness*. Noting how writers such as Barnes, Rebecca West, and Virginia Woolf defended the book, Scott rightly concludes that "we can appreciate the importance of sexuality as a subject matter for modernism."[13] Sexuality is a subject matter of importance for women's modernist diaries as well. Many diaries explore lesbian desire, in addition to themes and preoccupations that would be considered equally taboo, such as masturbatory fantasies, adulterous passions, incest, and bad mothering. It is my contention that many women wrote their diaries by keeping up a pretence that they were private, while intending them to be published at a later date. In this way they could communicate to an audience thoughts and feelings that were too personal or controversial to be revealed through their fiction, but which they wanted, and needed, to convey. The private-diary-as-public-text proves the perfect vehicle by which women can deliver their own versions of themselves. As Suzanne Bunkers acknowledges in "What Do Women *Really* Mean? Thoughts on Women's Diaries and Lives," "I've recognized that I write in my own journal as one way of shaping the story of my life ... I have a large stake in telling my story as I want it told."[14]

Women's inscriptions of taboo experiences, coupled with their "shaping" of stories within diaries intended for audiences, underscore my argument that women's diaries are subversive spaces. To appreciate this point further, we can return to Scott, who notes that, in the wake of *The Well of Loneliness*, Woolf, West, and Barnes "had become accomplished literary strategists ... They coped with legal structures to work around the censor, while simultaneously putting into question his authority. They anticipated different audiences, providing texts that could be read more or less personally. Genre structures also yielded to multiplication and combination, suitable to the complex perspectives pursued."[15] Scott's study focuses on the novels, stories, and essays of Woolf, West, and Barnes; however, issues of censorship, male authority, audience, personality, genre, and multiple perspectives inform the diaries of many modernist women, Woolf's among them. Diarists, too, are often "accomplished literary strategists."

Scott's comment that "Genre structures also yielded to multiplication and combination" has particular resonance for the study of the diary genre. Distinctions between the supposedly private text of the diary and public texts such as the autobiography and the novel are in fact blurred. Lensink remarks that it is the "gender-blindness of the current literary criteria that disregard diaries." She says that we must "overcome our fear of new forms when faced with dusty, scribbled narratives"; only then can we "expand the boundaries of our reading and thinking."[16] One scholar who has expanded these boundaries is Marlene Kadar; in *Essays on Life Writing: From Genre to Critical Practice*, she redirects attention to the more inclusive term "life writing." In her introductory essay she outlines her preference for a breaking down of boundaries between fiction and non-fiction, and between fiction and autobiography in particular. Kadar encourages us to view autobiography "as a continuum that spreads unevenly and in combined forms from the so-called least fictive narration to the most fictive." She defines life writing in this general way: "Life writing comprises texts that are written by an author who does not continuously write about someone else, and who also does not pretend to be absent from the [black, brown, or white] text himself/herself."[17]

Kadar believes that "life writing includes many kinds of texts, both fictional and non-fictional"; she adds that the only reason we focus on non-fictional works is because "they appear more 'true to life.'" Commenting that this writing obviously presents the story of a life, she states: "But life writing includes more than just life stories, and it has the potential to cross genre boundaries and disciplines. The narratives within life writing are linked by their common thematic concern with a life, or the self, but in recent years they have come to share a more complex feature: a philosophical and linguistic imperative that comes first ... and then a sincere, probing disregard for genre and its rules, which has the effect of blending genres, creating new genres."[18] Comparing the concept of genre to water, Kadar astutely observes: "Like water, genres assume the shape of the vessel that contains them. Also like water, genres tend to exhibit certain properties. But if you empty the containing vessels, the better to see what's inside, you are bound to be tricked. Like water, the shape of genres does not really exist, and their essence can never really be captured."[19] Drawing on this provocative theory, I will evaluate the diary not only as a genre in itself but also as one that is fluid, amoebically merging with the autobiography and the novel.

My selection of Virginia Woolf, Antonia White, Elizabeth Smart, and Anaïs Nin as subjects for this study was based on the fact that they are modernist novelists whose diaries have been published. To varying degrees, all four writers wanted, and in some cases planned and even oversaw, the publication of their diaries; and all four diaries in many ways resemble the respective writer's fiction. In addition to sharing some of the radical or taboo themes discussed above, the four diaries offer extensive insights into artistic process, painting a series of portraits of the women as they developed from inexperienced to professionally established writers. In this way the diaries are linked by the fact that they were begun when the writers were young and were kept until the women's deaths. In terms of cultural contexts, the four diarists lived and wrote in cities in which literary modernism flourished: Woolf and White were from London; Smart, a colonial Canadian, spent the greater part of her adult life in and around London; and Nin divided her time between Paris, New York, and Los Angeles. All four were white and from largely middle-class families.

Against this background is the fact that all four lived unconventional lives. In *Writing for Their Lives*, Gillian Hanscombe and Virginia L. Smyers stress, "Modernism, for its women, was not just a question of style; it was a way of life."[20] This observation has particular relevance for those who were diarists. Women who lived modernism as much as they wrote it necessarily inscribed that modernism within their diaries, for diaries are life texts. The modernisms inscribed are many. Taking my cue from scholars such as Scott, who argues for a consideration of modernism not as a "monological phenomenon" but as a pluralistic one,[21] I examine the diaries in light of several modernisms, including (post)-impressionism, Freudianism, allusion, symbolism, and surrealism. These respective strains of modernism are not limited to any one diary; for just as modernism is not a monolithic ideal, so the individual diaries here are not monolithic texts.

My selection of these particular diaries for study is thus based on the fact that they inscribe not only similar themes but also similar styles and techniques. While early on in my work I detected these parallels, after closer scrutiny I was surprised by the extensive degree to which the diarists resembled one another in terms of their experiences, concerns, and motivations in life writing. Because these connections become clear and meaningful only as my work unfolds, they will be discussed later in more appropriate contexts.

Despite their personal and creative affinities, Woolf, White, Smart, and Nin have been assigned by literary history to different positions along a continuum of literary value. This continuum is gender determined, an issue I discuss in detail in chapter 2. For now, it is enough to acknowledge that Woolf is one of the most well respected writers, and probably the most well respected female writer, of twentieth-century English literature. She is, for instance, the only woman canonized in *The Norton Anthology*'s list of "Heroic Age" modernist novelists. Nin resides at the other end of the spectrum. If Woolf is a major writer, Nin is a minor one, as her biographer Deirdre Bair attests: "I certainly agree with the view that Anaïs Nin will enter posterity as a minor writer." Bair does argue that Nin "must be judged a *major* minor writer," but her qualification offers only "minor" semantic compensation to Nin's reputation.[22] White and Smart lie closer to Nin, being relatively "minor" figures dependent upon feminist revisionism to (re-)establish their reputations.

The status of these writers is intricately linked to the genres in which they wrote. Woolf has been honoured first and foremost as a novelist, while her diaries have garnered scant attention as literary texts. Nin, on the other hand, has been recognized as a prolific diarist, but at the expense of becoming infamous and thus devalued. White and Smart are remembered as largely one-novel sensations: Smart for *By Grand Central Station I Sat Down and Wept*; White for *Frost in May*. Their diaries, like Woolf's, have inspired little scholarship.

Bradford K. Mudge emphasizes the connection between reputation and genre: "For as long as the distinction between literary and nonliterary remains operative, corresponding distinctions between major and minor follow logically. To rethink major and minor, one must rethink the ingrained systems of critical valuation which thus far have kept the concept of the 'literary' securely in place."[23] Mudge is echoing Kadar and Lensink, who posit that life writing has too often been relegated to "nonliterary status." Celeste Schenck similarly tells us, in "All of a Piece: Women's Poetry and Autobiography": "Traditionally viewed as purely aesthetic markers, genres have been highly politicized (not only gendered but also class biased and racially biased) in the long history of Western literary criticism, a phenomenon that has had enormous implications for the banishment of women writers (and other marginalized groups) from the canon." She rightly insists, "Genres ... are fairly drenched in ideologies," a view that makes sense given that genres are nothing but "cultural constructions."[24]

Mudge, like Schenck, Kadar, and Lensink, argues for "a critical practice whose system of valuation would be structured so as to accommodate diverse cultural artifacts – an obscure autobiographical fragment as well as the acclaimed *Three Guineas*." We must acknowledge "alternative modes of valuation, of other ways of mapping the 'literary' terrain so as to include the fragmentary remains of 'minor' women as well as the more polished 'works' of the 'highbrow' sisters."[25] The aim of my study is to do just that. Once we recognize that diaries deserve a place on the literary map, and once we trace their exclusion from this map to what Kathleen Blake calls "gender generics,"[26] we can begin to ignore the misleading signposts of "major" and "minor."

My analysis of the diaries is based on both the published volumes and the unpublished manuscripts. I must emphasize that my work on the original diaries focuses on their physical qualities, as my interest lies in showing how these women designed their diaries as books – in terms of title pages, prefaces, indexes, illustrations, and the like – and how elements such as handwriting, edited words and phrases, or torn-out pages contribute to an understanding of self-representation and self-preservation. I was to a large extent able to compare the texts of the published and original versions as well.

Woolf's diaries have for the most part been published in full.[27] *A Passionate Apprentice: The Early Journals of Virginia Woolf*, edited by Mitchell A. Leaska, complement the five-volume series *The Diary of Virginia Woolf*, edited by Anne Olivier Bell. Both editors have produced accurate transcriptions of Woolf's work, providing not only the main text but also her many marginal asides, notes, diagrams, added comments, spelling corrections, and the like. The diaries are part of the Henry W. aned Albert A. Berg Collection at the New York Public Library, with the exception of the seventh volume of the early journal, which is in the British Library. I have been able to examine all these manuscripts.

White's diaries were published in two volumes, edited by her elder daughter, Susan Chitty. In her introduction Chitty states that only one quarter of the original material was selected. She and her husband, Thomas Chitty, who hold the original diaries, generously invited me to their home in Sussex, England, to study the manuscripts. Susan Chitty informed me that she had tried to reproduce as many actual entries as possible, but that she drastically reduced the length of the entries, which were often repetitious and long-winded.

Smart's diaries are similarly presented in two volumes, *Necessary Secrets* and *On the Side of the Angels*, both edited by Alice Van Wart. Having seen the original diaries, which are housed at the National Library of Canada in Ottawa, I am able to note that Van Wart is a fairly scrupulous editor. Smart often wrote drafts of poems in her diary, in addition to shopping lists and other trivia. While Van Wart has excised these parts, she has not altered or deleted the main text of the diary.

Unlike the diaries of Woolf, White, and Smart, which have been transcribed from the originals to the published books in a fairly straightforward manner, those of Nin have not. Her diary has had a complicated and ongoing publishing history. Between 1966 and 1976 six volumes of *The Diary of Anaïs Nin* appeared, all heavily edited by Nin herself. Between 1978 and 1985 four *Early Diaries* and volume 7 of *The Diary* were published posthumously, but Nin had prepared their typescripts before she died. More recently, four unexpurgated volumes have come out: *Henry and June* (1986), *Incest* (1992), *Fire* (1995), and *Nearer the Moon* (1996). These were edited by Nin's common-law husband, Rupert Pole, by the in-house editor at Harcourt Brace Jovanovich, John Ferrone, and by Nin's personal editor, Gunther Stuhlmann. The original diaries are in the Anaïs Nin Special Collection at the University of California at Los Angeles. Those up to the date of the last unexpurgated published volume are available to qualified scholars. The later ones will be released over time, pending publication of further unexpurgated material.

My treatment of Nin's manuscripts differs from the approach taken with the others here in that, short of a few passages that were of special interest to me, I found the task of even attempting to compare the unedited and the various edited versions beyond the scope of my research. This is clearly the job of a thorough biographer, one recently undertaken by Deirdre Bair. The fact that Bair offers us a tome of more than five hundred pages and that it represents "less than a third" of her completed manuscript[28] underscores the intensity required to dissect Nin's published diary (appropriately once referred to as her "liary").[29]

At the time of my visit to Nin's archive, I was able to see the original volumes from 1914 through to 1934. I thus focus my analysis on the physical qualities of these diaries and for the most part on the texts found in the various published versions which correspond to the 1914–34 originals. I hold up this limited but representative selection from Nin's diary as an example of her diaristic modernism. I must note that, in working mainly with these evidently unreliable texts, I do not feel that I am undermining my scholarship, for as Bair writes, "One wonders ... why 'truth' is the primary criterion for judging diaries, especially those such as Nin's, which were intended from the beginning to represent one woman's view of herself and her life."[30] The versions of self which Nin constructed for her audience are what interest and inform my work.

One last general point that should be mentioned here concerns my method of documentation. Though I have in many instances taken material from the unpublished manuscripts, I have given page references to the published versions if the material is the same, for the simple reason that these latter versions are the ones readily available to other readers. Further, when quoting from these books, I have distinguished my ellipses from those of the editors by including them within square brackets; and I have indicated original misspellings with [*sic*].

My analysis is divided into seven chapters. In chapter 1, I establish a broad historical, critical, and theoretical base on which to examine the diary as a text distinct from, yet greatly similar to, the autobiography and the novel. In chapter 2, I consider the diary as a female form. Explaining why women turned to this space, I examine the roles of women in a patriarchal culture throughout history and then more specifically within the twentieth century. From here I move into a discussion of literary modernism in chapter 3, explaining how the diary can be evaluated as a modernist text, how female authors have inscribed modernist literary strategies within their diaries, and how these strategies are subversive.

Against this background, I draw on feminist theory, literary history, biography, and personal anecdote to discuss the specific diaries of Woolf, White, Smart, and Nin in chapters 4, 5, 6, and 7 respectively. Within each chapter, I evaluate the particular diary as a physical entity. I then establish that it has been crafted as a modernist work. Finally, I examine how and why the diary is used to construct various selves – selves which both inform and are informed by the life lived outside the text. In this way I hope to meet the challenge posed by scholars such as Mudge: to "rethink the ingrained systems of critical valuation which thus far have kept the concept of the 'literary' securely in place." Disrupting traditional concepts of "literary," I hope to show how the diaries of Woolf, White, Smart, and Nin are valid and valuable modernist achievements.

1 Blurring Boundaries: Mapping the Diary as Autobiography and Fiction

Diaries, as we traditionally think of them, are private records of a person's life. From the Heian period in Japan (794–1185), when women kept hidden "pillow books," to the twentieth century in the West, where girls keep their thoughts in books literally under lock and key, diaries have always seemed synonymous with secrecy. In contrast, though autobiographies are also texts about personal and private experiences, they, like novels, are written for a public audience. While this distinction may hold true in certain cases, a closer examination of diaries written by English-speaking literary women exposes the myth of genre specificity. The diary we conceive in theory does not necessarily exist in practice; rather, it can be read as autobiography, which itself can be seen as a kind of fiction.

I am not suggesting that each of these genres has no distinguishing features. Rather, I am proposing that the overlapping of elements such as plot, character, theme, and what Francis R. Hart recognizes as intention, form, and truth-telling calls for a reconsideration of the terms "diary," "autobiography," and "novel."[1] Redrawing traditional boundaries of categorization, I will establish a broad critical and theoretical range on which to map the diary as an aesthetic work. My aim is to arrive at a point where the diary is seen as distinct from, yet significantly similar to, the autobiography and the novel, in terms of textual production and character construction. To do so I will first situate it within a historical context, tracing the evolution of its own tradition.

The inception of such a tradition is best considered in light of the coining of the words "diary" and "journal." These terms are often interchangeable, despite attempts by various writers to make specific claims for each one. For instance, Arthur Ponsonby argues, "The word *Journal* should be reserved for the purely objective historical or scientific records, and the word *Diary* for the personal memoranda, notes and expressions of opinion."[2] Thomas Mallon accepts that the "two terms are in fact hopelessly muddled," but he suggests that "perhaps because of *journal's* links to the newspaper trade and *diary's* to *dear,* the latter seems more intimate than the former."[3] Felicity Nussbaum states that she is "using journal interchangeably" with diary, "though often diaries are considered to be the less elaborate form."[4] Judy Simons concurs that "the terms 'journal' and 'diary' themselves become interchangeable." As she explains, "Although strictly speaking 'diary' can be used as a generic term to cover both a daily record of engagements and more intimate writing, while 'journal' tends to refer more specifically to a personal chronicle, writers themselves do not always keep to such nice distinctions."[5]

The blurring of these terms can be traced to historical definitions which, though registering subtle differences, tend to conflate the two. According to the *Oxford English Dictionary*, the term "journal" preceded "diary." The original meaning of "journal," first recorded in 1355–56, was ecclesiastical: "A service-book containing the day-hours: = DIURNAL." The function shifted in 1540: "A daily record of commercial transactions, entered as they occur, in order to the keeping of accounts. a. In a general sense = DAY-BOOK." Shortly after, in 1552, the journal became associated with the journey: "A book containing notices concerning the daily stages of a route and other information for travellers; = ITINERARY." The year 1565 marked its appearance as "A record of public events or of a series of public transactions, noted down as they occur day by day or at successive dates, without historical discussion." The journal as specifically "private" was first described in 1610: "A record of events or matters of personal interest kept by any one for his own use, in which entries are made day by day, or as the events occur." What is particularly significant about this definition is the privileging of the journal's value over the diary. The entry says of the journal: "Now usually implying something more elaborate than a *diary*." Finally, beginning in 1728, the journal became synonymous with the newspaper: "A daily newspaper or other publication; hence, by extension, Any periodical publication containing news or dealing with matters of current interest in any particular sphere. Now often called specifically a *public journal*." This usage makes its reputation as a public text explicit.[6]

The first definition of "diary" offered in the OED equates it with the journal: "A daily record of events or transactions, *a journal*; specifically, a daily record of matters affecting the writer personally, or which come under his personal observation" (my emphasis). The term was first coined in 1581 in a letter written by William Fleetwood: "Thus most humbly I send unto yor good Lo. this last weeks Diarye." Later meanings of the term, circulated from 1605, include "A book prepared for keeping a daily record, or having spaces with printed dates for daily memoranda and jottings; also, applied to calendars containing daily memoranda on matters of importance to people generally, or to members of a particular profession, occupation, or pursuit." Although more attention is given to the journal, especially as a public document – the OED entry for "journal" is over three times as long as the one for "diary" – it is difficult to distinguish the two. Coined as a term more than two hundred years later than the journal, the diary seemed destined to develop in definitive ambiguity. It is recorded that in 1674 Heylin wrote, "A Diary or Journal, as the name imports, containing the Actions of each day." And in 1765 T. Hutchinson commented, "Goffe kept a journal or diary."[7] Given these ambiguities, I use the terms "journal" and "diary" interchangeably.

DEAR AUDIENCE

The diary emerged in direct relation to evolving conceptions of selfhood. In *A Poetics of Women's Autobiography*, Sidonie Smith traces the origins and development of autobiography in the late Middle Ages and early Renaissance. Although her discussion is limited to autobiography "proper," her historical data can be applied equally to the specific evolution of the diary.

Smith locates the inscription of an "ideology of individualism" in England and on the Continent during the fifteenth, sixteenth, and seventeenth centuries. The changes that took place during these centuries impacted upon the individual qua individual: among them were the erosion of the feudal system; progress in science, such as the discoveries of Copernicus and Galileo; the empiricism of Bacon; the philosophical speculations of Descartes, Locke, and Rousseau; a burgeoning interest in chronicle and family history; and increasing secularization. These historical factors stimulated an attitude during the sixteenth, seventeenth, and eighteenth centuries which essentially made autobiography possible: a new understanding of identity and an emphasis on the importance of the self led individuals to conceive their lives as significant and as stories worthy of being told.

Smith identifies "certain recurrent phenomena" generally agreed upon by historians: "the new recognition of identity as an earned cultural achievement, an arena of self-fashioning rather than an ascriptive, natural donnée, the corollary recognition of identity as simultaneously unique and yet dependent on social reality and cultural conventions; an increased willingness to challenge the authority of traditional modes of inquiry and to promote the hermeneutical responsibility and authority of the speaking subject." These phenomena "coalesced to foster an environment in which a realignment of the human subject occurred and in which autobiography as the literary representation of that human possibility became not only possible but also desirable."[8] Cinthia Gannett summarizes the corollary impact on the diary: "The primary incarnation of the journal as we know it, the personal journal or diary, will be born of the Renaissance and Reformation habit of mind that places value on the singular, knowing self."[9] The self-awareness fostered during the sixteenth to eighteenth centuries was that of the self as unified and knowable. It formed, as Smith tells us, the earliest conceptions of Western "'man' as a metaphysical entity."[10] The specific "man" is intended here, since Smith's valid complaint is that the "ideology of individualism" not only privileged but also universalized the male. In chapter 2, I retrace this history through the experiences of women.

Historical circumstances contributed to the formation of genres of self-documentation. In *Private Chronicles*, Robert Fothergill provides a detailed examination of an evolving English diary tradition.[11] The diary cannot be traced to any one originating source; rather, "It is best regarded as the coalescence of a number of pre-diary habits into a form that exceeds its component elements." These pre-diary habits are reflected in different kinds of diaries, categorized by Fothergill as "journals of travel, 'public' journals, journals of conscience, and journals of personal memoranda."[12] Before we consider these four types of diaries in detail, it is important to realize that concurrent with the development of the diary was the evolution of most other literary prose genres: the novel, the biography, the autobiography, and the modern essay. This concurrence supports the argument that genre boundaries have had, from the beginning, the potential to blur. Hence there is the need to reconsider the diary in terms of these other forms.

For example, Brian Dobbs believes the diary proper is indebted to the essay. He cites a book of essays by Michel de Montaigne as the text which marked a new consciousness of the self. Written in the 1580s, the *Essays* were original in that Montaigne described his own character, feelings, desires, and the like, making himself the true subject of his text.[13] Virginia Woolf was inspired by Montaigne's *Essays*, and in my chapter on her I discuss how their form and content impacted on her diary.

The diary developed alongside biography and autobiography as well. The term "biography" was coined by John Dryden in 1683 as "Biographia, or the History of particular Mens Lives"; this use was followed by "biographer," introduced by Joseph Addison in 1715, and "biographical," by William Oldys in 1738.[14] "Autobiography" first appeared in the *Monthly Review* in 1797. Just as "diary" is associated with "journal," so "autobiography" is defined in relation to "biography": "The writing of one's own history; the story of one's life written by himself."[15]

Several decades ahead of this definition, though, Daniel Defoe exploited the concept of autobiography in his novel *Robinson Crusoe* (1719). Acting as the mere editor of Crusoe's self-narrated life story, Defoe takes pains to inform his readers that he "believes the thing to be a just history of fact; neither is there any appearance of fiction in it."[16] He similarly announces the autobiographical stance of *Moll Flanders* (1722) on its title page, disclaiming his involvement: "Written from her own Memorandums."[17] Novelist Samuel Richardson likewise drew on life-writing genres, crafting *Pamela* (1740) and *Clarissa* (1748–49) in the form of letters and journals.

It may not be a coincidence that the novel emerged in the eighteenth century, the period during which the personal diary was reaching full fruition as a form and a practice. Not only did novels reflect the content of diaries, but they also offered new stylistic and imaginative possibilities on which diaries could be modelled. Marcia Landy easily associates the early novel with the diary: "In literature, the novel, in its portrayal of bourgeois society, its emphasis on romance and sentiment, on psychology, paved the way for a closer examination of social relations, particularly of male-female relationships. The biography and autobiography, the journal and the diary are inevitable counterparts of the novel."[18] Gannett observes, "The journal would carry with it the critical habits of mind associated with close observation of and reflection on the physical world, the social world, and the inner world of sense and sensibility" found in the novel.[19] One of the most crucial connections to be explored is the pervasive gendering of both the diary and the novel (in its devalued status of romance or sentimental fiction) as women's forms. This theme is taken up in chapter 2.

Concerned as I am with the autobiography and the novel specifically, and taking my cue from Hart's analysis of autobiography based on notions of intention, form, and truth telling, I now work through these terms in order to show how the diary approaches and encroaches on these other genres.

There is no dispute that the autobiography and the novel are intentionally written for a public audience. Even the letter, no matter how confidential, has an external addressee. Of all the literary genres, the diary is the only one that, to be imaged "authentically," must be written with no consideration of an audience beyond the writer herself. Further, by virtue of being defined as a daybook – to be recorded in regularly – it must be spontaneous and therefore unconstructed. However, it is possible to discuss the diary in terms of these other publication-oriented and audience-directed genres because the diary, no matter how private it has been assumed to be, has from its inception comprised its own self-conscious tradition. It is arguable that there has never been a time when all diarists truly wrote unselfconsciously, unaware of the implications embedded in the act of writing itself.

Simons notes that, "by their choice of mode as written documents all diaries imply readership, even if the reader and writer are one and the same."[20] More important here is the fact that reader and writer may also be different, as confirmed by a further investigation into the four types of diaries proposed by Fothergill. The first two kinds of diaries, journals of travel and public journals, are not purportedly private; the last two, journals of conscience and journals of personal memoranda, would seem by definition to be secretive in nature. Yet evidence suggests that each type of diarist was never wholly indifferent to the prescriptive functions of the text and thus never unaware of an audience for that text.

One of the earliest diaries was the itinerary. To recall the OED listing, the journal was defined in 1552 as "A book ... concerning the daily stages of a route and other information for travellers." Fothergill draws attention to Francis Bacon's 1625 essay "Of Travel" to highlight how formulaic these itineraries could be.[21] Bacon argues that for "young men" on continental tours, diaries should be "brought in use," since the men will behave well and study hard if they are encouraged to record their actions and thoughts. He offers a thorough catalogue of "The things to be seen and observed," including "the courts of princes," "the courts of justice," "the churches and monasteries," "the walls and fortifications of cities and towns," and "colleges, disputations, and lectures."[22]

Harriet Blodgett cites the equivalent for young women on their tours: in the nineteenth century, Anna Brownell Jameson begins her diary with the rhetorical question "What young lady, travelling for the first time on the continent, does not write a 'Diary'?"[23] Bacon's instructions and Jameson's self-consciousness indicate that the diary was not meant to be a wholly spontaneous document, for diarists were on the lookout for particular things to record in a distinctive manner.

Not only were travel diaries prescribed, but beginning in the sixteenth and seventeenth centuries, many were also published. Fothergill concludes that publication helped "to establish the diary convention as a way of structuring the presentation of first-hand material." More significantly, "an interesting dimension is added, at a very early stage, to the question of whether the concept of the diary can include the idea of its being intended for a reader."[24] Jameson's diary was certainly "intended for a reader," for it was in fact a fictional text written specifically for the marketplace. Turning to more legitimate diaries, we will see that Woolf and Smart, for instance, diligently recorded their thoughts, observations, and experiences during their extensive travels, intending them to be read by others at a later date.

The second class of diaries, the public journal, was unquestionably written for an audience. This diary was used for documenting information that would be of benefit to the public at large. While many of these diarists performed their jobs in fulfillment of "official" duties, others took it upon themselves to be the "self-appointed chroniclers of their times." These latter were a "persistent phenomenon in the diary genre." What is especially noteworthy about public diarists is that they often included personal information about themselves even though they were not required to do so. As a result, "Diaries of this kind are often either about to become, or appear to have grown out of, 'personal' diaries."[25] The interlapping of these forms is crucial, for it emphasizes the fact that an awareness of audience informed diaries which, notwithstanding their public nature, also had a personal component.

The third type of diary, the journal of conscience, was established as a genre in the late sixteenth and early seventeenth centuries by the Puritans and the Quakers. It provided a prescriptive place where the inner life of the conscience could be examined in religious terms. White and Nin at times wrote this kind of text, for they used their journals to evaluate their behaviour from rigidly Catholic perspectives. Like travel books, religiously oriented diaries were written very much to order, with manuals instructing diarists how to go about the task of recording and advising them on what material was fitting for their spiritual records. Fothergill rightly perceives that writing such a text was "an activity whose conventions were largely pre-established." To participate in this tradition, then, was often merely to follow a prescribed thought, tone, and style.[26]

Equally discernible in White's, Nin's, and others' spiritual diaries is the fact that private subject matter did not necessarily exclude the possibility of the journals being read by external audiences.[27] Lawrence Rosenwald informs us that, while it was not the practice of New England Puritans to show their diaries to their contemporaries, they were "injoined to preserve them for the use of their biographers and the edification of their descendants."[28] P.A. Spalding offers the example of the Quaker Dr Rutty, who "left directions in his will" for the publication of his diary so that "others might profit from his mistakes."[29] White especially echoes Rutty when she notes that her diary might be useful to others "who have suffered the same agonies of impotence and self-distrust" (D, 2:97).

The fourth type of diary, the personal memoranda, established in the seventeenth century and developed in the eighteenth, was the "record of things done and seen and heard." Not constituting "a diary *per se*, being no more than accumulations of jottings," it nonetheless contained "the germ of one."[30] This germ would grow into what Blodgett calls the "diary proper" of the eighteenth century, "the book reflecting the daily life and impress of an individual personality."[31]

It must be emphasized that the diary proper did not derive only or wholly from the personal memoranda. Men and women early on had begun to combine the personal memoranda with the diary of conscience, and these diaries in themselves may have contained descriptions of travels or information of historical or social value, such as those associated with public journals.[32] The personal-diary-cum-diary-proper must therefore be examined in all its complexities. We should also note that Fothergill qualifies his division of the diary into four categories by contending that "probably no 'major' diary is possible which draws its character from only one of the sources of impetus" identified.[33] As will be seen, the diaries of Woolf, White, Smart, and Nin draw their "character" from various combinations of these "sources."

WHAT A DIARY SHOULD BE

Writers of even the earliest personal memoranda exhibited traces of self-consciousness, in terms not only of what they wrote but of how they wrote. A case in point is Sir Henry Slingsby, who in 1638 introduced his diary by proposing to imitate the practice of Montaigne's father: this man "kept a journal Book, wherein he day by day registr'd the memories of the historys of his house; a thing pleasant to read, when time began to wear out the Remembrance of them... [My intention is] to sett down in this Book such accidents as befall me, not that I make my study of it, but rather a recreation at vacant times, without observing any time, method, or order in my wrighting, or rather scribbling."[34] By stating his intention within the very text which he proposes to write, as it were, without intention, Slingsby immediately draws attention to the self-reflexive nature of his project.

Coming on the heels of Slingsby's diary was John Evelyn's journal, and Samuel Pepys's personal record was immediately to follow. The publication in the nineteenth century of these latter two works inaugurated a tradition of marketable manuscripts. Evelyn's journal, which covers most of his life (1620–1706), was discovered and published in 1818. It was followed by portions of Pepys's diary (1660–69) in 1825[35] and by Byron's journals (1813–14, 1816, 1821) in Thomas Moore's *Memoirs* in 1830. Fanny Burney's diaries appeared soon after: *Diary and Letters ..., 1778–1840* was published in 1842–46 and her *Early Diary, 1768–1778* in 1889. Comprising as they do the foundation on which the personal-diary-as-published-text was erected, these four diaries need to be examined in order to ascertain just what kind of materials were used in their construction. Since they were the first published diaries of their kind, there can be no doubt that they served as blueprints for future diarists. Dobbs suggests as much when he notes the close timing of the publication of Evelyn's and Pepys's diaries with the production of personal diary books by John Letts in 1816. Letts's company "was supplying a new product, a commercially-produced diary, at just the time that diary-keeping was in the news and when people may have felt keen to emulate their distinguished predecessors."[36]

In his 1983 selected edition of *The Diary of John Evelyn*, John Bowle states: "John Evelyn is famous as a diarist ..." The sentence is completed with "or, more accurately, as the author of memoirs."[37] The first published text of Evelyn's life writing, edited by William Bray in 1818, was titled *Memoirs, Illustrative of the Life and Writings of John Evelyn, Esq. F.R.S.* The title page of this edition continues, "Comprising His Diary, From the Year 1641 to 1705–6, and a Selection of His Familiar Letters." The OED definition for "memoir" makes clear how these life-writing forms blur. Defining "memoir" as "A person's written account of incidents in his own life, of the persons whom he has known, and the transactions or movements in which he has been concerned; an autobiographical record," the entry then uses Evelyn as the first recorded illustration: "1673 Evelyn *Diary* 18 Aug., Nor could I forbeare to note this extraordinary passage in these memoires."[38] Since the definition equates "memoir" with "autobiography," it seems that from the beginning Evelyn's diary was associated with the deliberate crafting of self and text.

His memoir, originally subtitled a diary, eventually became specifically a diary, for not only is Bowle's own text titled as such, but so are all the editions published after Bray's 1818 version. In 1889 the version that followed Bray's is suddenly missing the "memoir" and is titled *Diary and Correspondence of John Evelyn*. In 1907 the work is called more simply *The Diary of John Evelyn*, and the definitive six- volume edition of 1955 is similarly entitled. Bowle underscores this change by consistently describing Evelyn's work as a diary. But then *The Oxford Companion to English Literature* refers to Evelyn's "*Memoirs* or *Diary*".[39]

Bowle seemingly reconciles the two terms when he discusses the work as both memoir and diary. Describing Evelyn's writing strategy, he notes that the author "revised his *Diary* twice: the bound up manuscript *Kalendarium*, the main source, covers his life from 1620 to 1697 and continues on loose sheets until 1706; but most of it was written up from contemporary notes retrospectively. The first part, from the beginning up to the visit to Rome in 1644, was written in 1660; the second, from 1644 to 1684, written in 1680–84, and only from 1684 onwards does it become a contemporary Diary. The *Kalendarium* is thus at once an unconscious self portrait and – principally – a considered memoir."[40] And yet Bowle's "principally" is misplaced, for the work has been marketed primarily as a diary. Coupled with the fact that "memoir" and "diary" become interchangeable, his observation suggests that early conceptions of the terms offered possibilities for blurring.

In its entry on Evelyn, *The Oxford Companion* makes this comparison: his diary is "less spontaneous and personal than that of Pepys." Mallon would support this view, for he maintains of Pepys, "If he cannot be said to have invented the form [of the diary] as we now think of it, he very nearly did, just as he more or less perfected it within months of starting his book on January 1, 1660."[41] William Matthews explores in detail just what kind of form Pepys "perfected." In his introduction to *The Diary of Samuel Pepys*, he makes it clear that this work is far more crafted than *The Oxford Companion* entry on Evelyn would have us believe. Matthews shows that Pepys often wrote up as many as fourteen days at one time, he relied not only on personal notes but on public papers such as news books for information, and he had a habit of rereading his entries, often for the purpose of revising them. Thus "the manuscript makes it fairly certain that Pepys's way of writing was more complex than is usually assumed, and consequently that his great diary is no simple product of nature, thrown together at the end of each succeeding day. In part at least, it is a product fashioned with some care, both in its matter and its style."[42]

Matthews's work has profound implications for the study of the diary because it undermines the foundation on which that study has been based. Pepys has so consistently been hailed as the first "real" diarist that critics obviously use his diary as a standard against which others are measured. For instance, Ponsonby – who condemns the crafted diary – praises Pepys's, claiming, "It fulfills all the conditions of what a diary should be."[43] Kate O'Brien, though admitting that she personally dislikes Pepys's work, states that "it seems clear enough" that his diary "was never intended for any other eyes besides its writer's" and that it "has become the most famous in the world."[44] James Aitken refers to Pepys's "incomparable diary," "'The most undress [sic] record in our literature,' as it has been called."[45] Spalding uses Pepys and Evelyn as examples of the "pure" diarist to support his argument against "false" ones.[46] And Dobbs, citing Pepys and Boswell as two of the rare few whose diaries "have achieved the status of great literature," takes great pains to defend their sincerity.[47] All the early diary critics use Pepys as their model of the genuine, true, sincere diarist, establishing from this model the equation between so-called spontaneity and truthfulness. It took Matthews's analysis to drive home to me the irony implicit in these studies. And it is from this less-naive perspective that Ponsonby's comment rings ironically true: Pepys's diary fulfills all the conditions, not of what a diary *should* be, but of what it more often *is*.

Likewise, Leslie A. Marchand, who edited the complete collection of *Byron's Letters and Journals*, provides historical information which suggests that Byron's diaries must have been written for eventual publication. Marchand tells us that Byron gave his first journal, written between 1813 and 1814, to Thomas Moore so that Moore could publish it. His second journal, kept on an Alpine tour in 1816, was specifically written for his sister, who in turn granted Moore permission to publish extracts. Because Byron had already given Moore one volume, it is likely that he wrote the second with publication in mind. And he also personally sent to Moore his third journal of 1821 as a supplement to what he had already offered.[48]

Finally, Fanny Burney's diary begins, in 1768, with an awareness of its audience: it is "Addressed to a Certain Miss Nobody," thereby implying that it is "addressed" to somebody. Simons reads Burney's address to "Nobody" as prophetic in that Burney was obviously "formulating her ideas with more than half an eye on her non-existent audience." And although she "began her journal as a semi-satirical chronicle of her life, purely for her 'most genuine and private amusement,' its purpose changed as she grew older." She began sending her diary entries to her sister, Susan, as a means of communication. When Susan died, Fanny took the advice of Susan's husband and continued the diary, but as a text which would secure her a place in posterity. Simons confirms that these diaries are consciously constructed, showing Burney's "literary powers at their height." In particular, there is a startling similarity between the writing style in the diary and the techniques and subject matter of her first best-selling novel, *Evelina*. That she crafted the diary is evidenced by her method of composition. Rather than recording events on a daily or immediate basis, she kept notes which she only later expanded and elaborated into journal entries.[49] In this, she followed the practices of Evelyn and Pepys.

What these four diaries have in common is essentially everything that we assume diaries not to be: comprised of daily entries written up en masse, aesthetically designed, and revised – in short, contrived. Two explanations obtain here. Either writers early on exploited a "pure" diary form to meet their own artistic and personal ends, or there never was such a form to begin with. While the diarist may start out with the best intention of recording only for herself or himself, the act of writing immediately undermines this unselfconscious stance. Rosenwald states: "To assert that journal accounts are governed only by the uncontaminated expressive impulses of the writer is false because it is impossible. All our utterances are mediated through our sophisticated or imperfect sense of some public, externally given form."[50]

In either case, the diary as a truly spontaneous, secret, uninhibited text remains at best an ambiguous reality. Fothergill suggests that the concept of the diary as a consciously crafted work was "a gradual development," implying that aesthetic intention, however slight, was in fact detectable early on. By the nineteenth century this "development" had fully matured, as diarists increasingly viewed their occupation as a literary one.[51] Rosenwald posits that, with the onslaught of published diaries in the first half of the nineteenth century, "well-read diarists were surely considering the prospect of posthumous independent publication and, thus, inevitably thinking of their diaries as *books*."[52] Recall Anna Brownell Jameson, the young traveller who thought of the diary as a "book." Relying on an increasing market interest in diaries and cultivating the diary's associations with the novel, Jameson penned the fictional *Diary of an Ennuyée*, which was published in London in 1826.[53] Only one year after the appearance of Pepys's diary and with Evelyn's still fresh from the press, Jameson exploited the form to meet her own imaginative ends.

Diaries that were published, and thus widely circulated, could serve as models or blueprints, influencing future diarists to follow stylistic suit. If Evelyn and Pepys launched the published personal diary at the beginning of the nineteenth century, Marie Bashkirtseff (Mariia Bashkirtseva) took it to new heights at the end of the century. Her journal, originally published in French in 1887, was translated into English by Mathilde Blind in 1891. Bashkirtseff was a French-Russian artist who died a Keatsian death from tuberculosis at the age of twenty-four. She began her diary in January 1873 and kept it until eleven days before her death in October 1884. Blind introduced the manuscript as a "literary event" because nothing like it had appeared before. It offers us "the momentary feelings and impulses, the uninvited back-stair thoughts passing like a breath across our consciousness, which we ignore for the most part when presenting our mental harvest to the public."[54] More importantly, it is one of the first publication-directed diaries. The *Journal* contains an "Author's Preface," in which the public design of the book is made explicit. Bashkirtseff unabashedly announces: "Why tell lies and play a part? Yes, it is clear that I have the wish, if not the hope, of remaining on this earth by whatever means in my power. If I do not die young, I hope to survive as a great artist; but if I do, I will have my Journal published, which cannot fail to be interesting."[55]

The posthumous publication of Bashkirtseff's diary was matched by the appearance in print of the journal of Bruce Frederick Cummings in 1919. A biologist by trade, Cummings was also an aspiring but unsuccessful writer who had determined that the only way he could get into the marketplace was via his diary. Rosenwald claims that Cummings, who published under the pseudonym Barbellion, "seems to have invented the species" of diary "edited for publication by its author." Of course, Rosenwald ignores the achievement of Bashkirtseff. But he does highlight the consequences of the personal diary being published by the author himself or herself: "Barbellion's 1919 coup gave precedent for living diarists' entering the literary marketplace; over the course of the century the precedent has become almost an obligation, as diaries have followed autobiographies in becoming not so much books published as intimate guides to famous men and women as books published by men and women interested in becoming famous."[56]

Appropriately, Barbellion often acknowledged his debt to Bashkirtseff. Another writer who similarly paid homage to her is Nin, one of the most self-reflexive diarists of all time. Fothergill is thus incorrect when he comments that Barbellion's recognition of Bashkirtseff is "a rare case of one diarist being 'influenced' by another."[57] By the twentieth century, with the publishing of diaries an accepted and expanding practice, diarists can often be found referring to, deferring to, and quoting from other diarists they have read. For example, Virginia Woolf acknowledged the diaries of Pepys, Evelyn, Burney, Barbellion, James Boswell, Dorothy Wordsworth, and André Gide. Antonia White read the diaries of Woolf and Nin, in addition to those by her friends, such as the poet David Gascoyne and the writer Emily Coleman. Elizabeth Smart referred to and quoted from those by Gide, Katherine Mansfield, and James Agate. And in addition to Bashkirtseff's, Nin drew on journals by Eugénie de Guérin, Henri Frédéric Amiel, Mansfield, and Pepys. It is particularly ironic that Spalding asserts that "diarists owe nothing to one another," not only in light of the proof offered here but because of his own evidence to the contrary. He states that Sir Walter Scott was "directly inspired by reading Byron's" diary, and in his endnote to this point he claims that "there is no 'purer' diary" than Scott's.[58] The fact that literary diarists include journals in their reading material shows how practitioners of the form perpetuate a self-conscious tradition.

Diarists may be influenced not only by other diaries but also by novels and short stories. In "The Diaries of Forgotten Women," Penelope Franklin emphasizes that "Diarists, inevitably, are readers. Moreover, they are people considerably under the sway of the written word." As a result, "they are likely to have developed both their habits of expression and their ideas about appropriate subject matter on the basis of their reading."[59] Franklin examines how even non-literary women style their diaries according to the novels and magazines they read, a point reinforced by Steven Kagle and Lorenza Gramegna in "Rewriting Her Life: Fictionalization and the Use of Fictional Models in Early American Women's Diaries" – "Just as a diary may inspire and direct fiction, so fiction and its patterns may inspire and direct a diary."[60] This symbiosis recalls how the diary and the novel developed as genres at similar historical moments, and it shows how they continued to nourish each other as they grew more established.

Some diaries may be written with the hope of publication, while others not necessarily intended for extended, impersonal audiences may be written for either a particular individual or a select group of family or friends. Diary keeping was commonly a collective activity among women in the eighteenth and nineteenth centuries. Either they wrote journals to each other, in the form of "diary-letters," or they shared portions of their private entries with sisters and friends by reading them aloud or passing them around.[61] Cynthia Huff notes that women were "frequently the designated chronicler of family records," and thus in addition to reading or listening to the diaries of their relatives, they may have transcribed them as well.[62] Gannett draws attention to the existence of "diary cycles: that is, multiple generations of women keeping diaries in the same family." In general, "a central and unique aspect of women's journal traditions" was that of a "social – or domestic – discourse network."[63]

A good example of this "network" is offered by Suzanne Bunkers and Judy Nolte Lensink, who have edited respectively the diaries of

Sarah Gillespie Huftalen and her mother, Emily Hawley Gillespie; these women lived and wrote in Iowa during the late nineteenth and early twentieth centuries. Bunkers affirms that these generational diaries "were collaborative and interactive."[64] Recall, as well, that Fanny Burney sent her initial diaries to her sister, Susan. In the twentieth century we shall see how Smart shared her journal with her sister Jane, and Nin with her childhood friend Frances. Women were not the only ones who exchanged journals. For instance, in his work on Emerson, Rosenwald found that New England transcendentalists "passed their diaries around as scholars pass around drafts of essays."[65]

Rosenwald is a helpful critic because his "Prolegomena" to his study on Emerson undermines assumptions of diaristic intention, form, and truth. Concerning intention, he uses the example of the transcendentalists to drive home what he rightly considers obvious: "the notion that diaries are necessarily private is simply false." While he acknowledges that not every diarist read other diaries or wrote his or her own to be published, Rosenwald does remark that, suspiciously, only a few diarists probably take the most deliberate step to preserve secrecy – destroying the text. He is anxious to expose the "myth of necessary secrecy" because he is aware that "its hold over us is very great." Referring to a tradition of audience-directed diaries, he insists that diaries be located within a system of production and distribution not unlike that of the novel – and, I would add, that of the autobiography. The diary is "a commodity within its author's power. Diarists distribute their texts to the readers they choose, novelists to the readers who can afford the publisher's price."[66]

That diaries are intended for distribution is widely corroborated. Thomas Mallon admits on a personal note that when he writes his diary, he finds himself correcting grammar and spelling. This practice, coupled with his examination of over four centuries of diary writing, leads him to no longer believe anyone who says that he or she does not write for an audience.[67] In her article "A Diarist on Diarists," Gail Godwin contends, in the suspicious spirit of Rosenwald, that if a diarist really did not want anyone to read her diary she would find a way to prevent it. Godwin surmises that the far more prevalent "breed of diarist" is the one "who writes for *some* form of audience." Like Mallon, she is convinced that diarists write for "some form of posterity," and she confesses that she finds herself "explaining" in her diary, "putting in that extra bit of information that I know quite well but cannot expect a stranger to know."[68]

Sarah Gristwood, in *Recording Angels*, wonders whether diary writing is "really the most private form of writing known to man – or woman – or a sneaky surfacing of the exhibitionist streak which lies at the heart of us all?" She considers the truth to be the latter, for she cites many examples which prove that "the possibility of the entries being read by someone else is always at the back of the diarist's mind."[69] Lyn Lifshin notes of the diarists she solicited for her anthology *Ariadne's Thread: A Collection of Contemporary Women's Journals*: "When it came to talking about whether thoughts of publishing occurred to them, the most common answer seemed to be some variation of 'no, but ...' or 'no, not really,' blending with an almost unconscious, or not quite admitted, 'well, maybe sometime, when I'm famous or dead.'"[70] These "no, but" and "well, maybe" tensions underscore my central argument about diaries in general and Woolf's, White's, Smart's, and Nin's diaries in particular: they are often written for some form of posterity.

Oscar Wilde would certainly agree, for soon after the arrival of Bashkirtseff's diary, he was lampooning a journal's genre claims in his play *The Importance of Being Ernest* (1895). A discussion between the characters Cecily and Algernon deserves to be quoted at length:

Cecily. ... If you will allow me I will copy your remarks into my diary. (*Goes over to table and begins writing in diary.*)
Algernon. Do you really keep a diary? I'd give anything to look at it. May I?
Cecily. Oh no. (*Puts her hand over it.*) You see, it is simply a very young girl's record of her own thoughts and impressions, and consequently meant for publication. When it appears in volume form I hope you will order a copy. But pray, Ernest, don't stop. I delight in taking down from dictation. I have reached "absolute perfection." You can go on. I am quite ready for more.
Algernon. (*Somewhat taken aback.*) Ahem! Ahem!
Cecily. Oh, don't cough, Ernest. When one is dictating one should speak fluently and not cough. Besides, I don't know how to spell a cough.
(*Writes as Algernon speaks.*)[71]

Wilde exposed as myth the ideas that the diary is a private text and that it is a spontaneous, immediate recording of events.

THE DIARISTIC CONTRACT

It is particularly surprising that the diary is so often dismissed in studies of autobiography primarily because it is assumed to have no audience. This has been the case even with early feminist revisionists of life writing. Sidonie Smith, for instance, defines autobiography "as written or verbal communication that takes the speaking 'I' as the subject of the narrative, rendering the 'I' both subject and object." But she excludes diaries, confining her study to texts "written to be published and thus addressed to that arbiter of all cultural ideologies, the public reader."[72] Similarly, in "Selves in Hiding," Patricia Meyer Spacks asserts that autobiography claims the authority and significance of the life and self recorded by virtue of its public orientation, whereas the diary does not.[73]

Beyond the issue of audience, Estelle Jelinek discriminates against "marginal" forms of life writing in her preface to *The Tradition of Women's Autobiography*. She states that, although "I occasionally refer to diaries, letters, and journals (to place them in historical context), I rarely discuss them because I do not consider them autobiographies ... Autobiography is an amalgam of one's self-image, one's process of thinking and feeling, and one's talent as a formal writer."[74] Jelinek thus implies that these are not qualities of the diary. But like Smith and Spacks, she is working within predetermined boundaries. Though she makes the crucial case for women's own tradition of autobiography, she does not challenge traditional definitions of genre which exclude the diary.

What are these traditional definitions with their male paradigms? One must first understand how autobiography has been evaluated in critical and scholarly terms in order to appreciate how these terms are inadequate to describing life-writing texts by both men and women. As Kadar put it, the "essence" of genres "can never really be captured."

Rosenwald defines the diary thus: "In form a diary is a chronologically ordered sequence of dated entries addressed to an unspecified audience. We call that form a diary when a writer uses it to fulfil certain functions. We might describe those functions collectively as the discontinuous recording of aspects of the writer's own life." The diary "must be a book of time"; it "must be conceived as a book of days and dates and intervals." "Whatever functions a diary serves, the writer of it chooses for them a form articulated by dates in chronological order, and a mode of writing spaced over time." Based on this interpretation, autobiographies are "obviously" excluded from the diary's definition.[75]

Rosenwald echoes Georges Gusdorf, whose seminal article "Conditions and Limits of Autobiography" appeared in 1956. Gusdorf's only reference to the "diary is to note its difference. While the diary asks its author to record his "impressions and mental states from day to day," fixing "the portrait of his daily reality without any concern for continuity," the autobiography "requires a man to take a distance with regard to himself in order to reconstitute himself in the focus of his special unity and identity across time."[76]

And in *Design and Truth in Autobiography*, Roy Pascal claims: "There is an autobiographical form, and indeed a convention, which one recognises and distinguishes from other literary modes." His exploration of autobiography emerges out of his belief that there is a "true" autobiography. Comparing the diary and the autobiography, Pascal is confident that the formal differences are "obvious. The latter is a review of a life from a particular moment in time, while the diary, however reflective it may be, moves through a series of moments in time." Unlike the autobiographer, the diarist fails to present a fully rounded picture of himself. Though the diarist deposits his "uncertainties," the autobiographer shapes his life into a "coherent" story. To do so, the autobiographer must take a "standpoint of the moment at which he reviews his life, and interprets his life from it."[77] From this standpoint, the autobiographer must choose and discriminate between experiences and feelings – while, presumably, the diarist does not. For Pascal, the diarist does not write from a specific standpoint because he writes in a continuum of time. The diary is spontaneous, fragmentary, and immediate, whereas the autobiography is consciously patterned in the way novels are.

In "The Autobiographical Contract," Philippe Lejeune approaches autobiography from the point of view of the reader, a logical position to interpret the function of the text, he feels, given that autobiographies are written for others. He offers this working definition of the genre: "a retrospective prose narrative produced by a real person concerning his own existence, focusing on his individual life, in particular on the development of his personality."[78] Lejeune tells us that he arrived at this definition "through a series of oppositions between the various texts which are available for reading" – those texts including memoir, biography, first-person novel, autobiographical poem, self-portrait or essay, and diary.

He determines that the only difference between the diary and the autobiography is that the latter's narration is retrospectively oriented. In this, he recalls Gusdorf and Pascal. Lejeune, however, affords flexibility, qualifying his statement by observing that "the orientation should be *mainly* retrospective, but this does not exclude," among other things, "passages of ... diary." He considers genre classification "a matter of proportion," admitting that "there are natural transitions to the other genres of *littérature intime* (memoirs, diary, essay), and a certain latitude is left to the classifier in the examination of particular cases."[79]

Lejeune further joins the diary to the autobiography as he opposes them both to the biography and the personal novel. In the former two, unlike the latter, author and narrator are the same, as are narrator and protagonist. This observation feeds into the crux of his argument: identity is verified by way of the title page, and it is this title page which constitutes the "autobiographical contract" between writer and reader.[80] The author's "signature" on the title page, which must be honoured as such, is measured against the names of narrator and protagonist within the text in order to determine and verify "identity." Once identity is established, the author's intention becomes clear. While Lejeune goes on to explain this concept in detail, I am interested in two points that reflect on the status of the diary.

First, he admits that the reason he has gone outside the text, to examine autobiography from the position of the reader, is that an internal analysis alone is not enough to distinguish autobiography from the novel: "All the devices that are used in autobiography to convince us of the authenticity of the story can be imitated by the novel, and that has often been done."[81] Indeed, we should recall Daniel Defoe's *Robinson Crusoe* and *Moll Flanders*. Because Lejeune has been forced by his criteria to include the diary in his basic definition of autobiography, what he is saying here about autobiography and the novel can be applied to the diary and the novel as well. Many novels take the diary as their form – consider the examples of Doris Lessing's *The Golden Notebook*, Dostoevsky's *Notes from the Underground*, and Lawrence Durrell's *The Black Book*. More provocatively, what can be extracted from Lejeune's comment is that the diary itself might employ "devices ... to convince us of the authenticity" of the life recorded.

Secondly, once a diary has been published and stamped with the author's signature on the front, it, like an autobiography, announces itself as a "*contractual* genre."[82] In the case of the diary, the contract invites the reader to enter a private document. But in an extreme case such as Nin's, where the intention of the diarist was to produce a text specifically for public consumption, the foundation of "genuine" authorship on which the diaristic project is based is eroded; the author's signature on the title page is no longer a sign of sincerity but, rather, a testament to the diarist's manipulation and exploitation of that intention.

This possibility is taken up by Elizabeth W. Bruss in *Autobiographical Acts: The Changing Situation of a Literary Genre*. Here she follows Lejeune's interest in how the reader "takes" the autobiographical text. She posits that the title page may issue a satisfactory contract, but she also cites Gertrude Stein as an example of twentieth-century manipulation of conventional expectations which undermines Lejeune's contract. Stein is able to "invoke and frustrate" notions of genre by using subversive titles such as *The Autobiography of Alice B. Tok-*

las by Gertrude Stein and *Everybody's Autobiography* by Gertrude Stein.[83]

Lynn Z. Bloom and Orlee Holder, in "Anaïs Nin's Diary in Context," are among the first scholars to adequately consider the diary in the autobiographical context. They point to the rich diversity of content in both forms: "autobiographies and diaries may present, among other materials, narrative incidents, vignettes of personal relationships, character sketches, accounts of travels, essays on various topics, dialogues, copies of letters sent or received." Bloom and Holder do, however, distinguish between the genres in two ways: autobiographers speak "softly to an audience," whereas "diarists usually talk to themselves"; and while diarists present events chronologically, writing entries under specific dates, autobiographers can follow a chronological or a thematic pattern.[84] These last points echo the essentialist definitions of Gusdorf and Pascal. As I have argued in contradiction, many diarists talk to an implied audience, either a general, public one or a "dear diary" or a "dear friend." And as I will show, diarists often manipulate structure according to theme.

Francis H. Hart is a scholar who goes further by opposing genre essentialism. He reacts against critics such as Gusdorf and Pascal who, in an effort to identify a "true autobiography," become restrictive and limited in their selections of texts. Hart warns of the dangers of excluding works that do not fit prescribed criteria. Having examined nearly forty (male) autobiographies, he concludes that it is impossible to speak of only "one" autobiography. Like Bruss, he is convinced that the only way to make generalizations about the genre is through studies of specific texts. It is only when "recognitions of individual autobiographies have accumulated and undergone testing and sorting" that it will "be possible to make real and meaningful descriptive generalizations about the historical development of modern autobiography."[85]

Although Hart bases his argument on the general or formal category of autobiography, he slips in a reference to journals. While autobiography proper involves the writer in a tension between "life and pattern, movement and stasis, identification and definition, world and self," the diary heightens and intensifies this conflict.[86] He locates the diary on the same ranges of construct as autobiography proper. The truth of an autobiography "demands its own discrimination and conflation of perspectives, and hence its own narrative mode"; likewise, the diary is "an artifice of multiple perspectives – levels of retrospect, minglings of dramatic and real anticipation, operations of significant selection."[87] This is a potent observation, and it indicates that a subtler approach to both autobiographies and diaries is necessary.

AUTODIARY

Just as there is no "one" autobiography, so there is no "one" diary. An examination of issues such as time, selection and shaping of material, and closure highlights the complexities within and similarities between these genres.

A consideration of the notion of time, for instance, demands that certain points made by Rosenwald, Gusdorf, and Pascal be refuted. There is no disputing that the diary is conceived as a book of days. Yet many diarists use this diurnal structure strategically, writing up several days' entries at once, relying on notes for information after the fact, or transferring and expanding brief jottings into full, comprehensive narratives later. The most crucial corollary to this observation is that the autobiography, purportedly written from one position at one particular moment, is often produced over a long stretch of time.

In his insightful argument that "autobiographical truth is not a fixed but an evolving content," Paul John Eakin draws attention to the "evolution of the autobiographical *act*"[88] as well (my emphasis). Commenting that completed autobiographies result only from a series of drafts which have undergone editing and revisions over an extended period of time, Eakin is perceptive to the reality that they often take years to write. He explains that this "evolution" is "usually masked by the publication of only a final draft."[89] This masking is partially responsible for overgeneralized distinctions between the diarist, who records every day, and the autobiographer, who sits down to write only once. Antonia White proves the inapplicability of such binary oppositions: she spent the last fifteen years of her life working on her autobiography, revising it with the consistency with which she made entries in her diary.[90]

Time is an issue in terms not only of when a diary is written but also of how the self is presented. Blodgett asserts, "The diarist's urge ... is not the autobiographer's." For while the autobiographer reconstructs what she once *was*, the diarist is concerned with what she *is*, which is a "self in process."[91] But the autobiographer who sits down to write is recording what she or he is at that instant no less than is the diarist. Autobiography is just as much about the person who writes in the present as about the person who lived in the past, for the past per se is never recoverable. In "Full of Life Now," Barrett Mandel argues: "The past may appear to rule the present; but in fact all genuine power resides in the *moment* of creativity" (my emphasis). This distinction is understood by the reader of the text, who "is constantly sensing the impact of the author's present historical moment and the present message of his culture."[92] Gusdorf, too, recognizes that the autobiographer imposes meanings on an event which were not evident at the time: "This postulating of a meaning dictates the choice of the facts to be retained."[93] The "postulating" is done from the present position of writing. Memory selects according to the "meaning," or version, of the past dictated to it from the present.

The diarist also selects and, in selecting, imposes meaning on the past, however recent that past may be. Lejeune's notion of "retrospective orientation" can be applied in principle as much to the diarist's task as to the autobiographer's, for the diarist who records at 9 p.m. what happened at 9 a.m. is, to a degree, "retrospectively oriented." It is true that she must generally select on a more consistent basis and over less-extreme gaps in time. But if we heed Mandel's assertion that the past exists only as an "illusion created by the symbolizing activity of the mind,"[94] and if we invoke Heraclitus's adage that it is not possible to step into the same stream twice,[95] we see how diarist and autobiographer are equally charged with inventing their past at the precise moment they seek to record it – or step into it – whether twelve hours or twelve years later.

The future is perhaps the most difficult aspect of time to reconcile comparatively. The autobiographer writes about the past with full knowledge of its outcome up to the present point of writing, whereas the diarist supposedly cannot know what will happen tomorrow. Of course, he or she can anticipate the future. But often the diarist does more: she or he may make entries for a day after that day has passed, so that the writing is informed by what has occurred since. This is the case with writers such as Pepys and Burney and, as will be shown, with Woolf, White, Smart, and Nin.

Moreover, if the diary charts the "self in process," so too does the autobiography. Though the diary's claims to immediacy are more pronounced than the autobiography's, the self that evolves within the totality of each text is equally a "self in process." As Bruce Mazlish suggests, "autobiographies, to convince us, ought ideally to deal with the self as a developing entity."[96] In *Metaphors of Self: The Meaning of Autobiography*, James Olney states that an autobiography is "intentionally or not, a monument of the self as it is becoming, a metaphor of the self at the summary moment of composition."[97] Elsewhere he indicates that the best way to interpret life is "to view bios as a process the whole of which the autobiographer is in a position to see, recall, and compose." He notes that "it is up to the autobiographer to cut it where he will so that the process will be complete and unified."[98]

This last point is particularly significant because Olney is pointing to another feature typically associated with the autobiography as against the diary: the notion of closure. The autobiography, unlike the diary, is assumed to move towards a summing-up in a "unified" whole. But diarists make similar moves. It is appropriate to recall here that they often conceive of their lives as books to be written. Posing the question of whether the diary can be considered a "formally completed whole," Fothergill answers that it can. He admits that many diarists are committed to the "*exercise* of diary-writing," and he emphasizes that the "major diarists" are committed "to the *book* that their living nourishes." Fothergill contends that "as a diary grows to a certain length and substance it impresses upon the mind of its writer a conception of the completed book that it might ultimately be, if sustained with sufficient dedication and vitality."[99] On the practical side of creating such a product, diarists "cut" the process at the two most obvious places: at the end of individual books or volumes and at the end of the year. They acknowledge that they have reached an "end" (as Smart did in explicitly making "Finis" her last word in her 1933 journal) and generally look back both on what has happened and on what they have written. They tend to make summarizing comments and to offer various resolutions for the future.

The diary's status as a finished work must further be considered in terms of editing. Diarists edit their texts themselves, from the mental process of selecting what to include and exclude to rewriting and crossing out words and passages and, in the most extreme cases, to preparing typescripts of their diaries, as writers such as a young Anne Frank and a young and an older Nin did. But what also needs to be examined is how the text is altered when it is prepared for publication by someone other than the diarist. The editor is likely to proceed according to her or his prejudices and on the basis of the image of the subject that she or he wants to project. The editor wields a great deal of power, and our reading of this kind of prepared diary must take into account that the "completed book" may be a distorted version of the diarist's own vision. For example, Anne Olivier Bell, the editor of the unexpurgated diaries of Woolf, has charged that Leonard Woolf's earlier abridged edition, *A Writer's Diary,* "probably did a good deal to create or reinforce that popular journalistic image of Virginia Woolf, the moody, arrogant, and malicious Queen of Bloomsbury."[100]

The other side to notions of completion and closure is that the "process" can never cease so long as the life is being lived. Gusdorf acknowledges that autobiography is "never the finished image or the fixing forever of an individual life: the human being is always a making, a doing."[101] Roland Barthes concurs, for at the end of his autobiography he asks, "And afterward? – What to write now? Can you still write anything?" He answers in the affirmative: "One writes with one's desire, and I am not through desiring."[102] Domna C. Stanton under-scores the organic quality of the autobiography in her distinction between it and biography. The biography can be considered a closed text, possibly describing the death of its subject, whereas autobiogra-phy cannot, for it is "necessarily un-ended, incomplete, fragmentary, whatever form of rhetorical closure it might contain."[103]

This is the point that Rosenwald makes about the journal. He remarks, "During the lifetime of the diarist," the diary "remains unfin-ished and open; something can always be added." It remains "within its author's power" for the duration of her or his lifetime.[104] This is true, if to a more limited extent, of the autobiography, for an autobi-ographer accrues material with experience. In addition to White, who spent fifteen years revising her autobiography, Leonard Woolf is a good example of what might be called the diaristic autobiographer. He published five volumes of autobiography between 1960 and 1969, a period as long as many diaries last. His five volumes of autobiography complement the five published volumes of the diary written by his wife, Virginia Woolf.

The diary's remaining "within its author's power" has implications with regard to the diarist's ability to impose structure not unlike the autobiographer's and novelist's. The fact that diarists may write more than one entry in a single sitting, coupled with their likely habit of rereading entries, makes it possible for them to impose not only closure but also narrative continuity and thematic pattern, practices tradition-ally ascribed to the autobiographer and the novelist. Rosenwald encourages the assessment that diarists are, or can be, "readers and shapers of their texts." Thus he provides the necessary contradiction to Gusdorf's claim that they have no concern for continuity. Stressing that we cannot "presume diaries as wholes are composed at random," Rosenwald instructs us to examine each text individually: "diarists' relations to their diaries present a wide spectrum of varying degrees of control and awareness, and in studying any individual diarist we will need to ascertain where in that spectrum the diarist is to be found."[105]

Fothergill draws attention to the most basic level of "control and awareness." Disagreeing with William Matthews's dismissal that "a diary which has a consistent pattern is a literary work and no diary at all," he points out that nobody begins each day with a tabula rasa, having erased everything from his or her thoughts during the night. Thus "one of the most important effects of keeping a diary is the awareness thereby generated of patterns and processes at work in the life of the writer. Channelled back into the diary, this awareness becomes the source of structural 'themes' that may give to the work a highly sophisticated design."[106]

For the most part, rather than focusing on literary diarists, anthologists such as Blodgett and Lifshin devote their time to non-literary diarists, or those who do not appear to be writing for a reading audience. Perhaps, then, it is easier for them to doubt that aesthetic motives inform the author's agenda. But in *Read This Only to Yourself: The Private Writings of Midwestern Women, 1880–1910*, Elizabeth Hampsten, denying that "ordinary" women wrote with any literary concerns, nonetheless adds in the conclusion to one of her chapters, "there is frequent evidence that individual writers were conscious of shaping what they wrote."[107] Helen Buss, too, in *Mapping Our Selves,* affirms that the diary of Canadian pioneer Elizabeth Simcoe, written in 1792–96, "was carefully shaped in moments of leisure from detailed notes recorded on the scene earlier in the day or week."[108]

In her introduction to *British Women's Diaries: A Descriptive Bibliography of Selected Nineteenth-Century Women's Manuscript Diaries*, Huff provides further illumination on the motivations of diarists. Her study of unpublished manuscripts reinforces how diary writing cannot be dissociated from other literary constructions. Huff's survey of fifty-nine manuscripts reveals a clear, recurring pattern of self-reflexivity. Features of this kind include diarists' tendencies to address a reader, reread entries and edit them, and trace over in ink any entries written in pencil, thereby indicating their desire to render their creations fixed for posterity.[109]

Likewise, in her article "What Do Women *Really* Mean? Thoughts on Women's Diaries and Lives," Bunkers examines manuscript diaries of nineteenth-century Midwestern women. Referring to the schoolteacher Louise Bailey, Bunkers asserts that Bailey "saw her diaries as her 'life's story,'" which was deliberately "shaped" as such. And "her decision to save all of her diaries and donate them to historical society archives is a strong indication that she had a larger purpose and intended audience than herself alone in mind." Bunkers "can reasonably speculate" that Bailey's "preservation of her diaries and her commitment of them to the 'public' realm lend credence to her designation of her diaries as her autobiography."[110]

And in her study of the nineteenth-century diarist Emily Hawley Gillespie, Lensink skilfully demonstrates how a non-literary diary approaches autobiography. She offers convincing research which suggests that Gillespie consciously selected her material to project a carefully constructed persona of "the striving sufferer"; by addressing a "dear reader," she was aware of a reading audience; she employed intratextuality and used this technique to create thematic structure; she described people in such a way as to render them "characters"; and she imposed closure. Lensink radically redefines Gillespie's project: "this never was intended to be a diary that recorded life. Rather, it was a book in which to frame an authorized version of life – selective, mutable as the ideology driving it, eventually vocal and judgmental."[111] The fact that it is possible to point to design in texts such as these makes it even more appropriate to consider the aesthetic quality of diaries written by literary women.

Diaries and autobiographies written with narrative considerations are further connected to the novel in that, as scholars now generally agree, the autobiography shares a certain amount of fictionalizing with the novel. Roland Barthes, for instance, introduces his autobiography *Roland Barthes* with the epigraph: "It must all be considered as if spoken by a character in a novel." Patricia Meyer Spacks probes this relationship in *Imagining a Self: Autobiography and Novel in Eighteenth-Century England*. Investigating a range of both genres, she finds an interconnectedness inherent in their presentation and formation of identity, such that "substantial distinctions between fictional and factual renditions of personality have always proved difficult to maintain." Both autobiographers and novelists "necessarily depend upon artifice – shaping, inventing, selecting, omitting – to achieve their effects." Though "Autobiographers rely mainly on artifices of selection; novelists, on those of invention," "both communicate vital truths through falsifications." These "falsifications," practised by diarists as well, have continued to be invoked into the twentieth century.

Any story is comprised of characters, and both autobiographers and diarists conceive of themselves as such. Though Spacks considers the autobiographical and novelistic enterprises equally based on "falsifications," she does qualify this position by stating that for the autobiographer, unlike the novelist, "the raw material of his narrative remains himself," and "Despite all decorum, he risks exposure in a way the novelist does not." The same holds true for the diarist. In fact, the diarist risks exposure of herself or himself to an even greater degree. Comparisons between the novel, the autobiography, and the diary must therefore acknowledge distinctions such as these.

If, on the one hand, life writers draw on fiction, on the other, fiction writers draw on life, specifically their own lives. As Spacks proposes, "Twentieth-century novelists write thinly veiled autobiography, call it a novel, then complain if readers suspect some direct self-revelation."[112] (This statement need not be restricted to the twentieth century.) Perhaps it was easy to sever the author entirely from her or his creation – it was certainly prescribed – during the impersonal reign of the New Critics, but critical approaches since the nineteen fifties and sixties have allowed for, and even urged, more biographical and referential textual readings. The fall of this New Critical power has contributed to a rise of appreciation for documents such as diaries which, not withstanding their autobiographical bases, may be appreciated as valuable and legitimate works of art.

TEXTUAL/REFERENTIAL SELVES

In *Fictions in Autobiography*, Eakin emphasizes the fictional aspects of autobiography, reminding us that, while scholars early on believed that autobiography was factually verifiable, they now often treat it as a genre "indistinguishable" from the novel. His argument proceeds from the more balanced position that the autobiographer negotiates "a narrative passage between the freedoms of imaginative creation on the one hand and the constraints of biographical fact on the other." Autobiographers in the twentieth century "readily accept the proposition that fictions and the fiction-making process are a central constituent of the truth of any life." Autobiography is accepted in its dual status as "an art of memory and an art of imagination." Speaking for himself and on behalf of the subjects of his study, Eakin explains how they reject traditional notions of "fiction as a potential threat to the success of the autobiographical process, antithetical to the truth they propose to tell," regarding fiction instead "as a central feature of that truth, an ineluctable fact of the life of consciousness."[113]

In like manner, Hart concludes, "Truth is a definitive but elusive autobiographical intention."[114] He is complemented by Shari Benstock, who concludes that "autobiography reveals the impossibility of its own dream: what begins on the presumption of self-knowledge ends in the creation of a fiction that covers over the premises of its construction."[115] Gusdorf suggests that autobiography shows the person, "not as he was, not as he is, but as he believes and wishes himself to be and to have been." Whether autobiography be "fiction or fraud," of more significance is that "its artistic value is real."[116] Timothy Dow Adams believes, "The truth in autobiography ... can be better understood if we think of it as narrative rather than historical truth." Since all autobiographies are "stories," they "all partake of narrative truth."[117]

The assumption that the self could know itself and relate "truths" about itself may be historicized, as we have seen earlier in Smith's work, to the late Middle Ages and especially to the Renaissance, when humanism was lending itself to the development of life-writing genres. In *Being in the Text: Self-Representations from Wordsworth to Roland Barthes*, Paul Jay traces a historical shift in self-representation specifically within literary autobiographies by male writers such as St Augustine, William Wordsworth, Thomas Carlyle, Henry Adams, T.S. Eliot, and Barthes. Not only was the humanist self-conceived of as being "whole," a stable entity capable of becoming fully known to itself, but so was the form of the autobiography which contained that self; that is, early, traditional autobiographies have been described as being chronological, linear, appropriate to the self becoming "whole" and fixed within them. As concepts of the self evolved over time – from the Romantic to the postmodern period – the self has supposedly become increasingly fractured, less knowable, and so the forms of autobiography, reflecting this breakdown, have become more and more disjointed in their narrative structures.

While Jay ignores the presence of women's autobiographies in this hypothesis, in chapter 2 I consider how such texts are an essential component of any study of life-writing selves. Further, it is important to note that the choice of a linear or a fragmented mode of narration in autobiography has been linked not only to history but also to gender. Jelinek, for instance, contends that women write differently from men; unlike those of men, women's autobiographical styles tend to be "episodic and anecdotal, nonchronological and disjunctive."[118] And after surveying a wide range of autobiographies and diaries by women, Bloom and Holder agree with Jelinek and also with Suzanne Juhasz that "Diffuseness is indeed the common organizational mode." They consider this "diffuseness" a significant factor distinguishing women's autobiographies from men's. More specifically, they locate these "diffuse" origins in women's diaries.[119] However, not everyone agrees. Stanton refutes such claims with the convincing evidence that some men write in a fragmented form, some women in a chronologically linear one.[120] And Lensink has shown, as I will also, how the diary can be narratively ordered.

Jay emphasizes that even the earliest autobiographies, such as that by Augustine, contained "internal contradictions" which highlighted how the act of writing, of using language, impinges on the representation of a pure or authentic self: "the personal and psychological goals animating a retrospective self-analysis like Augustine's – or Wordsworth's – nearly always become conflated with compositional and rhetorical problems at cross-purposes to those goals. The personal and psychological resolutions that these texts seek to mediate are often disrupted, or even displaced, by the aesthetic problems of translating a psychological subject into a literary one."[121]

These tensions increased over time, so that by the late nineteenth-century, Nietzsche was articulating how the self is nothing but a construct within the realm of language. In The Will to Power, as Jay notes, Nietzsche argued that "the 'subject' is not something given, it is something added and invented and projected behind what there is."[122] Nietzsche's dismantling of the Western self would be complemented by Freud's constructed division of the supposedly unified subject into the ego, the id, and the superego.

Not merely dividing the self but deconstructing it in the spirit of Nietzsche, Paul De Man argues that the self within autobiographies is textual rather than referential. A passage from his often-cited "Autobiography as De-facement" bears quoting here: "are we so certain that autobiography depends on reference, as a photograph depends on its subject or a (realistic) picture on its model? We assume that life *produces* the autobiography as an act produces its consequences, but can we not suggest, with equal justice, that the autobiographical project may itself produce and determine the life and that whatever the writer does is in fact governed by the technical demands of self-portraiture and thus determined, in all aspects, by the resources of his medium?"[123]

Eakin takes up this question in "Narrative and Chronology as Structures of Reference and the New Model Autobiographer," in which he argues that the subject within autobiography may indeed have a referent beyond the text. He uses as an example *Roland Barthes* by Roland Barthes to illuminate how narrative design contributes to the representation of the subject. Eakin shows how Barthes's text resists sequential, narrative connectedness, but he then undermines this conclusion by demonstrating that no matter how diligently Barthes tried to avoid a traditional linear autobiographical discourse depicting a coherent self, he failed; and no matter how much it appears a patchwork, Barthes's text displays an underlying pattern of narrative continuity. For not only does his text includes "many a micronarrative and microchronology of autobiographical retrospect, but it is framed by sections of narrative and chronology invoking the novel ... and biography."[124]

There must be, as Eakin appropriately concludes, an inevitable human drive to constitute the self as somehow coherent and existing within the temporal chronology of life. This drive logically motivates not only autobiographers suceh as Barthes but also, as will be evidenced, diarists such as Woolf, White, Smart, and Nin. The diary, like Barthes's text, is, on the one hand, fragmented and piecemeal by virtue of the fact that it is ordered as a book of separate entries; on the other, like Barthes's text, many diaries contain connected narratives, both within and between entries.

Eakin focuses on narrative structure as a means of supporting his argument against scholars such as Paul De Man who contend that the self in language has no referent beyond that language. Eakin maintains that "'the picture' is an intrinsic part of 'the thing itself' and cannot be separated out of it."[125] His discussion is important because in our postmodern times, when the self has been declared to be unknown to itself and even to be non-existent, he gives us back our selves, for he considers the "announcements of the death of the unified subject are premature." Eakin believes that, contrary to its assertion "Do I not know that, in the field of the subject, there is no referent?" Barthes's *Roland Barthes* consistently attaches itself to its referent self. In fact, Barthes's "making of a textual self here and elsewhere in Barthes' later work became a central feature of his biographical experience," and so "The concept of a self-reflexive textuality wholly divorced from biography and chronicity is only a wishful fiction and nothing more."[126] The notion that the unified self actually "lives" is especially significant for women, who, as we shall see, have only in recent historical and critical times come into their own as "whole" and central subjects.

Investigations of self today tend to focus on issues arising out of post-structural, psychoanalytic, and linguistic analyses which would allow the self some knowledge about itself but also a capacity to deceive itself; which would admit that the self is always in part invented by and perpetuated through its linguistic and textual configurations but also by its social, cultural, and historical contexts. This is the point made by Eakin, who finds that "the most promising contemporary treatments [of the autobiographical self] suggest that the self and language are mutually implicated in a single, interdependent system of symbolic behaviour."[127] It is from this interdependent perspective that I examine the textual and historical selves of Woolf, White, Smart, and Nin. It should be emphasized that features of selfhood are also determined by gendered codes, and I will explore these in detail in chapter 2.

Rosenwald recognizes how autobiographical selfhood is problematized in the diary specifically, and he offers a mode of analysis for investigating interpretive mysteries. A subject's self may best be uncovered, not by looking for blatant "truths of assertion" made by the writer, but by detecting her or his subtle "signs of behavior." Specifically, the diary's "status as a continuous record of comparable gestures" is what makes detection possible. The reader of a diary must examine not simply one entry but the series of entries that make up the text. In such a comparison, habits and hence aspects of personality are revealed. Instructing us on what to look for in a diarist's "modus operandi," Rosenwald insists that not only the written words "but also their incarnation and format" should be taken as evidence.

He offers the most comprehensive checklist of behavioural signs that I have found to date; since my analysis of diaries gratefully works through this list, it needs to be quoted in full. To begin, life-writing scholars must consider "the sort of book a diarist buys or makes to write in, and what it costs; how a volume of the diary is presented *qua* volume, what span of time it characteristically includes, whether it is given a formal beginning or ending; whether the text is immaculate or scribbled over with revisions; whether the page is exploited as a unit of organization; where dates are placed relative to the entries they govern; what non-verbal marks accompany the words."

Next, scholars must evaluate "how long the average entry is, and how frequently and regularly entries are made; which subjects are treated at length, which in passing, which not at all; how entries are organized, whether by order of association or order of occurrence or order of exposition; what use is made of first- and second-person pronouns; what areas of the entry are habitual and which free ...; how sentences are punctuated and words capitalized." Once a modus operandi is identified, we need to interpret variations, deviations, and changes "at every level of organization, for it is as true from the diachronic perspective as from the synchronic that a set of habits is a way of being, and even the slightest modification registers a considerable tremor."[128] Fothergill likewise labels the information gleaned through habit the "imprint" of the author, that "mark on the page" revealing either intentional self-expression or unconsciously dropped nuggets of personality.[129]

Before we proceed to an examination of specifically female "marks on the page," it is fitting to end this chapter with a working definition for the term "diary literature." Though I have argued that it is not appropriate, or even possible, to limit genres to single definitions, I can put forward certain qualities which might suggest the diaristic direction of a text. The diary is a book of days presented in chronological sequence, though not necessarily recorded as such. It inscribes the thoughts, feelings, and experiences of its author and may depict the social, historical, and intellectual period in which she or he lives and writes. Aspects of the author's character may be denied or repressed, or acknowledged and celebrated. The author is identical to the protagonist in this life story, though the author necessarily narrates it through varying layers of personae or invented, fictive selves. The diary is an open-ended book, but it may include internal closures and summations. By virtue of its status as a book of days, it is disconnected, yet it may offer structural and thematic patterns and connectives. Though likely written spontaneously, it is a consciously crafted text, such that the diarist often takes content and aesthetics into account. Finally, though composed in private, the diary is not necessarily a secret document. It may be intended for an audience: an individual, a small group of people, or a general public, and either contemporary with or future to the diarist's lifetime.

This definition is broad and flexible, reflecting the fluid nature of generic distinction. The diary is grounded in assumptions of what it should be, yet it is a space in which these assumptions can be undermined, appropriated, manipulated. These are the qualities that made the diary so attractive and useful to Woolf, White, Smart, and Nin.

2 "That profoundly female, and feminist, genre"

I was fourteen when I received the book which I made my first diary. It came in my stocking on Christmas morning, a book of blank, unlined pages that was titled simply *The Next to Nothing Book*. I put it aside in favour of bigger, more exciting gifts, but that night I opened it and wrote, "Dear Nothing," and it became something – just as hundreds of years earlier Fanny Burney had addressed her diary to "Dear Nobody" and made it a "Somebody." At that moment I had no idea that such a small stocking stuffer would become perhaps the biggest, most exciting gift, not that my mother gave to me, but that I gave to myself – a first expression of and to my self. I now think of Anaïs Nin, also beginning her diary as a schoolgirl: "Nothing comforts me like being able to tell all my sorrows, my joys and my thoughts to a silent friend" (*ed*, 1: 39–40). Though I long ago bid farewell to "Dear Nothing," twenty years after that Christmas night I am still telling "all my sorrows, my joys and my thoughts" to my listening diary.

It was as if by instinct that I entered a tradition of female diary-keeping, and yet once in, I gradually came to appreciate how the journal has been, and remains, an ideal and perhaps unprecedented space for girls and women. Adrienne Rich rightly refers to it as "that profoundly female, and feminist, genre." Historicizing a nineteenth-century division between private and public spheres, she makes clear that "fundamental to women's oppression is the assumption that we as a group belong to the 'private' sphere of the home, the hearth, the family, the sexual, the emotional, out of which men emerge as adults to act in the 'public' arena of power, the 'real' world."[1] Given this situation, one can understand how the diary would become a more crucial outlet for women than for men, since women could find in its private, unassuming pages a place to express themselves, confirm their value, and paradoxically comply with and challenge the silence prescribed for respectable feminine conduct.

Harriet Blodgett maintains that the diary is a characteristic female form, while others, such as Gannett and Nussbaum, suggest that it is a genre more generally practised by women, marketed to women, and acytually created by women. The purpose of this work is not to focus on women versus men or to pit women's diaries against men's. However, in exploring the diary as a female space, and in charting a specifically female diaristic tradition, I will necessarily examine not only women's particular hold over this genre but also the subsequent neglect and devaluing of their diaries despite this hold.

PEPYS'S SISTER

Women have legitimate claims to a diaristic history. One of the first diarists was Lady Margaret Hoby (1571–1633), whose extant diary from 1599 to 1605 evolved during these years from a Puritan spiritual and moral account into the kind of book we now generally assume a diary to be: a record of daily thoughts and activities.[2] Blodgett argues that, "As the first English female diarist, she anticipates much of what is to come in women's diaries – besides stealing a march on Pepys's 'and so to bed.'"[3] Of this particular sign-off, Fothergill writes, "It will be observed that Lady Hoby was using Pepys's most famous contribution to English idiom sixty years before he began to write."[4] Both statements show how women's contributions are not made famous but are devalued, for if Hoby was writing sixty years before Pepys, she was not "using" anything of his.

Hoby's divergence from the typical Puritan regimen expected of her in favour of more personal and domestic recordings signals the fact that, from the beginning, women played a crucial role in the development of the genre. In "The Emergence of Women's Autobiography in England," Cynthia Pomerleau states: "The idea that oneself, one's feelings, one's spouse and domestic relations were properly and innately worth writing about was essentially a female idea, however tentatively conceived at the time. There is little or no precedent for such a notion, at least in English, in male thinking or practice."[5] In the same spirit, Felicity Nussbaum discusses early-eighteenth-century diarists. She identifies women such as Elizabeth Bury, Deborah Bell, and Mrs H. Housman, whose respective published journals represent some of the first works of private, interior examination. Not surprisingly, then, it is "possible that women invented such a form, that they began the idea of private, and later, public articulation of quotidian organization of internal experience."[6]

If Hoby was among the first English diarists, and if women played a major role in the development of the genre, why are men's diaries privileged over women's in the variety of ways they are? Domna Stanton wonders, incredulously, how to reconcile women's absence from critical discourse on autobiography "with the age-old, pervasive decoding of all female writing as autobiographical"; and why, if women have historically been associated with autobiography, their writings are viewed negatively, while men's possible appropriation of the genre is viewed positively.[7]

Addressing these queries with specific regard to the diary, Cinthia Gannett struggles to connect two opposing realities: the first, that male diarists such as Pepys and James Boswell hold canonical rights to founding and influencing the diaristic tradition, which has consequently been recognized and perpetuated as largely a male one; the second, that women buy and read more diaries than men, blank diaries in stores are marketed for women, more adolescent girls receive diary books than boys[8] – in short, as Thomas Mallon recognizes, the diary is "a genre to which women have always felt especially drawn." This dichotomy is well illustrated by the fact that Elizabeth Smart penned some of her entries in manufactured diary books which were titled "Pepys Lady's Diary."

Mallon notes that Western women began to keep diaries in order to express themselves "in centuries when their attempts to practice other forms of literature – say, produce a play – were considered presumptuous or silly." He believes that the "social history of all people is more detailed than it would otherwise be because of women's attention to the texture of the everyday in the diaries their men permitted them."[9] This last phrase is particularly striking, all the more so given that Mallon ends his paragraph here and offers no elaboration on what he means by "permitted." But he does imply that the diary was the one form which women were authorized to write in, a silent text which presumably did not threaten to claim for itself a more "serious," legitimate literary status. His comment contributes to the perception that women's writings have in the past been controlled, however subtly, by men.

Further evidence drives home the truth of such speculations. Though Evelyn and Pepys were among the first published sensations in the world of diaries, their journals had been written more than one hundred years before they were found and published. Pepys, for instance, by virtue of being a man who had received the benefit of a formal education, entrusted his diaries to his alma mater, Magdalene College, Cambridge. There they were sealed in privileged safety until the time came when someone took an interest in them and decoded them.[10] Unfortunately, time has obliterated the possibility of our knowing what other diaries were found and decidedly not published.

In her introduction to *Private Pages: Diaries of American Women, 1830s–1970s*, Penelope Franklin articulates the gendered fate of diaries: "What I found amazed me. The vast majority of published journals were those of men. The thousands of unpublished women's diaries were in archives across the country – thousands more, I realized, were in attics like my own."[11] In researching working-class women's diaries from the period 1880–1910, Elizabeth Hampsten corroborates this picture: "because it is generally assumed that what is worth keeping is what has historical value, and because historical value is measured by accounts of discrete events (boundaries laid, lands bought and sold), which men are more likely than women to participate in and to describe, the writings of men are likely to be kept and to find their way to permanent archives. How many times has someone said that writings of a particular woman had no historical value because they were merely about daily events?"[12] In the past, more women were illiterate than men, but of the women who could write, the private, non-threatening journal was, along with the letter, the genre they would most probably have practised. And yet these journals by women were not likely to be preserved the way the men's were.

Virginia Woolf, in *A Room of One's Own*, asks us to consider the fate of William Shakespeare's fictitious sister, Judith Shakespeare. If William enjoyed the privileges of a formal education and the ability to enter a profession, Judith was denied these privileges simply because she was female. Woolf paints a bleak picture of Judith; she winds up killing herself after her hopes for her own theatrical career are cruelly thwarted by the actor-manager Nick Greene, who, rather than giving her a job, seduces her and makes her pregnant.[13]

With Judith's fate in mind, we must wonder what happened to Evelyn's or Pepys's sister. While we do not know about Pepys's sister, we do know about his wife, Elizabeth. She also kept a diary, but hers was not to be valued the way her husband's was and is. Enraged by certain passages about their marriage which his wife read aloud to him, Pepys took it upon himself to destroy her diary. He recorded this brutal act within his own diary (unaware of the irony implicit in the fact that he, unlike his wife, still had a diary to turn to): "She now read it [the diary], and was so picquant, and wrote in English and most it true, of the retiredness of her life and how unpleasant it was, that being writ in English and so in danger of being met with and read by others, I was vexed at it and desired her and then commanded her to teare it – which she desired to be excused it; I leapt out of the bed and in my shirt clapped them into the pockets of my breeches, that she might not get them from me; and having got on my stockings and breeches and gown, I pulled them out one by one and tore them all before her face, though it went against my heart to do it, she crying and desiring me not to do it."[14] Of this passage, Judy Simons comments: "The violence of Elizabeth Pepys's reaction to the rape and pillage of her diary ... suggests the value of the papers as an extension of self, the physical violation equivalent to an assault on her person."[15] Pepys's "assault" on his wife's diary parallels Nick Greene's assault on Judith Shakespeare's body.

Gannett calls attention to further references to violence, in this case in the diary of Jane Carlyle, wife of Thomas Carlyle; in the nineteenth century Jane opened her diary thus: "I remember Charles Buller saying of the Duchess of Praslin's murder, 'What could a poor fellow do with a wife who kept a journal but murder her.'" Carlyle did not murder his journalizing wife, but like Pepys, he did destroy many of her diaries.[16] Henry James, in similar mood, rejected the idea of his sister Alice's journals being published, even after her death, despite the fact that she had written them specifically for such a purpose.[17] Simons quotes Margaret Cavendish, the seventeenth-century woman of letters, who explained that men resist women authors "because they think thereby, women incroach too much upon their prerogatives; for they hold *Books* as their *Crowne*, and the *Sword* their *Scepter*, by which they rule, and governe."[18] Cavendish helps us to begin to understand the actions of husbands and brothers such as Pepys, Carlyle, and James. Her assertion, backed up with the evidence of the actions of these men, also contradicts Mallon's assumption that diaries were "permitted" to women by men.

Obviously, though, not all men responded as brutally as the murderous Duke of Praslin or the destructive Pepys to women diarists. And as Franklin has found, there are "thousands of unpublished women's dairies" waiting to be discovered. It has been only recently, in the last few decades, that this mass of buried matter has begun to be unearthed and made available to interested readers. But of those that do get published, many have been distorted. Husbands and family members who edit the diaries of their wives or daughters are particularly susceptible to charges that they have tampered with the writer's intentions.[19] As noted in chapter 1, Anne Olivier Bell has argued that Leonard Woolf's abridged *A Writer's Diary* presents an unflattering portrait of Virginia

Woolf.[20] And Simons suggests that John Middleton Murry, who in 1927 edited the diary of his wife, Katherine Mansfield, has created "a sentimentalised portrait of his wife as pure, childlike and romantic," a writer limited to, and limited by, the short story genre.[21]

Problematic approaches to the preservation and publication of women's journals have been exacerbated by critical devaluation and neglect. It is well beyond the middle of his introduction to *English Diaries* before Arthur Ponsonby mentions that women are diarists too, and he does so by confining this apparently rare bit of information to two paragraphs.[22] In his updated *More English Diaries*, his occasional references to women are in the vein of this remark: "Lady Knightley of Fawsley, for instance, wrote sixty volumes, no part of which has any sort of merit."[23] P.A. Spalding is blatant in his dismissal of women diarists in *Self-Harvest: A Study of Diaries and the Diarist*. Less than ten pages from the end of his book, he reminds us that "the principles analyzed in this study have been drawn" from the diaries of Pepys, Boswell, James Woodforde, Benjamin Haydon, and Francis Kilvert. Only at this point does he comment, "It will be noted that the list contains no woman," for "despite the number of good feminine diarists, not one, except possibly Lady Eleanor Butler, equals our five men in total effect. They lack, as it were, *solidity*, a third dimension."[24]

In *Dear Diary ...: Some Studies in Self-Interest*, Brian Dobbs affirms that there is "undoubted literary equality of the men and women who have kept diaries."[25] But like Ponsonby and Spalding, he reserves his attention to women until later, in this case the last chapter before the epilogue. Entitled "The Female of the Species," this chapter is specifically set aside for the analysis of women's diaries. In the forty pages he offers here, Dobbs does give a fair treatment to the diarists under consideration, but the fact that he relegates women not only to their own chapter but also to the end of his book suggests that they are to be isolated, set apart from the more universal, gendered-masculine study of diaries.

Women's writings have often been devalued in light of men's, a practice which may be traced to the establishment of a canon of sacred religious texts in the Middle Ages, and which extended over time to embrace secular, literary works, predominantly those written by men.[26] Women's diaries in particular have suffered the fate of being gendered "feminine" and thus of less historical, cultural, and literary value than "masculine" works. In *A Day at a Time*, Margo Culley summarizes the historical conditions which sealed this fate. Though her work is confined to American diaries, her comments can be read to reflect circumstances in Canada and Britain as well. Like Adrienne Rich, Culley attributes "a split between the public and private spheres" of experience to the nineteenth century, such that things private became synonymous with women. At the same time, the "content and function of the diary" was shifting from the public to the private in reaction to historical events such as the industrial revolution, movements such as Romanticism, and scientific approaches to the psyche such as psychoanalysis, all of which contributed to a redefining of the self.

Specifically, "As the modern idea of the secular diary as a 'secret' record of an inner life evolved, that inner life – the life of personal reflection and emotion – became an important aspect of the 'private sphere' and women continued to turn to the diary as one place where they were permitted, indeed encouraged, to indulge full 'self-centeredness.' American men, unused to probing and expressing this inner life in any but religious terms found, as the secular self emerged as the necessary subject of the diary, the form less and less amenable to them."[27]

By the nineteenth-century's close, further feminizing of the diary was brought about by the proliferation of "etiquette books," which were designed to instruct young women how to gauge and improve their feminine conduct through particular diary-keeping habits and techniques. These etiquette books, aptly described by Blodgett as "potent weapons of socialization," armed women in their diaristic fight against their moral weaknesses and urged them to celebrate their moral victories and domestic conquests.[28] The nineteenth-century gender split, coupled with the prevalence of instruction manuals, heralded a new order, so that by the twentieth century, women were probably keeping more diaries than were men.[29]

It should be clarified that this kind of journalizing was defined not only by gender but also by class and race, for it was a specifically white, upper-class privilege to linger over one's activities and the fashionable recording of them.[30] This is not to imply that women of the lower classes did not keep diaries. Hampsten has uncovered a rich history of working-class journals, offered to us in *Read This Only to Yourself*, as have archivists such as Huff and Franklin. Their findings underscore the notion that the diary has been a genre familiar to women of diverse backgrounds. However, the fact that it was more prominently a "feminized" site for upper- and middle-class women is of greater relevance to my work on Woolf, White, Smart, and Nin, for they were raised within largely privileged environments and were educated in and had access to a diary tradition which reflected these privileges.

Though women may have been more directly associated with diaries by the early twentieth century than were men, this association was not properly acknowledged in early critical studies. Women's contributions to the genre have only within the past few decades begun to be celebrated fully. Feminist revisionism has increased interest in both the writings of marginalized writers, such as White, Smart, and Nin, and the marginalized writings – such as diaries – of established writers like Woolf. White is a good example of this change. Her highly praised *Frost in May* was originally published in 1933, and though it was a success at the time, it eventually went out of print. It was not until 1978 that it became the first Virago Modern Classic, launching as it did "a list dedicated to the celebration of women writers and to the rediscovery and reprinting of their works."[31] Once White's novels were (re)introduced into the literary marketplace, they could generate interest in her other work, so that the publication of her diaries became a commercial possibility.

Presses such as Virago, dedicated to reprinting forgotten women's works; publishers eager to promote marginalized genres such as the diary, a genre always available to and practised by women; and feminist revisionism of literary history that seeks to admit women into a canon that has for too long excluded them – all these factors contribute to a new fascination with women's diaries, so that when we think of the genre, we no longer only or automatically think of Pepys but also of Woolf, Nin, Sylvia Plath, and Anne Frank, for instance. Who can we name among the men? André Gide, of course, and there is Franz Kafka. Other twentieth-century male diarists include Arnold Bennett, E.M. Forster, W.H. Auden, David Gascoyne, and Graham Greene. But their journals are not as readily familiar as the now more famous and popular diaries by the women. Plath's journal illustrates just how true this statement is. An entire industry of perhaps unprecedented biographic scrutiny has been built around her diaries, obsessed with what was burned by her husband, Ted Hughes, and what unpublished portions have been denied to the public's eyes. This passion similarly drives the industries of Nin and Woolf studies – though unlike Nin's, Woolf's diary has until recently been rather ignored as a literary work.

This twentieth-century surge of interest in women's diaries has more to do with the increased attention given to women than with their increased productivity. It is not that women's association with the genre has dramatically changed, but that critical and biographical scrutiny has more fully recognized this association. Motivations for journal keeping in the twentieth century reflect those of earlier diarizing times. In order to appreciate this fact, it is helpful to return to Sidonie Smith, whose discussion of the development of autobiography reflects that of the diary as well.

MOTHERS OF THE DIARY

Smith proposes that most women of the late medieval and Renaissance periods dutifully restrained themselves and did not write for the public. Those who did write, however, can be credited with helping to develop the autobiography genre. She also mentions that women kept diaries, but she posits that they confined their texts to private and domestic themes and thus did not challenge their prescribed silence in the way that the "going public" autobiographers were doing. Smith has only the autobiographer in mind when she writes: "Stealing words from the language, she would know and name herself, appropriating the self-creative power patriarchal culture has historically situated in the pens of man."[32]

Smith's conclusions could and should be read to suggest that it is the very act of writing, as opposed to the act of writing publicly, that symbolizes challenge and empowerment. The diarist as much as the autobiographer steals the "pens of man" and affirms, however silently, the value of her presence. Gannett would agree, for she lauds early diarists who "created texts out of their lives and new lives out of their texts. Texts are marks on the world; they are physical objects, and journals and diaries, while silent, are visible, potentially permanent markers of a life lived."[33] Blodgett also sees that it is the *act* of writing a diary which is particularly meaningful to women: "I suggest that diary keeping has been practised so extensively by women because it has been possible for them and gratifying to them ... A diary is an act of language that, by speaking of one's self, sustains one's sense of being a self, with an autonomous and significant identity."[34] It is necessary not only to consider that the act of writing is a vocalizing statement but also to recognize that diaries have often been written deliberately for some form of public audience. This perception makes women's challenges all the more dramatic and determined.

Concurrent with the development of women's autobiography was that of women's fiction, and in order to understand the one, we need to consider the other. I will briefly trace the history of women writing novels because, in discussing the diary as a modernist work, my main interest is to show how it resembles the modern novel specifically. This is not an arbitrary comparison. The diary has often been classified and dismissed as a female form, but so has the novel. Similar historical, social, and cultural factors impacted upon women becoming novelists and diarists.

In *Mothers of the Novel*, Dale Spender challenges the canonized version of literary history that celebrates five men as the founders and exemplars of the novel: Daniel Defoe, Henry Fielding, Samuel Richardson, Tobias Smollett, and Laurence Sterne. Strikingly reminiscent of those feminists who unearthed a plethora of diaries doomed to archival neglect, Spender "discovered" hundreds of novels by eighteenth-century women similarly collecting dust. Having spent her intellectual life accepting that Jane Austen was among the first women novelists, Spender was stunned to realize that Austen was in fact the inheritor of a female tradition that had essentially been obliterated. The explanation that her research led her to make is that women's work is not differentiated from men's on the basis of the quality of the writing; rather, a devaluation occurs "based on sex and power."[35] This conclusion echoes those made by Gannett, Franklin, and Hampsten about the (lack of) preservation of women's diaries.

Jane Spencer explores women's relation to the novel in *The Rise of the Woman Novelist: From Aphra Behn to Jane Austen*, and like Spender, she recognizes a discrepancy: "Eighteenth-century England witnessed two remarkable and inter-connected literary events: the emergence of the novel and the establishment of the professional woman writer. The first of these has been extensively documented and debated, while the second has been largely ignored."[36] Though Spender is devoted more to establishing women as the founders of the novel, while Spencer sees them contributing to it, they offer complementary analyses of the complex connections between history, gender, and the novel.

Novels first appeared in England at the beginning of the eighteenth century and were informed by and inscribed with features historically associated with women. Spender considers the novel "a logical extension of women's role," for novels were written in the form of letters, and letters were what women most often wrote.[37] Women also wrote journals, and thus early novels assumed the diary form as well. Note that Fanny Burney, one of the earliest and most successful and eminent novelists, was also one of the first diarists to be published. In writing novels, women were using what was available to them to gain recognition. Unlike literary classics such as the epic, which was inherited from ancient cultures and available only to those with learning – namely, men – the novel presupposed no education or cultivated intellect among its practitioners and readers.

Celeste Schenck points out that women may have been especially drawn to the novel because, at the time of its inception in the early eighteenth century, poets were busy conducting the revival of classical, Augustan themes and forms.[38] Women may arguably have translated their private writings into the new form of the novel, which enabled them to invest it with what was not already established as, and encoded with, cultural authority. As Woolf observed in *A Room of One's*

Own, "The novel alone was young enough to be soft" in women's hands.[39]

Not only did early novels reflect the life-writing forms practised by women, but they also were made possible within the sphere inhabited by women: novels were written in homes. Woolf explains the ramifications of this circumstance upon generations of women who wrote: "Writing was a reputable and harmless occupation. The family peace was not broken by the scratching of a pen. No demand was made upon the family purse. For ten and sixpence one can buy paper enough to write all the plays of Shakespeare – if one has a mind that way. Pianos and models, Paris, Vienna, and Berlin, masters and mistresses, are not needed by a writer. The cheapness of writing paper is, of course, the reason why women have succeeded as writers before they have succeeded in the other professions."[40]

It is therefore understandable why writing was the preferred profession for women in the eighteenth and nineteenth centuries. Why they needed a profession at all was the result of changing economic conditions. Before the eighteenth century, women had enjoyed some status as contributors to the family income through various cottage industries. These home industries, however, were taken over by the increasing trade and industrialization of the eighteenth century, which effectively rendered women not only idle but also dependent on husbands for economic support. Women were confined to the (unproductive) home, and they were given carefully scripted roles to play within it.

Woolf provides a vivid description of the leading role, as performed by the actor she named the "Angel in the House": "She was intensely sympathetic. She was immensely charming. She was utterly unselfish. She excelled in the difficult arts of family life. She sacrificed herself daily ... In short she was so constituted that she never had a mind or a wish of her own, but preferred to sympathize always with the minds and wishes of others. Above all – I need not say it – she was pure." Of greatest consequence was that this "Angel" was trained to prevent women such as Woolf from writing, as Woolf herself complained: "It was she who used to come between me and my paper when I was writing reviews. It was she who bothered me and wasted my time." In chapter 4, we shall see how Woolf defended herself against the angel and "at last killed her." For now, though, we must consider how this angel "bothered" Woolf's literary precursors. Woolf historicizes this meddling phantom to "those days – the last of Queen Victoria," when "every house had its Angel."[41] Spencer finds her lurking around even earlier, situating "the rise of a new ideology of femininity" within the late seventeenth and early eighteenth centuries, as the result of the rupture between work and home.

Women in the home, who were supposed to be devoted to it and their families, would seem defiant in aspiring to things beyond. But they could manipulate their domestic, private spaces into ready-made work facilities, a task that was easy enough given that their start-up and maintenance costs were, according to Woolf, negligible. By writing at home, women did not have to give up their household duties. A novel could be written, like a diary, during whatever spare moments they could find for themselves. Woolf's comment that for women writing prose, "interruptions there will always be," is well supported.[42] Nin, for instance, was only too well aware of how the time she spent writing her diary had to be accommodated to the time spent performing domestic chores (from which her two brothers were excused). Consider this entry made when she was eighteen: "I opened my Diary and laid it on the table with my pen and ink ready to use. I would make a bed and write five lines; I would wash dishes and write 10 lines – the compensation according to size of task!" (*ed* 2: 285, 293). Nin was proving how she was fulfilling what was expected of her as a woman, but she was also underscoring, with her sarcastic tone, how these expectations were gendered ones, and how they threatened her development as both a diarist and a novelist.

Moreover, Schenck tells how Adrienne Rich tried to write poetry as a new mother in the 1950s: "the poem was jotted in fragments during children's naps, brief hours in a library, or at 3:00 A.M. after rising with a wakeful child." Rich described her poem as being composed of "fragments and scraps,"[43] appropriate images which call to mind women's diaries as well. What they also bring to mind is the modernist preoccupation with the fragmentary, perhaps best illustrated in T.S. Eliot's now-famous assertion at the end of *The Waste Land*: "These fragments I have shored against my ruins." The connections between modernist and diaristic fragments, and how women "shored them" against their ruins, are explored in chapter 3.

In general, women writers had to pay a heavy price for their profession. There is a paradox implicit in the notion of women writing novels for money: "writing, at the same time as it was being professionalized, was also being domesticated." That is, novels not only were written in the home but had to be *about* it and the virtues that the woman in the home represented and upheld. This was the main way that women could be accepted in the marketplace. Domestication was propagated through conduct books, which instructed women how best to achieve and maintain their femininity, within both their real and their written lives.[44] Recall that manuals were also published to assist girls and women on how to perfect their moral and gendered sensibilities in their diaries.

During the eighteenth century, women were strongly associated with the novel and were well recognized for their achievements. But as the novel became more respected as a form, men possibly began to appropriate it. Spender makes much of this possibility, arguing that it was after the eighteenth century that women's accomplishments began to be devalued and their novelistic heritaghe denied. It was in the nineteenth century "that the pervasive notion of silly novels by silly women novelists has held such sway," the consequence being that many women wrote under closer personal guard – as evidenced by the use of pseudonyms such as Currer, Ellis, and Acton Bell (Charlotte, Emily, and Anne Brontë), George Eliot (Mary Ann Evans), and George Sand (Amandine-Aurore Lucille Dupin). Consider also that Jane Austen's novels were initially attributed to an anonymous author, and that Elizabeth Barrett Browning's personal love poems, *Sonnets From the Portuguese*, were presented as mere translations rather than her own original work. Recognizing that they could not prevent women from writing, men developed a strategy, as Spender describes it, of "containing" their words. Just as eighteenth-century novelists inscribed in their texts a femininity as a pay-off to patriarchy, so their nineteenth-century siblings were advised to limit their imaginative scope to emotional, domestic tales.

Not surprisingly, then, the canon makers of the nineteenth and twentieth centuries could look back and dismiss many novels produced by women as being "mere" romance.[45] But men have also always written love stories. Their novels are filled to the point of preoccupation with female characters – and female characters in domestic settings. Spender appropriately concludes that it is not the subject of the text which is being devalued but the sex of the author. At the same time as the novel was subjected to this kind of gender division, so too was the diary. In the nineteenth century, "journal" became associated with men and public value, and "diary" devalued as domestic and feminine.[46]

The fate of women's works is made clear in *How to Suppress Women's Writing*, where Joanna Russ provides a broad and ironic list of accusations levelled against the female author in order that her writings be kept out of, or be devalued within, the marketplace: "She didn't write it. She wrote it, but she shouldn't have. She wrote it, but look what she wrote about. She wrote it, but 'she' isn't really an artist and 'it' isn't really serious, of the right genre – i.e., really art. She wrote it,

but she wrote only one of it. She wrote it, but it's only interesting/
included in the canon for one, limited reason. She wrote it, but there
are very few of her."[47]

While a male fear of a female threat may account for women's
limited presence in the canon, more needs to be said about the fact
that women did, complicitly, inscribe traditional narratives in pre-
twentieth-century autobiography, diaries, and novels – we might say
in line with Russ, "She wrote it the way she thought she should."
Women's lives have certainly been, and arguably still are, largely
focused on and around men. This focus is manifested in women's
preoccupation with things domestic, with their appearance and fashion, and with love. Women generally aspired to marriage as their
most significant adult goal; once wed, they were then expected to
produce children in fulfillment of their female destiny. Many women
accepted not only these roles but also the personality that accompanied them – "feminine," frail, emotional, passive, devoted. On the
other hand, Blodgett provides much evidence to support the view
that women often recorded in their diaries their desires for and
active struggles to achieve political, social, sexual, and economic
equality. And yet in her final analysis, she must concede that women
too often either bought into or did not challenge enough the male
myths of women, and instead, accommodated themselves to male
expectations and desires.[48]

Smith describes a bind that pre-twentieth-century female autobiographers were caught in as they accepted or rejected self-determination
by male myths, becoming either womanly women or manly women.
Women who accepted traditional conditioning wrote through the myth
of the ideal woman – as identified by Spender and Spencer – embrac-
ing prescribed roles of femininity and narrating their stories passively,
effacing themselves and the value of their experiences as they presented themselves as good, humble, unambitious. But these writers were
likely devalued and dismissed because they were "just" writing about
women, and women could not tell central stories within a patriarchy
which relegated them to the margins. Rather, the stories they inevitably
told positioned women "in relationship to a life cycle tied to biological
phenomena and the social uses to which those phenomena are put:
birth, menarche, maidenhood, marriage, childbirth, menopause, widowhood." The result was the obliteration of any possibility for individuality.

Women who rejected traditional roles were no better off. Though
many may have openly and unabashedly celebrated themselves and
their accomplishments, flaunting their derring-do for all to see, they
would probably have been judged harshly by the public, which would

have dismissed them as selfish, aggressive, manly, and not "real" women at all. Further, these women would have ostracized themselves from their own gender because they were necessarily narrating stories which inscribed, not women's marginal, but men's central experiences. As Smith posits, to write with authority is to write "like a man," and thus women could be branded unfeminine in the process of "posturing" as men.[49]

If until the nineteenth century essentialist conceptions of textual selfhood trapped women in a Catch-22, these concepts were less confining as the twentieth century unfolded. Smith suggests that autobiographies at this time afforded women "more flexible, more self-conscious, more experimental" possibilities for self-representation. This change was in part due to the spread in the first part of the century of Nietzsche's epistemological skepticisms, which posited that the self is merely a social construct, and Freud's theories, which destabilized the unified self, fracturing it into knowable and unknowable parts and limiting its authority, and to the emergence in the second part of the century of structural, post-structural, psychoanalytical, and linguistic methods of critical evaluation, which further called into question the authenticity of textual selves. Because autobiography had traditionally established itself as a contract to honour the unified self, the breakdown of this self also fractured what had been an "androcentric contract." "Twentieth-century destabilizations of the notions of self, author, representation, narrative, and gender have thus opened up fault-lines in the ideology of a unitary self through which alternative ideologies of self and narrative have seeped."[50]

The modern novel is one site on which these alternative ideologies have been registered, as demonstrated by Rachel Blau DuPlessis in *Writing beyond the Ending: Narrative Strategies of Twentieth-Century Women Writers*. Her argument arises from the notion "that woman is neither wholly 'subcultural' nor, certainly, wholly main-cultural, but negotiates difference and sameness, marginality and inclusion in a constant dialogue."[51] To this end, DuPlessis shows how twentieth-century women rewrite traditional narratives in such a way as to critique their androcentric origins and meanings. Nineteenth-century women writers generally provided accepted narrative endings. Protagonists who were successful in their femininity were rewarded with marriage; those who failed to meet societal standards were judged to be corrupted or failures or were made invalids and often doomed to death. Twentieth-century writers broke with this binary hold over predictable endings and wrote "beyond" them.[52]

DuPlessis focuses on "writing beyond the ending" of the romance plot in particular because she identifies diverse women writers across the twentieth century who have similarly chosen this plot as their site of "scrutiny, critique, and transformation of narrative." This shared selection makes sense in light of her contention that "the romance plot ... is a trope for the sex-gender system as a whole." "As a narrative pattern, the romance plot muffles the main female character, represses quest, valorizes heterosexual as opposed to homosexual ties, incorporates individuals within couples as a sign of their personal and narrative success." Writing beyond this kind of ending results in narratives that challenge scripted, limited roles and experiences of women.[53] These narratives are rewritten to a great extent within diaries as well. The storylines that plot the journals of Woolf, White, Smart, and Nin consist of, among other things, travels of adventure, professional ambition, lesbian love, adulterous passion, and unconventional parenting.

POLYVOCAL PLAYGROUNDS

Smith's and DuPlessis's analyses show that the twentieth century offered new possibilities for writers. This view must be qualified, however, because women's options remained loaded ones, so that in choosing to be alternative or radical or different, a writer was still threatened with ostracism, castigation, and criticism. Smith describes the modern autobiographer as one who "begins to grapple self-consciously with her identity" – the word "grapple" underscoring the inner struggle that ensues when a woman confronts her absence within cultural and linguistic representations of selfhood.[54]

It is arguable that modernist women were more consciously aware of – or better able to articulate – how gender is a construct and how women have been handed predetermined narratives through which their lives are to unfold.[55] Nowhere is this awareness more evident than in *Orlando*, Woolf's elaborate parody not only of the art of biography but also of the art of gender performance. Having transformed her eponymous protagonist from a man into a woman at the start of the eighteenth century, Woolf gives her this profound insight: "She remembered how, as a young man, she had insisted that women must be obedient, chaste, scented, and exquisitely apparelled. 'Now I shall have to pay in my own person for those desires,' she reflected; 'for women are not (judging by my own short experience of the sex) obedient, chaste, scented, and exquisitely apparelled by nature. They can only attain these graces, without which they may enjoy none of the delights of life, by the most tedious discipline.'"[56]

Orlando's plight, brought to light for twentieth-century readers, reflects modern women's struggles as they "grappled" with the self-conscious knowledge of how they had been socially gendered. The notion that "grappling" went on at all in the supposedly modern period may be tied to the argument put forward by Kadar: "Most often in this century life writing is exploited by women writers."[57] Stanton questions whether women, by choosing to write in devalued life-writing forms, may have encouraged the myth of their being unable to write in anything else. And yet she suggests that the only way they could gain entry into the literary marketplace was to write in forms non-threatening to men.[58]

The question that obtains from this historical query is why, in the modernist period of the twentieth century, when women seemed to have unprecedented access to the marketplace, they would still feel the need to exploit private – and hence devalued – forms for public ends. The answer may lie in the possibility that, within this century, women still inhabit a patriarchal culture. As we shall see in the next chapter, even the most unconventional modernist women were pitted against a conventional society. Like their nineteenth-century sisters before them, they continued to negotiate between what they had been led to believe was appropriate and expected behaviour and expression, on the one hand, and thoughts and actions which were uncensored and unconditioned, on the other.

Kadar's contention that women have exploited life-writing forms in the twentieth century echoes the point made by Culley that women in this century have dominated the diaristic field. In "All of a Piece: Women's Poetry and Autobiography," Celeste Schenck states that the genre of autobiography – and, I would argue, by extension that of the diary – "may be paradigmatic of all women's writing" because of its "concern with constituting a female subject."[59] It is for this reason that theorists are so eager to formulate a poetics of the genre. This concern is crucial, for changing theories about the nature of the self and how that self can be known and represented have problematized, in particular, how women's subjectivity has not been adequately represented throughout history and within texts.

According to Smith, though Renaissance humanism allowed men to reconfigure themselves as individual, complex beings, women were not offered such self-fashioning possibilities. Rather than being permitted or encouraged to explore unique sensibilities of self, they were limited to and determined by the "four predominant life scripts available to women in the late medieval and Renaissance periods: the nun, the queen, the wife, and the witch." Though this is not an exhaustive list – additional stereotypes include the angel, the martyr, the whore, the mistress, the muse, the abandoned woman, the fallen woman – what is significant is that women emerge from history as having had difficulties configuring themselves outside the roles assigned to them by society. Women necessarily became the "other" against which the "new" men were able to define themselves.[60] Woolf states the case simply: "Women have served all these centuries as looking-glasses possessing the magic and delicious power of reflecting the figure of man at twice its natural size."[61]

Humanism further diminished women's sense and "size" of self by constituting the subject capable of full self-knowledge as a universally male one, consequently negating, ignoring, or marginalizing female selfhood. In *A Room of One's Own*, Woolf highlights what she perceives to be the phallocentrism inherent in the "I" of male-created protagonists. Glancing through a novel by "Mr. A," Woolf's persona – "call me Mary Beton, Mary Seton, Mary Carmichael or by any name you please" – admits: "One began to be tired of 'I.' Not but what this 'I' was a most respectable 'I'; honest and logical; as hard as a nut, and polished for centuries by good teaching and good feeding." But she is bored because these I's "celebrate male virtues, enforce male values and describe the world of men."[62]

Not only fiction but also autobiography theory and criticism have tended to focus on the male. Not surprisingly, feminist scholars have for the past few decades been working to dismantle these paradigms and erect in their place a structure of selfhood that fully and justly supports the experiences of women and the realities of their lives. Susan Stanford Friedman, in "Women's Autobiographical Selves: Theory and Practice," exposes the patriarchal assumptions underlying interpretations of the autobiographical text. Acknowledging the importance of Gusdorf's contributions to the genre, she nonetheless challenges his individualist perspective. Using Sheila Rowbotham's historical and Nancy Chodorow's psychoanalytic studies, she makes clear that individualistic models of the self cannot be used to identify women and minorities. While Gusdorf dismissed identification, interdependence, and community as issues informing the autobiographical self, Rowbotham, Chodorow, and Friedman bring them back, privileging them as key elements in the formation of women's identities.

Rowbotham equates individualism with the dominant white male heterosexual culture. A man in this position of power can afford to "think of himself as an 'individual.'" Women, on the other hand, defined by this power, are forced to see themselves as "other" and think within a "group consciousness." Chodorow further explains how men's and women's personalities are formed in dramatically different ways: "girls come to define and experience themselves as continuous with others; their experience of self contains more flexible or permeable ego boundaries. Boys come to define themselves as more separate and distinct, with a greater sense of rigid ego boundaries and differentiation. The basic feminine sense of self is connected to the world, the basic masculine sense of self is separate."[63] Whereas men oppose themselves to others, women see themselves in relation to others, living an interdependent existence. Friedman argues that women's identities, unlike men's, evolve from a collective consciousness of self and are defined by interpersonal relationships within a community at large.[64]

Similarly, Stanton conceives an "autogynography" whose purpose is to constitute the female subject, for she realizes that within a phallocentric system a woman is defined as the object to the male subject, and thus a woman's textual self is necessarily "constructed through the relation to mother and father, mate and child." Like Friedman, Stanton acknowledges that the female "I" represents "a denial of a notion essential to the phallogecentric order: the totalized self-contained subject present-to-itself."[65] Smith, as well, reinforces the notion that representation is a problematic practice because it encodes a patriarchal agenda. She refers to Alice Jardine's argument that it reflects an imperialistic desire for "naming, controlling, remembering, understanding."[66] Old criteria for evaluating autobiography must give way to new ones which will take into account the fact that women have historically not been in positions of significant power.

The old criteria of individualism have been replaced with those of post-structuralism, but these new criteria are equally problematic for women. As Shirley Neuman makes clear, while post-structuralism seeks in various ways to fracture the subject and limit its authority, only those who have power and full self-confidence in the first place can afford to surrender it. These agendas thus seem particularly poorly timed for women and minorities, who are coming into their own sense of self and power at the critical moment that the self is declared unfixed and de-authorized.

Neuman explains how theorists of autobiographical texts, interested in redefining a poetics, "have challenged and relinquished what disables them in both humanist and poststructuralist poetics, and have taken what enables them." Specifically, "they have appropriated the poststructuralist project of decentring the universal subject for precisely such decentring has made space for the experience of racial minorities, the working classes, colonial and postcolonial peoples, women, non-heterosexuals. At the same time they have refused to relinquish the possibility of a unified self: why give up a visibility and a position from which to act, a visibility and a position just beginning to become available in either social praxis or literary theory to those who are not Euro-American, white, middle-class and male?"[67] While the subjects of my study are white and middle class, they are women and thus arguably have lacked "a visibility and a position" within society and within texts, if to a lesser extent than women who are, for instance, non-Euro-American and or non-white.

Though she only gestures towards it in an endnote, Neuman identifies this selective taking and discarding as "the fundamental strategy of feminism."[68] Bella Brodzki and Celeste Schenck have employed this strategy in their collection *Life/Lines: Theorizing Women's Autobiography*. In their introduction they outline the critical and political agenda of the essays, which advocate a feminist enterprise that negotiates "the tension between life and literature ... selfhood and textuality."[69] Schenck reiterates this agenda in her contribution "All of a Piece." She emphasizes that autobiographical criticism "requires working on two fronts at once, *both* occupying a kind of center, assuming a subjectivity long denied, and maintaining the vigilant, disruptive stance that speaking from the postmodern margin provides." She concludes that we must read women's autobiography as well as women's other texts which inscribe this autobiography "both as records of historical marginality and, increasingly, as vocative evidence of potential self-presence."[70]

Smith is equally interested in exploring how women, traditionally denied the privilege of the centre, may be granted authority from the margins. In a recuperative gesture, she contends: "While margins have their limitations, they also have their advantages of vision. They are polyvocal, more distant from the centres of power and conventions of selfhood. They are heretical." Celebrating twentieth-century female autobiographers, she recognizes how they have defied concepts of an essentialist, unified self by writing through their multiple, polyvocal selves,[71] appropriating as they go "bits and pieces" of patriarchal "fictions of man and woman."[72] While prescriptive roles may be inhibiting, they also provide women life-writers with culturally condoned covers under which they hide subversive expressions and depictions of self within their texts. It is precisely this appropriating that I identify as a central strategy of Woolf, White, Smart, and Nin, for in constructing and narrating their lives, they borrow to subvert scripted "fictions of man and woman," as well as making use of themes and techniques of modernism generally attributed to its male practitioners.

However, Smith's point, raised earlier, that women grapple with

identity must constantly be kept in mind. Modernist writers, specifically diarists, may have confronted and then abandoned male myths of
women, adopting their own versions of female experience. But at times
they may have embraced these myths, which prescribed how they
should perceive themselves as daughters, wives, mothers, and lovers.
Whether Woolf, White, Smart, and Nin seem to be challenging or
accepting, radical or conservative, they were perpetually struggling
with their selves as they tried to make sense of and reconcile traditional gender roles with recent dismantlings of gender construction. These
struggles were enacted on the diary site, which is at once a textual battlefield, a playground, and a no *man*'s land.

Ironically, a woman is perhaps most vulnerable to the charge of self-
centredness when she writes in her journal, and it is this charge which
forces her to do battle with herself and with her text. The act of diarizing registers concern and respect for one's self, life, feelings, and experiences. The possibility of such registration is likely a major motive for
diary keeping. But such self-validation does not go unqualified; it gets
reduced to inappropriate egoism. As Blodgett observes, "Diaristic egoism smacks of simple vanity and self-assertion, which go contrary to
female training; it implies selfishness when one has been trained not to
do for oneself what one could be doing for others."[73] Women, in moving forward to centre stage to claim starring roles, are quickly reas-
signed to the margins to play supporting ones.

As Smith and Schenck suggest, though, women do not necessarily
remain silent, but use their positioning offside to critique and/or
subvert the roles assigned to them by those still at the centre. To
compensate for an apparently unacceptable preoccupation with their
selves, many writers use the diary as a place where the deeds of
the day can be marked and given value, in confirmation that it
was spent in domestic work and not in self-obsession. For instance,
entries such as this were common for Nin: "Today was such a busy
day that I could not study. I swept and dusted and tidied. Writing
letters for Mother in between, I cooked and washed and mended;
then we went marketing, and I wrote more for Mother" (ED,
2: 58).

Even more significant is the fact that diarists often convert the pleasure of the diaristic enterprise into a duty itself, a task that must be performed. In this way, the act of writing becomes legitimized as work.
White bracketed one entry with "(as I do *not* enjoy writing in this big
bumpy notebook)" (D, 2: 216). The fact that she kept a diary for over
five decades suggests that she must have enjoyed, or benefited from,
the practice on some level. But thinking that she did not enjoy it elim-
inated the guilt that came from perceived self-indulgence. In addition,

diarists often make apologies for not writing regularly, thus reinforcing the construction of a work ethic.

Conversely, Woolf is an example of a writer who, admitting her pleasure in diarizing, made the diary a duty in order to justify its allotted time in her schedule: "Give it a name & a place, & then perhaps, such is the human mind, I shall come to think it a duty, & disregard other duties for it" (D, 3: 6). Moreover, Simons observes that "women created for themselves a literary format that helped to justify an otherwise unforgivable obsession with self."[74] The diary can ostensibly be conceived as a book not for the diarist but for others to enjoy, as in the cases of women who passed their journals around to friends or family members. In this way, the diarist subversively recapitulates the stereotype that women live by and for others, gaining pleasure in doing things for anyone except themselves.

Diarists do not spend all of their time in textual struggles. Much space in their journals is devoted to play, specifically, the playing of multiple roles. Smith's conception of women as polyvocal can be appreciated by considering once again Woolf's Orlando. Transformed into a woman in the eighteenth century, Orlando comes in the twentieth century to the realization that "Nothing is any longer one thing" and that she is composed of many selves: "for everybody can multiply from his own experience the different terms which his different selves have made with him." Questioning of herself, "Who then?" she answers, "a woman. Yes, but a million other things as well."[75] Through Orlando, Woolf was urging women to celebrate their polyvocal selves and rejoice in their capacity to play different roles and assume complex identities. It is in this light that the diary may be illuminated as a playground of subjectivities.

Penelope Franklin, writing about diaries of American women kept between the 1830s and the 1970s, notes how the diary "can be a 'safe place' where new roles can be tried out, protected from censure."[76] Nin proved the truth of this idea throughout her diary, admitting how in her journal she was "Always imagining another role. Never static" (HJ, 119). The roles performed by Woolf, White, Smart, and Nin within their diaries influenced how they presented themselves outside their texts. Conversely, how they conceived themselves in their real lives directed how they configured these selves in their written lives. This relationship will be considered in terms of De Man's suggestion in "Autobiography as De-facement" that just as a life may produce a text, so a text may produce a life.

If women occupy within their diaries a battlefield on the one hand and a playground on the other, they ultimately position themselves in the no man's land between margin and centre, negotiating between the self as other and as subject; between the self as absent and as present; between minor genres such as the diary and major ones such as poetry and fiction; and between the diary genre in particular as raw outpouring and as constructed narration. Recall DuPlessis's argument that women novelists occupy a similar position, voicing "difference and sameness, marginality and inclusion in a constant dialogue."

PERMEABLE BORDERS

The diary is perhaps the quintessential site for women's negotiations of these kinds, and it is the relationship between gender and genre which makes this significance clear. In her foreword to *Revelations: Diaries of Women*, Mary Jane Moffat suggests that women write diaries because the form "is an analogue to their lives: emotional, fragmentary, interrupted, modest, not to be taken seriously, private, restricted, daily, trivial, formless, concerned with self, as endless as their tasks." Women exploit this form, though, using it to voice their dissatisfaction with the ways that society has scripted their lives, writing their own versions of self instead.[77] More specifically, in *Mapping Our Selves: Canadian Women's Autobiography in English*, Helen Buss uses the example of Lucy Maud Montgomery to show how the diary "offers creative women an outlet not offered by public genres." Forced to care for her ill husband and thus prevented from pursuing her career as a novelist, Montgomery spent whatever spare time she had making notes for her diary, thereby turning it into her "principal literary tool."[78]

DuPlessis, in "For the Etruscans: Sexual Difference and Artistic Production – The Debate over a Female Aesthetic," likewise perceives the strategic element of diary keeping. Although she is concerned specifically with Nin, her argument is applicable to women diarists in general: "Her [Nin's] diary as form and process is a strategem to solve a contradiction often present in acute form for women: a contradiction between the desire to please, making woman an object, and the desire to reveal, making her a subject." DuPlessis notes that male productions are usually cast in lasting forms, such as books, statues, paintings, and architecture, whereas women's, such as diaries, are traditionally "ephemeral." Yet she sees ephemerality as being "permanence in impermanence."[79] Nin wrote supposedly private journals (impermanence) for public audiences (permanence), making certain that no matter how absent or "other" her selves may have been, they would ultimately become "present" to the world.

These negotiations between self and text may be considered along-side the psychoanalytic investigations of Chodorow, who has shown how girls' "experience of self contains more flexible or permeable ego boundaries." The relational, borderless female is embraced by Diane P. Freedman, who is inspired by the work of Judith Kegan Gardiner. It focuses on women's "continual crossing of self and other" and on how "women's writing may blur public and private" distinctions. In light of this perception, Freedman explains that "For women, borders – of ego, genre, discipline, geography – are made to be crossed." She discovers how women's relational connections can be used to challenge and rewrite traditionally limiting or prescribed academic discourse which would keep its practitioners at an impersonal distance from their subject matter: she affirms, "Many contemporary writers want an intimacy with their readers and subjects as well as with themselves."[80]

Buss shares that opinion, turning her metaphor of *Mapping Our Selves* onto herself as she reveals her own subjectivity and how it impinges on her reading. I agree with her that it is especially necessary for scholars to risk a more intimate dialogue when engaging with private texts such as diaries, memoirs, and autobiographies, for not only are these texts more immediately personal than novels, for instance, but the nature of the material often demands decoding and thus requires that the researcher state upfront her own biases pertaining to culture, history, class, race, and gender.[81]

Freedman and Buss are both interested in life-writing genres, especially in how, to quote Buss, women's texts "transgress the generic bounds" established by privileged "paternal" texts.[82] This interest is of particular relevance to my and others' arguments that genre distinctions no longer carry the authority they once had. Such disruption has called for the inclusion of the diary in the canon of literature, to be regarded as a form that can and must be evaluated alongside other more established genres such as poetry and fiction. And it highlights how diarists may cross genres within their texts as they ignore traditional public and private boundaries.

Moreover, the notion that "For women, borders ... are made to be crossed" establishes a bridge between them, the diary, and modernism. One of the defining figures of that period is the artist in exile, the artist who crosses borders literally, spiritually, imaginatively. As we shall see, women lived their lives in perpetual and multiple states of exile, in terms not only of geographical but also of gendered dislocations. They exiled themselves to various foreign lands, and they were exiled by others to marginal positions within society and the family. How these expressions of exile (fleeing to and from the borders) have become inscribed in twentieth-century literary diaries specifically is examined in chapter 3.

The diary is the perfect medium for the permeable female ego, because it is itself permeable, a supposition which further links the diary to modernism. Rebecca Hogan makes these points evident in "Engendered Autobiographies: The Diary as a Feminine Form," where she pursues the connection between the diary as a favoured female text and as a feminine form. Arguing that "the diary is *par excellence* the genre of detail," Hogan finds confirmation of the historical equation of "detail" and "feminine" in Naomi Schor's *Reading in Detail: Aesthetics and the Feminine*. Schor defines detail as encompassing both the ornamental (associated with "effeminacy") and the everyday (associated with women's domestic sphere).[83] Hogan locates these qualities within the structure of the diary, drawing for support on Elizabeth Hampsten's evidence that women laboured as much over the design of their diaries as over their dressmaking, embroidery, baking, decorating, and gardening,[84] and on Suzanne Juhasz's comment that the diary is the "classic verbal articulation of dailiness.[85]

Hogan then turns to French theorists such as Hélène Cixous, Luce Irigaray, and Julia Kristeva and their notion of *l'écriture féminine*, which is perceived as being "potentially subversive of the structures, logic, and syntax of masculine language."[86] She links this "feminine" style to women's autobiographical writing, in that both have been described as, for example, unended, fragmented, and fluid – terms also used to define a modernist aesthetic. (It is important to note, though, that these terms are only potentially descriptive of women's writing, for to embrace them wholly recapitulates inappropriate binary divisions between men's linear and women's disjointed autobiographies.) Women's diary writing may also be subversive, like *l'écriture féminine*, in the way that it blurs traditional divisions between self and others, writer and reader, text and experience, art and life.[87]

Hogan ultimately draws attention to the diary as a specifically feminine form by referring to Chodorow's contention that women's egos are permeable.[88] She also cites DuPlessis, who, in "For the Etruscans," speaks of a unique form of writing that women can create: "Something I call an emotional texture, a structural expression of mutuality. Writers know their text as a form of intimacy, of personal contact, whether conversations with the reader or with the self. Letters, journals, voices are sources for this element ... expressing the porousness and nonhierarchic stances of intimate conversation in both structure and function."[89] DuPlessis's concept of porousness echoes Chodorow's definition of the permeable female ego, effectively linking the diary and the woman writer.

The diary can be an innovative text for expression, at once linguistically sophisticated and rooted in everyday experience. It is a liberating place where women can challenge and redefine "language, genre, and self."[90] In this way the diary is a quintessential feminist and, as we shall see, modernist space.

3 Life Writing a Modernist Text

The various poems, novels, and plays that have recently been inserted into the [autobiography] genre – all of which, significantly, are either modern or else particularly susceptible to modernist interpretation – do seem, despite their fictiveness, to address the same problems of self-definition that have taxed autobiographers ever since Augustine discovered that the self is a hard ground to plough. Indeed, the modernist movement away from representational discourse toward self-enacting, self-reflexive verbal structures and the critical theories that have been devised to explain this movement conspire to make the very idea of literary modernism seem synonymous with that of autobiography.[1]

In *The Forms of Autobiography*, William C. Spengemann focuses on issues which I have taken up in chapter 1, but which bear repeating here because of their implications for an investigation of diaries as modernist texts. Specifically, he describes the two most pervasive approaches to autobiography as being an acknowledgment, on the one hand, of its inescapable grounding in biography and, on the other, of its inevitable turning towards fiction. As Spengemann suggests in the passage quoted above, modernism's practitioners and critics were especially preoccupied with the self and how it was rendered in literary works, and this concern makes it all the more appropriate to evaluate the diary as a classic modernist text, inscribed as it is with biographical and fictional representations of selfhood.

In order to appreciate the diary's modernist character, it is necessary first to consider the period within which Woolf, White, Smart, and Nin were writing. As current debates among postmodern critics abound, highlighting the impossibility of theoretical consensus, what also comes to light is the impossibility of restricting modernism to one definition. There is no such thing as one modernism. Like concepts of genre and self, it is a construct, and it is consistently being reconfigured as such. We can speak of many modernisms; those under consideration here include largely Anglo-American ones. They historically originate from around the 1880s but are primarily situated in the years between the two world wars and within the movement commonly termed "high modernism."

My approach is filtered through recent feminist studies which have revealed that, contrary to their claims to impersonality and universality, many modernisms in fact encode a white, male, heterosexual perspective.[2] In her introduction to *The Gender of Modernism*, Bonnie Kime Scott serves as a representative voice when she states: "Modernism as we were taught it at midcentury was perhaps halfway to truth. It was unconsciously gendered masculine ... Though some of the aesthetic and political pronouncements of women writers had been offered in public, they had not circulated widely and were rarely collected for academic recirculation." Scott suspects "that modernism is not the aesthetic, directed, monological sort of phenomenon sought in their own ways by authors of now-famous manifestos – F.T. Marinetti (futurism), Ezra Pound (imagism and vorticism), T.E. Hulme (classicism), Wyndham Lewis (vorticism), T.S. Eliot ('Tradition and the Individual Talent'), and Eugene Jolas (the 'revolution of the word') – and perpetuated in new critical-formalist criticism through the 1960s."[3] Feminist revisionism of modernism redresses these "half truths" by putting women back at the centre of modernism, a space they inhabited in many ways during the period. And more pertinently here, by exposing and redefining "unconsciously gendered masculine" aesthetics, it encourages the study of heretofore marginalized "feminine" texts such as the diary.

DIARISTS IN EXILE

In "Expatriate Modernism: Writing on the Cultural Rim," Shari Benstock argues that stylistic features of modernism are directly related to the exiled or expatriated conditions of the artists who penned them.[4] I would like to focus on ideas of exile because modernist women who wrote were exiled within male-centred literary movements, and women who wrote diaries were exiled even further in terms of genre. My discussion is indebted to the provocative collection of essays in *Women's Writing in Exile*, edited by Mary Lynn Broe and Angela Ingram, which examines from multiple perspectives various states of women's voluntary and involuntary exiles, such as geographical, spiritual, sexual, and generic ones.

In "Exile in the American Grain: H.D.'s Diaspora," Susan Stanford Friedman places the terms "exile" and "expatriate" within a modernist context: "The prerequisite to adulthood is leaving home. The founding gesture of American Modernism seems to have been expatriatism, a self-imposed exile from the parochial and provincial for the cosmopolitan and international. The two are not so unrelated, for Victorianism in both its English and American forms is akin to parentalism, a cultural dominance, a parental superego prescribing duty over pleasure, obligation over freedom, social order over personal rebellion ... The young moderns growing up in the Victorian era had to leave home."[5]

This definition aptly describes the experiences of Woolf, White, Smart, and Nin. In the literal sense, when they became young adults they left home. Woolf moved within London from her parents' conservative Kensington mansion to the "bohemian" neighbourhood of Bloomsbury, setting up a liberal household with her siblings. White, similarly raised in Kensington, married early and moved to the artistic neighbourhood of Chelsea. Smart, from the Canadian counterpart to Friedman's parochial America, left colonial Ottawa for London upon graduating from high school. And Nin, who like White was young when she married, moved with her husband from the suburb of Queen's, New York, to the coronary centre of modernism, Paris. In this way, all four women situated themselves within the international scope of modernism, unfolding as it was within and between cities such as Paris and London. Though Smart and Nin were expatriates in the traditional sense of leaving their "fatherland," Woolf and White may be considered expatriates to the extent that they left the homes of their fathers (*ex patria*) and moved within London to districts which were more likely to be inhabited by artists of diverse nationalities, and they travelled throughout the Continent, where international ideas flourished.

Women's flights from their conservative, traditional homes and cities were concomitant with men's flights from similarly restrictive environments to and within Europe. Moreover, for both women and men such escapes were not only geographical but also psychological. As Friedman confirms, "an artist's survival depends upon an internally imposed exile – upon, in other words, alienation – the state of being alien, that is, foreign, outside, exiled from belonging to the larger *communitas* of family, religion, and nation – to which we might add class, sex, and race."[6] She draws attention to probably the most famous modernist articulation of exile, that made by James Joyce's persona, Stephen

Dedalus, as he takes his physical and spiritual leave from his native Dublin in *A Portrait of the Artist as a Young Man*: "I will not serve that in which I no longer believe whether it call itself my home, my fatherland or my church: and I will try to express myself in some mode of life or art as freely as I can and as wholly as I can, using for my defence the only arms I allow myself to use – silence, exile, cunning."[7]

Joyce was not the only modernist figure who forsook his past to create the art of his future. Women were "making it new" (as Pound would have it) in modernism contemporaneous with their now more famous male counterparts, as recent scholars continue to show.[8] But modernism arguably meant – had to mean – more for women than for men, because in "making it new," women were being innovative in terms not only of how they wrote but of how they lived and conceived themselves. Their challenges to prescriptive feminine behaviour and feminine self-definitions were an essential component of women's modernisms.

Shari Benstock, in *Women of the Left Bank*, exposes a large group of Anglo-American expatriate and French women writing in Paris between 1900 and 1940, living in lesbian, bisexual, asexual, or alternative heterosexual – non-marital, non-monogomous – relationships, and registering these alternatives within their texts. In *Writing for Their Lives: The Modernist Women, 1910–1940*, Virginia L. Smyers, also focusing on Anglo-American writers, comes to the overall conclusion that "None of them seemed to live conventionally."[9] It is important to remember that these women shared a privileged middle-class background. What they also shared was an "anti-conventionality" in their personal lives, "at a time when the overwhelming social expectation was that a woman should marry, bear children, and remain both married and monogamous." Comparing the literary experimentalism of male and female writers, Gillian Hanscombe and Virginia Smyers rightly observe of high-modernist heroes such as Pound, Lawrence, Joyce, and Eliot that "however radical or innovatory or 'creative' their respective literary genius," they "lived conventionally male heterosexual lives; perhaps wild, sometimes, or eccentric or egoistic, but somehow within the norm." In contrast, the women were as experimental in how they lived as in how they wrote.[10]

Friedman emphasizes how women's exilic "flight from femininity" was a precondition to their becoming artists: "For women, the pressure to conform centered on the question of gender. Freedom of mind and spirit meant above all freedom from family pressure to conform to conventional feminine norms."[11] Women aspiring to be artists who did not kill the "angel in the house" thus ran away from her instead; even Woolf, who confessed to such a murder, had to escape to Bloomsbury to try to evade the angel's haunting spectre. We can appreciate the need for escape by considering the example of Smart. That she was trapped in a feminine snare is clear from her comment about her lack of artistic freedom at home in Canada: "Having to camouflage books, read poetry secretly, pass ashtrays gracefully, be a Blonde" (A, 140). Trading in her ashtrays for a steamer ticket, Smart broke away to Europe and there developed as a writer.

It must be emphasized, though, that if Smart and others like her found creative and intellectual freedom in foreign places, they were, as Woolf can attest, plagued by the ghosts of their past. Women can never completely exile themselves *from* a patriarchy because they are always being exiled *by* that patriarchy. Benstock notes: "For women, the definition of patriarchy already assumes the reality of expatriate *in patria*; for women, this expatriation is internalized, experienced as an exclusion imposed from the outside and lived from the inside in such a way that the separation of outside from inside, patriarchal dicta from female decorum, cannot be easily distinguished."[12] In this sense, then, modernist women who took to their heels were fleeing not only the conservatism of their families but the very ideologies of femininity that made these families so in the first place. But because these ideologies were intrinsic to society, women remained confined to and by them.

Women continued to "grapple" with their identities, constantly doing battle with their internalized sense of femininity. Moreover, they still had to engage with the external world. Smart recalled the London art scene of the thirties: "The London pubs were great places for literary activity. Everyone gathered at the various places to talk and drink. Women sort of kept back on the edge of the crowd as the men discussed all the exciting things that were happening."[13] Smart as a woman and as an artist was relegated to "the edge" of the male world, a position which continually threatened her confidence as a writer. Her self-imposed exile to London, where she might have benefited from certain freedoms, was undermined by the exile imposed on her there, which limited those freedoms.

Smart's use of the word "edge" is appropriate, for it is synonymous with "margin," and we have seen how women's lives have traditionally unfolded there. In discussing the American in London Hilda Doolittle, Friedman argues, "Being foreign was an externalization of an interior difference, the very difference that fueled her writing."[14] Like Doolittle, Woolf, White, Smart, and Nin were writers in multiple states of exile; they were in many ways marginalized on the basis of gender and genre; and their experiences of these conditions fuelled their modernist texts, including their diaries.

TRADITION AND THE INDIVIDUAL DIARIST

Women's exile within modernism derives from the movement's repudiation of them, and aspects of the feminine and the relational associated with them. Anglo-American artists James Joyce, T.S. Eliot, Ezra Pound, and Wyndham Lewis, otherwise known, as Lewis saw fit to label them, as "the men of 1914,"[15] are particularly implicated in their personal and professional denigrations of women. All four lived expatriate lives, and all four were central to the construction of modernism as a "directed, monological sort of phenomenon," in terms of what art they produced and how that art has been reproduced and thus preserved by canon makers. Several scholars offer in-depth examinations of these stars of 1914, and the purpose of my work here is not to tread such sprawling ground.[16] Rather, I will focus on Joyce and Eliot – perhaps the most familiar pillars of Anglo-American modernism – touching upon the aesthetics which informed their work and which consequently impacted on women writing diaries.

Benstock contends, "Women writers of this period and place both mimed and undermined Modernist principles, and we have yet to discover whether the 'Modernist Mime' constituted an enforcement of the patriarchal poetic law or a skillful subversion of it."[17] The answer, I suggest, is that women did both, in their fiction and, more importantly here, in their diaries. The purpose of this chapter is to show how. Women's modernist practices may be connected to those of recent autobiographical theorists who, as Neuman and others point out, take what empowers them and reject what disempowers them.

Eliot's 1919 essay "Tradition and the Individual Talent," a touchstone of modernist aesthetics, exiles women from the great Western literary tradition. He defines this tradition as containing, "in the first place, the historical sense," which "involves a perception, not only of the pastness of the past, but of its presence. The historical sense compels a man to write not merely with his own generation in his bones, but with a feeling that the whole of the literature of Europe and of Homer and within it the whole of the literature of his own country has a simultaneous existence and composes a simultaneous order." Eliot outlines what has become perhaps the most talked-about shift in literary history: "The existing monuments form an ideal order among themselves, which is modified by the introduction of the new (the really new) work of art among them. The existing order is complete before the new work arrives; for order to persist after the supervention of novelty, the *whole* existing order must be, if ever so slightly, altered; ... and this is conformity between the old and the new."[18]

For women, the problem of this pronouncement is that they have not been part of the tradition which Eliot invokes. His reference to "the whole of the literature of Europe and of Homer" excludes women because they have not enjoyed the privileges of education which men have had, and hence they would not have been introduced to past literatures, especially those in foreign languages. This was one of the reasons that women found the novel so amenable to them – writing one did not require formal training.

The reference to "the whole of the literature of his own country" is equally exclusive. For even though women did begin writing novels contemporaneously with the genre's emergence, they were not appropriately recognized for their achievements, as Spender, Spencer, and Russ have shown. Even Eliot's literary world denied any meaningful recognition to women's contributions. Eliot himself, as assistant editor, commented on *The Egoist* in 1917: "I struggle to keep the writing as much as possible in Male hands, as I distrust the Feminine in literature."[19] And Pound, speaking on behalf of himself and others at the *New Age* journal a year later, attested: "Not wildly anti-feminist we are yet to be convinced that any woman ever invented anything in the arts."[20] Statements such as these imply that Eliot's privileging of "the new" discounts women's new art.

It is therefore likely that he had only those "monuments" created by men in mind when he suggested his "ideal order." This interpretation is reinforced when we recall DuPlessis's contention that men's productions are judged to be permanent – monuments – whereas women's are dismissed as impermanent, as things that would disintegrate if even nudged by a more solid work of male art. DuPlessis has the diary specifically in mind as an ephemeral work, and thus not only women writers but women diarists seemed to have no chance of making it into Eliot's canon.

This is not to say that they did not yearn to be part of it. For instance, Emily Coleman, a novelist, poet, and diarist like her close friend White, asserted in her diary: "I want to be among the English poets" – the "poets" being those monumental ones like Shakespeare and company.[21] Coleman's desire was shared by White, who later in life complained that she had not been, in effect, canonized: "I'm 55 now and would like a status" (D, 1: 276). Woolf, echoing Coleman, asked hopefully in her diary: "do I think I shall be among the English novelists after my death?" (D, 4: 251). Though she remained uncertain about the answer, Woolf, who, as Scott suggests, "probably satisfies more traditional definitions of modernism than any other woman writer," has certainly enjoyed monumental status of late.[22]

Beyond, or against, women desiring to be inducted into a men's hall of fame was their daring to make their own traditions based on their revising of Eliot's agenda, which they knew full well to be a sexist one. Dorothy Richardson, a once-prominent but now often-ignored modernist, voiced her critique of the Tradition via the thoughts of her fictional persona, Miriam Henderson. In *Oberland* (1927), the ninth volume of Richardson's autobiographical *Pilgrimage*, Henderson wonders: "'Art,' 'literature,' systems of thought, religions, all the fine products of masculine leisure that are so lightly called 'immortal.' Who makes them immortal?" She answers, "A few men in each generation who are in the same attitude of spirit as the creators, and loudly claim them as humanity's highest spiritual achievement, condoning, in those who produce them, any failure, any sacrifice of the lives about them to the production of these crumbling monuments."[23]

Henderson's phrase "crumbling monuments" ironically suggests that at the moment when critics such as Eliot were waxing nostalgic about timeless monuments, revisionist women such as Richardson were trying to tear them down. So too was Woolf, as we have seen in her refusal to tolerate any longer those works which reflected only a masculine "I." And in *Three Guineas* she advocated her famous "outsiders society" of women. Although she was suggesting that women position themselves outside a male politics of war, I would apply this location by extension to a male politics of literary tradition. Earlier, Miriam Henderson had complained, "It was history, literature, the way of stating records, reports, stories, the whole method of statement of things from the beginning that was on a false foundation."[24] Richardson was highlighting how value is an arbitrary construct, and from her observation we may glean the fact that Eliot's male monuments as much as women's diaries may be ephemeral. The other side to this view is that diaries, if erected on a new "foundation," may become prized as monuments to female creativity and selfhood.

Another essay by Eliot which warrants reflection is "*Ulysses*, Order and Myth," his 1923 review of Joyce's *Ulysses*. Praising the book, he celebrates its structural and thematic ties to Homer's *Odyssey*: "In using the myth, in manipulating a continuous parallel between contemporaneity and antiquity, Mr. Joyce is pursuing a method which others must pursue after him. It is simply a way of controlling, of ordering, of giving a shape and a significance to the immense panorama of futility and anarchy which is contemporary history."[25] Eliot coined the term "the mythical method" (as opposed to the "narrative method") to describe Joyce's strategy, and I will return to this concept later. For now, I would like to consider why he believed that contemporary history needed "controlling" and "ordering."

I suggest that this need was bound up with his and others' anxiety towards women, manifested in their imaging women – especially those who wrote – as chaotic forces that had to be "controlled" and "ordered." Just as Spender and Spencer have shown, Elaine Showalter contends, in *Sexual Anarchy*, that by the 1870s and 1880s, "women writers constituted a set of frightening rivals in the literary market-place." As a result, "What seemed to many like the feminization of literature created identity problems for male artists."[26] And indeed it did, as Andreas Huyssen explains in *After the Great Divide*. Discussing the *fin de siècle* opposition between high art and mass culture, he argues that aesthetic modernism "constituted itself through a conscious strategy of exclusion, an anxiety of contamination by its other: an increasingly consuming and engulfing mass culture."[27]

Given Showalter's evidence that women constituted a literary threat, it is not surprising that Huyssen is able to equate them with a mass-culture threat. He shows that the only way women could be prevented from gaining access to male sites of privilege was by devaluing them: "It is indeed striking to observe how the political, psychological, and aesthetic discourse around the turn of the century consistently and obsessively genders mass culture and the masses as feminine, while high culture, whether traditional or modern, clearly remains the privileged realm of male activities." The masses are gendered feminine to the extent that they are seen as a raging threat – hysterical, instinctive, and chaotic.[28]

Richardson, perceptive to the gendering of tradition, was equally aware of the gendering of masses, as she revealed in a 1924 article,"Women and the Future." "To them [certain men], feminism is the invariable accompaniment of degeneration. They draw back in horror before the oncoming flood of mediocrity. They see ahead a democratized world, overrun by hordes of inferior beings, organized by majorities for material ends; with primitive, uncivilizable woman rampant in the midst."[29] Richardson's persona, Miriam Henderson, concurs, for in discussing how men have conceived women as being uncivilized and chaotic, she tells us: "There isn't any 'chaos.' Never has been. It's the principal masculine illusion."[30]

It is possible that Eliot bought into, and perpetuated, this "illusion," and it is to this "illusion" that we can trace at least some of his concerns over what he saw as anarchic contemporary history.[31] Huyssen suggests that the modernist artist, afraid of his domain being infiltrated, "tries to stake out his territory by fortifying the boundaries between genuine art and inauthentic mass culture." The result is the "persistent gendering as feminuine of that which is devalued." It follows that modernism "begins to look more and more like a reaction formation" against feminine masses and masses of women.[32] Eliot's call for control and order may be aimed at quelling not only the anarchic masses but the masses of writing women. We might also reconsider in this light his insistence that great art constitutes an "ideal order," an order of male art which, by virtue of its solidity and strength, keeps the chaos of women's productions at bay.

Huyssen defines the "great divide" as a barrier raised within modernism and subsequently lowered during postmodernism. He finds that women and their contributions are far more valued in our present society than they were in the modernist period. For, "where modernism's great wall once kept the barbarians out and safeguarded the culture within, there is now only slippery ground." Starting in the 1960s, art movements began to wrestle with the high-modernist stranglehold on culture, as Huyssen makes clear: "One of the few widely agreed upon features of postmodernism is its attempt to negotiate forms of high art with certain forms and genres of mass culture and the culture of everyday life."[33] This negotiation is crucial where the diary is concerned, for in being a genre accessible to anybody, it is necessarily considered a genre of (feminine) mass culture.

If, however, postmodern artists and critics are now blurring boundaries and accepting a "slippery ground" of value, their modernist counterparts had already been negotiating the divide between "high" and "low" art, as current popular-culture studies show.[34] More specifically, the distinction between canonical male texts and devalued "feminine" diaries breaks down as it becomes apparent that both were directed by the thematic and stylistic concerns of literary modernism. In fact, many of the aesthetic imperatives used to keep the masses out of the modernist stronghold were already entrenched within the excluded texts.

For instance, modernist classics such as *Ulysses*, *The Waste Land*, and Pound's "Hugh Selwyn Mauberly," along with Woolf's *Mrs Dalloway* and Smart's *By Grand Central Station I Sat Down and Wept*, draw on early-twentieth-century mass commodity culture, mixing popular songs, advertising jingles, newspaper slogans, and the like with more esoteric references and allusions. In a more general sense, many modernists advocated a democratic levelling of subject matter. If Yeats memorialized in his poetry those national heroes who fought for Ireland's independence, William Carlos William celebrated a red wheelbarrow.

Diarists similarly negotiate such a range. They may literally divide their text, creating a section at the back in which they record their accounts, shopping lists, telephone numbers, and memoranda, or they may intersperse these jottings throughout their daily passages. Incorporating the banal with the meaningful, diarists consistently invoke the democratic principle. White, for example, took the time in her diary to note: "Washed garbage pails and counter tops" (D, 2: 258).

In her essay "Modern Fiction," Woolf urged the modern writer to focus on "an ordinary mind on an ordinary day," because "'The proper stuff of fiction' does not exist; everything is the proper stuff of fiction, every feeling, every thought; every quality of brain and spirit is drawn upon; no perception comes amiss."[35] Attention to "an ordinary day" is reflected in works such as *Ulysses* and *Mrs Dalloway*, in which the lives of the protagonists – like the lives of diarists – unfold within a single day. Further, in depicting his characters Stephen Dedalus and Leopold Bloom in *Ulysses*, Joyce offers us intimate accounts of their bodily functions, what food they eat, even what Bloom has in his pockets. The details reflect what is the natural "stuff" of the diary, as we recall Rebecca Hogan's assertion that "the diary is *par excellence* the genre of detail."[36]

Though literary modernism might incorporate forms of "low art," it also inscribed "high art" as a strategy to keep the practitioners of this "low art" out. One way to exclude them was through the creation of manifestos and "isms" which outlined in political jargon the artistic platforms of respective artists and their movements. Peter Nicholls observes that between 1886 and 1924, there were fifty "isms"[37] – among the more important are naturalism, symbolism, impressionism, post-impressionism, imagism, futurism, vorticism, dadaism, and surrealism. It is significant to note Philippe Lejeune's description of the preface that Marie Bashkirtseff wrote to her diary in 1884: "This preface, published in the 1887 edition, is a sort of 'manifesto' for the diary" which highlights how the text was crafted for an audience. Her diary was "ahead of its time" and helped to mark "the way to modernity" in its inscriptions of a woman's unabashed concern for and celebration of herself and her work.[38] As we shall see, the diarist, as much as any other artistic figure, was central and not marginal to modernist expressions and enterprises.

THE EMOTION OF ART IS (IM)PERSONAL

Among those manifestos identified by Scott as leading to an "aesthetic, monological" modernism was that of impersonality, a manifesto that had significant implications for women writers. If modernist men had to create fraternities with the specific aim of keeping women out, what better term than "impersonality" to blackball the sex historically defined by all its antitheses? If women were relational, regarding themselves in terms of others and writing their lives in terms of the personal, what better means to exclude them from artistic authority than an aesthetics of detachment? We can here appreciate Margo Culley's statement that more women write diaries in the twentieth century than men; modernists had made life writing unworthy of aesthetic pursuit. It was a period that valorized aesthetic pursuit for its own sake and as an effective means, according to Huyssen, of preserving an elitist patriarchy.

In *Portrait of the Artist*, first serialized between 1914 and 1915, Stephen Dedalus proclaims what would become a quintessential credo for modernism: "The artist, like the God of the creation, remains within or behind or beyond or above his handiwork, invisible, refined out of existence, indifferent, paring his fingernails."[39] Dedalus is echoed by Eliot in "Tradition and the Individual Talent." Having asserted the importance of tradition, Eliot emphasizes how the poet must "develop or procure the consciousness of the past. What happens is a continual surrender of himself as he is at the moment to something which is more valuable. The progress of an artist is a continual self-sacrifice, a continual extinction of personality." That is, "The emotion of art is impersonal."[40]

What Eliot had in mind was an artist who sacrificed himself to his art and to the tradition which housed it, a kind of technical and inter-textual submission. He believed that art was rooted in emotion, but emotion of a particular kind: there should be "an expression of *significant* emotion, emotion which has its life in the poem and not in the history of the poet."[41] Nicholls states that Eliot was concerned with "the need for clear boundaries to be drawn around the self," and that Anglo-American modernists were interested in "developing models of psychic order which reinstate the divide between art and life."[42] This agenda led to an art that was self-reflexive and self-referential, one in which the author's "I" was sacrificed to a persona that had no being beyond the text. Moreover, this "I" was fractured into multiple personae, so that identity was unfixed, unstable within the text, thus further undermining the authority of the author. It is because of this concern with representations of self that Spengemann contends that "literary modernism seems synonymous with that of autobiography."

The self-reflexive text is autonomous; aware of itself, it is thus about itself as a text. Its detachment is due in part to the preoccupation of the writer with style. Nicholls states that "the true work of aesthetic modernity depends on the assiduous cultivation of style, on that 'atrocious labour' of which Flaubert was to become an exemplary practitioner ('Last week I spent 5 *days writing one page*')."[43] Diaries are inevitably self-reflexive, for diarists frequently address their texts with variants of "Dear diary." More importantly, not only do they, like Flaubert, cultivate style, but they do so within the very text they are styling. The most obvious example is Woolf's often-cited entry of 20 April 1919, in which she examines her method of diarizing. Asking, "What sort of diary should I like mine to be?" she answers that, although she should "write as the mood comes or of anything whatever," "A little effort is needed to face a character or an incident which needs to be recorded. Nor can one let the pen write without guidance" (D, 1:266).

If a text is autonomous, then the writer may be excised from that text. We can see detached presence in Eliot's "The Love Song of J. Alfred Prufrock." When the protagonist invites us at the start of the poem, "Let us go then you and I," we willingly follow, only to discover that Prufrock's "I" has no substance or meaning beyond the personae he adopts within the poem. He tells us, "There will be time ... / To prepare a face to meet the faces that you meet," and he spends his time in the poem in just such cosmetic application, painting on one mask only to cover it over with another one.[44] Prufrock – via Eliot – achieves his goal of impersonality through allusion, endlessly quoting from and referring to other literary sources and personae, thus ensuring that identity has only intertextual referents.

The Waste Land is another example of a poem in which meaning is created through allusion, and it fractures Prufrock's "I" into the subjectivities of characters such as Marie, Madame Sosostris, Lil, the Phoenician sailor, Tiresias, and the Fisher King. Both male and female novelists similarly created multiple narrators to disrupt the omniscience of a narrator and to depersonalize the organizing and controlling presence of the author. Such is the case with Ulysses, William Faulkner's As I Lay Dying, Woolf's To the Lighthouse and The Waves, Gertrude Stein's The Autobiography of Alice B. Toklas, and Djuna Barnes's Nightwood, to name a few.

Examples of this narration are found in women's journals as well. Smart crafted a diary that is at many times as allusive and as esoteric as Eliot's poetry, with meaning revealed only to those readers learned enough to pick up the references. She becomes like Prufrock, her identity unfixed because it is consistently being deferred to fictional sources. However, these sources contribute to an understanding, not of a "universal" (and hence male) narrative, but of a female one of her own making. By shifting identities, Smart refuses to be pegged as any one kind of woman. In a different way, White detaches herself from her own narrative by casting herself as the subject/object of a Freudian case study, her memories and experiences mediated through the impersonal words of her analysts. And Nin fabricates so many stories within her diary, tells so many lies about who she is and what she does, that it is difficult to unravel who the "I" of the text really refers to – as her two biographers, Deirdre Bair and Noël Riely Fitch, have proven.

It is likely that women found an aesthetic of impersonality empowering. In *Feminine Fictions: Revisiting the Postmodern*, Patricia Waugh suggests that "'impersonality' has much to offer, aesthetically and ultimately politically, to women writers." Drawing on the work of Patricia Spacks, she notes that women may have felt liberated by an aesthetic that allowed them to cut loose from traditional bindings which associated women with the personal and the relational. Waugh also draws attention to Woolf's essay "Women and Fiction," in which the writer hails a new impersonal regime which promises women long-awaited political and personal freedoms: "The change which has turned the English woman from a nondescript influence, fluctuating and vague, to a voter, a wage-earner, a responsible citizen, has given her both in her life and in her art a turn toward the impersonal. Her relations now are not only emotional; they are intellectual, they are political ... Hence her attention is being directed away from the personal centre which engaged it exclusively in the past to the impersonal, and her novels naturally become more critical of society, and less analytical of individual lives."[45] Woolf is a good example of this new impersonal writer, for she scripted in her journals (even more than in her fiction) her social critiques and political concerns. Her later diaries are especially important as documents which chart her and England's increasing fear of fascist invasion.

If the personal no longer engaged women as "exclusively" as it had in the past, it nonetheless continued to attract them. There is an implicit irony in Eliot's conception of the successful artist as one who continually sacrifices himself, continually extinguishing his personality, for Eliot was unwittingly describing the successful woman. Recall what Woolf said about the angel of the house, that arbiter of feminine ideology: "She sacrificed herself daily." Or consider how Woolf's protagonist, Mrs Ramsay, feels in *To the Lighthouse*: "So boasting of her capacity to surround and protect, there was scarcely a shell of herself left for her to know herself by; all was so lavished and spent."[46] But Eliot valued an emotion "which has its life in the poem and not in the history of the poet." In contrast, women's sacrifices – and the expression of them in their art – are made in very real terms. The life of a woman's "emotion" is often precisely "in the history of the poet."

Eliot drew boundaries between art and life, and this differentiation brings to mind the psychoanalytic and sociological issues discussed in chapter 2. Men think of themselves as separate, as having clearly demarcated borders between self and others, whereas women see themselves as relational, as having fluid, permeable ego boundaries. Based on this perception, women would probably not be as able as men to produce the kind of "impersonal" art envisaged and honoured by modernists such as Eliot and Joyce. Even Woolf in her concept of "impersonality" recognized that women are grounded in the "real" world. She reiterated this understanding in *A Room of One's Own*: "fiction is like a spider's web, attached ever so lightly perhaps, but still attached to life at all four corners. Often the attachment is scarcely perceptible; Shakespeare's plays, for instance, seem to hang there complete by themselves. But when the web is pulled askew, hooked up at the edge, torn in the middle, one remembers that these webs are not spun in mid-air by incorporeal creatures, but are the work of suffering human beings, and are attached to grossly material things, like health and money and the houses we live in."[47]

Women diarists were consistently pulling the web askew and acknowledging the "grossly material things" behind it. As much as diarists experimented with stylistics within their texts, they wrote literally about "health and money and the houses" they lived in." White, for instance, in addition to doing her financial accounts in her journal, documented with great detail the times she redecorated her various flats. The diarists' narratives in these cases reflect the "low art" of modernist mass culture discussed earlier, concerned as it is with the ordinary "stuff" of fiction.

In general, Woolf, White, Smart, and Nin often rejected a modernism of detachment and instead used their diaries to document more historically grounded narratives of their real lives, refusing to erase or deny the conditions which contributed to their marginal status in society. Eliot, in "Tradition and the Individual Talent," emphasized that "Impressions and experiences which are important for the man may take no place in the poetry, and those which become important in the poetry may play quite a negligible part in the man, the personality."[48] Women, whose "impressions and experiences" have traditionally not been considered "important," were not going to exclude them from their diaries or other texts at a time when feminism was on the rise. In taking what empowered them, these diarists practised one of the strategies noted by Shirley Neuman of postmodern theorists of women's autobiography.

Moreover, many male writers obviously did not ascribe to a theory of impersonal emotion, and those who propounded it did not necessarily practise it. Autobiographical elements in D.H. Lawrence's novels are often easily identifiable, in keeping with his theoretical rejection of an art disconnected from life. In *Women in Love*, for example, he created the "little insect" Loerke, a "detached" artist to whom Lawrence, through the voice of Ursula, could object. Looking at a photogravure of one of Loerke's productions, a statuette of a girl astride a horse, she believes the thing to be a picture of Loerke himself. To which he replies: "It is a work of art, it is a picture of nothing, of absolutely nothing. It has nothing to do with anything but itself, it has no relation with the everyday world of this and other, there is no connection between them, absolutely none." Ursula, refusing to be shaken, affirms, "The world of art is only the truth about the real world, that's all."[49] It is interesting to note that Lawrence had a profound effect on Nin and influenced Smart as well.

There are strains of autobiography that could not be transcended in the works of Joyce or Eliot, a fact that makes it appropriate to reconsider modernism in terms of Kadar's notion of life writing as "a continuum" which spreads "from the so-called least fictive narration to the most fictive." Joyce ends *A Portrait*, the very text in which he inscribes his advocacy of detachment, with the diary entries of Stephen. Even as he goes off alone to create like his impersonal God, Stephen cannot transcend his own self and instead offers us the very kind of writing he has come to deplore. More surprisingly, by the middle of *Ulysses*, he negates his theory by delivering a lecture on the necessary fusion of author and protagonist. Addressing an audience at the National Library, Stephen argues that Shakespeare is both Hamlet and Hamlet's ghostly father. He posits the view that, in general, Shakespeare "has hidden his own name, a fair name, William, in the plays ... as a painter of old Italy set his face in a dark corner of his canvas. He has revealed it in the sonnets where there is Will in overplus."[50] We may similarly find Joyce "revealed" in his works.

Likewise, in *T.S. Eliot's Personal Waste Land: Exorcism of the Demons*, James E. Miller Jr illuminates the extent to which Eliot's poem is informed by – comes directly out of – his personal experiences.[51] But Miller does more: he suggests that Eliot's aesthetic of impersonality was a carefully constructed credo designed specifically to draw attention away from his need to write autobiographically. Miller does a thorough job tracing and identifying biographical material in *The Waste Land*, but the actual content of the poem is not my concern here. Rather, what proves fascinating is Miller's analysis of Eliot's critical writings and how they reveal his autobiographical urge.

Miller begins his work by discussing Eliot's 1936 essay "In Memoriam," because it strikes him as so antithetical to poet's earlier tenets on impersonality.[52] Having seen how "Tradition and the Individual Talent" serves to devalue the diary as a legitimate form of literature, we cannot be anything but surprised here. Eliot introduces his subject simply: "Tennyson is a great poet, for reasons that are perfectly clear." He describes "In Memoriam" thus: "It is unique: it is a long poem made by putting together lyrics, which have only the unity and continuity of a diary, the concentrated diary of a man confessing himself. It is a diary of which we have to read every word." Tennyson is great, and he is so precisely because he writes like a confessional diarist. The diary as a form is elevated to literary heights, as possessing the "unity and continuity" one expects from the most revered of genres, poetry. (One also expects "unity and continuity" in traditional, linear autobiography.) Eliot continues: "It happens now and then that a poet by some strange accident expresses the mood of his generation, at the same time that he is expressing a mood of his own which is quite remote from that of his generation." Miller posits the argument that Eliot is speaking not only of Tennyson but of himself, offering his readers the clue that his own "mood" is preserved in *The Waste Land*.[53]

To support this interpretation, Miller quotes fragments by Eliot from various sources. The facsimile manuscript of *The Waste Land*, edited by Eliot's wife Valerie and published in 1971, provides insights into his intentions. Valerie Eliot's choice of an epigraph – a statement made by Eliot at an unspecified date – is especially significant: "Various critics have done me the honour to interpret the poem in terms of criticism of the contemporary world, have considered it, indeed, as an important bit of social criticism. To me it was only the relief of a personal and wholly insignificant grouse against life; it is just a piece of rhythmical grumbling." And in a 1959 interview in the *Paris Review*, Eliot responded to a question about intention, "I wonder what an 'intention' means! One wants to get something off one's chest."

In his 1951 lecture "Virgil and the Christian World," Eliot acknowledged: "A poet may believe that he is expressing only his private experience; his lines may be for him only a means of talking about himself without giving himself away." Miller wonders: "Could it possibly be that Eliot believed that in 'The Waste Land' he was 'expressing only his private experience'? ... Could it be that ... 'Tradition and the Individual Talent,' with its elaborate and tortured 'impersonal theory' of poetry, had been a sophistic or sophisticated defense for someone wanting to write poetry 'talking about himself without giving himself away'?"[54]

Miller explores just what it was that Eliot may have been afraid to "give away," and he is convincing in his argument that Eliot was expressing his love for Jean Verdenal, a young friend killed during World War I. The supposition that the poem encodes a necessary outpouring of autobiographical material and devotional emotion has a major impact not only on how we read "Tradition and the Individual

Talent" but on how we re-evaluate the status of women writing contemporaneously with Eliot. What, in fact, his poem suggests is that good poetry – and, by extension, good art in general – is not dependent upon the extinction of personality. Women writers – in particular, literary diarists – were arguably doing nothing that writers such as Joyce and Eliot were not also doing to some degree. Eliot was encoding his "diary" in his poetry, just as women were employing modernist strategies in their diaries.

SETTING THE SELF IN ORDER

One reason that Eliot turned to the public forum of poetry to carry out personal explorations may have to do with the notion that, by the twentieth century, men were increasingly associated with public activity and not psychological introspection. He may have felt embarrassed cultivating the requisite private spaces for such introspection. To appreciate this dilemma, we need to consider modernism's responses to Freud and modern psychology.

Freud began publishing his research in 1895, and during the first decades of the twentieth century he continued to offer seminal studies on the subjects of hysteria, dreams, and the workings of the unconscious. It was not until after World War 1, however, that he "became known to millions of people throughout the world." In *A Primer of Freudian Psychology*, Calvin S. Hall summarizes the impact of Freud's work at this time: "Psychoanalysis was the rage, and its influence was felt in every theater of life. Literature, art, religion, social customs, morals, ethics, education, the social sciences – all felt the impact of Freudian psychology. It was considered fashionable to be psychoanalyzed and to use such words as subconscious, repressed urges, inhibitions, complexes, and fixations in one's conversation."[55]

Scott argues, "The psychological was a focus far less acknowledged by the 'men of 1914'" than by the women of the period,[56] a point borne out by the plethora of psychologically driven characters and narratives in many works of women's fiction. Woolf, for instance, relied on dreams as a means of representing her characters' repressed thoughts in novels such as *The Voyage Out* and *The Years*. Rebecca West used the notion of free association to "cure" her protagonist in *The Return of the Soldier*. Djuna Barnes's Dr Matthew O'Connor in *Nightwood* is a Freudian figure to whom the other characters come to confess and learn truths about themselves. Nin's novella "The Voice" delivers reflections of a psychoanalyst. And White's story "House of Clouds" and her novel *Strangers* treat psychological breakdown and recovery.

Woolf, White, and Nin, as well as many others, were directly involved with the psychoanalytic profession, and many contemporaries underwent analysis. Virginia and Leonard Woolf were the first to publish Freud in English through their Hogarth Press. Hilda Doolittle was psychoanalyzed by Freud in 1933 and 1934, and her *Tribute to Freud* was published in 1954. White underwent analysis throughout her adult life, as did Nin, who also worked as an analyst for several months in 1935. Novelist May Sinclair was interested in psychoanalytic texts and helped to establish the Medico-Psychological Clinic of London in 1913.

The introduction of psychoanalysis as a tool for exploring the mind radically changed the diaristic project. While earlier diarists may certainly have used their textual spaces to contemplate their feelings, question their motives, and examine their personalities, they could not have done so with the same degree of awareness as these modernists. Probing the self became a more conscious pursuit done in the new light of scientific legitimacy. Psychoanalysis became the redeeming religion of the early twentieth century, shifting the Puritan diary of spiritual examination to the modernist plane of secular introspection.

Psychology itself was likely gendered feminine in the way that the anarchic masses storming the gates of modernism were, a notion we can appreciate in terms of the diary and by recalling Culley, who has noted that the "split between the public and private spheres" of activity rendered the diary a feminine space, one which privileged the inner life "of personal reflection and emotion." The advent of psychoanalysis was significantly one of the causes of this rupture.[57] If "the life of personal reflection and emotion" was associated with women's lives, and if "personal reflection and emotion" can be considered a subject of psychoanalysis, then women would be more amenable than men to its probing methods.

"The men of 1914" were perhaps less interested in psychology because of this feminization of it, and because Freud himself was preoccupied with the female gender. He made this focus clear in a number of works, including his 1933 lecture "Femininity," where he informed his audience that his talk "deals with a subject which has a claim on your interest second almost to no other. Throughout history people have knocked their heads against the riddle of the nature of femininity." He emphasized to the male portion of the audience, "Nor will *you* have escaped worrying over this problem – those of you who are men," while he condemned the female section: "to those of you who are women this will not apply – you are yourselves the problem."[58] Freud's lifelong frustration was articulated thus: "The great question that has never been answered and which I have not yet been able to answer, despite my thirty years of research into the feminine soul, is 'What does a woman want?'"[59]

I would argue that women found the diary an ideal space in which to seek their own answers to Freud's question. If at times they accepted his misogyny (evident in "Femininity" and throughout his work), writing through a sense of the female self as "the problem," they also called into question that misogyny by offering their own analyses of patriarchy and of womanhood. If Eliot labelled Joyce's style the "mythical method," I would label that of Woolf, White, Smart, and Nin the "psychoanalytic method." Drawing on their intellectual knowledge of and/or personal experiences with analysis, they turned to this method as a way of "ordering and controlling" the chaos and anarchy of their often-troubled psyches, using their diaries to chart their ongoing "grappling" with identity. Like post-structuralist feminists who negotiate enabling and disabling discourses, these modernists gained from psychoanalysis the ability to explore in unprecedented ways and gain profound insights into their selves and lives, which empowered them to voice their wants and needs. Freud ended his "Femininity" lecture with these instructions: "If you want to know more about femininity, inquire from your own experiences of life, or turn to the poets, or wait until science can give you deeper and more coherent information."[60] I would add, if you want to know more about women, turn to their diaries.

Psychoanalysis impacted on diaries and on the modern fiction and poetry which these diaries emulated. May Sinclair, involved with psychological research, is perhaps most famous for her contribution to modernist terminology. Drawing on the work of American psychologist William James,[61] she coined the term "stream of consciousness" for a particular literary style. In reviewing the first three volumes of Richardson's *Pilgrimage* in 1918, Sinclair stated: "'In this series there is no drama, no situation, no set scene. Nothing happens. It is just life going on and on. It is Miriam Henderson's stream of consciousness going on and on. And in neither is there any grossly discernible beginning or middle or end."[62] The stream-of-consciousness method allows the author, like the analysand and the diarist, to let thoughts come as they will. Reading a diary becomes analogous to reading a modernist novel, both of which enact the process of Freud's "free association." We are immediately, and for the duration of the "story," immersed in the mind of the character.

The representation of time is consequently revolutionized, for rather than being restricted to the conventional sequence of beginning, middle, and end, the modernist text merges past and future by representing the multiple layers of consciousness that constitute every present moment for any individual. This is precisely what occurs in a diary: the continual thoughts of the diarist are released in kaleidoscopic fashion in the calendrical spaces that go "on and on." Likewise, Freud noted: "Linear presentation is not a very adequate means of describing complicated mental processes going on in different layers of the mind."[63]

Modernist fiction and diaries alike inscribe the isolated, individual consciousnesses of their protagonists. These consciousnesses are often multiple, just as I discussed earlier how writers created various personae when they crafted "impersonal" texts. The notion of a split selfhood is attributed to Freud, for it was he who divided the psyche into the knowable consciousness and the knowable and unknowable unconsciousness (which would later become the tripartite ego, superego, and id). The self not fully or always present to itself is represented in the fragmented psyches of fictional characters and, further, in the fragmented form of their texts. Techniques for rendering such states of knowledge include unpunctuated (and thus unmediated) dialogue or monologue, ellipses or dashes to indicate a fluid or interrupted stream of thought, and gaps or divisions within or between passages or whole sections.

These techniques are basic to the diarist. She often ignores the dictates of formal punctuation, writing a stream-of-consciousness prose replete with ellipses and dashes that would make authors such as Joyce or Jean Rhys proud. DuPlessis calls the diarist's method "radical parataxis,"[64] and it may be considered, once again in terms of Freudian "free association" as well as in light of the modernist penchant for juxtaposition, the placing side by side of disparate ideas or phrases without (logical) transitions. While Eliot (and Pound as editor) went to great lengths to remove connectives from *The Waste Land*, Kafka shows how the diarist could be swifter, recording in his journal on 1 August 1914: "Germany has declared war on Russia. – Swimming in the afternoon."[65] The failing to privilege one event over another, a common feature of diarizing, echoes the democratizing principles of modernism.

The technique of employing gaps or divisions is fundamental to the diarist's regime of making separate entries on different days. The diary may be considered the quintessential text of modernist fragmentation, for the perpetual starting and stopping of entries, their varying lengths, the differences in time passed between each one, and the mingling of retrospect and anticipation in each one highlight the real fragmentation of lived experience which modernism sought to emulate.

Moreover, the diary is ostensibly written by as many narrators as there are entries. Assuming that the self is not fixed, the self the diarist brings to one entry varies from that which she brings to the next. Nussbaum contends: "The self presented in diary lacks an obvious center and a smooth continuity in its intermittent form and content, and thus may call into question the dominant humanist assumption that man is the center of meaning." From its developments from the seventeenth century, the diary has all along been a site on which the unitary self has been contested and multiple subjectivities registered.[66] The diary, then, may be the ur-modernist text.

If the self is fragmented, it nonetheless strives to be whole. Freud believed that unity, or self-knowledge, could be achieved when the repressed material of the unconscious, which was the cause of the division (neurosis), became known. It was to this end that he sought to "cure" his patients. I would argue that, although in a radically different manner, writers such as Joyce and Eliot "cured" their fragmented texts and made them whole as well.

In *Ulysses*, Joyce created a complex narrative and set of characters which had their allegorical counterparts in Homer's *Odyssey*. Worried that his audience would not appreciate the connections, he handed over his detailed charts of these connections to critic Valery Larbaud, who then gave explicating lectures on the book. Acknowledging that the eighteen sections of the novel create a fragmented appearance, Larbaud emphasized how "the whole forms none the less an organism, a book ... We begin to discover and to anticipate symbols, a design, a plan, in what appeared to us at first a brilliant but confused mass of notations, phrases, dates, profound thoughts, fantasticalities, splendid images, absurdities, comic or dramatic situations."[67]

Similarly, Eliot was apparently worried that *The Waste Land* would be misconstrued as a work which was wholly fragmented, and like Joyce, he wanted to draw attention to its unity. In "T.S. Eliot's New Critical Footnotes to Modernism," Michael Edward Kaufmann traces the history of Eliot's writing footnotes to *The Waste Land*. He shows how these footnotes were inspired by Eliot's wanting his work to have the perceived patterning that Joyce's was given. With respect to *Ulysses*, which we have heard Eliot praise for its "giving a shape and a significance" to his contemporary history, Eliot saw how Joyce turned "heterogeneity into a paradoxical homogeneity," and he wanted to do the same with his poem.[68] Kaufman notes that Eliot, who provided extensive documentation of his references, used "the opportunity afforded by the footnotes to present *The Waste Land* as a unified, coherent work, establishing links and arguing for larger patterns structuring the poem."[69]

These descriptions of Joyce's and Eliot's intentions could easily be applied to diaries and their authors' intentions. Though diaries employ "radical parataxis," at the same time they establish narrative continuity. Woolf, White, Smart, and Nin consistently acknowledged that they reread past entries, and they then established links to those entries. They also habitually filled in narrative gaps if necessary, or they wrote whole portions in one sitting if they had missed any days, all in the interests of unifying theme and content. Recall that Eliot praised Tennyson's diary-poem for its "unity and continuity." Larbaud's assertion that with *Ulysses* "we are before a much more complicated book than we had supposed"[70] speaks just as clearly to the diary.

Eliot's protagonist asks at the end of *The Waste Land*, "Shall I at least set my lands in order?" and he attests, "These fragments I have shored against my ruins." It is likely that he was seeking order not just for his lands/text but also for his chaotic psyche. So too were diarists. Nin lamented, "I suffer most of all from a breaking up of myself, from a lack of wholeness" (*ED*, 4: 77). We shall see how she and others used the fragmented spaces of their journals to gather up their fragmented selves, shoring them against societies which would negate or ignore them.

A WOMAN'S ONLY HOPE

If developments in psychology encouraged women to investigate their psyches, then social and moral laxities, especially on the Continent, encouraged them to explore their bodies. Writing about artists in France, Benstock affirms: "One common denominator among women's writing of this period is the mark not only of gender but of female sexuality. Heterosexual and homosexual women expatriates, for instance, discovered *sexualized* writing identities in expatriation – and in doing so they changed the history of modern women's writing, charting the terrain of female sexuality from female perspectives."[71] This is especially the case for Smart, Nin, and White, who engaged in heterosexual and homosexual relationships and then poetically and politically recorded them in their diaries.

In opposition to often liberating experiences of sexuality, Nin, White, and Woolf were probably victims of incest, and these hideous experiences also made their way into their journals, though in remarkably different ways, as we shall see. In *Father-Daughter Incest*, Judith Herman describes the incest victim: "No one could understand better than she what it means to undergo emotional torment. No one knows better what it means to be an orphan, to be driven too soon from one's home, to live as an outsider, to feel like an exile in normal society." Drawing on the same metaphor in "My Art Belongs to Daddy: Incest as Exile, the Textual Economics of Hayford Hall," Mary Lynn Broe associates incest with perhaps the most brutal form of exile imposed upon a woman – exile within her family and from her own body by her abuser. As Broe argues in a literary context, narratives of these abuses may be considered modernist in that incest survivors transform their textual spaces into metaphoric bodies, of which they may assume or regain control. In so doing, women challenge Freud, who initially formulated a "seduction theory" in a belief that incest was real, but who later abandoned it in favour of incest as fantasy.[73]

Broe quotes Djuna Barnes, one such survivor, who emphasized the importance of writing for healing: "It's getting the awful rust off the spirit that is almost insurmountable. It's why working every day is important – one may write the most lamentable balls but in the end one has a page or two that might not otherwise have been done. Keep writing. It's a woman's only hope, except for lace-making."[74] Though Barnes was referring to fiction, her insistence that women should write every day has clear implications for the diurnal diarist as well. Her conviction that writing is "a woman's only hope" may also be considered within the context of Eliot's "shored fragments." For women who were shattered with profound physical and psychological trauma, the diary was, if not their "only hope," certainly one site for shoring against their ruins.

Inscriptions of lesbian, heterosexual, and adulterous loves, in addition to abuses such as incest, underscore how radical the content of diaries may be, an important point in terms of yet another kind of exile experienced by women. Being experimental – "making it new" – has become a truism of modernism. While there is no disputing the prevalence of the "new," what is generally made and valued as such is form. It is arguable that form becomes privileged over content, so that what may constitute bold content is passed over, particularly when it comes to canon-making. In "Exiled by Genre: Modernism, Canonicity, and the Politics of Exclusion," Celeste M. Schenck analyzes how women's work specifically suffers from this hierarchical and arbitrary ruling. Although she focuses on poetry, her conclusions reflect the problematized fate of the diary as well.

The aim of her article is to recover a position within modernism for the neglected poets Anna Wickham, Charlotte Mew, Sylvia Townsend Warner, Alice Meynell, and Edith Sitwell. They are dismissed, Schenck argues, because they wrote in traditional rather than experimental verse. That they did so, however, is precisely what made poetry possible for them: "conventional form, although alive and well in genteel Georgian verse, was the *bête noire* of the Modernist movement in poetry, and therefore, although devalued, comparatively open to women poets." Recall Stanton's suggestion that women continued to write in devalued life forms in order to be accepted in the marketplace.

But if women retained conventional form in their work, they were not necessarily conservative in their content. Taking up the point made by Georg Lukács and certain feminist critics that "the radical poetics of Modernism often masks a deeply conservative politics," Schenck boldly inverts the equation and wonders if "the seemingly genteel, conservative poetics of women poets whose obscurity even feminists have overlooked might pitch a more radical politics than we had considered possible?"[75]

In her introduction to *Women's Writing in Exile*, Angela Ingram acknowledges that, while some women are exiled by geography, others are exiled in terms of genre. Revisionism "risks perpetuating a hierarchy of genre" whereby value is ascribed to "formal experimentation but not to radically new content." Excluding the seemingly traditional, non-experimental poets identified by Schenck "diminishes and homogenizes the multiplicity of modernisms."[76] Ingram, like Scott, recognizes that there is no such thing as one modernism, no "monolithic phenomenon," and thus the non-experimental form has as much place in the modernist program as the experimental.

It is in this context that the diary finally needs to be examined. Schenck's line that "recourse to convention does not always constitute a desire for constriction"[77] may well serve as a motto for the modernist diarist. While diarists employ modernist experimental techniques within their texts, the text itself remains on the most basic level conventional, perhaps the most traditional female space available. The challenges made by diarists are twofold. They exploit the traditional diaristic space by converting it into a site for literary experimentation. But they also challenge this experimentation – the technique of mainstream modernism – by marking on their calendrical spaces subversive female preferences and perspectives.

Women's diaries, perhaps more than any other modernist works, were written in states of multiple exile. Friedman chose as an epigraph to her essay on exile a quotation by H.D.: "I can't write unless I am an outcast."[78] This statement applies to the diarists under study here, offering a means of understanding why they turned to their journals, and why they turned their journals into modernist works. White once commented on her approach to writing, "I can only write if I think it is not going to be published" (D, 2: 131). Nin likewise confessed: "I have no faith in myself. Which does not mean that I will stop writing, but which means that I can never look at writing as a profession, as a 'public' work. I think I am doomed to loving and practicing it in secret" (ED, 3: 159). Women's diaries were thus written defensively, out of their need to tell their stories within societies which continued to regard such telling with suspicion. Women found in the diary a place to write "in secret." By exiling themselves to this genre, they escaped the censure that met them in the public marketplace. They used the diary, to answer Benstock's query, to both mime and undermine modernist principles, creating texts which are at once aesthetically autonomous and historically honest. Woolf, White, Smart, and Nin used well the modernist "arms" available to them: "silence, exile, cunning."

4 Virginia Woolf's Diary: "the proper stuff of fiction"[1]

On 3 January a nearly fifteen-year-old Virginia Stephen made this first entry in her 1897 diary: "We have all started to keep a record of the new year – Nessa, Adrian and I" (PA, 5). Though siblings Vanessa and Adrian began such diaries as well, their sister's journals are what hold our attention one hundred years later.[2] The first extant texts, from 1897 to 1909, were edited by Mitchell E. Leaska and published in 1990 as *A Passionate Apprentice: The Early Journals*. They complement the five-volume series *The Diary of Virginia Woolf*. Edited by Anne Olivier Bell and Andrew McNeillie, it spans the years 1915 to Woolf's death in 1941 and was published between 1977 and 1984. This complete work restores the bulk of material excised by Leonard Woolf in his initial offering of *A Writer's Diary* in 1953.

Since the nineteen sixties and seventies, Woolf has been the focus of much feminist revisionism in literary history. Scholars and publishers around the world drive the current Woolf industry and show no sign of easing up on production. More pointedly, as H. Porter Abbott notes, "Recent years have brought an appreciation of the uniqueness of Woolf's modernism." And yet, as he continues, "One thing still overlooked in this revaluation is how, early on, the development of Woolf's modernist oeuvre was deeply inflected by her personal writing – in particular, by her practice of keeping a diary."[3]

Though countless articles and books on Woolf's fiction, and increasingly on her life, are generated each year, her diary continues to attract relatively minimal attention in and of itself. Despite the fact that Quentin Bell, in his introduction to volume 1 of the *Diary*, hailed it as "a major work," "a masterpiece," and "a literary achievement,"[4] there is at present not one scholarly book on the diary, and the chapters and articles devoted to it are remarkably few in number. It remains a classic illustration of how diaries have been traditionally mined for information about the lives of the famous and for insights into how their authors' "real" literature may have been conceived and developed. If Woolf is a major writer, her diary has remained a minor text.

I do not believe, however, that she considered her journal in this limited sense, and nor should its readers. The Indigo Girls, an American folk-rock duo, tell Woolf at the start of their 1992 song "Virginia Woolf": "they published your diary and that's how I got to know you." Publication of the whole diary has allowed people from all over the world to get to know Woolf at almost every stage of her life and to interpret that life (and life's work) in a variety of ways. As one of her biographers, Hermione Lee, comments: "Virginia Woolf's story is reformulated by each generation. She takes the shape of difficult modernist preoccupied with questions of form, or comedian of manners, or neurotic highbrow aesthete, or inventive fantasist, or pernicious snob, or Marxist feminist, or historian of women's lives, or victim of abuse, or lesbian heroine, or cultural analyst, depending on who is reading her, and when, and in what context."[5]

Reading her diary in the context of a tradition of literary diaries, I have found a Woolf who used her journal to play out the multiple roles identified by Lee. In so doing, she provides us with an answer to her query in 1919: "What sort of a diary should I like mine to be?" (D, 1:266). By charting her self and her life through such a range of personae, Woolf has produced a text which treats many of the social, psychological, and aesthetic concerns of an Anglo-American modernism she not only practised but helped to define. Moreover, the various identities she gave herself in her diary reflect the diversity of her writing styles, so that just as she can never be relegated to one self, so her diary cannot be reduced to one genre. In considering her theories of modern fiction, coupled with an examination of her strategies for other types of writing – especially as discussed within the diary – I have found that for Woolf there was little distinction in her conception and execution of the myriad of genres she employed, including diary, memoir, biography, essay, and fiction. In breaking down the barriers between genres, and in disrupting the concept of a single selfhood, Woolf emerges from her diary as one who, in the spirit of modernism, made her life and work "new."

She herself valued her journal immensely. In the darkest sense, her severe bouts of mental illness kept her from her journal, but it was often the case that her milder and more consistent "moods" led her to her diary, for she found comfort and catharsis in dealing with them there. Although the text is in some ways a reticent one, it offers an investigation of a woman's lifelong struggle with depression, thereby inscribing the modernist preoccupation with self-analysis.

In a lighter vein, the diary was a place where Woolf could practise and sharpen her lively, sarcastic wit, which was directed at the scores of famous people with whom she had contact. But she was just as interested in her domestic world, so that her housekeepers Nelly Boxall and Lottie Hope earned as much space as the likes of T.S. Eliot and Katherine Mansfield. In this way the diary practises the modernist penchant for democratization of subject matter. In general, it proves a fascinating record of the vibrant and innovative literary, intellectual, and social period in which Woolf lived. She was well aware of the diary's function as such, since she took great care to fashion it as an enduring document.

The diary served several professional and artistic functions as well. It was a space in which Woolf could loosen her pen for the benefit of her commercial and fiction writing, and it was to serve as source material for her future memoirs. In a different sense, Woolf used the diary to construct herself as a writer and as a professional businesswoman. It was the canvas on which she painted her self-portrait of an artist. It was also to be a book that would fight her battle against the "race of time" (D, 1:304). She wrote her diary, as much as her other works, in a creative attempt to "stay this moment" (D, 1:135). As will be seen with White, Smart, and Nin, the fact that Woolf persevered in her diary, returning to it over and over again, reinforces how sustaining a text it was. It was a place in which she could affirm the reality and value of herself, her art, and her life.

THIS DUSTY BOOKISH ATMOSPHERE

In order to appreciate how the diary functioned for Woolf in these diverse and complementing ways, it is necessary to consider first the physical qualities of the volumes. At the time that I began to research Woolf's diaries, my husband and I rather suddenly found ourselves with the opportunity to spend a year in England. We had only a few months to prepare for our move, and in this period of hectic upheaval I was forced to dash off to New York City to examine Woolf's archive there. The irony of having to go to New York, before I left for England, to see the manuscripts of one of Britain's most famous writers was not lost on me or on my husband, who volunteered to drive me from Toronto to conserve our travel funds.

Before we left for the United States, I had spent some time waiting
for the New York Public Library, which houses the archive, to grant me
permission to see the actual manuscripts. I had been informed that the
collection had been placed off-limits to most scholars, since it had been
so over-handled that librarians were concerned about its physical survival. Limiting the number of scholars was made easy by the fact that
the entire collection had been microfilmed. But having explained in a
letter the importance to my research of seeing the physical aspects of
each volume, I fortunately received in the mail permission to do just
that.

As the brochure for the microfilmed series states, "The Woolf
materials at the Henry W. and Albert A. Berg Collection of English
and American Literature in the New York Public Library is the
largest selection of Woolf writings in the world." The brochure goes
on to emphasize that this collection is "Crowned" by the holograph
"volumes of diaries acquired from Leonard Woolf." As I entered the
doors of the New York Public Library one hot summer morning, I
certainly felt that I had come to see a precious, personal jewel. And
I was treated accordingly. I was first directed to a security office,
where I had to fill out a lengthy form which demanded all sorts of
information about myself and my business at the library. I was finally given a pass, which I had to press against the window of a locked
door down the hall so that the librarian behind it could identify who
I was. A click sounded, the door snapped open, and I was admitted
to a reading room.

I entered a plush chamber full of burgundy leather chairs, old yellow
lights, and dark wooden tables. Looking around, I thought of Woolf
and the hours and hours she had spent reading and researching in the
British Museum library. One of her sardonic descriptions came to
mind: "I to the Brit[ish] Mus[eum]; where all was chill serenity, dignity & severity [...] I like this dusty bookish atmosphere. Most of the
readers seemed to have rubbed their noses off & written their eyes out.
Yet they have a life they like – believe in the necessity of making books,
I suppose: verify, collate, make up other books, for ever" (D, 3:80).
I was eager to get down to work on my own book.

Unlike my experiences with the Smart and Nin archives, where the
sets of diaries had been brought out on trolleys so I could freely study
any volume at any time, Woolf's diaries were nowhere in sight. Rather,
I had to order one volume at a time and wait for the librarian to bring
it to me, and as soon as I finished my work, it was whisked away while
I waited patiently for the next one. Again I remembered Woolf writing
in her diary, "I used to feel that the British Museum reading room was
going on for ever. I felt I could take 15 years over a book; I wanted to

take longer & longer" (D, 4:208). Time for me was limited, as I had thirty-six volumes of diary to go through.

One other volume, the last of her early diaries, is the only one housed at the British Library. I was able to examine this notebook during my year in England. Thinking about my visits to both libraries – seeing Woolf's original diaries, holding them, feeling them, being "alone" with them – I turn to Woolf herself, whose words echo my sentiments: "I shall spend my day at the British Museum. (This is one of those visual images, without meaning when written down, that conveys a whole state of mind to me)" (D, 3:321). Based on my own "visual images," I will try to convey the physical character of Woolf's diaries and what it suggests about her state of mind at the time she was producing them.

SOME WORTHY & ANCIENT WORK

It is helpful to recall Lawrence Rosenwald from chapter 1, where his notion of the diarist's modus operandi was outlined. This modus operandi includes not only what words are used by the diarist but how they are presented: their "incarnation and format."[6] By taking factors such as these into account, we may discern the diarist's habits and intentions. My analysis of Woolf will place her at the far end of Rosenwald's spectrum of diaristic control, for she was an assiduous reader and shaper of her text.

Before I proceed to discuss the manuscripts, two points should be noted in order to explain why there are no diaries for certain periods of Woolf's life. First, in the most basic sense, she may have lacked the time to record. She was a prolific writer and often had no energy left to give to her diary. The more significant and lengthy gaps may be attributed to her periods of psychological depression, which prevented her from writing even in her diary. Woolf suffered several major breakdowns in her life, and although her biography may be familiar to many readers, these episodes bear acknowledging here to the extent that they impacted on her journal keeping. The first collapse occurred in 1895 after the death of her mother, Julia (Duckworth) Stephen. The recovery was slowed by the death two years later of Woolf's half-sister Stella Duckworth, who had assumed the role of mother after Julia's death. Woolf noted Stella's death in her diary with the words, "it is impossible to write of" (PA, 115), thus hinting at how the diary would peter out as she grew increasingly unable to cope. Though it was well maintained in 1903, the death of her father, Leslie Stephen, in February 1904 and her suicide attempt that May brought the diary to a close for the rest of the year.

In November 1906 her elder brother, Thoby, died, and the following February her sister Vanessa married Clive Bell. Though these events made Woolf feel abandoned, she was finding strength in her new career as a professional writer, and there are diaries for these years. There are none, however, between 1910 and 1915. By the former year she was once again ill. Virginia married Leonard Woolf in August 1912, but in September 1913, having tried to kill herself, she descended into a severe depression which lasted through to 1914. She began a diary on 1 January 1915, yet in February was forced to break off because of another breakdown. This episode debilitated her until 1917, at which point the diary picks up again; it would be sustained until her suicide on 28 March 1941.

Woolf's early diaries (1897–1909) are contained within seven note-books; the adult diaries (1915–41) within thirty. The first extant volume, for 1897, is in fact the only standard diary that she used. It is a small, brown leather book, whose pages are gold-rimmed. Most notable is its lock (now rusted and without a key), the hallmark of a girl's diary – Woolf was nearly fifteen years old at this point. Confined to one page per day, her writing reflects how the diary was more a site of disciplined recording than a space in which to let loose. She often registered her disappointment in this regard; for example, "This diary is too small to allow of very much prose, and that is quite inadequate" (*PA*, 73).

Her next diary, which she began keeping two years later, is a medium-sized book with a hard leather cover, onto which she has stuck a piece of paper with the title "Warboys Summer Holidays 1899."[7] From this point, Woolf would make it a habit to paste on a title giving a place and/or date. The rest of her early diaries are green or blue, soft or hard-covered, medium-sized notebooks, and all are unlined, making it easier for Woolf to write in her painstakingly small script.

What Rosenwald refers to as the "sort of book a diarist buys or makes to write in" is an important factor in determining the aesthetic quality of the work, and this second early volume was handmade by Woolf, and made to be beautiful. Impossible to appreciate in the published version is how she pasted what were original diary sheets onto the pages of *Logick: or, The Right Use of Reason*, by Isaac Watts D.D. She devoted most of her entry for 18 September 1899 to explaining this transfer. Referring to the diary in its initial state, she commented: "The work heretofore was contained in one modest paper book, that fronted the world in a state of nature – naked but not ashamed. Boards it recked not of, now it boasts boards that amount to the dignity of a binding, being ancient tooled calf – the tooling resplendent today as a hundred years ago." Woolf continued, "A sudden idea struck me, that it would be original useful & full of memories if I embedded the fore-going pages in the leaves of some worthy & ancient work [...]." One reason she chose the Watts volume was "because its back had a certain air of distinction among its brethren" (PA, 159–60).

Woolf's actions may be interpreted in several ways. As noted, she had been in a fragile state of mental health from 1895 to 1897 and had been under medical supervision. By the time of the 1899 diary, she had recovered. She may have chosen to preserve that diary in the particu-lar text of *Logick: or, The Right Use of Reason* to prove to herself (and to her future readers) that her recorded thoughts were those of a logi-cal, reasonable, and hence sane person.

Her actions may also be considered in terms of creating a palimpsest, a manuscript "on which the original writing has been effaced to make way for other writing."[8] In *The Madwoman in the Attic*, Sandra Gilbert and Susan Gubar contend that throughout history women have "produced literary works that are in some sense palimpsestic, works whose surface designs conceal or obscure deeper, less accessible (and less socially acceptable) levels of meaning." Through this strategy they "managed the difficult task of achieving true female literary authority by simultaneously conforming to and subverting patriarchal literary standards."[9] Woolf's 1899 diary is certainly a palimpsest, for she effaced Watts's text to "make way" for her own. She arguably did so to achieve the "literary authority" mentioned by Gilbert and Gubar. By transferring her diary from loose sheets to a bound book, she was mak-ing clear her subversive desires. She wanted the diary's appearance to "boast" of "dignity" and "distinction"; and if her entries were con-tained within "some worthy & ancient work," then they would them-selves take on the respected qualities of such a work. In this way she could approach the "patriarchal" literary status of Watts, and her diary – a traditionally devalued and feminine genre – would be elevat-ed to literary status.

Woolf's attention to the aesthetic construction of her journal coin-cided with its becoming more of a writer's notebook. The Watts diary's entries have become longer and more formally executed. For instance, she titled her entry for 18 August "Warboys Distractions." And not only did she call 3 September "A Chapter on Sunsets," but she wrote the date again, with her initials, at the end (PA, 156), suggesting how she conceived the entry as a finished "piece." Leaska appropriately concludes that in this volume Woolf "was practising the art of essay writing for the first time" (PA, 135).

The third diary, for June to October 1903, continues to reveal a developing writerly sensibility in that it opens with an "Index," listing by page the contents to follow, such as "A Dance in Queens Gate 1,"

"An Artistic Party 33," "Life in the Fields 120," and so on (book 3). Though the material is presented in essay form, Woolf has provided some dates, just as she would for diary entries, underscoring how early on she was blurring genre boundaries.

The fourth diary, for Christmas 1904 to May 1905, is more like the first one in that there are short entries which record rather than elaborate on the day's events and accomplishments. But unlike the 1897 volume, this later one celebrates a young woman who has become a professional writer. At the end of 1904 Woolf first had her work published: one essay and two book reviews appeared in the *Guardian*. By February 1905, she was writing reviews for the *Times Literary Supplement*, a job she would continue to do until the last years of her life. Her writing energies were likely being directed towards her new employment, a fact that could account for the brief diary passages.

In addition to the regular entries, at the back Woolf has listed several books and checked off those read. On another back page, under the heading "Work Done," she has registered all her book reviews. She further provided a "Notes" section, documenting various hotels visited and their cost, and she has penned a detailed commentary on her reading of Edward A. Freeman's *History of the Norman Conquest*. Using the back of the journal as a miscellaneous space would become a habit for Woolf, one which equates the diary with any modernist text running the gamut from "high" to "low" culture.

The last three of the early journals were written sporadically, during various holidays. The diary of August to September 1905 documents Woolf's summer in Cornwall, while the final two record travels spanning the years 1906 to 1909. The entries within each volume are long and descriptive, proving that the diary had once again become a place in which Woolf was honing her writing skills. It is important to note that it was at the end of 1907 that she began "Melymbrosia," the manuscript which would become her first novel, *The Voyage Out*. The diary's literary development was therefore concomitant with her becoming a novelist.

By the start of her later diaries on 1 January 1915, then, Woolf had long been established as a professional writer of book reviews and essays, and *The Voyage Out* was due out in March of that year. Her artistic consciousness is reflected in "the sorts of book" she "bought or made to write in," for she bought diaries that were physically appealing, and she further made them, or transformed them, into aesthetic caches. She used, for the most part, two kinds of books, both of which were unlined. The first are medium-sized, and are distinguished by their multicoloured, marbled cardboard covers, which give them a rich, luxurious appeal. The second, and more frequently used, are large, floppy books. Woolf covered many of these with a variety of wrapping papers, sheets printed with the simple, yet striking designs made for and by the Hogarth Press.[10] The diary for 1922, for instance, has a burgundy pattern set against a cream background; that for 1935 has a small blue and black floral pattern against a white background. These printed covers are beautiful, and they elevate the diaries from ordinary store-bought books to personally decorated ones. There were also some occasions when Woolf made her diaries from scratch, taking ordinary paper, punching two holes, and then threading the pages into a cardboard spine. Alternatively, she fitted paper into a ring binder and then covered it with her own decorative paper.

Almost every cover has a small, usually white, piece of paper glued on the front, with "Diary" and the appropriate date written on it. Likewise, on the first page is always written the places at which the respective diaries were kept, such as "Hogarth House, Paradise Road, Richmond Oct. 1917." Most of the books are made with white paper, but some have light blue pages. On an even more colorful note, Woolf had a penchant for writing in different colours of ink, often changing colours within a single volume. Her preferred shades were black, peacock blue, and bright purple. For me, this combination made reading the diaries a visually playful and engaging activity, and it draws attention to her fascination with pens, a topic she constantly mentioned within the diaries.

It was interesting to see not only the colour of Woolf's words but their angle: her handwriting always slants upwards. Gilbert and Gubar, in their discussion of palimpsest, mention Emily Dickinson as one of the many women who wrote subversively. They cite as an example of her strategy her poem that begins, "Tell all the Truth but tell it slant."[11] This poem came to my mind as I followed Woolf's words diagonally across the pages of her journals. While I am not suggesting that she deliberately wrote on an angle, we might consider her penmanship as an unintentional representation of Dickinson's dictum. That is, I am arguing that Woolf used her private diary to deliver certain "truths" about herself – in what either she wrote or withheld – which she intended others to discover or decode at some later date, and this was her "slant."

If her writing was slanted, her margins were straight. Though her books were unlined, she took the time to rule margins for every page of a volume, in red ink or pencil, light blue pencil, or peacock blue ink. By the time I reached Woolf's final diary, I had become so accustomed to this habit that I received an emotional shock. In the published diary, Woolf's last entry logically comes at the end of the last volume, number 5. In the original manuscript, however, her last entry is in fact near the beginning of a new diary volume, in which she had ruled her own margins on every page. This format illuminates the fact that Woolf had set up the diary as a book which she had intended to fill, and it underscores a life stopped short. The experience of seeing a majority of pages left blank was deeply moving.

In consideration of Rosenwald's interest in "how a volume of the diary is presented *qua* volume," we have seen how Woolf valued each diary as a unique physical entity. The issue of whether each volume was "given a formal beginning or ending" is also at least in part affirmed, for she took the time to label each volume and to ground it in her place or places of residence. Moreover, from the start of her diarizing, Woolf acknowledged where and when a new diary volume began and an old one ended. Having introduced her first diary – "We have all started to keep a record of the new year" (PA, 5) – she ended that year with "Here then comes the 'Finis' [...] Here is a volume of fairly acute life [...] ended locked & put away [...] The End of 1897" (PA, 134). Such closure became a lifelong gesture. On 27 July 1918, for instance, she wrote, "But first one must pause to say that here a new volume starts, the third" (D, 1:171); and on 29 December 1931, "I will finish this book, & begin another for 1932" (D, 4:57). The "end" was often further marked by a summing up of the particular year, or volume, as in September 1899, when a young Woolf bid farewell to her summer diary: "The day has come at last of which I have thought so much. It is my habit, on this the last page of the book, to sum up my judgment & deliver my verdict on the summer entire" (PA, 160).

While Woolf's diary may have been conceived as separate volumes, each was simultaneously part of a larger whole. The diary thus follows the agendas of the likes of Joyce and Eliot, whose *Ulysses* and *The Waste Land*, as we have seen, are at once fragmentary and unified. Woolf opened her 1915 book on 1 January thus: "To start this diary rightly, it should begin on the last day of the old year [...]" (D, 1:3). Interested in maintaining narrative continuity from the previous year, she was determined that the diary function in a manner conducive to this flow. This was a concern of hers from the start of her diary keeping. Not only did she make countless references to her "lapses" or "gaps" in the diary, but she often went back and tried to make up for them. In an entry for 10 July 1897 she noted, "(This is where I left off writing my diary – I fill in these days from memory, this afternoon Tuesday July the 27th.)" (PA, 113). True to her word, she proceeded to reconstruct a record of her missed diary days, a practice she would sustain throughout her life. Recall that Pepys similarly wrote up to fourteen days in one sitting.

Another indication of narrative drive is Woolf's penchant for inserting diary fragments, or diaries kept elsewhere, into the corresponding diary proper. In the middle of her diary for 1930–31, she attached to the spine a small "volume" made of loose sheets bearing the title: "Diary of Tour to La Rochelle, Brantome etc. April 16th 1931" (book 20). Woolf went so far as to inform her journal, "Here I will paste in – though it is hardly worth the trouble, the fitful flying notes I made" (D, 4:17). But she did trouble to paste in the extraneous diary, suggesting that it was important for the story to be as complete and unfolding as possible. It was also worth the trouble to paste twenty-eight small white sheets onto the larger blue pages of the main diary, kept during her travels in Greece between 18 April and 11 May 1932 (book 21). And again, she inserted a miniature volume kept on a trip to Holland, Germany, Italy, and France between 6 and 31 May 1935 (book 24). In May 1937, upon returning home from France, she took the time to type out her travel notes. She then inserted this typed version into the diary proper, an act which implies that she not only wanted narrative continuity for herself but that she wanted her prose to be readable for others (book 26).

Woolf sought to preserve narrative within and between entries in other ways as well. In 1903 she broke off a passage about London, only to return with "London (continued)" (PA, 210). More imaginatively, she closed her entry for 17 September 1935 with this description: "London yesterday: a violent storm of wind all night. Garden a litter of apples & branches." A few days later she updated it: "Yes it was a terrific storm; a storm to mark, I suppose. All the trees chocolate brown on the wind side; little leaves like chipped potatoes" (D, 342).

Woolf was able to preserve such continuity because of her passion for rereading past entries. She reread her diary so frequently as to suggest that it had become her favourite book, as she affirmed: "Oh yes, I've enjoyed reading the past years diary, & shall keep it up" (D, 1:317). Another time, she "spent the whole morning reading old diaries, & [was] now (10 to 1) much refreshed" (D, 4:167). These examples support Rosenwald's claim that a diarist is in control of her text, for in rereading her diary, Woolf could shape future entries in a thematic manner. Simons believes that Woolf's penchant for narrative flow "suggests her need of a structural principle, however slight, to assure herself of her own control over the medium of her life."[12] I would add that she was just as determined to assert control over the medium of her diary as art.

Rereading afforded Woolf the opportunity to edit her diaries. She did so at different stages of writing. In the most basic sense, she edited at the moment of composition or thought. In her entry for 18 December 1921, she began a sentence "Our circumst" and then crossed out "circumst" and wrote "luck" instead (book 10). Though the change from "circumstances" to "luck" is insignificant in itself, it highlights the fact that Woolf was determined to chose her words precisely, as would any conscientious writer. She drew attention to her intentions in December 1938: "I will spend the last morning [...] in summing up the year. True, there are 10 days or so to run; but the liberty of this book allows these – I was going to say liberties, but my meticulous conscience bids me look for another word. That raises some questions; but I leave them; questions about my concern with the art of writing" (D, 5:192). While I will, along with Woolf, "leave" these "questions" to be considered in detail later on, we can here appreciate that even on the most basic level she wrote her diary with aesthetic awareness.

She also went back and added to, deleted, or corrected words and phrases already written. She would have done so either at the time of writing or later, as evidenced by a change in pen. Discussing Lytton Strachey's "lack of physical warmth," Woolf conceded, "Mentally of course it produces that metallic & conventionally brilliant style which prevents his writing from reaching the first rate, to my judgment." She has changed the last words with arrows to "from reaching, to my judgment, the first rate" (book 7). While alterations such as these are common, one last example is perhaps of greatest import. Woolf's diary entries for 20, 22, and 24 January 1919 were originally composed in the book for 1918. Wanting to transfer them to the start of a new diary for the following year, she copied out the entries, but she made revisions as she did so (D, 1:233, 325, appendix 2). She saw her diary as a work which could be improved, and which would reflect and satisfy her professional, writerly sensibilities. We must see it as one which forces us to challenge assumptions that the diary is a spontaneous and uncrafted text.

A LITTLE BOOK

It is likely that Woolf's aesthetic sensibilities were aroused by the plethora of published journals which she read. As Rosenwald has documented, "Before 1800 few diaries were published *qua* diaries ... But the independent publication of Evelyn's diary won respectful reviews in 1818, that of Pepys's considerable popularity in 1825, and that of Byron's ... European acclaim in 1830."[13] The diary in its published form had been, by the time Woolf began her own journal, elevated to literary status, a fact of which she was well aware.

Only three months into her 1897 book, she recorded her progress in
reading the diary of Samuel Pepys (PA, 62, 65, 66, 67, 69), in 1903 she
read Boswell's *Journal of a Tour to the Hebrides* (PA, 206), and in her
later diaries she made further references to both these works (D, 3:237,
239). She also alluded to Pepys on more than one occasion, as the clos-
ing of this 1915 entry testifies: "Home & finished Pope, & so to bed"
(D, 1:29). While Woolf may have been merely parodying Pepys's
famous "& so to bed," she may also have been allying her diary with
his published and publicly celebrated text. She certainly honoured him
in her 1918 essay "Papers on Pepys": "Insatiable curiosity, and unflag-
ging vitality were the essence of a gift to which, when the possessor is
able to impart it, we can give no lesser name than genius."[14]

Woolf mentioned reading other diaries as well, including those of
Fanny Burney (D, 1:14; 3:199–200) and Alice James (4:248). When she
read the published journal (1868–92) of social reformist Beatrice Webb
in February 1926, she was concomitantly rereading her own: "Mrs
Webb's book has made me think a little what I could say of my own
life. I read some of 1923 this morning" (D, 3:62). In August 1934 she
noted an affinity with André Gide: "then Gide's Journal, again full of
startling recollection – things I cd have said myself" (D, 4:241). By
November 1939 she was comparing her diary writing unfavourably
with his: "How compete with the compression & lucidity & logic of
Gide writing his Journal? Well, the plain truth is I cant" (D, 5:244); and
in February 1940: "I wish I could conglobulate reflections like Gide"
(5: 263). Woolf consistently made connections between her private and
others' published diaries.

In addition to that on Pepys, she wrote numerous reviews and essays
about published diaries, establishing herself as one of the first, most-
informed, and prolific critics of this "new" literary genre. In a 1920
essay on Evelyn's journal, she commented that reading a diary is "a
profitless occupation which no critic has taken the trouble to investigate," but we must take this statement with a grain of salt, for here and
elsewhere she did take a great deal of "trouble to investigate" it.[15] She
was able to affirm of Evelyn, for instance, that "he writes a diary; and
he writes it supremely well"; and "He was not an artist ... but as an
artistic method this of going on with the day's story circumstantially ...
has its fascination."[16]

Some of Woolf's earliest reviews were of diaries. In 1908 she wrote
"The Journal of Elizabeth Lady Holland" for *Cornhill Magazine*. Lady
Holland (1791–1811), previously Lady Webster, was examined thus:
"From her earliest youth Lady Webster seems to have had a quality
which saved her diary from the violent fate of diaries, and spared the
writer her blushes; she could be as impersonal as a boy of ten and as

intelligent as a politician."[17] Woolf criticized the eighteenth-century diary of Lady Charlotte Bury in her 1908 review for the *Times Literary Supplement*: "As it is, the size of the volumes is sufficiently formidable, and were it not for the watery Georgian atmosphere which they preserve we might wish that Lady Charlotte's sentiments had been curtailed."[18] In a *TLS* review of Emerson's *Journals* in 1910, Woolf recognized its literary quality: "In the pages of his diary one can see how his style slowly emerged from its wrappings."[19]

Of Anne Chalmers (1813–91) and her travel journal, Woolf wrote for the *Nation and Athenaeum* in February 1924, "her freedom of spirit seems to have survived, and the book, for those who like such old wives' tales, is full of amusement."[20] It was in an appreciative mood that she ended a 1926 essay on the diaries of nineteenth-century painter Benjamin Haydon: "finally we catch ourselves thinking, as some felicity of phrase flashes out or some pose or arrangement makes its effect, that his genius is a writer's," and that "Always his painter's eye lights up his phrases."[21] Similarly, in 1932 she praised Dorothy Wordsworth's journals: "Even in such brief notes one feels the suggestive power which is the gift of the poet rather than of the naturalist."[22]

In "Reading Other People's Diaries," Andrew Hassam contends that once a diary has been published, it has become a work of literature and so subject to the same critical scrutiny as other literary texts.[23] Woolf's many reviews and essays support this view, for they prove that she regarded diaries and journals as works worthy of such scrutiny. From the beginning, she wrote her diary with the knowledge of a tradition of published diaries behind her. In light of the new market potential for diaries, Rosenwald concludes: "by the 1830s, then, well-read diarists were surely considering the prospect of independent publication and, thus, inevitably thinking of their diaries as *books*."[24] Woolf, well aware of the diary's elevated status, must have considered her own as just such a "book."

She both knew about and perpetuated a critical, diaristic literary tradition, and so it is not surprising that her own journal often appears intended for a reading audience other than herself. Fothergill's assertion that diarists may "address themselves to a putative reader" is proven by Woolf early on. In May 1897 she made this entry: "In the morning, I went out by myself – Nessa was at her most ——— (to be filled in as desired) studio" (PA, 91). Woolf seems to be playing with an audience, inviting it to participate in her text. More explicitly, by August 1899 she admitted: "(I suppose a reader sometimes for the sake of variety when I write; it makes me put on my dress clothes such as they are)" (PA, 144).

It is likely that the audience she envisioned was largely an unknown, distant one. For, as we shall see, though White, Smart, and Nin shared their diaries with their closest friends and/or relatives at various times, Woolf for the most part did not. When reading aloud a memoir to a Bloomsbury gathering in the early twenties, she did include passages from her diaries of 1904–05 and 1909, but this was a rare incident.[25] Acknowledging that many of her friends similarly kept journals, she told her diary in January 1918: "The diary habit has come to life at Charleston. Bunny sat up late on the Old Year's night writing, & Duncan came back with a ledger, bought in Lambs Conduit Street. The sad thing is we daren't trust each other to read our books; they lie, like vast consciences, in our most secret drawers" (D, 1:95).[26] Woolf was just as reserved with her husband, admitting, "As I cannot write if anyone is in the room, as L[eonard]. sits here when we light the fire, this book remains shut"; and "(L. is getting logs so I cant write)" (D, 5:338, 342). In contrast, Nin nightly read her diary to her husband, while Smart often allowed her lover to respond to entries about him.

If Woolf resisted sharing her journal with her intimates, she seemed amenable to sharing it with future generations. By the time she was accustomed to seeing her works of criticism and fiction in print, she understandably considered the public direction that her diary might take. In August 1938 she had "half a mind one of these days to explain what [her] intention is in writing these continual diaries. Not publication" (D, 5:162). And yet she frequently revealed intentions to make her diaries somehow public. In March 1926 she wondered: "But what is to become of all these diaries, I asked myself yesterday. If I died, what would Leo make of them? He would be disinclined to burn them; he could not publish them." She then countered: "Well, he should make up a book from them, I think; & then burn the body. I daresay there is a little book in them" (D, 3:67). In November 1928 she commented on her journal, "And this shall be written for my own pleasure," but was forced to acknowledge, "that phrase inhibits me: for if one writes only for one's own pleasure, – I dont know what it is that happens. I suppose the convention of writing is destroyed; therefore one does not write at all" (D, 3:201). Given that she wrote these words in 1928 and would continue until her death more than ten years later, she must have been writing, on some level, for someone else's "pleasure" as well.

To appreciate Woolf's public intentions, we can turn to her short story "The Legacy," which she wrote six months before her death. The plot of the story is of interest here only to the extent that it involves a widower who learns important truths about his late wife by reading her diary. Of particular significance is this early description of the couple: "Ever since they were married, she had kept a diary ... When he came in and found her writing, she always shut it or put her hand over it. 'No, no, no,' he could hear her say, 'After I'm dead – perhaps.' So she had left it for him, as her legacy."[27] These lines mirror Woolf's own tendency to cover the pages of her journal when Leonard was in the room, and they reinforce her intention that he would inherit her diaries when she died and "make up a book from them," as he did when he published *A Writer's Diary*. We can thus see Woolf's diary not only as a legacy to her husband but as one to us, the readers she intended for that "book" which Leonard was to make.

Virginia Woolf arguably wanted her legacy published in order to give others pleasure and also to ensure her posterity. She once noted: "At this point it would be useful could I command the pen of some intelligent & well informed diarist, with an eye for the future; someone who could put down what were the really interesting things that Sir Wm Tyrrell, Camile Huysman, & the Sidney Webbs said" (*D*, 1:145). In like manner, she mused, "I open this, forced by a sense of what is expected by the public, to remark that Kipling died yesterday; & that the King (George 5th) is probably dying today" (*D*, 5:8). Though tongue-in-cheek, the passages reveal Woolf to be conscious of the diary's potential to establish herself as an important social historian.

At other times, she was directed towards her future literary reputation, as when she wrote: "(I go on to wonder whether any one else is thinking of Carlyle's birthday, & if so whether it gives him any pleasure; & again of the curious superstition, haunting literary people, of the value of being remembered by posterity – but I had better reign myself in)" (*D*, 1:223). Perhaps Woolf had to "reign" herself in because she was getting too close to her own desire to be remembered, which she may have considered shameful arrogance. On the other hand, she did write "reign" rather than "rein," and if her mistake was an intentional pun, we can read the line another way. Perhaps she wanted to set herself up as a literary sovereign in her own right, enjoying all the power and prestige traditionally granted to male rulers of the cultural realm. A well-written diary, a "legacy" to her reputation, could help her achieve that regal status.

Woolf often suggested that her diary would be useful to her in the future, not primarily as a work in itself, but as the raw material from which she would compose her memoirs. As early as 1905 she had written of her entries: "These are rough notes to serve as land marks" (*PA*, 291). In 1919 she made reference to a "Virginia Woolf at the age of 50" who would sit down "to build her memoirs out of these books [...]" (*D*, 1:234). And in 1940 she paused to observe: "I may as well make a note I say to myself; thinking sometimes who's going to read all this scribble? I think one day I may brew a tiny ingot out of it – in my memoirs" (D, 5:269).

While we must take heed of Woolf's stated intentions, I would suggest that she was protesting too much. Her need to rationalize why she was writing the diary could be taken as an apologia for keeping a daily book of the self which was supposedly, in itself, of no value and hence a waste of time. Blodgett argues that, in terms of motive, women who claim they are keeping a diary for purposes such as memory recall for the writing of memoirs are not being fully honest. She contends: "The truth is rather that diarists, even in public diaries, are taking an interest in self," and because such interest runs counter to expected female behaviour, "diaristic ego usually retreats behind justifications that are entirely self-acceptable: utility and need – a memoir for posterity, a record for my children, a self-improving discipline to make me more acceptable to others."[28]

Though Woolf had no children, she did assert over and over again the diary's useful function – that it would be mined for her memoirs. But by the end of her life she had in fact barely begun, let alone completed, them. We do have the fragment of this intended work, which she introduced in this way: "Two days ago – Sunday 16th April 1939 to be precise – Nessa said that if I did not start writing my memoirs I should soon be too old."[29] What follows, the posthumously published "A Sketch of the Past," is described by Abbott as "a kind of antimemoirs, a diarylike text written with her left hand and intentionally balanced on the cusp between reminiscence and the accidental intrusion of present thoughts."[30]

The memoir is certainly "diarylike," for it is divided into passages which are dated like diary entries over an extended period of time, from 15 May 1939 to 15 November 1940. Regarding these markers, Woolf acknowledged, "I write the date, because I think that I have discovered a possible form for these notes." The diary also "has its form, which one learns" (D, 1:304). And her description of her sketch as "notes" for her memoir is precisely how she described the diary: "These are rough notes" (PA, 291).

Despite all the other works that Woolf finished, she was never able to complete the memoir. She seems to have been always in a state of making notes for it. And yet with the diary she was actually producing not the notes but the very stuff of a memoir. Her conflation of genres reminds us of John Evelyn, who, as we saw in chapter 1, was described as being "famous as a diarist or, more accurately, as the author of memoirs." And just as his life writing was eventually titled simply *The Diary of John Evelyn*, so Woolf's diary assumed dominant status for Woolf herself. Abbott speculates about the fate of the "Sketch" memoir: "What had happened was that the conventional idea of her diary as something to be plundered for the story of her life was gradually displaced by Woolf's sense that her diary was a rather extraordinary object in its own right, with its own life and its own integrity."[31]

Given both Blodgett's and Abbott's arguments, we can find a Woolf who, on the one hand, tried to justify her unfeminine preoccupation with the self, while on the other, refused to deny her diary its central status as a literary work. By considering Blodgett's point that female diarists often retreat behind the justification that their journals are "a self-improving discipline," we can further appreciate how Woolf reconciled what was expected of her as a woman and what she wanted as a writer. She consistently wrote about duty, but she was interested in making herself not so much "acceptable to others" as acceptable to herself. In focusing on her professional, creative self, she subverted the tradition of femininity that instructed women to use their diaries only to improve their moral and spiritual sensibilities.

As a highly conscientious writer, Woolf used her diary to chart her stringent work ethic, as this proposal for *The Hours* testifies: "I am now saying that I will write at it for 4 months, June, July, August & September, & then it will be done, & I shall put it away for three months, during which I shall finish my essays; & then that will be – October, November, December – January: & I shall revise it January February March April; & in April my essays will come out; & in May my novel. Such is my programme" (D, 2:301).

While such a program might be expected for professional writing, Woolf devised an equally stringent one for her diary as well. Part of her regime entailed recording at a particular time of day, either in the morning before lunch or just after tea in the afternoon. If she was unable to write, she rarely failed to mention those times of neglect. But that was not all: she offered excuses, as in this opening: "Just back from Rodmell [...] And I should explain why I've let a month slip perhaps" (D, 3:57). Woolf conceived her diary writing in terms of expectations that must be met, chastizing herself in 1897: "This diary has been woefully neglected lately – what with one thing & another – Improvement must be made! (hear hear)" (PA, 112). Her sense of duty informed her later diaries as well, as she confessed in 1918: "I am overwhelmed with things that I ought to have written about" (D, 1:219). On 19 July 1922 she decided: "I will seize the opportunity of tea being done, Ralph gone, & Leonard writing letters, to pay some of my dues here" (D, 2:182). And three days later, "My conscience drives me again to write" (D, 2:184).

Woolf at times expressed guilt for attending to the diary rather than doing some other more "serious" or "legitimate" work: "The truth is that I have an internal, automatic scale of values; which decides what I had better do with my time [...] How I come by this code of values I dont know. Perhaps its the legacy of puritan grandfathers. I suspect pleasure slightly" (D, 2:94). In order to atone for this guilt, and in order to continue writing the diary for its own sake, she affirmed: "the truth is, I must try to set aside half an hour in some part of my day, & consecrate it to diary writing. Give it a name & a place, & then perhaps, such is the human mind, I shall come to think it a duty, & disregard other duties for it" (D, 3:6). This last point suggests a subversive strategy on Woolf's part, for by making the diary into a task, it, like any other chore, had to be done.

Perhaps one of the main reasons that Woolf would give as to why the diary had to be done was that it was a training ground for her "real" writing. She added to one entry: "(It strikes me that in this book I *practise* writing; do my scales; yes & work at certain effects. I daresay I practised Jacob here, – & Mrs D. & shall invent my next book here [...])" (D, 2:319). She typically noted that she "must use this page as a running ground" (D, 5:90).

But for all the "running" Woolf did in the diary, she consistently slowed down so as to contemplate the diary as an artistic product in itself and to hone the skills required to produce it. On 10 January 1897 she commented: "It is a week today since I began this diary. How many more weeks has it to live – At any rate it must and shall survive Nessas Collins and [Adrian's] Renshaw. It has a key, and beautiful boards, and is much superior" (PA, 10).[32] Soon after, she exclaimed, "This diary today beats my 1896 diary – Wonderful creature!" (PA, 16).[33] Woolf was as interested in her journal as a text as she was in the life that went into it.

As a young woman she referred to diary writing as an "art" (PA, 139), and from this early stage she was already beginning to theorize the genre. In August 1899 she paused to remark: "Oh dear – the style of this work ought to undergo a radical change. All these details will swamp me in time" (PA, 136). By 1908 she had come to recognize, "There are many ways of writing such diaries as these. I begin to distrust description [...] I should like to write not only with the eye, but with the mind; & discover real things beneath the show" (PA, 384).

On 20 April 1919, with over twenty years of diarizing behind her, Woolf made her most intellectual investigation of the journal as a genre. Though telling herself that the diary was meant only for her "own eye," and that it was a place only in which to practise writing, she went on to observe:

there looms ahead of me the shadow of some kind of form which a diary might attain to [...] What sort of diary should I like mine to be? Something loose knit,

& yet not slovenly, so elastic that it will embrace any thing, solemn, slight or beautiful that comes into my mind. I should like it to resemble some deep old desk, or capacious hold-all, in which one flings a mass of odds & ends without looking them through. I should like to come back, after a year or two, & find that the collection had sorted itself & refined itself & coalesced, as such deposits so mysteriously do, into a mould, transparent enough to reflect the light of our life, & yet steady, tranquil composed with the aloofness of a work of art.

Woolf cautioned, "The main requisite" "is not to play the part of censor, but to write as the mood comes or of anything whatever." But ultimately, she profoundly acknowledged, "A little effort is needed to face a character or an incident which needs to be recorded. Nor can one let the pen write without guidance; for fear of becoming slack & untidy [...]" (D, 1:266). She reiterated in October the same year, "even this unpremeditated scribbling, has its form, which one learns" (D, 1:304). Woolf's insistence that her diary must be written with "guidance" and must be shaped into an appropriate "form" necessarily places it at the far end of Rosenwald's continuum of diaristic control and self-consciousness, underscoring its status as a constructed work of art.

A NEW FORM

Virginia Woolf's diary is a "form" in itself. Moreover, it is a testament to the way in which she consistently fused genres. We can appreciate how this form resembles that of her fiction by considering the language she used to discuss her conception and composition of both, such that it becomes difficult to distinguish between the two.

In the simplest sense, she conceived her life as a story, for she referred to it in novelistic terms. In her early journal of 1903 she concluded an entry: "Tomorrow I shall open at a new chapter" (PA, 187). In Constantinople in 1906 she playfully invoked the fiction writer in herself when describing a "crowded pool of the river, where the Golden Horn branches off from the Bosphorus [sic]." She went on: "But here my point of view was certainly eclipsed; nor do I remember any more, as novelists say, & they have all the best devices [...]" (PA, 348). Woolf's imagination persists in her later diaries as well. She commented on one entry, "Now there's a chapter in a novel!" (D, 2:137), while she opened another, "I think I shall initiate a new convention for this book – beginning each day on a new page – my habit in writing serious literature" (3:62).

Her "habit in writing serious literature" resembles that of writing the diary in more significant ways than merely opening a page. On 26 January 1920 Woolf documented arriving "at some idea of a new form for a new novel," and she wondered: "Suppose one thing should open out of another – as in An Unwritten Novel – only not for 10 pages but 200 or so – doesn't that give the looseness & lightness I want: doesnt that get closer & yet keep form & speed, & enclose everything, everything?" (D, 2:13). "An Unwritten Novel" was a short story that Woolf included in her 1921 collection *Monday or Tuesday*. The new novel in question was *Jacob's Room*, which would be published in 1922. *Jacob's Room* marked her transformation from a rather conventional novelist into a modernist one. She could not have chosen a more appropriate date, since 1922 also brought readers Eliot's *The Waste Land* and Joyce's *Ulysses* in bound novel form. While I will later explore in detail the connections between Woolf's diary and her modernist aesthetics, for now I would like to continue to focus on how the diary resembles the fiction in more general terms.

Her statement that she wanted *Jacob's Room* to have "looseness & lightness" echoes her April 1919 description of her diary as being "loose knit." And her feeling that this approach would, for the new novel, "get closer & yet keep form & speed, & enclose everything, everything," parallels her description of the diary as "not slovenly" and "so elastic that it will embrace any thing." Further, in January 1919 Woolf acknowledged: "I have just reread my years diary & am much struck by the rapid haphazard gallop at which it swings along, sometimes indeed jerking almost intolerably over the cobbles. Still if it were not written rather faster than the fastest typewriting, if I stopped & took thought, it would never be written at all; & the advantage of the method is that it sweeps up accidentally several stray matters which I should exclude if I hesitated, but which are the diamonds of the dustheap" (D, 1:233–4). The "rapid gallop" of the diary suggests the "speed" with which she hoped to compose her new novel. And the fact that the diary "sweeps up" "stray matters" relates to the novel, which should "enclose everything, everything."

Further comparisons abound. Despite Woolf's confession, heard earlier, that "I suspect pleasure slightly" (D, 2:94), the diary was often a site of pleasure, as she admitted: "I sit down to this page instead of to the sterner one of duty & profit at some minutes after ten a.m." (D, 2:57). She employed many terms to describe both the site of the diary and diary writing as pleasurable. She conceived the diary as a space in which to relax from her more "serious" writing: "What a mercy to use this page to uncramp in!" (D, 5:80); "I think it would be a relief to write a free sentence here, after so much churning" (5:90); and "Oh how gladly I reach for this free page for a 10 minutes scamper" (5:244).

Those sentiments also describe Woolf's fictional writing. More pointedly, if her diary was "loose knit," composed at a "gallop," and thus "free," so too were her novels. She wanted *Jacob's Room* to embody "looseness & lightness" (D, 2:13), and she once remarked, "I've reached the party in Jacob & write with great pleasure" (2:67). Woolf examined the technical development of *The Hours*: "It is reeling off my mind fast & free now [...] I feel as if I had loosed the bonds pretty completely & could pour everything in" (D, 2:302). She similarly detailed the progress of *To the Lighthouse*: "I am now writing as fast & freely as I have written in the whole of my life [...] Amusingly, I now invent theories that fertility & fluency are the things: I used to plead for a kind of close, terse, effort" (D, 3:59). It is important to note here that Woolf described her memoir "A Sketch of the Past" in like terms of artistic freedom: "And thus as I dribble on, purposely letting my mind flow"; "I return to this free page"; and "I will go on with this loose story."[34] She also applied these theories to her living as well – "I am more & more attracted by looseness, freedom, & eating one's dinner off a table anywhere" (D, 3:316) – underscoring Hanscombe and Smyers's point that women such as Woolf lived modernism as much as they wrote it.

Woolf contemplated her next book, *Orlando*, in a state of excitement: "I want to kick up my heels & be off [...] I think this will be great fun to write" (D, 3:131) This image recalls how the diary was a place in which to "scamper." Not long after, she updated her diary on "this farce," noting: "I enjoy [it] as much as I've ever enjoyed anything; & have written myself into half a headache & had to come to a halt, like a tired horse" (D, 3:162). Her reference to a horse calls to mind that her diary was being written at a "gallop." In November 1928 Woolf looked back on *Orlando*: "People say this was so spontaneous, so natural [...] I think a kind of ease & dash are good" (D, 3:209). She began her next diary entry, "Here is a note barely dashed off" (D, 3:210).

Woolf's eagerness to "dash off" both diary and novel was, as I have mentioned, matched by her awareness of the diary as necessarily swinging along at a rapid "gallop." Appropriately, then, she used the term "gallop" over and over again to describe her fiction: "I am now galloping over Mrs Dalloway" (D, 2:323), while *The Years* was "written at a greater gallop than any of my books" (4: 245). Galloping implies speed, and so she stressed of *The Waves*, "what is essential is to write fast & not break the mood" (D, 3:282). In this spirit she marvelled at Shakespeare's writing pace: "I never yet knew how amazing his stretch & speed & word coining power is, until I felt it utterly outpace & outrace my own [...] Even the less known & worser plays are written at a speed that is quicker than anybody else's quickest" (D,

3:300–1). This comment parallels Woolf's earlier observation of her diary style: "Still if it were not written rather faster than the fastest typewriting [...] it would never be written at all."

The "gallop" allowed the "diamonds of the dustheap" to be collected not only within her diary but within her fiction. Woolf commented on *Jacob's Room*: "nature obligingly supplies me with the illusion that I am about to write something good: something rich, & deep, & fluent & hard as nails, while bright as diamonds" (D, 2:199). She described the process of *The Hours* as a search for another precious substance: "I may have found my mine this time I think. I may get all my gold out [...] To get it I must forge ahead, stoop & grope. But it is gold of a kind I think" (D, 2:292). In less-glittering terms, she wrote of "Pointz Hall" (published as *Between the Acts*): "Began P. H again today, & threshed & threshed till perhaps a little grain can be collected" (D, 5:289).

In addition to searching for such nuggets, Woolf considered the atoms around her as equally valuable. Formulating "The Moths," the novel that would become *The Waves*, she related: "The idea has come to me that what I want now to do is to saturate every atom. I mean to eliminate all waste, deadness, superfluity: to give the moment whole; whatever it includes [...] I want to put practically everything in; yet to saturate [...] It must include nonsense, fact, sordidity: but made transparent" (D, 3:209–10). Her new novel had been prefigured in her description of the diary as a "capacious hold-all, in which one flings a mass of odds & ends," and which would, in time, coalesce "as such deposits so mysteriously do, into a mould, transparent enough to reflect the light of our life." Woolf's diary, imaged as a "deposit" that would coalesce into a brilliant, hard object, illuminates her fascination with the diamonds of art.

Her desire to "saturate every atom" in the novel echoes her call to the modern writer in the 1925 essay "Modern Fiction." She asked this writer to heed the "incessant shower of innumerable atoms" as they fall because "the accent falls differently from of old; the moment of importance came not here but there."[35] This image was repeated in her April 1930 meditation on Shakespeare: "Evidently the pliancy of his mind was so complete that he could furbish out any train of thought; &, relaxing lets fall a shower of such unregarded flowers" (D, 3:301). And in "Papers on Pepys" she affirmed that Pepys was modern in part because of his language, "which catches unfailingly the butterflies and gnats and falling petals of the moment."[36] Likewise, Woolf commented in her diary in 1932: "I like writing. I like change. I like to toss my mind up & watch to see where it'll fall" (D, 4:86). In her diary she was tossing up not only her mind but also her sense of genre, and where genre falls is anywhere but settled, for she was able to find parallels in the writing strategies of novelists, playwrights, and diarists from diverse literary periods.

Woolf employed similar terms to describe the work of Shakespeare and Pepys – appropriately so given that, in addition to reading her diary as fiction and memoir, we can also read it as drama. In "Mimesis: The Dramatic Lineage of Auto/Biography," Evelyn J. Hinz argues that (auto)biographical documents share three qualities with dramatic art: "an element of conflict and dialogue, a sense of performance and/or spectatorship, and a mimetic or referential quality."[37] Woolf's passion for drama is evidenced throughout her diary, and it inspired her to conceive her entries in the theatrical terms observed by Hinz.

She frequently used dialogue to bring life and action to plot and character. Within one entry she observed: "By the way, on re-reading this book I resolved to write rather more carefully, & to record conversations verbatim [...] As for recording conversations, nothing is harder. Let me try" (II: 251-2). She then followed with what appears to be a script for a play, with characters and setting outlined at the start:

Desmond
Janet
Leonard   Scene tea-time Friday, 6th.
Virginia

Woolf here reminds me of the young Cecily in Oscar Wilde's play *The Importance of Being Ernest*. In chapter 1 I drew attention to Cecily, who not only kept a diary but went to great lengths to "record conversations verbatim," to use Woolf's words. Recall Cecily's instructions to Algernon as she struggled to catch his dialogue: "Oh, don't cough, Ernest. When one is dictating one should speak fluently and not cough. Besides, I don't know how to spell a cough." If Cecily was a character in a play who wrote a diary, Woolf was a woman in a diary who wrote a play.

In a different sense, Woolf calls to mind James Boswell; Hinz uses him to illustrate affinities between dramatist and biographer: "the first great biographer, Boswell, employed distinctly dramatic metaphors to describe his objectives in his life of Johnson: to enable the reader 'to see him live,' and to 'live o'er each scene' with him, as he actually advanced through the several stages of his life."[38] Woolf, in the above and other entries, strove to bring not only herself but her friends and acquaintances – many of them famous like Johnson – to dramatic life. As she once noted, "I told Lytton [Strachey] I should try to write down his talk – which sprang from a conversation about Boswell" (D, 2:201).

Hinz also mentions Leon Edel, whose biography of Henry James is "so convincing" because it creates not only setting but also action, showing James "'moving' in these settings – we see him climbing stairs, riding horseback, entering apartments."[39] Woolf drafted another diary script in like manner, re-enacting an evening that she and her husband had spent with friend Augustine Birrell and his sons, Francis and Anthony: "Persons: Aug. Birrell: Francis B. Tony B. L. & V. Scene 70 Elm Park Road: first dark pannelled dining room; later the library, a room just beneath the grass of a large garden. Books all round; regular, back to back books in series & editions. Framed autographs on walls." In addition to providing such details, she gave her characters stage directions: "Tony Birrell in a high shrill falling voice, he squints rather, is pale, wears spectacles, & suddenly disappears to range about the garden alone"; and, "Tony goes & fidgets at the sideboard" (D, 2:253, 255, 256). Just as Edel made James "move," so Woolf animated the characters on her diaristic stage.

In broader terms, she often employed the language of the theatre in her entries. She closed her volume for 1903 with this description: "October begins work & pleasure lifts the curtain on that particular act of our drama which is played in London. Actors may change – their parts may be different but the sameness of scene gives a certain continuity to the whole, & does in fact influence our lives to no little extent" (PA, 213). As a director, she frequently offered a variety of settings: "Scenes now come to mind" (D, 2:79); "Let the scene open on the doorstep of number 50 Gordon Square" (2: 222); "Some little scenes I meant to write down" (3: 153); and "The scene has now changed to Rodmell" (4: 303). She would eventually incorporate drama into her fiction, as she commented on the early stages of *The Years*: "I am now seeing that the last 200 pages will assert themselves, & force me to write a play more or less [...] (I meant to make a note about the dramatic shape which forces itself upon me)" (D, 4:319). This dramatic shape was explicitly manifested in her last novel, which ended with a play and was published under the title *Between the Acts*. Her diary similarly took on dramatic shape, both within and between the acts of her life and others' lives.

In addition to drama, Woolf's journal shares affinities with her essays, such as her 1925 collection *The Common Reader*. In June 1929 she "read through the Common Reader" and evaluated it thus: "I must learn to write more succinctly. Especially in the general idea essays like the last, How it strikes a Contemporary, I am horrified by my own looseness. This is partly that I dont think things out first; partly that I stretch my style to take in crumbs of meaning" (D, 3:235). Woolf's detested writing is described in terms reminiscent of her diary. But within a few years, her "horror" changed to respect.

She began an entry for 10 September 1933 wondering: "why am I sitting here at 10:30 on a Sunday morning [...] writing diary, not novel?" She answered: "Because of dear old Tom largely. 24 hours (short interval for sleep) solid conversation." Referring to T.S. Eliot, she went on in a rather rambling way to relate the content of their conversation, which included some of Eliot's thoughts on his work. She followed this account with her responses to his ideas, as well as with a brief biographical sketch of him. At the end of the entry she asked: "(why not write a book – of Cr[itics]m in this style?)" (D, 4:177–9) – that is, she was suggesting she should write criticism in the form of a diary entry. She later clarified this idea: "I wish I cd. invent a way of dashing down criticism, *as I do here*" (D, 5:36; my emphasis).

Returning to the subject, Woolf reiterated: "I wish I cd invent a new critical method – something swifter & lighter & more colloquial & yet intense: more to the point & less composed; more fluid & following the flight, than my C. R. essays. The old problem: how to keep the flight of the mind, yet be exact. All the difference between the sketch & the finished work" (D, 5:298). Once again we can see how her "new critical method" resembles her diary style. Her sense that she must "keep the flight of the mind, yet be exact" in her essays recalls the diary, which should be written "as the mood comes," but with "A little effort." In terms of Woolf's comment that this balance marks "All the difference between the sketch & the finished work," we can consider that years earlier, while composing *Mrs Dalloway*, she had asserted: "Suppose one can keep the quality of a sketch in a finished & composed work? That is my endeavour" (D, 2:312). If a diary entry possesses "the quality of a sketch," then the diary as much as the "new" essay can resemble this "finished & composed work." Indeed, Woolf once wrote that she hoped her diary would "suggest finished pictures to the eye" (PA, 384).

PRESENT MOMENTS

I have been pressing for a consideration of the diary as a work which in many ways is akin to Woolf's other forms of writing. Of course, the argument could be made that the diary was not edited and revised to the extent that these other genres were. For example, after finishing the playful *Orlando* Woolf acknowledged, "There will be three months of close work needed" (D, 3:176), while she revelled in the diary, "which thank God in heaven, needs no re-writing" (4: 141). On this last point, however, we must keep in mind the fact that she did rewrite the diary at various stages of its production. My initial treatment of the physical journal reveals that it is a highly self-conscious, intentionally crafted text, in that Woolf consistently took its form and content into consideration when she sat down to write. She implied as much when discussing her diary: "It is all very well, saying one will write notes but writing is a very difficult art [...] Writing is not in the least an easy art" (D, 4:156). And just as she felt that her brain was "knotted by all that last screw of The Waves" (D, 4:37), so she asserted of the diary that "writing, even here, needs screwing of the brain" (2: 94). These points make it even more appropriate to suggest that there is not as much "difference between the sketch & the finished work" as one would assume.

Specifically, the similarities between the diary and other "finished works" which concern me here are modernist ones, for the diary is shaped by the aesthetic philosophies dictating the modernist direction of those other works. Throughout her diary, her countless essays, and even her fiction, Woolf was constantly theorizing her art, and I would now like to offer a thorough analysis of these ideas in order to illuminate her modernism. Within this discussion, I will show how she used the diary to construct various identities for herself. Such an analysis will drive home the extent to which she negotiated the divide between the public and the private and the intellectual and the emotional aspects of herself and her life. As my discussion of modernism will be thematic rather than chronological, so will my treatment of her biography.

We can begin to apprehend Woolf's diaristic modernism through a consideration of how her fiction and essays reflect the diary, and how all three respect modernism's interest in time. One of her earliest pieces of fiction presents the life of its protagonist, Joan Martyn, through her diary entries. Left untitled and unpublished after its completion in 1906, the story, which was printed in 1979, was called by its editors "The Journal of Mistress Joan Martyn." In keeping with her interest in the recorded flow of days, Woolf named her second novel, which appeared in 1919, Night and Day. In May 1923, she indicated that she might call her new book "The Hours" (D, 2:242). Eventually published as Mrs Dalloway in 1925, this novel, like an extended diary entry, presents one day in the life of its two protagonists. Her novel The Waves also suggests the diary in so far as she had once described a journal entry as being "the little waves that life makes" (D, 3:165). The title of her work in progress, "The Pargiters," was changed to "Here and Now" (D, 4:176) and then "Ordinary People" D, 4:266). Finally brought out as The Years in 1937, the novel retains its titular theme of time.

Of greater significance is her short story "Monday or Tuesday," published in the 1921 collection of the same name. The story consists of only six brief paragraphs, which poetically trace a day from morning to night, so that its offering of a single day's events is in keeping with a diary entry. Woolf made the connection in her 1932 essay on the diary of the eighteenth-century parson James Woodforde: "For forty-three years he sat down almost daily to record what he did on Monday and what he had for dinner on Tuesday."[40] The issue of calendrical time – whether it be Monday or Tuesday and so on – becomes explicitly linked to modernism in the essay "Modern Fiction," included in her *Common Reader* (1925). Here Woolf gave instructions to the writer of modern fiction: "Examine for a moment an ordinary mind on an ordinary day. The mind receives a myriad impressions – trivial, fantastic, evanescent, or engraved with the sharpness of steel. From all sides they come, an incessant shower of innumerable atoms; and as they fall, as they shape themselves into the life of Monday or Tuesday, the accent falls differently from of old; the moment of importance came not here but there."[41] Her repeated references to "Monday or Tuesday" highlight how time shapes the material not only of the diary but of modern fiction.

The essence of Woolf's call to the modern writer echoes the theories of literary impressionism put forward by writers such as Henry James and Joseph Conrad and furthered by others, such as Ford Madox Ford and Katherine Mansfield. In his 1884 essay "The Art of Fiction," James asserts, "A novel is in its broadest definition a personal, a direct impression of life."[42] And in the preface to his *Nigger of the "Narcissus"* (1897), Conrad outlines the task of the artist, who must first "snatch in a moment of courage, from the remorseless rush of time, a passing phase of life." He or she must then "hold up unquestioningly, without choice and without fear, the rescued fragment" in order "to show its vibration, its colour, its form; and through its movement, its form, and its colour, reveal the substance of truth – disclose its inspiring secret: the stress and passion within the core of each convincing moment."[43]

Conrad's friend Ford, in his 1913 article "On Impressionism," asserted that "any piece of Impressionism ... is the record of the impression of a moment."[44] He elaborated in his 1924 piece "Joseph Conrad: A Personal Remembrance" that he and Conrad accepted the label of "Impressionist" because they saw that "Life did not narrate, but made impressions on our brains. We in turn, if we wished to produce on you an effect of life, must not narrate but render ... impressions."[45] Similarly, throughout her fiction, journals, letters, reviews, and stories, Mansfield, Woolf's professional rival and personal friend, advocated a kind of literary impressionism. In one letter she explained: "If I had been well I should have rushed off to the darkest Africa or the Indus or the Ganges or wherever it is one rushes at those times, to try for a change of heart ... to gain new impressions. For it seems to me we live on impressions – really new ones."[46]

Ford's and Mansfield's explorations of impressionism were concurrent with Woolf's own development of a theory of modern fiction, expressed in her 1925 essay "Modern Fiction" as well as in its earlier version of 1919, "Modern Novels." Her observation, made in both essays, that "The mind receives a myriad impressions" and that these should be accounted for by the modern novelist takes on greater meaning in light of her hope, noted in April 1925, that she would use her diary as a place in which to "get down some of the myriad impressions which I net every day" (D, 3:6). Moreover, as we have seen, Conrad's and Ford's emphasis on things "altogether momentary" is reiterated by Woolf in her "Modern" essays, and also in her celebration of Pepys, whom she lauded for catching the "falling petals of the moment." And as we shall see, her own fiction and diary are preoccupied with unique moments isolated in time – as are Mansfield's stories and journals.

Woolf's and modernism's interest in such moments is indebted to the Victorian aesthetician and literary critic Walter Pater, who advised attuning our senses to each moment because that is all we have at any given time: "Every moment some form grows perfect in hand or face; some tone on the hills or the sea is choicer than the rest; some mood of passion or insight or intellectual excitement is irresistibly real and attractive for us, – for that moment only. Not the fruit of experience, but experience itself, is the end." Pater asserted: "To burn always with this hard, gemlike flame, to maintain this ecstasy, is success in life."[47]

The Paterian moment would inform, perhaps most famously, the Joycean epiphany in the early twentieth century. Joyce outlined his conception of art as epiphany in his first version of *Portrait*, *Stephen Hero* (1904–06), as expressed by his protagonist, Stephen Dedalus: "By an epiphany he meant a sudden spiritual manifestation, whether in the vulgarity of speech or of gesture or in a memorable phase of the mind itself." These epiphanies constitute "the most delicate and evanescent moments."[48] Though Woolf would not have read this description – the manuscript was not published until 1944 – she would have been familiar with the enactment of epiphany in the well-known "bird-girl" scene on the beach in *Portrait*, in which Dedalus experiences "an instant of ecstasy."[49]

Woolf would also have been aware of Mansfield's version of epiphany, described by her in one review as a "spiritual event" and "one blazing moment," and in her journal as " 'glimpses', before which all that one has ever written [...] pales ... The waves [...] and the high foam, how it suspended in the air before it fell ... What is it that happens in that moment of suspension? It is timeless. In that moment [...] the whole life of the soul is contained. One is flung up – out of life – one is 'held,' and then, – down, bright, broken, glittering on to the rocks, tossed back, part of the ebb and flow."[50] Mansfield died of tuberculosis in 1923, and her journal was published four years later. Woolf, in her review of it ("A Terribly Sensitive Mind"), invoked the literary impressionism of this entry: "It is not the quality of her writing or the degree of fame that interest us in her diary, but the spectacle of a mind – a terribly sensitive mind – receiving one after another the haphazard impressions of eight years of life." (Recall the "haphazard gallop" at which Woolf's own diary "swings along.") Woolf also noted how diverse "moments" in Mansfield's journal "suddenly put on significance."[51]

She was inspired by Pater to create her own kind of significant moment. In March 1905 she informed her journal that she had bought a book of his, for the purpose of studying it (PA, 251), and at the end of that diary, under the section "Books," she has ticked off as read Pater's *Renaissance*, the work in which the passage quoted above about moments and ecstasy is found (PA, 274). Years later, in her essay "The Moment: Summer's Night," she would ask: "Yet what composed the present moment?" She answered that "everybody believes that the present is something, seeks out the different elements in this situation in order to compose the truth of it, the whole of it."[52]

Her version or interpretation of this present moment is illuminated by her fictional characters, such as Mrs Ramsay and Lily Briscoe in *To the Lighthouse*. During the famous *boeuf en daube* dinner scene, Mrs Ramsay sits back and contemplates the artistic success not only of her meal but of her ability to unify a group of otherwise disparate family members and guests. She suddenly realizes: "there is a coherence in things, a stability; something, she meant, is immune from change, and shines out ... in the face of the flowing, the fleeting, the spectral, like a ruby ... Of such moments, she thought, the thing is made that remains for ever after." The painter Lily Briscoe, fondly remembering the now-deceased Mrs Ramsay, articulates Ramsay's sentiments: "The great revelation had never come. The great revelation perhaps never did come. Instead there were little daily miracles, illuminations, matches struck unexpectedly in the dark ... Mrs Ramsay making of the moment something permanent ... this was of the nature of a revelation."[53]

Mrs Ramsay's and Lily's "revelations" echo Pater. His insistence that "Every moment some form grows perfect in hand or face" is reflected in their sense that there are moments which are stable, coherent, and permanent. Mrs Ramsay's moments "shine out ... like a ruby," while Lily's are "matches struck unexpectedly in the dark," both images that call to mind not only the "hard, gemlike flame" that burns brightly in Pater's description but the "diamonds" of Woolf's diary. Pater's conviction that a moment lasts "for that moment only" is found in Mrs Ramsay's epiphany at the end of the evening: "With her foot on the threshold she waited a moment longer in a scene which was vanishing even as she looked ... it had become, she knew, giving one last look at it over her shoulder, already the past." Lily comes to accept this view at the very end of the novel. Though she finishes her painting, she reports its completion after the fact – "I have had my vision" – underscoring that it too "was already the past."[54] Pater affirms, and Mrs Ramsay and Lily understand, that "Not the fruit of experience, but experience itself, is the end."

While these ideas are superbly handled by Woolf in her fiction, their genesis can be traced to a younger, diarizing Woolf. Holidaying at Warboys, she wrote on August 1899, "I am, at the present moment (the emotion is fleeting I know, so I must chronicle it) in love with a country life" (PA, 137). And at Giggleswick in 1906 she examined her diary writing: "With a purpose I make use of words implying some thing handed down to me, as it were, from on high; because the hours seemed so complete in themselves, so little the result of what had gone before or the prelude to that which was to be that one might figure them simply thus – as a gift set down in the course of an ordinary day" (PA, 306). What she was celebrating was the "present," and her ability to record it as such. In "The Journal of Mistress Joan Martyn," written the same year, Woolf's protagonist revels in the early morning: "May it be mine to taste the moment before it has spread itself over the rest of the world!" Martyn goes on to observe, "Let us, then, who have the gift of the present, use it & enjoy it."[55] Here the "gift" of writing the present and the "gift" of experiencing it fuse, both realized in and through the medium of a diary.

This fusion is made at other times as well. In December 1932 Woolf acknowledged: "If one does not lie back & sum up & say to the moment, this very moment, stay you are so fair, what will be one's gain, dying? No: stay, this moment. No one ever says that enough. Always hurry. I am now going in, to see L. & say stay this moment" (D, 4:135). And in January 1940 she wrote, "I cling to my tiny philosophy: to hug the present moment" (D, 5:262). In these passages the act of experiencing the moment in life is simultaneously the act of staying, or hugging it, in the diary.

A moment, however, is at best fleeting, as Woolf wondered: "Now is life very solid, or very shifting? ... This has gone on forever: will last for ever; goes down to the bottom of the world – this moment I stand on. Also it is transitory, flying, diaphanous. I shall pass like a cloud on the waves" (D, 3:218). (Recall that she described her diary as "the little waves that life makes.") What is especially interesting is that in this entry Woolf had just mentioned the deceased Mansfield, and as the passage shows, she went on to echo Mansfield's own diaristic sentiments about time – "One is flung up – out of life – one is 'held' and then, down, bright, broken, glittering on the rocks, tossed back, part of the ebb and flow."

Elsewhere, Woolf played with the notion of "present." She began: "The present moment. 7 o'clock on June 26th: L. printing: hot: thunderous: I after reading Henry 4 Pt one saying whats the use of writing; reading, imperfectly, a poem by Leopardi; the present moment, in my studio." Continuing in this vein, she concluded: "so to dine, & read Archibald Marshall's memoir; & music; thunder, I dare say; & so to open my windows, & go up: the moment done" (D, 4:165–6). Like Lily's "vision," Woolf's "present," by the time it was put down, "was already the past."

As well as those of time, there are significant "moments of being." Woolf was preoccupied with how people are linked in the physical and spiritual realms. In her novel *Mrs Dalloway* she created Clarissa Dalloway, who frequently experienced epiphanies. She was, for instance, able to perceive her self as an isolated and unique entity: "It was her life, and, bending her head over the hall table, she bowed beneath the influence, felt blessed and purified, saying to herself ... how moments like this are buds on the tree of life." She was likewise able to appreciate how her self could be transcended and fused with the world around her: "sitting on the bus going up Shaftesbury Avenue, she felt herself everywhere; not 'here, here, here'; and she tapped the back of her seat; but everywhere. She waved her hand ... She was all that. So that to know her, or any one, one must seek out the people who completed them; even the places."[56]

In a more autobiographical mode, Woolf reflected on her childhood in "A Sketch of the Past." She recalled the moment when she began to translate the "shocks" or "blows" dealt to her by life into the "revelations" she referred to as a "philosophy." "[T]he shock-receiving capacity is what makes" her a writer. Lily's "revelation" and Stephen's epiphany are echoed in Woolf's explanation of the shock's value: "it is or will become a revelation of some order; it is a token of some real thing behind appearances; and I make it real by putting it into words." She perceived "that behind the cotton wool is hidden a pattern; that we

– I mean all human beings – are connected with this; that the whole world is a work of art; that we are parts of the work of art."[57]

Woolf's "moments of being," as she called them, are acutely registered within the diary. Her acknowledgment that she could sense "some real thing behind appearances" is manifested in her agenda for writing her early journal – to "discover real things beneath the show" (PA, 384). In this way she was enacting the impressionist aesthetic, which, according to Conrad, holds up a "fragment" of life in order to "reveal the substance of truth – disclose its inspiring secret: the stress and passion within the core of each convincing moment." As a young woman, Woolf received impressions which dug down to the "core" of various moments. She wrote in 1903: "I read some history: it is suddenly all alive, branching forwards & backwards & connected with every kind of thing that seemed entirely remote before. I seem to feel Napoleons influence on our quiet evening in the garden for instance – I think I see for a moment how our minds are all threaded together – how any live mind today is of the very same stuff as Plato's & Euripides [...] Then I read a poem say – & the same thing is repeated. I feel as though I had grasped the central meaning of the world, & all these poets & historians & philosophers were only following out paths branching from that centre in which I stand" (PA, 178–9).

Not only do Woolf's "moments of being" suggest a "terribly sensitive mind" – to use her description of Mansfield – but they also recall the theory of interdependence put forward by Chodorow. Woolf's ego here is clearly permeable, flowing interchangeably to and from the minds of figures throughout history. On the other hand, Woolf did not consistently lose herself in others: just as the "present moment" is instantaneous, so for her interdependence was often followed by independence. One example, written in April 1939, illuminates this: "the severance that war seems to bring: everything becomes meaningless: cant plan: then there comes too the community feeling: all England thinking the same thing – this horror of war – at the same moment. Never felt it so strong before. Then the lull & one lapses again into private separation" (D, 5:215). Woolf's ego is at once typically female in its permeability and classically modernist in its state of isolation and disconnection.

If Woolf rendered significant moments in time and being, in the spirit of modernism, she also offered significant moments in thinking that incorporated the past, present, and future in one long, drawn-out stream of consciousness. May Sinclair's 1918 review of Richardson's Pilgrimage bears repeating here: "In this series there is no drama, no situation, no set scene. Nothing happens. It is just life going on and on. It is Miriam Henderson's stream of consciousness going on and on.

And in neither is there any grossly discernible beginning or middle or end."[58] Woolf had studied this review[59] and then incorporated Sinclair's terms and Richardson's methods into her own writing.

She discussed her work in progress, "The Moths," accordingly: "I am not trying to tell a story. Yet perhaps it might be done in that way. A mind thinking. They might be islands of light – islands in the stream that I am trying to convey: life itself going on" (D, 3:229). She conceived her diary in similar manner, describing it as containing the "drifting material of life" (D, 1:266) and stating: "I have got into another stream of thought, if thought it can be called. Let me collect a few logs, drifting in my mind, to represent the past few days" (3: 128).

And in "Modern Fiction" she praised Joyce for achieving in *Portrait* a style which comes "closer to life" than that of his predecessors, setting him up as the model modern novelist who "record[s] the atoms as they fall upon the mind in the order in which they fall," and who "trace[s] the pattern, however disconnected and incoherent in appearance, which each sight or incident scores upon the consciousness."[60] This call for atoms to be "disconnected and incoherent" articulates not only the concept of the stream-of-consciousness technique but modernist juxtaposing. While I have earlier discussed how Woolf ensured narrative continuity within her diary, it is just as important to acknowledge that she concomitantly produced a fractured text.

For example, she noted of an entry in June 1922: "But I sketch this, partly from discretion, partly from haste, & so leave out the links" (D, 2:177–8). By "leav[ing] out the links," she produced a text which in part resembles the "disconnected and incoherent" *Waste Land*. The relationship between the June entry and Eliot's poem is in fact implied by Woolf, who immediately went on to recount: "Eliot dined last Sunday & read his poem. He sang it & chanted it rhymed it. It has great beauty & force of phrase: symmetry; & tensity. What connects it together, I'm not so sure." She then identified the poem as *The Waste Land* (D, 2:178). Woolf thus used her diary to enact the juxtaposing of the very poem she was celebrating.[61]

Juxtaposing allows an author to treat the ordinary alongside the extraordinary. It is this democratic quality which Woolf noted in Joyce, and which she asked her readers of "Modern Fiction" to appreciate: "Let us not take it for granted that life exists more fully in what is commonly thought big than in what is commonly thought small."[62] Her sentiments reveal her focus on the life – and stream-of-consciousness thoughts – of an "ordinary mind." Remember that her working title for *The Years* was "Ordinary People." Interest in the everyday was inspired by her diary, the quintessential text of dailiness – as scholars such as Hogan and DuPlessis have shown. In her early journal of 1906

Woolf described her "use of words" as being "a gift set down in the course of an ordinary day" (PA, 306), a description that anticipates her essay "Modern Fiction," in which she asked the writer to "Examine for a moment an ordinary mind on an ordinary day." The new fiction writer, as much as the diarist, values what is "ordinary."

Woolf elaborated on what she intended by the term "ordinary." We find her pitying the poor writer who is "constrained, not by his own free will but by some powerful and unscrupulous tyrant who has him in thrall, to provide a plot, to provide comedy, tragedy, love interest." She rejected prescribed content because we should, as she bid us, "Look within and life, it seems, is very far from being 'like this'" – that is, life is far from being categorically a comedy or a tragedy. Instead, she urged the writer to take heed of the realistic fall and arrangement of atoms, for "'The proper stuff of fiction' does not exist; everything is the proper stuff of fiction, every feeling, every thought; every quality of brain and spirit is drawn upon; no perception comes amiss."[63] Woolf's words remind us of those used by Ford in his treatment of impressionism. Just as he "saw that Life ... made impressions on our brains," so Woolf affirmed that life consists of "every quality of brain and spirit" we perceive.

The belief that "everything is the proper stuff of fiction" echoes her hope that her "new novel" (*Jacob's Room*) would "enclose everything, everything" (D, 2:13). The statement also brings to mind her April 1919 claim that she writes in her diary "as the mood comes or of anything whatever." Recalling her comment, made in January 1919, that her diary-writing method "sweeps up several stray matters" which are "the diamonds of the dustheap," we can see how these "diamonds," coupled with the assertion that she writes "as the mood comes," are the proof that "no perception comes amiss." Woolf's reflections upon the hierarchy of value emphasize how the impressionistic, modernist work is fully grounded in the realm of everyday life, such that everything is the "proper stuff of fiction."

Her aesthetic theory was directly informed by her long-standing approach to diary writing. In documenting a trip to Athens in 1906, she promised: "I will deal deliberately with the days adventures, whether they are significant or irrelevant" (PA, 321). It is just such democratic levelling which she lauded in the diaries of others, and which marked them – despite their dates – as relevant modern works. For example, in "Papers on Pepys" she wrote: "And thus it comes about that the diary runs naturally from affairs of State and the characters of ministers to affairs of the heart and the characters of servant girls; it includes the buying of clothes, the losing of tempers, and all the infinite curiosities, amusements, and pettinesses of average human life." So "if ever we feel ourselves in the presence of a man so modern that we should not be surprised to meet him in the street ... it is when we read this diary, written more than two hundred and fifty years ago."[64] Likewise, we feel ourselves in the "presence of a [woman] so modern" when we read Woolf's diary.

MR BENNETT AND MRS WOOLF

Her emphasis on Pepys's "characters of ministers" and "characters of servant girls" reminds us that Virginia Woolf valued above all the accurate rendering of character in the modern novel. In the 1924 essay "Mr. Bennett and Mrs. Brown" she stated: "I believe that all novels ... deal with character, and that it is to express character – not to preach doctrines, sing songs, or celebrate the glories of the British Empire, that the form of the novel, so clumsy, verbose, and undramatic, so rich, elastic, and alive, has been evolved." Using as a model for character the fictional Mrs Brown, Woolf addressed readers of fiction: "Your part is to insist that writers shall come down off their plinths and pedestals, and describe beautifully if possible, truthfully at any rate, our Mrs. Brown." It is the modern Georgian writers (such as Forster, Lawrence, Joyce, and Eliot), as opposed to the Edwardians (Bennett, Galsworthy, and Wells), who have come closest to "a complete and satisfactory presentment of her."[65]

And of course, Woolf herself was one who had achieved a relatively "complete and satisfactory presentment" not only of the characters who people her fiction but of the people she knew and met. In her diary her talent for observation fused with her wit, enhancing her genius for characterization. She recognized that "many portraits are owed to" the diary (D, 2:170) – we shall see that Nin similarly referred to the "portraits" she created within her diary. In April 1918 Woolf described, for example, Harriet Weaver, who had come bearing the manuscript of *Ulysses*, hoping to convince the Woolfs to publish it at their Hogarth Press. "I did my best to make her reveal herself, in spite of her appearance, all that the Editress of the Egoist ought to be, but she remained inalterably modest judicious & decorous. Her neat mauve suit fitted both soul & body; her grey gloves laid straight by her plate symbolised domestic rectitude; her table manners were those of a well bred hen. We could get no talk to go. Possibly the poor woman was impeded by her sense that what she had in the brownpaper parcel was quite out of keeping with her own contents" (D, 1:140). Woolf brilliantly offers not only the materiality of Weaver but also the spirituality.

Just as Pepys's diary "runs naturally" from "the characters of ministers" to "the characters of servant girls," so Woolf's runs from the characters of well-respected women such as Weaver to her own "servant girls," such as Nelly Boxall, whose long service with the Woolfs began in 1916. In fact, Woolf went so far as to acknowledge that Nelly made the diary especially vital: "I thought (as I so often think of things) of many comments to be written. One remains. If I were reading this diary, if it were a book that came my way, I think I should seize with greed upon the portrait of Nelly, & make a story – perhaps make the whole story revolve round that – it would amuse me. Her character – our efforts to be rid of her – our reconciliations" (D, 3:274).

Woolf's tribute to Boxall is important in terms of modernism's tendency to democratize its subject matter and also in terms of her relationship with her own father, Leslie Stephen. The editor of the *Dictionary of National Biography* from 1882 to 1891, Stephen raised his daughter in an intellectual climate which not only included his talented friends, such as George Meredith and Henry James, but which also stressed the value of the written lives of famous men. As Woolf would later recall of her childhood, "Great figures stood in the background."[66] Lee appropriately suggests that Woolf's "concept of traditional life-writing was derived from her father's major life's work, the *Dictionary of National Biography*." But as Lee also points out, Woolf used her diary as a space in which to challenge the patriarchal privileging of these male lives, subverting notions of DNB "greatness" by offering biographies of both men and women, and often from her raw and irreverent perspective.[67]

If one measure of the modern novelist's success was the degree of accuracy with which she or he presented character, this character was assumed to be wholly separate from that of the author, for "impersonality" was one of the most stringent edicts for the modern writer. As I have noted in chapter 3, Joyce and Eliot are generally regarded as the major disseminators of a theory of detachment, but Woolf would likely have found their aesthetics to be, at best, reflections of her own theories. Consider her response to Milton's *Paradise Lost* in 1918: "I am struck by the extreme difference between this poem & any other. It lies, I think, in the sublime aloofness & impersonality of the emotions [...] What poetry! I can conceive that even Shakespeare after this would seem a little troubled, personal, hot & imperfect" (D, 1:192–3). We have seen that it was exactly this "aloofness" that Woolf would hope to find in her diary less than a year later.

In her 1926 article "Life and the Novelist" she considered "the relation of the novelist to life and what it should be," confirming that the greatest writers are the ones who "have mastered their perceptions, hardened them, and changed them into the fabrics of their art." That is, they must expose themselves to life and absorb it, but then retire to a private room in order to transmute this life into a permanent work of art. This transformation is what Woolf wanted for her diary: to be able to "come back, after a year or two, & find that the collection had sorted itself & refined itself & coalesced." (D, 1:266).

Her prescription for the artist is elaborately outlined in *A Room of One's Own*, where Eliot's "extinction of personality" is matched by her delight that the more recent women writers' "impulse towards autobiography may be spent." And just as Joyce argued for the artist to remain "invisible, refined out of existence, indifferent, paring his fingernails," so Woolf called for similar distancing: "The writer, I thought, once his experience is over, must lie back and let his mind celebrate its nuptials in darkness ... he must pluck the petals from a rose or watch the swans float calmly down the river."[69] As I have discussed in chapters 2 and 3, however, impersonality for Woolf was synonymous with androgyny. Weary of the superiority of the universalized male "I," she implored the writer to use "equally" both the feminine and the masculine sides of his or her mind.[70]

Woolf's agenda for the androgynous artist can be considered against her earlier celebration of Richardson, a specifically "feminine" writer. In reviewing the seventh volume of Richardson's *Pilgrimage* in 1923, Woolf paid strong tribute to her "egotistical" enterprise: "There is no one word, such as romance or realism, to cover, even roughly, the works of Miss Dorothy Richardson. Their chief characteristic, if an intermittent student be qualified to speak, is one for which we still seek a name. She has invented, or, if she has not invented, developed and applied to her own uses, a sentence which we might call the psychological sentence of the feminine gender ... It is a woman's sentence, but only in the sense that it is used to describe a woman's mind by a writer who is neither proud nor afraid of anything that she may discover in the psychology of her sex."[71]

Woolf's claim that she was "an intermittent student" of Richardson suggests that she had been learning from her. Yet in 1920 she had recorded in her diary that she had "arrived at some idea of a new form for a novel," but she went on to worry: "I suppose the danger is the damned egotistical self; which ruins Joyce & Richardson to my mind: is one pliant & rich enough to provide a wall for the book from oneself without its becoming, as in Joyce & Richardson, narrowing & restricting?" (D, 2:13–14). Woolf reissued her indictment of "the damned egotistical self" at the end of *A Room*, arguing that "it is fatal for anyone who writes to think of their sex ... It is fatal for a woman ... in any way to speak consciously as a woman." Ultimately, "anything written with that conscious bias is doomed to death."[72] It was this bias which Woolf had previously found in the work of Joyce and Richardson, and which resurfaced when she set about developing her theory for a sentence that was simultaneously masculine and feminine.

In chapter 3 we have heard Woolf explain, "The change which has turned the English woman from a nondescript influence, fluctuating and vague, to a voter, a wage-earner, a responsible citizen, has given her both in her life and in her art a turn toward the impersonal. Her relations now are not only emotional; they are intellectual, they are political." Because a woman's "attention is being directed away from the personal centre which engaged it exclusively in the past to the impersonal," her "novels naturally become more critical of society, and less analytical of individual lives."[73]

Woolf's aesthetic response to the intellectual and political gains of women informed even her diary, the one place in which she might be expected to be personal and emotional. She explained in her journal in November 1924: "What I was going to say was that I think writing must be formal. The art must be respected. This struck me reading some of my notes here, for, if one lets the mind run loose, it becomes egotistic: personal, which I detest" (D, 2:321). Recall that in 1899 Woolf had imagined a reader of her diary who made her "put on [her] dress clothes such as they are" (PA, 144). "Dress clothes" would be worn to reflect her sense that "writing must be formal." Further, it is important to remember that in her 1908 review she had praised Lady Webster for the fact that, within a diary, Webster "could be as impersonal as a boy of ten and as intelligent as a politician."

Woolf's rejection of the personal was thus an artistic, intellectual, and political one. It was also likely due to more subtle and complex social and psychological reasons as well. In October 1924 she acknowledged in her diary: "Odd how conventional morality always encroaches. One must not talk of oneself &c; one must not be vain &c. Even in complete privacy these ghosts slip between me & the page" (D, 2:317). This "conventional morality" would have been tied to her "legacy of puritan grandfathers" (D, 2:94), and the legacy of her puritan father as well. As Lee argues, Leslie Stephen instilled in his young daughter "one obstinate and enduring conception; that nothing is so much to be dreaded as egotism."[74]

Woolf clarified what hold this "legacy" had over her – and over women in general – when she offered her now-famous description of the angel in the house: this angel was a "phantom" "who used to come between me and my paper when I was writing reviews" (exactly as the "ghosts [of conventional morality] slip between me & the [diary] page"). After much struggle, Woolf was able to kill the angel; however, she remained haunted by her. Of the "two adventures of [her] professional life," Woolf conceded that if she had solved the problem of the angel, she nonetheless remained unable to tell the "truth about [her] own experiences as a body."[75]

Nowhere is her inability to articulate those truths more clearly manifested than in her diary, the one place she might have felt free. Feelings of inhibition are testament to the lingering presence of the angel, and to her feminine edicts to be good, to be unselfish, and above all never to dwell on the self – edicts that, according to Blodgett, have prevented many diarists from conceiving their texts as egoistic enterprises. Woolf's theories of impersonality may thus have developed out of necessity, and they may be seen as subversive, providing her with the means, to paraphrase Eliot, of telling the truth about herself without giving herself away, or – to connect her angled handwriting with Emily Dickinson – of allowing her to "Tell all the Truth but tell it slant." I will explore this interpretation in detail, but it is first necessary to establish that running counter to theories of impersonality were those of personality. As much as Woolf tried to shun the subject of herself, she constantly embraced it in a manner that similarly reflected both her artistic and her feminine sensibilities.

If in works such as "Life and the Novelist" Woolf argued for the writer to assume, in the end, a position of impersonality, when the issue was considered from the point of view of the reader, she emphasized personality. She affirmed in the aptly titled "Personalities," "the critics tell us that we should be impersonal when we write, and therefore impersonal when we read." As a critic herself, she had to confess that she could not always do so, and that she thus was guilty of "critical malpractices," for in the case of a work such as Keats's "Love Letters," his "personality affects us." She concluded: "The legacy of a negligible novel is often an oddly vivid sense of the writer's character, a fancy sketch of his circumstances, a disposition to like or dislike which works its way into the text and possibly falsifies its meaning. Or do we only read with all our faculties when we seize this impression too?"[76] Here the "impression" netted by the reader parallels the impressions which "the mind receives" and which the modern novelist should seek to capture.

In chapter 3 I showed how modernism's quintessential impersonal works may be interpreted as personal ones, a point that Woolf underscores with regard to *The Waste Land*. After listening to Eliot read his poem, she observed, "Mary Hutch, who has heard it more quietly, interprets it to be Tom's autobiography – a melancholy one" (D, 2:178). Woolf significantly found this strain in her diary as well, for some of her "notes here" seemed "egotistic: personal" (D, 2:321), while another time she confessed: "I have wrapped myself round in my own personality again" (3: 74). These admissions prove that her diary is not entirely the "aloof" work of art she had wanted it to be.

Neither are her other works "aloof." Woolf questioned whether she was able to keep her self out of her novels: "I wonder, parenthetically, whether I too, deal thus openly in autobiography & call it fiction" (D, 2:7). Examining character development in *The Hours*, she asked, "Have I the power of conveying the true reality? Or do I write essays about myself?" (D, 2:248). And of the *The Moths*, she suggested, "Autobiography it might be called" (D, 3:229). Charting the progress of her biography of Roger Fry, she tells us she finished her "first 40 pages – childhood &c – well under the week; but then they were largely autobiography" (D, 5:214). She furthered the confusion of genres by noting that *Fry* is "too like a novel" (D, 5:215).

Personality may also be revealed in the essay, as Woolf makes clear in her 1925 piece "Montaigne." Given my argument in chapter 1 that the diary's development can be linked to Montaigne's *Essays* of the 1580s, it is appropriate that she praised these essays as she would a diary: "After all, in the whole of literature, how many people have succeeded in drawing themselves with a pen? Only Montaigne and Pepys and Rousseau perhaps." She foreshadows the theorizing of scholars such as Kadar, in that she heralded the inclusive term "life writing" as she fused essay, diary, and autobiography under the rubric "literature."

It is Montaigne whom Woolf viewed with the highest regard: "this talking of oneself, following one's own vagaries, giving the whole map, weight, colour, and circumference of the soul in its confusion, its variety, its imperfection – this art belonged to one man only: to Montaigne"; "No fact is too little to let it slip through one's fingers."[77] Montaigne, then, is like the diarist, who is like the fiction writer, for he "examines for a moment an ordinary mind on an ordinary day," and he proves that "no perception comes amiss."

In "Modern Fiction," Woolf castigated the Edwardian writers Bennett, Galsworthy, and Wells "because they are concerned not with the spirit but with the body." Bennett's work was particularly dismissed because "Life escapes; and perhaps without life nothing else is worth while."[78] In contrast, not only does Montaigne "follow" the "circumference of the soul," but his essays "are an attempt to communicate a soul." Woolf twice referred to him as "this great master of the art of life," reiterating that in his *Essays*, "It is life that emerges more and more clearly ... It is life that becomes more and more absorbing as death draws near, one's self, one's soul, every fact of existence."[79]

Woolf defined this "life" thus: "Life is not a series of gig lamps symmetrically arranged; life is a luminous halo, a semi-transparent enve-

lope surrounding us from the beginning of consciousness to the end."
She asked rhetorically, "Is is not the task of the novelist to convey this
varying, this unknown and uncircumscribed spirit?"[80] Likewise, in
Montaigne's work "we have heard the very pulse and rhythm of the
soul, beating day after day, year after year, through a veil which, as
time goes on, fines itself almost to transparency."[81] Woolf admitted the
spirit of life into her diary, calling one entry "human life" (D, 3:95),
while another was "A page of real life" (3: 282). Her conception of life
as "a semi-transparent envelope" and her description of Montaigne's
soul beating "through a veil" which "fines itself almost to transparency" echo her hope that her diary would become "transparent enough
to reflect the light of our life" (D, 1:266).

Like Montaigne, Woolf was able to register "the very pulse and
rhythm of the soul." As with the ego or personality, she struggled to
repress or deny her soul. Experience, though, proved over and over
again the impossibility of doing so. In November 1917, in speaking of
her journal to Lady Ottoline Morrell, Woolf commented: "Ottoline
keeps one by the way, devoted however to her 'inner life'; which made
me reflect that I haven't an inner life" (D, 1:79). But in June 1924 it
was "time to cancel that vow against soul description. What was I
going to say? Something about the violent moods of my soul. How
describe them, even with a waking mind? I think I grow more & more
poetic. Perhaps I restrained it, & now, like a plant in a pot, it begins to
crack the earthenware" (D, 2:304). In August she exclaimed, "But oh
the delicacy & complexity of the soul – for, haven't I begun to tap her
& listen to her breathing after all?" (D, 2:308).

From a young age, Woolf had been turning the tap to her inner and
personal life both off and on. For aesthetic and intellectual reasons, she
advocated detachment. But we can see in her theory of androgyny how
she urged writers to tap both the feminine and the masculine sides of
their minds, and thus she challenged other writers who preached
impersonality while encoding their work with the male or masculine
universal – a point well argued by scholars such as Benstock and Scott.
At the same time, her celebration of Montaigne's "art of life" and her
diary, which captures "real life," reminds us of a passage in A Room,
where she explains, "Fiction is like a spider's web, attached ever so
lightly perhaps, but still attached to life at all four corners."[82] In the
spirit of scholars such as Schenck and Smith, Woolf refused to give up
a position of subjectivity from where she could critique male-dominated centres of literary production, and from where she could articulate
the concerns of women, including herself, who had for too long been
silenced or ignored.

It was in this empowered mode that she advocated the personal:

"When Desmond [MacCarthy] praises East Coker, & I am jealous, I walk over the marsh saying, I am I; & must follow that furrow, not copy another. That is the only justification for my writing & living" (D, 5:347).[83] On a more humorous note, Woolf once described how she and Leonard had been invited to Eliot's for cake and tea, during which "We discussed the personal element in literature. Tom then quietly left the room. L. heard sounds of sickness. After a long time, he came back, sank into the corner, & I saw him, ghastly pale, with his eyes shut, apparently in a stupor." She concluded that the episode had been "One of those comedies which life sometimes does to perfection" (D, 2:278). So too did Woolf write the comedy to perfection in her diary. I can think of no better way for her to have relieved the constant tension in her text between the personal and the impersonal than to have juxtaposed Eliot, propounder of the impersonal, vomiting over a conversation about the personal.

LOCKED & PUT AWAY

The comic relief provided by Eliot was an isolated event, for the tension persisted. It can be traced to Woolf's first extant diary, where we find a young Woolf both revealing and concealing herself, making herself, in the terms set out by DuPlessis, at once subject and object. She had suffered her first breakdown following the death of her mother in May 1895 and was in the process of recovering when the diary opens. Remarkably, there is not one mention of her mother, and the only indications of an illness are two cryptic references to her taking "medicine" (PA, 13, 27) and the comment that Dr Seton "says I may do some Latin with Nessa in the mornings, but as far as I can make out, nothing else" (PA, 44).

Woolf filled her diary with her Victorian upper-middle-class social life, documenting her outings within London to places such as the National Gallery, Albert Hall, Kensington Gardens, and the zoo. Her entries are organized according to the time of day, so that we are told when she awoke, what she did in the morning, where she had lunch, where she went afterwards, and so on. She also noted the activities of others; for example, "After luncheon Nessa went back to her drawing; Stella to the work house, and Father to Wimbledon. Thoby and Adrian took off the top of the old organ" (PA, 12). The regimented presentation of the material is thus somewhat detached, offering no significant insights into Woolf's thoughts and feelings. Her preoccupation with where she and others were at any given time, however, does suggest a need to map and order an otherwise confusing world.

When her half-sister Stella Duckworth became ill at the end of April, Woolf updated her diary each day on the state of her health in terse lines such as: "Stella had a good night, & was better in the morning" (PA, 96)." Tragically, Stella died on 19 July, and for Woolf the loss was "impossible to write of" (PA, 115). After noting on 24 July that she had gone to Stella's grave, she made only one more reference to her half-sister in this diary, indicating how fully she was keeping her emotions at bay. Even earlier, in less-traumatic circumstances, expression was reined in: "We (Nessa and I) have resolved to be calm and most proper behaved, as if Stellas marriage were nothing at all touching us" (PA, 66). But it would touch her and Vanessa profoundly, for Stella's marriage to Jack Hills meant that she would move out of the Stephen household, leaving the children once again without a mother figure. Woolf's treatment of Stella reinforces how she was using her diary as a means of suppressing or controlling the chaos of her life.

Though the diary often conceals her feelings, it occasionally breaks down into either one- to two-line entries – in which Woolf frequently admitted that she "forgot" what had been happening – or blank spaces, which reveal how debilitated she had become. Further, her reticence following Stella's death was occasionally countered by moments of release, such as "Very strange & unhappy" (PA, 129) and "everything is miserable & lonely" (PA, 130). By October she was lamenting: "Life is a hard business – one needs a rhinirocerous [sic] skin – & that one has not got" (PA, 132).

The last entry of this book is a summation: "Here is a volume of fairly acute life (the first really *lived* year of my life) ended locked & put away. And another & another & another yet to come. Oh dear they are very long, & I seem cowardly throughout when I look at them" (PA, 134). The structure of this sentence is odd, for she was referring to reading volumes in the present – "when I look at them" – which in fact had not been written – "yet to come." Like Macbeth's "tomorrow and tomorrow and tomorrow," Woolf's allusive "another & another & another" suggests the weariness of spirit and psyche which was overwhelming her and which she was projecting onto her future state of mind. That this year was "locked & put away" underscores how diary and self were fused, for the stuff of the soul, as much as a book, could be put into storage.

The question that obtains is why Woolf would have had to "lock & put away" personal responses. It can be answered in part by recollecting that she lived with the angel in the house as well as with the father *of* the house, both of whom warned the young writer against self-expression. In subversive compensation, though, Woolf constructed a persona she named "Miss Jan." In "As 'Miss Jan Says': Virginia

Woolf's Early Journals," Louise DeSalvo sees Miss Jan as "a private self whom she allows to express her feelings. It is an unfortunate necessity, but an accommodation, none the less, to the way that women are socialised to silence their own voices."[84] Woolf introduced this other self in the journal's first entry, establishing that the diary would not be so much about "me" but about "her": "There was a great crowd of bikers and lookers on – Miss Jan rode her new bicycle, whose seat unfortunately, is rather uncomfortable [...]" (PA, 5). As the diary advances, we learn more about Miss Jan. For instance, a play that she had seen was "very good Miss Jan thought" (PA, 6).

The likelihood that Woolf used Miss Jan to express her feelings is most evident in the entry for 1 February 1897, one which DeSalvo rightly singles out. In the first person, Woolf explained that she was being asked to accompany Stella to Eastbourne, since Stella wanted to be her with her fiancé Hills. Woolf did not want to go, but she recognized that Stella could not go without a chaperone and that she, Woolf, would be made to go. She recorded, "I have been in a dreadful temper all day long, poor creature." In the process of expressing a desire contrary to what was being expected of her, Woolf slid from "I" to "her" – "poor creature." The elision – and loss of self – was completed in the last line: "This is a dreadful fix – Poor Miss Jan is bewildered" (PA, 27).

Miss Jan made her final appearance early, on 2 May 1897, but in many ways the disappearance was only nominal, for Woolf continued to write through a detached, third-person persona. We can read Miss Jan as a manifestation not only of Woolf's early aesthetic of impersonality but also of her awareness that the self is fractured into multiple personae (a point I will take up later). By writing through Miss Jan, Woolf was constructing herself as an object, one that was often dominated by the adults and the hostile world around her. But she was also making herself the subject by virtue of the fact that she was authoring herself as a character within her own narrative. In this way she was telling all the truth, but telling it slant.

DeSalvo argues that the main narrative of this early diary is one of pain, that beyond respecting the feminine self-denial traditionally expected of women, Woolf was locking and putting away the trauma of incest. In *Virginia Woolf: The Impact of Childhood Sexual Abuse on Her Life and Work*, DeSalvo convincingly shows that Woolf's diaristic reticence in 1897 and onwards was consequent to having to deny the abuse inflicted on her by her step-brothers, George and Gerald Duckworth.

We have heard Woolf make reference in her first journal to her taking medicine. During the period of her breakdown, her family and doctor had subdued her with drugs – subdued her rages, which DeSalvo sees as symptoms of abuse. Woolf could have been eager to be silent and good at the point at which the diary opens so as to avoid further medication.[85] We should also note that some time between the early 1880s and the 1890s, her half-sister Laura Stephen had been committed to an "idiot asylum," though the cause of her "illness" was not then, nor is it now, known.[86] Laura's fate may have inspired fear in Woolf, who had exhibited volatile behaviour, and may also be alluded to in her comment that the unhappy year recorded in her diary was "locked & put away."

Another sign of encoding may be found when Woolf, vacationing in Warboys in 1899, recounted in her journal a boating accident in which she was involved, from the detached position of a journalist reporting on the event. Headlining the story "Extract from the Huntingdonshire Gazette. TERRIBLE TRAGEDY IN A DUCKPOND," she delivered the news: "Our special correspondent who was despatched to that village has had unrivaled [sic] opportunities of investigating the details as well as the main facts of the disaster, & these we have a melancholy pleasure in now presenting to the reader." "Miss Emma Vaughan, Miss Virginia Stephen & Mr. Adrian Leslie Stephen" were nearly drowned by the "angry waters of the duck pond," which was "covered at all times by a carpet of duckweed" (PA, 150–1).

DeSalvo interprets this piece as a cry for help. As well as pointing out that references to "duck" represent the threatening Duckworths, she draws attention to the fact that Woolf copied out this passage, adding further images of "duck," and sent it to her cousin Emma Vaughan, instructing her: "Do you see? You must read my work carefully – not missing my peculiar words."[87] Vaughan either missed or ignored her "peculiar words," and Woolf remained imprisoned in an abusive home.

It bears noting that even as an adult she did not write about incest directly in her diary. One entry, recorded in March 1920, may offer a clue as to why. At "the 2nd meeting of the Memoir Club,"[88] Woolf explained, "I subjective & most unpleasantly discomfited. I dont know when I've felt so chastened & out of humour with myself [...] 'Oh but why did I read this egotistic sentimental trash!' That was my cry, & the result of my sharp sense of the silence succeeding my chapter." And she elaborated: "It started with loud laughter; this was soon quenched; & then I couldn't help figuring a kind of uncomfortable boredom on the part of the males; to whose genial cheerful sense my revelations were at once mawkish & distasteful. What possessed me to lay bare my soul! Still, the usual revulsion has now taken place" (D, 2:26).

It is possible that "this egotistic sentimental trash" was Woolf's "22 Hyde Park Gate," the memoir that she delivered to the club at a date impossible to fix, but around the time of the March entry. It was here that she exposed the truth of her past, ending the piece with the shocking exposure: "Yes, the old ladies of Kensington and Belgravia never knew that George Duckworth was not only father and mother, brother and sister to those poor Stephen girls; he was their lover also."[89] The "uncomfortable boredom on the part of the males," and their "sense that my revelations were at once mawkish & distasteful" would be consistent with the nature of the information released in "22 Hyde Park Gate." Woolf's admission that "the usual revulsion has now taken place" could signal a return of shame and self-blame that had silenced her early on. Having voiced the truth, she was again reminded, through ostracism, that certain truths are better left unsaid – and in the case of the diary, a text which reflected herself, better left unrecorded.

Sexual abuse exiled Woolf from her body and from her family, and later from her friends, who were unable to cope with the psychological implications of her revelations. As Broe emphasizes, "home" for such a victim "is a stark, threatening prison of intimates in power over her. She is a commodity, an object, a prisoner of silence."[90] Woolf's reluctance to treat the issue of incest directly in her diary confirms this status of herself as an object who conceals, "a prisoner of silence," and it relates to the taboo placed by her father – clearly an "intimate" with "power over her" – on egoistic self-expression. Unlike Nin, who used the diary to graphically depict incest with her father, and White, who used it to explore the possibility of such abuse, Woolf did not, on the surface, use her diary for "dis-closure, for re-membering and releasing the woman's body," as Broe would have it.[91] But in passages such as the Duckpond report, she may have been working on a deeper level to reveal herself as a subject who could regain control of her body and her fractured psyche through the aesthetic of detachment ,which served her both artistically and emotionally.

CROSSING THE GULF

Woolf's explicit treatment of her social life and implicit treatment of her inner life in her early diaries may be a reflection of the physical environment in which she lived. For the first twenty-two years of her life, she resided at 22 Hyde Park Gate in the fashionable, conservative neighborhood of Kensington. When I was in London, I found this house, on a dead-end street directly across from Hyde Park and off the Kensington Road. I stood in front of it and marvelled at its size, a narrow but huge six-storey mansion, freshly painted white and with a blue heritage plaque by the front door announcing that this had been the home of Sir Leslie Stephen. It was a typically chilly and grey London day, and whether because of the climate, Woolf's writings, or both, I regarded the house as a cold and hostile place.

I had been reading "A Sketch of the Past," and as I stood there, I thought about Woolf's description of her life in that house: "The division in our lives was curious. Downstairs there was pure convention; upstairs pure intellect. But there was no connection between them."[92] "Downstairs" was where Woolf was conditioned to behave as a feminine angel. As she recalled, "Victorian society began to exert its pressure at about half past four," that is, at tea time, when Virginia and Vanessa "became young ladies possessed of a certain manner."[93] In the evening, "Society – upper middle class Victorian society – came into being," when "the pressure of the [social] machine became emphatic," and the sisters were forced to put on their fancy clothes.[94]

This social decorum had its counterpart in Woolf's aesthetics, for she believed that "writing must be formal" and that she should "put on [her] dress clothes" when she wrote the diary (D, 2:321; PA, 144). We can further consider the impact of such socialization in terms of Du-Plessis's notion of the romance plot. Contending that Victorian women novelists were conditioned by their families and by the marketplace to write traditional narratives for their female characters, she shows how the endings to their stories typically involve a (re)inscription of domesticity and femininity. In compliance, then, Woolf had told her diary in 1903, "Success is always able to move my admiration; & really no success seems so rounded & complete as that which is won in the drawing room. The game requires infinitely delicate skill, and the prize is of the subtlest possible" (PA, 168). Her early diaries are in general woven with the threads of this romance plot, for she consistently performed and charted her social and domestic activities. In many ways she wrote what Smith would define as a womanly woman's narrative, conforming to the roles scripted for her gender.

But as DuPlessis and Smith also posit, by the early twentieth century many women were writing beyond the romance ending, and rebelling instead of conforming as they "grappled" with their identities. Thus, if "downstairs" represented the superficial social life that Woolf's family was trying to impose on her, then "upstairs" was her room, the creative and intellectual space that she was designing for herself. Against those shallow afternoon and evening rituals she pit a morning world of art and self-expression: "From ten to one Victorian society did not exert any special pressures upon us." While Vanessa painted, Virginia "read and wrote"; "For three hours we lived in the world which we still inhabit."[95] Rooms became for Woolf the symbolic site on which her Victorian upbringing of docility was both staged and contested.

From the start of her diary, it can be seen how she went about constructing, often subversively, the "upstairs" room of her future modernism. In addition to reading as many books as she could, she tried to secure for herself a formal education. In May 1897 she "went to High St & bought some braid & something else which I cannot remember – a catalogue of the classes at King's College – that was it – which I may go to" (PA, 82). Woolf's casual tone carefully belies the significance of her actions and desires. For although her father allowed her free reign over his library, he did not believe in university education for girls. By taking the initiative to bring home the catalogue, she was challenging her father while asserting her intellectual needs. And it was likely because of her persistence that they were briefly met, for in October 1897 she did attend King's College (PA, 132). Further, at the end of the summer of 1899 she started Greek and Latin lessons with Clara Pater, Walter Pater's sister (PA, 135), and in 1902 continued her studies with Janet Case (163).

Woolf's desire to learn was intricately tied to her passion to write. She ended her 1897 diary with a hint of the powerful artist she would become: "Nessa preaches that our destinies lie in ourselves, & the sermon ought to be taken home by us. Here is life given us each alike, & we must do our best with it: your hand in the sword hilt – & an unuttered fervent vow!" (PA, 134). Woolf vowed to fight for a life in which she believed, one in which she could be intellectually and artistically free. She would be a swordswoman or, more to the point, a wordswoman, carving out her destiny with her pen.

We have heard Friedman argue that "Victorianism is akin to parentalism, a cultural dominance, a parental superego prescribing duty over pleasure, obligation over freedom, social order over personal rebellion," and that within such an environment "young moderns" "had to leave home" in order to realize their art.[96] As a writing woman on the warpath, Woolf clearly needed to free herself from the downstairs world of Hyde Park Gate in more profound ways than simply exiling herself upstairs. When in February 1904 her father – her literal "parental superego" – died, she and her siblings Vanessa, Thoby, and Adrian moved in December from Kensington to "start life afresh in Bloomsbury. It was thus that 46 Gordon Square came into existence."[97] Self-imposed exile from their conservative heritage allowed the Stephen children to come into "existence" as autonomous beings. After reading a book by Edith Sichel, Woolf would later recount in her diary: "She makes me consider that the gulf which we crossed between Kensington & Bloomsbury was the gulf between respectable mum[m]ified humbug & life crude & impertinent perhaps, but living" (D, 1:206).

In her memoir "Old Bloomsbury," Woolf described how "The light and the air after the rich red gloom of Hyde Park Gate were a revelation." The siblings decorated and lived in the place according to their own tastes and habits, being "full of experiments and reforms. We were going to do without table napkins [...] we were going to paint; to write; to have coffee after dinner instead of tea at nine o'clock. Everything was going to be new; everything was going to be different. Everything was on trial."[98] Her description anticipates how she would not only write but live "beyond the ending," and it establishes how, according to Hanscombe and Smyers, she would both live and write modernism in particular.

Not surprisingly, it was in this refreshing and independent atmosphere that Woolf's intellectual world expanded in the direction she so longed for it to go. While in the social world of Hyde Park Gate, she and her sister "were not asked to use [their] brains much," but in Bloomsbury they "used nothing else."[99] Thus did their "flight from femininity," to borrow Friedman's phrase, pay off. On 8 March 1905 she arrived "Home & found [Clive] Bell, & we talked the nature of good till almost one!" (PA, 249). On 16 March "Sydney Turner & Gerald" came over, thus launching "the first of our Thursday Evenings!" (PA, 253). These "Thursday Evenings" were gatherings hosted by the four siblings and attended by Thoby's Cambridge friends, such as Bell, Sydney-Turner, Leonard Woolf, and Lytton Strachey. Woolf acknowledged: "These Thursday evening parties were, as far as I am concerned, the germ from which sprang all that has since to be called – in newspapers, in novels, in Germany, in France – even, I daresay, in Turkey and Timbuktu – by the name of Bloomsbury."[100] The initial group of guests would later be complemented by friends such as E.M. Forster, Roger Fry, Duncan Grant, and John Maynard Keynes. Taken together, the members of "Bloomsbury" would prove Woolf's claim that "Everything was going to be new," for they would revolutionize ways of seeing and thinking about writing, art, economics, politics, history, and sexuality.

Exile to Bloomsbury gave Woolf the creative freedom she needed, for it was here that she began her career as a professional writer. While we can read her earlier creation of Miss Jan and her Duckpond article as convincing signs of trauma repressed and expressed, we could and should also read them as the inventions of an aspiring journalist and novelist. The two may be intricately related, especially in light of Djuna Barnes's orders: "Keep writing. It's a woman's only hope." Woolf certainly needed to write with "hope," for she had made her first suicide attempt in the middle of 1904 and had been recovering from her depression when she moved to Bloomsbury.

Her stint as the Duckpond reporter heralded her career as a reviewer and essayist; her first works began appearing at the end of 1904. The following January she also began lecturing "about books &c" at Morley College (PA, 217). The 1905 diary presents a young woman constructing herself as a dedicated, hard-working professional. She hid the part of herself that had suffered breakdowns and abuses behind the persona of this confident writer, whose identity was fully bound to a work ethic.

On 10 January she received her "first instalment of wages [...] for Guardian articles, which gave [her] great pleasure" (PA, 219), and by February she was hoping for "more steady work at reviews, for the sake of [her] purse" (232) – she needed money in excess of her inheritance in order to cover the medical costs of her illness.[101] I believe that "steady work" was just as important to her sense of "steady" self. When the *Times* agreed to send her books to review, Woolf responded, "& thus my work gets established" (PA, 234), and, I would add, so too did her sense of self as a writer.

Her identification of self with work can be appreciated by even a quick scan of her diary entries for any given week. To take the week of Monday, 6 March, to Saturday, 18 March, a period in which Woolf recorded every day, we can see how her professional persona dictated the direction of each entry, begun thus: "Wrote my review"; "Worked at Sophocles"; "Worked at my evening lecture"; "Read my Sophocles"; "Finished my Oedipus Tyrannus"; "Wrote"; "Read all the morning"; "Wrote my review"; "Wrote this morning"; "Wrote all the morning"; "Started my Sichel review"; "Worked" (PA, 248–53). Just as revealing is the impact of not working. On 24 January she was "ashamed to say that I did very little work" (PA, 227). On 19 February she was "Down late, as usual & legitimate on Sunday" (PA, 239), but the next week she confessed "Sunday is the most melancholy day of the week – because I dont work I suppose" (PA, 243). No wonder, then, that she seemed to resent friends and visitors: "All the morning gone! [...] I grudge time" (PA, 229).

Woolf's obsession with work reminds me of Charlie Marlow, the narrator of Conrad's *Heart of Darkness*. Trying to survive the darkness not only of Africa but of his and others' souls, Marlow informs us, "What saves us is efficiency – the devotion to efficiency"; and he affirms, "I don't like work . . . but I like what is in the work, – the chance to find yourself."[102] Woolf was arguably saved from a painful past by her devotion to her rigorous schedule, just as she was able to find and define herself as a capable, talented young writer, as opposed to being relegated to the margins as a fragile, "mad" patient and victim of abuse. Further, Blodgett posits that women turn to their diaries to give the value to their selves that patriarchal society fails to give. By documenting her professional agenda within the diary, then, Woolf was reinforcing the significance of her accomplishments.

She lived not only through her work but through words. In the 1897 diary she listed every book she had read that year, a practice that would become a lifelong habit. She often personalized a relationship with the text; for example, "my beautiful Lockhart" (PA, 25), "my beloved Macaulay!" (PA, 87), and "my dearly beloved Hawthorne" (PA, 90). And of course, her journal was addressed as "my dear diary" (PA, 6). In 1903 she admitted, "books are the things that I enjoy – on the whole – most" (PA, 178). The genres she was reading during these years were fiction, history, biography, and diary (both her own and published ones), so that her creative faculties were developing alongside her awareness of and passion for written lives, or life writings.

Given the 1903 passage quoted earlier, in which her readings had made her feel connected to "all these poets & historians & philosophers," we can appreciate in Chodorow's terms how her ego was becoming interdependent with the words of others. The fact that she was charting in her diary what work she did and what books she loved alongside many of her personal, social, and historical inscriptions highlights how she conceived herself and the world around her as being literarily determined. Her diary may thus be read in the context of Brodski and Schenck's scholarship, which demonstrates how women in their autobiographies negotiate the divide between reality and fiction, defining themselves as products of their social and historical environments, while simultaneously constructing themselves as characters inhabiting autonomous textual spaces.

MULTIPLE DIMENSIONS

Woolf used words in an attempt to fix her identity. She told her diary about a "profound" realization: "about the synthesis of my being: how only writing composes it: how nothing makes a whole unless I am writing" (D, 4:161). For twenty-two years she had lived, as I have shown, both "upstairs" and "downstairs," and if she insisted that "there was no connection between" those two worlds, she certainly tried to connect the divisions in her psyche. As she admitted in April 1939, "Happily I'm interested in depression; & make myself play a game of assembling the fractured pieces" (D, 5:215). Nowhere are these fractured pieces more "assembled" than in her diary, a text which provides a detailed record of Woolf's many states of mind and being and her ultimate determination to unify them.

She recognized that the self in the early twentieth century was no longer the unified whole that it had been from the time of Renaissance humanism, and to some extent she appreciated the possibilities that a multiple selfhood could offer her as a woman and as a writer. She acknowledged in 1935: "I see that there are 4? dimensions; all to be produced; in human life; & that leads to a far richer grouping & proportion: I mean: I: & the not I: & the outer & the inner [...] New combinations in psychology & body – rather like painting" (D, 4:353). Specifically, her attention to "4? dimensions" can be considered alongside Freud's division of the mind into the tripartite ego, id, and super-ego, as well as in light of the post-impressionist movement in painting, both of which challenged traditional conceptions and representations of selfhood.

While Woolf did not meet Freud or begin reading his works intensely until 1939, she had become familiar with his ideas as early as 1914, when her husband was not only reading him but writing a review of the *Psychopathology of Everyday Life*.[103] By early 1924 Virginia and Leonard Woolf had become the first to bring Freud to an English audience, printing translations of his work on their Hogarth Press. As for post-impressionism, it was her friend Roger Fry who introduced the movement to England, in the first exhibit in London in November 1910 and the second in October 1912, where artists such as Cézanne, Matisse, Picasso, Van Gogh, and Gauguin were displayed. Woolf's response to the initial show is registered in her often-quoted statement that "in or about December, 1910, human character changed."[104] (Consider, for instance, how Picasso transformed the traditional representational portrait into one in which the subject was no longer whole but fractured into multiple, often distorted pieces.) Woolf made that statement in "Mr. Bennett and Mrs. Brown," her essay about rejuvenating character in fiction, thus effectively linking painting and fiction.

She also drew on these developments in her novels, such as *The Waves*, where her protagonist, Bernard, understands that he is "not one and simple, but complex and many. Bernard, in public, bubbles; in private, is secretive." Elsewhere he notes, "There are many rooms – many Bernards"[105] – just as there was one Woolf "upstairs" and another "downstairs." The complexity of any person can at best be appreciated when looked at through a many-sided lens. Bernard makes this fact clear while at a dinner party with his six friends: "We have come together ... to make one thing, not enduring – for what endures? – but seen by many eyes simultaneously. There is a red carnation in that vase. A single flower as we sat here waiting, but now a seven-sided flower, many-petalled ... a whole flower to which every eye brings its own contribution."[106] Lily Briscoe reiterates this sentiment when she thinks of Mrs Ramsay: "One wanted fifty pairs of eyes to see with, she reflected. Fifty pairs of eyes were not enough to get round that one woman with, she thought."[107]

Woolf's diary is similarly a carnation which assumes as many sides as there are readers. It is also a testament to the many eyes with which she viewed herself. Registering a conception of herself as split, she found it "extremely interesting having to deal with so many different selves [...] But how queer to have so many selves – how bewildering!" (D, 4:329). From her first extant diary, she donned masks, writing herself through the persona of Miss Jan. Even her name, Virginia Woolf, assumed the status of a persona: "now, as Virginia Woolf, I have to write ... to the Vice Chancellor of Manchester Un[ivers]ty" (D, 4:147). By the end of her life she had noted that each commercial book she wrote "accumulates a little of the fictitious V.W. whom I carry like a mask about the world" (D, 5:307). Like Eliot's Prufrock, Woolf spent her life "preparing faces," so that, to return to Brodski and Schenck, we can further see how she lived at once as a historically real and a textually created being.

Woolf ended "A Sketch of the Past" with a final comment about the worlds she inhabited: "I could not make them cohere; nor feel myself in touch with them. And I spent many hours of my youth restlessly comparing them. No doubt the distraction and the differences were of use; as a means of education; as a way of showing one the contraries."[108] She learned early how to harness these contraries in the service of her art, as she told her diary in 1908: "I attain a different kind of beauty, achieve a symmetry by means of infinite discords, showing all the traces of the minds passage through the world; & achieve in the end, some kind of whole made of shivering fragments" (PA, 393).

With a nod to Freud and post-impressionists such as Picasso, and anticipating post-structural theories which decentre the subject from its text, Woolf used her diary as a place in which she could play multiple roles, refusing, even when she referred to herself as "Virginia Woolf," to be fixed to any one identity. Recall Franklin's observation that many women turn to their diaries for the purpose of trying on new selves and Nussbaum's contention that the self in diary resists being pinned down. But for Freud a fractured personality was a neurotic one; and for feminist post-structuralists, loss of central authority at the moment when women are coming into that authority can be frustrating and even debilitating. It is in light of these consequences, then, that we can interpret Woolf's ultimate quest for unity, a need to be "whole" which drove her to write. If Eliot's protagonist used the fragments of *The Waste Land* to shore against his ruins, so Woolf used the "shivering fragments" of her psyche stored in the diary to "achieve in the end, some kind of whole."

Her comment that she was "interested in depression" and that she played the game of "assembling the fractured pieces" is realized through the diary, where her determination to acknowledge and explore her bouts of mental illness is manifested. The diary inscribes a Freudian attempt to make sense of the psyche, as she implied when she wrote: "its largely the clearness of sight which comes at such seasons that leads to depression. But when one can analyse it, one is half way back again" (D, 1:298).

In the following 1926 entry, entitled "A State of Mind," we observe Woolf's self-analysis: "Woke up perhaps at 3. Oh its beginning its coming – the horror – physically like a painful wave swelling about the heart – tossing me up. I'm unhappy unhappy! Down – God, I wish I were dead. Pause. But why am I feeling this? Let me watch the wave rise." She went on, "Wave crashes. I wish I were dead!" She urged herself: "take a pull of yourself. No more of this. I reason. I take a census of happy people & unhappy. I brace myself to shove to throw to batter down [...] I say it doesn't matter. Nothing matters. I become rigid & straight, & sleep again, & half wake & feel the wave beginning & watch the light whitening & wonder how, this time, breakfast & daylight will overcome it." Finally, she could "hear L. in the passage & simulate, for myself as well as for him, great cheerfulness; & generally} am cheerful, by the time breakfast is over. Does everyone go through this state? Why have I so little control? It is not creditable, nor lovable. It is the cause of much waste & pain in my life" (D, 3:110–11). Shortly after, she confirmed her role as self-analyst when she stated, "I want to trace my own process" (3: 113).

Part of this process involved documenting her dreams, and Woolf's diary (like White's) is certainly Freudian in its presentation of them. For instance, in November 1929: "dreamt last night that I had a disease of the heart that would kill me in 6 months. Leonard, after some persuasion, told me. My instincts were all such as I should have, in order, & some very strong: quite unexpected, I mean voluntary, as they are in dreams, & thus an authenticity which makes an immense, & pervading impression." Her responses were, "First, relief – well I've done with life anyhow (I was lying in bed) then horror; then desire to live; then fear of insanity; then (no this came earlier) regret about my writing" (D, 3:264). Here and elsewhere Woolf was acknowledging Freud and his *Interpretation of Dreams* (which Leonard had read in preparation for his review mentioned earlier).

We need to realize, though, that Woolf's relationship to Freud and his work was, to use his term, ambivalent. She also used the term:

"Shopping – tempted to buy jerseys & so on. I dislike this excitement. yet enjoy it. Ambivalence as Freud calls it. (I'm gulping up Freud)" (*D*, 5:249). If she borrowed – and benefited from – his approaches to the unconscious, she also rejected them in countless denigrating comments such as this one: "For my part, I doubt if family life has all the power of evil attributed to it, or psycho-analysis of good" (*D*, 2:242).

   Woolf's ambivalence is not unlike the aesthetic tension which pulled at her acceptance and rejection of the personal. She wanted to detach herself from "typical" expressions of female sentimentality and egoism, but she also resisted doing so in an impersonal language created by and for male perspectives. Where psychoanalysis is concerned, I agree with Lee, who believes that Woolf sought a "language of her own, in fiction and in autobiographical writing, which could explain her illness to her and give it value"; she turned to private phrases which could challenge and defeat "a clinical or psychoanalytical language for madness."[109] Returning to the diary entry "A State of Mind," we can see that by employing non-clinical words such as "horror," "tossing," and "painful waves swelling" within the context of a self-analysis, Woolf becomes an example of the female writer who, according to Benstock, "both mimed and undermined Modernist principles" – in this case, Freudian ones. Woolf took what empowered her from Freud – the notion, for instance, that introspection can be healthy and productive – and rejected the constraints that a more formal discourse would have imposed on her aesthetic and emotional freedoms.[110]

A WOMAN'S SENTENCE

Virginia Woolf experienced ambivalence in other ways as well. Keeping in mind Smith's work on autobiographical scripts, we can see Woolf in her diary grappling with her identity as a woman who was also a writer, struggling to reconcile a Victorian desire to embrace traditional roles with a modernist determination to reject them.(In discussing how she and her sister were socialized in "A Sketch of the Past," Woolf explained that their ladylike behaviour was learned "partly from remembering mother's manner; Stella's manner, and it was partly imposed upon us by the visitor who came in." She emphasized, "We both learnt the rules of the game of Victorian society so thoroughly that we have never forgotten them. We still play the game."[111]

   This passage underscores what Woolf so brilliantly parodied in *Orlando*, that gender is constructed, learned. But even when this fact is realized, as in Woolf's acknowledgment that she played a game, early inscriptions of gendered dictates proved insidious. She not only continued to "play" through them, but she had absorbed them to the point that she could not always distance herself from them, in that she was often concerned about fulfilling her feminine destiny.

Perhaps the most explicit indication of her giving in to such a future is the manner in which Virginia Stephen responded to Leonard Woolf's marriage proposal. She accepted him, but made it clear that their marriage would not be a passionate one: "As I told you brutally the other day, I feel no physical attraction in you. There are moments – when you kissed me the other day was one – when I feel no more than a rock."[112] She was thirty years old now, and perhaps her decision to marry was in some part the result of a sense that this might be her last chance to heed conventional society's edict that a woman must marry. Consequently, she scripted herself into the plot of the romance narrative, privileging the desire to please others and thus rendering herself an object (according to DuPlessis) or the ideal woman (according to Spender and Spencer).

In many ways the story in the diary is therefore predictable, with Woolf often defining herself in terms of her husband, her ego interdependent with his. She chose to identify herself, not only as a woman but as a writer, by his name – Mrs Woolf – and she revelled in her married status: "At anyrate today I am the wife of an Editor" (D, 1:190); and "you see it is an enormous pleasure, being wanted: a wife" (5: 115).

Intellectually, she compared herself unfavourably with Leonard: "Sometimes I think my brain & his are of different orders. Were it not for my flash of imagination, & this turn for books, I should be a very ordinary woman. No faculty of mine is really very strong" (D, 2:309). Domestically, Woolf compared other marriages unfavourably with hers. She described planning a trip to Rodmell: "(there was a little skirmish between us, for when I saw the snow falling I said, what about putting it off? At this L. was I thought unduly annoyed; so that we went – but Lord what a quarrel most old married couples would have made of it" (D, 4:287). Her concession elevates her relationship above "most old married couples." But it also illuminates the fact that harmony was maintained because Woolf played the womanly woman, suppressing her desires – "what about putting it off?" – and giving in to those of her husband – "so that we went."

Blodgett posits that "However much a fighter against women's devaluation, [Woolf] also genuinely underestimates herself because she still lives in the shadow of the misogyny which has historically led women to low self-esteem and male identification."[113] One of the clearest signs of low self-esteem is a preoccupation with one's physical – physically unsatisfactory – self. Woolf constantly denigrated her appearance, acknowledging at one point that it was "bad" for her to see her photograph (D, 3:21). And shopping for clothes, she was "struck by my own ugliness. Like Edith Sitwell I can never look like other people – too broad, tall, flat, with hair hanging. And now my neck is so ugly" (D, 3:132).

Her conviction that she was unattractive was connected to her fear of aging. The 24 January 1918 entry read, "The last day of being 35. One trembles to write the years that come after it: all tinged with the shadow of 40" (D, 1:112). And when, in 1929, "The occultist said to [her] this afternoon 'Perhaps you're not as young as you were,'" she realized, "This is the first time that has been said to me; & it seemed to me an astonishing statement. It means that one now seems to a stranger not a woman, but an elderly woman" (D, 3:230). She later questioned, "Why am I so old, so ugly [...]" (D, 5:208).

Tied to the issue of aging is Woolf's documentation of her menopause. While she had made it a habit to record her menses cryptically – "Owing to the usual circumstances, I had to spend the day recumbent" (D, 1:66) – her descriptions of menopause, which she referred to as "t of l," or "time of life," are far more revealing. Contemplating growing older, she wondered, "will there not be the change of life? And may that not be a difficult & even dangerous time?" (D, 3:254). It certainly proved to be, as she experienced "the old symptoms – t. of l., cant get rid of it – the swollen veins – the tingling; the odd falling; feeling of despair" (D, 5:35).

Smith has described the womanly woman's narrative as one which confines the author to a life cycle of "birth, menarche, maidenhood, marriage, childbirth, menopause, widowhood," reducing her to a series of "biological phenomena" and thus erasing individuality. In addition to touching on marriage, menarche, and menopause, Woolf often wrote about her childless state and how it made her feel as if she had wrongly deviated from her biological path. Her sense of failure as a woman was constantly measured against the "success" of her sister Vanessa Bell, who was both an artist and the mother of three children. Woolf typically reflected: "I am in one of my moods [...] And what is it & why? A desire for children, I suppose; for Nessa's life" (D, 2:221). Most denigrating is her comment of September 1926, in which she assumed responsibility for her condition: "my own fault too – a little more self control on my part, & we might have had a boy of 12, a girl of 10: This always rakes me wretched in the early hours" (D, 3:107). Woolf had rejected a physical union with her husband because she feared intercourse (a fear DeSalvo links to trauma inflicted by childhood sexual abuse), but her self-blame underscores how she had wanted to complete the child-bearing phase of a woman's traditional life cycle.

In compensation for not having children, Woolf, like many other artists who were women (such as White, Smart, and Nin, as we shall see), conceived her work in terms of mothering. While writing *The Waves*, she "had a day of intoxication when I said Children are nothing to this" (D, 3:298). The release of *Three Guineas* was "the mildest childbirth I have ever had" (D, 5:148). And having written the biography of Fry, she felt "intimately connected with him; as if we together had given birth to this vision of him: a child born of us" (D, 5:305). In this light, Woolf emerges as a woman who has written her story beyond the conventional ending, so that the natural consequence of marriage is giving birth not to babies but to a career. Her subversion of the notion of mothering may have freed her from feeling only an absence where children were concerned, and it may also have allowed her the freedom to develop as a writer.

Professional success brought Woolf at least one satisfaction denied to traditional stay-at-home wives and mothers: the ability to earn her own living. She told her diary in 1928: "I am happy to say I have still a few pounds in the Bank, & my own cheque book too. This great advance in dignity was made in the autumn. Out of my 60 [pounds] I have bought a Heal bed; a cupboard, a fur coat, & now a strip of carpet for the hall ... [A]nd I pan out articles so as to write one & earn 30 [pounds] a month" (D, 3:175).

Thus if her marriage reflected conventional norms, it also challenged them – not surprisingly, given that Leonard Woolf entered Virginia Stephen's life via Bloomsbury. In addition to being financially self-sufficient, Woolf generally refused the role of worshipping wife, regarding and depicting her husband as human rather than divine. Although she could praise him highly, she also noted his faults, as when they "quarrelled yesterday, about my jug of cream; & L. was unreasonable" (D, 1:135). That this negative comment was radical can be understood in the context of her parents' relationship. Woolf quoted her mother saying, "Your father is a great man," and she implied that Julia Stephen's death was the consequence of exhaustion, brought on by years of serving the man she considered a genius, a man she would never have dared to question, challenge, or find fault with.[114]

In contrast, Woolf did not allow herself – nor did Leonard ask her – to be such an angelic figure. Instead, she entered into her marriage as into a partnership. Together they ran the Hogarth Press, which they purchased in 1917. And Leonard Woolf was a productive in fluence on her writing, for he "may be severe; but he stimulates. Anything is possible with him" (D, 3:273). Perhaps most significantly, they were friends, as Woolf could marvel, "But my God – how satisfactory after, I think 12 years, to have any human being to whom one can speak so directly as I to L.!" (D, 3:49). She depicted their relationship in poetic, complementing terms: "But I was glad to come home, & feel my real life coming back again – I mean life here with L. Solitary is not quite the right word; one's personality seems to echo out across space, when he's not there to enclose all one's vibrations. This is not very intelligibly written; but the feeling itself is a strange one – as if marriage were a completing of the instrument, & the sound of one alone penetrates as if it were a violin robbed of its orchestra or piano" (D, 1:70).

Virginia Woolf therefore wrote beyond the Victorian romance plot, constructing in her diary not an ending but an ongoing story of a twentieth-century union in which the woman figures as an agent of her own destiny as much as the complement to her partner's. If at times she effaced herself as object in the service of her husband, she also revealed herself as subject in the service of her art and autonomy. She once noted that she was always a "woman" when she wrote (D, 3:231), and many of her diary entries testify that she wrote as a modern woman, utilizing both the feminine and the masculine sides of her mind and heart.

Woolf went beyond the romance ending when, as I have mentioned, she refused a physical connection with her husband. In fact, the sexual element had been one of her main reservations about marriage, for she informed Leonard, "Then, of course, I feel angry sometimes at the strength of your desire."[115] She rejected the sexual imperatives of a heterosexual union, and rather than sharing a bedroom with her husband, she occupied a room of her own. And in a further challenge to heterosexuality, she engaged in a lesbian relationship. Once again, though, her diary registers the tension of giving in to and resisting unconventional behaviour.

Woolf met author Vita Sackville-West, who was married to Harold Nicolson, at a dinner party in December 1922. Shortly after their first meeting, she announced: "had a surprise visit from the Nicolsons. She is a pronounced Sapphist, & may, thinks Ethel Sands, have an eye on me, old though I am."[116] Woolf traced these passions "500 years back, & they become romantic to me, like old yellow wine" (D, 2:235–6). Within a few years their relationship had developed into a physical one. On 7 December 1925 Woolf ended her entry: "Ethel Sands comes to tea. But no Vita." She began her next one: "But no Vita! But Vita for 3 days at Long Barn, from which L. & I returned yesterday" (D, 3:51). It was these "3 days" that marked the beginning of their affair.

Though Woolf was willing to testify in court on behalf of Radclyffe Hall's novel *The Well of Loneliness*, in her diary she was reticent with details pertaining to her own lesbian experience. On the one hand, she focused on Sackville-West's "Sapphism" in a seemingly derogatory way, distinguishing between Sackville-West and herself: "These Sapphists *love* women; friendship is never untinged with amorosity." On the other hand, though, she went on to praise Sackville-West's "maturity & full breastedness," and she judged her to be "in short (what I have never been) a real woman. Then there is some voluptuousness about her; the grapes are ripe." She admitted that Sackville-West "lavishes on me the maternal protection which, for some reason, is what I have always most wished from everyone" (D, 3:51–2). If Woolf distanced herself from the "Sapphists" by asserting that her interest in Sackville-West was based on maternal needs, she was simultaneously encoding a psychological basis for her passionate response to her.

On the eve of Sackville-West's coming to lunch in 1926, Woolf felt "amused at my relations with her: left so ardent in January – & now what? Also I like her presence & her beauty. Am I in love with her? But what is love? Her being 'in love' (it must be comma'd thus) with me, excites & flatters; & interests" (D, 3:86–7). In November, Sackville-West was sitting on the floor, while Woolf was "knotting her pearls into heaps of great lustrous eggs. She had come up to see me – so we go on – a spirited, creditable affair, I think, innocent (spiritually) & all gain, I think" (D, 3:117). Her reference to "great lustrous eggs" suggests the sexual element in their relationship, while the emphasis on "innocent (spiritually)" hints that it may not have been "innocent" in a physical sense. This latter point is encouraged by the fact that Woolf wrote *Orlando*, which is replete with bi- and transsexual escapades, as a tribute to Sackville-West.

Whatever the relationship was, she tended to discuss it in ambivalent terms. When Sackville-West was away in 1926, for instance, Woolf examined her feelings: "then I shall want her, clearly & distinctly. Then not – & so on" (D, 3:57). Perhaps not surprisingly, then, the lesbian element of their relationship petered out, and their platonic friendship suffered periods of disillusionment and hostility.

Unlike White, Smart, and Nin, who could be graphic in describing both heterosexual and homosexual eroticism, Woolf was reserved in her diary. Her reticence may seem at odds with the fact that she revelled in the uninhibited atmosphere that Bloomsbury offered her. She tells us in her memoir "Old Bloomsbury" how Strachey came in to the drawing room: "He pointed his finger at a stain on Vanessa's white dress. 'Semen?' he said. Can one really say it? I thought and we burst out laughing. With that one word all barriers of reticence and reserve went down."[117]

It was in this spirit that Woolf was able to record a visit with Strachey in January 1918: "Among other things he gave us an amazing account of the British Sex Society which meets at Hampstead. The sound would suggest a third variety of human being, & it seems that the audience had that appearance. Notwithstanding, they were surprisingly frank; & 50 people of both sexes & various ages discussed without shame such questions as the deformity of Dean Swift's penis: whether cats use the w.c.; self abuse; incest – Incest between parent & child when they are both unconscious of it, was their main theme, derived from Freud. I think of becoming a member." She added, "Lytton at different points exclaimed Penis: his contribution to the openness of the debate" (D, 1:110–11).

Woolf's recognition of the "surprisingly frank" audience and its lack of "shame" is not matched by any detailed "contribution to the openness" of the subject of lesbianism – nor, as we have seen, of incest – in her diary. Her reticence reminds me of her comment that, even after she left the confines of Kensington, she continued to play the game of social propriety. Her "legacy of puritan grandfathers," as well as the angel in the house, seems particularly haunting here, forcing Woolf to shun egoistic, taboo content in the place where she should have been afforded the greatest liberation: her diary. In May 1940 she did note in her diary: "Oh & I've forgotten I think Vita's visit [on 23 April], & can only assure whoever may read this page that we've seen & talked a great deal" (D, 5:283). This concern to "assure" reinforces my argument that Woolf was aware of an audience for her diary. It also indicates the enduring importance of Sackville-West to Woolf, and Woolf's desire to see this significance documented on a more personal site than in Orlando.

INSIDE AND OUT

Beyond domestic and sexual tensions, Woolf occupied the dichotomous position of being at once an insider and an outsider, especially in terms of the Bloomsbury group, patriarchal society, and a Western literary tradition. Bloomsbury itself may be seen as being both inside and outside a patriarchy. Composed of writers, painters, and intellectual thinkers who lived in homosexual or alternative heterosexual relationships, the group, marginal to conservative British society as a whole, was clearly living its modernism as much as creating it. But these same radical members were also well-educated, upper-middle-class people who did not always have to work for a living, who employed a plethora of servants, and who could thus advocate a "bohemian" way of life because they could afford to do so in style. Their elitism (often denigrated, then as now, as sheer snobbery) meant that they were in a central position in society, protected by the walls that privilege had built around them.

Woolf was a vital member of this coterie, as she told her diary in 1924: "All our Bloomsbury relationships flourish, grow in lustiness. Suppose our set to survive another 20 years, I tremble to think how thickly knit & grown together it will be" (D, 2:326). But if she was on the inside, she could also be relegated to the outside because she was a woman. Scott tells us: "Feminist critics have demonstrated ways that the Bloomsbury association devalued Virginia Woolf, noting that men such as E.M. Forster and Lytton Strachey had homosocial relations that excluded her, even as they were marginalized by a more virile modernist ethos."[118]

Not only did homosocial relations exclude her from Bloomsbury, but politically gendered relations shut her out from patriarchy. For instance, Woolf reported to her diary in 1935 how she had met Forster at the London Library, and he had informed her, as a member of the library committee, that it had just been "discussing whether to allow ladies" to join the committee, but had decided against them. Woolf recorded her response: "See how my hand trembles. I was so angry" (D, 4:297). In chapter 3 we heard Benstock state: "For women, the definition of patriarchy already assumes the reality of expatriate in patria," and Woolf's situation can be appreciated according to that definition. Growing up in Kensington, she was exiled from her intellectual self when she was forced to play the game of social manners. She later exiled herself to Bloomsbury, where that self could be more fully realized. But within Bloomsbury she was exiled once again because she was a woman and not a gay man, and because male members such as Forster wielded patriarchal powers of exclusion over her.

In 1940 Woolf returned to the issue of the committee: "Morgan asks if he may propose me for the L[ondon] L[ibrary] Committee. Rather to my pleasure I answered No. I dont want to be a sop – a face saver. This was a nice little finish to a meeting with EMF years ago in the L.L. He sniffed about women on Cttee. One of these days I'll refuse I said silently. And now I have" (D, 5:337). Woolf was denied positions of authority because she was a woman, but concomitantly she was determined to reject those positions because they were patriarchal. Her stance is further evidenced by her declining the offer of doctoral degrees from universities such as Manchester and Liverpool (D, 4:147; 5: 206). She refused to have a superior status conferred on her from institutions which had not so long ago denied women any status at all.

In an early diary entry, she had observed the people at a garden dance: "You at once conclude that they are remarkably ugly or remarkably dull – or remarkably ill dressed. At any rate you lump them together under some common head. This is just what I did tonight, feeling pleasantly detached, & able to criticise the antics of my fellows from a cool distance" (PA, 170). Nussbaum and Smith have both argued that women on the margins (especially in their diaries, where the self is inevitably decentred) are in fact in an advantageous position, for it is from the margins that they can critique the centre, which would deny their presence there. This is precisely what Woolf did. Her ability to stand back from the centre of social activity and "criticize" parallels her later desire to detach herself from and "criticise the antics of [her] fellows," who decided whether or not women could become members of male-dominated committees and the like.

Woolf was positioned at the margins and the centre not only of society but of literature. As one of the greatest innovators of twentieth-century fiction, she was inside a modernism that was itself outside a traditional literary history. In 1919 she observed: "I can't help thinking that, English fiction being what it is, I compare for originality & sincerity rather well with most of the moderns" (D, 1:259). Strachey ranked her ""the best reviewer alive, & the inventor of a new prose style, & the creator of a new version of the sentence" (D, 1:277), so that she believed she was "in the forefront of contemporary literature" (1: 310)

But within modernism she could be an outsider as well as an insider. On the one hand, this position was debilitating. Pound, for instance, was convinced that no woman "ever invented anything in the arts," a sentiment that Woolf mocked via the serpent-like Charles Tansley in To the Lighthouse, who hissed his mantra "Women can't paint, women can't write."[119] At times, though, she took this assertion seriously and personally, such as in 1921 when she was certain that "I'm a failure as a writer. I'm out of fashion; old; shan't do any better" (II: 106). Twenty years later she implied, in comments made about Joyce and already-established masterpieces such as Ulysses, that she had been left out of the Tradition: "Then Joyce is dead – Joyce about a fortnight younger than I am ... And now all the gents are furbishing up opinions, & the books, I suppose, take their place in the long procession" (D, 5:352–3). Woolf's sarcasm does not dispel her longing to be included in that "procession," especially when she queries, "do I think I shall be among the English novelists after my death?" (D, 4:251).

On the other hand, she problematized her desire to be identified as one belonging to that "long procession." She noted in 1932: "Two books on Virginia Woolf have just appeared – in France & Germany. This is a danger signal. I must not settle into a figure" (D, 4:85). She wanted to remain outside the control of others who might categorize and thus delimit her. It was for this reason that she most valued the independence that her Hogarth Press offered her: "Yet I'm the only woman in England free to write what I like. The others must be thinking of series & editors" (D, 3:43).

Remembering a younger Woolf's credo to forge her own destiny – "your hand in the sword hilt – & an unuttered fervent vow!" – we can read her as a writer who, if ambivalent about her status as a writer, was nonetheless able to assert her warrior side. She did not always want to adhere to the group ethos of Bloomsbury, as she wrote of her friends, "I see myself now taking my own line apart from theirs" (D, 2:81). In May 1938 she claimed: "I am an outsider. I can take my way: experiment with my own imagination in my own way. The pack may howl, but it shall never catch me. And even if the pack – reviewers, friends, enemies – pays me no attention or sneers, still I'm free" (D, 5:141). She reiterated in November: "I'm fundamentally, I think, an outsider. I do my best work & feel most braced with my back to the wall. Its an odd feeling though, writing against the current: difficult entirely to disregard the current. Yet of course I shall" (D, 5:189). Once again we can see how Woolf exiled herself from the centre that she also had access to, preferring to remain detached and critical on the sidelines as she forged her own brand of modernism. She thus proves Friedman's contention that for women there is a "link between expatriatism, modernity, and marginality."[120]

The issue of expatriatism is most explicitly treated by Woolf in *Three Guineas*, her political indictment of war in general and World War II in particular. Urging women to be pacifistic and to resist getting caught up in the jingoistic celebrations of England's war efforts, she appeals to the fact that within a patriarchy women have heretofore been devalued. Thus they should not now allow their country to place a value on their abilities to promote a nationalism which would lead to the slaughter of human beings. She writes that women must identify themselves as the outsiders that society has always considered them to be: "'For,' the outsider will say, 'in fact, as a woman, I have no country. As a woman I want no country. As a woman my country is the whole world.'"[121] Within her diary Woolf affirms that she is "in a stew about war & patriotism" (D, 4: 338), and that she is a pacifist (5: 17).

She believed that a woman's – in fact, all of civilization's – survival depended upon the deliberate rejection of fighting in the name of a nation. To this end, she filled her diary with evocative images describing the war's hideous progress. For instance, she reported in June 1940 how Harry West, the brother of their cook-housekeeper Louie, returned from the battle at Dunkirk: "It pours out – how he hadnt boots off for 3 days; ... the bombers low as trees – the bullets like moth holes in his coat ... He saw his cousin dead on the beach; & another man from the street. He was talking to a chap, who showed him a silk handkerchief bought for his joy lady. That moment a bomb killed him" (D, 5:297–8). Closer to home Woolf told about the devastation wreaked by a London air raid: "Stood by Jane Harrison's house. The house was still smouldering. That is a great pile of bricks. Underneath all the people who had gone down to their shelter. Scraps of cloth hanging to the bare walls at the side still standing. A looking glass I think swinging. Like a tooth knocked out – a clean cut" (D, 5:316).

Woolf's treatment of war in her diary reminds me of her essay "Women in Fiction." There she celebrated the impersonal in writing, which allowed women to focus less on the emotional and to emphasize the political, to the extent that they might "become more critical of society." However, it is the personal that ultimately infiltrates her pages on war. On 6 September 1939 she had noted the first air-raid warning: "But Lord this is the worst of all my life's experiences" (D, 5:234). From this point on, the diary only validates that statement.

Increasing doubts about her artistic abilities were exacerbated by the fear of fascist invasion, to the extent that Woolf's mental health irreparably declined. By September 1939 "Civilisation has shrunk" (D, 5:237), and by February 1941 she was living "without a future" (D, 5:355). But it was specifically a future without writing that terrified her, a fact that is not surprising given that her identity was so determined by words. Working on the Fry biography, she confessed: "The week end was sheer drudgery & has left me out of temper out of mood. Roger seems hopeless. Yet if one cant write, as Duncan said yesterday, one may as well kill oneself. Such despair comes over me – waking early" (D, 5:239). This despair led her to observe in June 1940: "It struck me that one curious feeling is, that the writing 'I,' has vanished. No audience. No echo. Thats part of one's death" (D, 5:293).

Woolf's anxieties increased, and the next month, at Charleston, she confronted them: "Threw another stone into the pond. And at the moment, with P[ointz] H[all] only to fix upon, I'm loosely anchored. Further, the war – our waiting while the knives sharpen for the operation – has taken away the outer wall of security. No echo comes back. I have no surroundings. I have so little sense of a public that I forget about Roger coming or not coming out. Those familiar circumvolutions – those standards – which have for so many years given back an echo & so thickened my identity are all wide & wild as the desert now." She added: "We pour to the edge of a precipice ... & then? I cant conceive that there will be a 27th June 1941" (D, 5:299). Tragically, Woolf's fears proved prescient. Nervous about the spring publication of her new novel, Between the Acts, and increasingly depressed, she drowned herself on 28 March 1941.

Three weeks earlier, on 8 March, she had promised: "I will go down with my colours flying" (*D*, 5:358). It is in her diary that these colours are most vibrant, for the diary is so closely tied to Woolf's identity as a textual and historical being. She ended her 1897 volume with this reference to all her potential diaries: "Still, courage & plod on – They must bring something worth the having – & they *shall*" (*PA*, 134). "[C]ourage & plod on" was as much a challenge to Woolf to face life as it was to record it.

The diary, like Woolf herself, was capable of both living and dying. She admitted in 1897: "This poor diary is lingering on indeed, but death would be shorter & less painful" (*PA*, 128). And in 1905, "So ominous a silence means – what I recognised before, that my Diary sinks into a premature grave" (*PA*, 273). But the diary was too much a reflection of herself for Woolf to bury it. She stressed in May 1918 that "to take up the pen directly upon coming back from Asheham shows I hope that this book is now a natural growth of mine – a rather dishevelled, rambling plant" (*D*, 1:150) – recall that she had described her soul as "a plant in a pot" (2: 304). She began a new book in July of that year, "& therefore there is every appearance of a long, though intermittent life" (*D*, 1:171–2). Lamenting that she had been separated from her diary because of travel and illness, she welcomed it back in 1918: "My chief complaint is that I was divorced from my pen; a whole current of life cut off" (*D*, 1:119). Another time, she announced, "I will signalise my return to life – that is writing – by beginning a new [diary] book" (*D*, 3:317).

Woolf consistently fought for and celebrated the survival of the diary; thus her own well-being was both determined by and reflected in that of the text. Such symbiosis can be further appreciated in light of her fascination with pens and ink. DeSalvo would concur, for she says of Woolf: "if anything happened to one of her pens, it was almost as if something happened to herself, and, conversely, when she herself was feeling unwell, she often describes how her pen is not well."[122] Woolf's inability to write was presented from the point of view of the pen: "This pen is terribly infirm" (*PA*, 119); "This pen grows worse & worse" (120); "My pen, I must add, is rather unwell at present" (139).

She was preoccupied with the state of her diary because it offered her sustenance. She turned to it over and over again as her one site of salvation. Writing in it "seems the proper channel for the unsettled irritable condition one is generally in" (*D*, 1:134), and it could "solace [her] restlessness" (1: 237). Her diary was a "refuge" (*D*, 2:53), "a kindly blank faced old confidante" (2: 106), and a place in which to "write away" "an intolerable fit of the fidgets" (2: 132). She could be comforted: "I want to lie down like a tired child & weep away this life of care – & my diary shall receive me on its downy pillow" (D, 3:48). And noting "my mind is agitated," she told her diary that "to soothe these whirlpools, I write here" (D, 3:155).

It is appropriate for us to read Woolf's diary as a text which constructs and reflects self and life, for this is how she often read the diaries of others. She closed her review of James Woodforde's journal with the acknowledgment that through this book "Parson Woodforde lives on,"[123] and she ended a review of John Evelyn's diary by noting that it "fills the mind with Evelyn's presence and brings him back, in the sunshine, to walk among the trees."[124] And she commented in 1929: "There are 18 volumes of Boswell's diaries now to be published. With any luck I shall live to read them. I feel as if some dead person were said to be living after all" (D, 3:237–8). Virginia Woolf's diary is a testament to the battle she waged against time and her victory in "staying it," so that she too "lives on," and continues to "walk among" us. If she revelled in the publication of Boswell's diaries, so over half a century later we can revel in the publication of hers. For with them and through them, we can prove to Woolf that her "writing 'I'" can never vanish. She will always have an audience and an echo.

5 "Still waiting for revelation: key to unlock" The Diaries of Antonia White, a Literary Case Study[1]

In a diary entry for 24 June 1964, the sixty-five-year-old Antonia White raised the issue of publishing the diary which she had been keeping for most of her adult life:

It worries me that I have not yet had the chance to tell Sue about my will and this notebook [...] I know that it seems conceited to imagine that anyone might ever want to publish any extracts. And I can most truly say that nothing in all these volumes covering, I suppose, something well over 30 years [...] has been written with any idea of publication [...] I ought perhaps to have put in my will that they should all be burnt at my death. On the other hand, if anything of my writing survives, other writers might find things of interest to them in it ... people interested in religion. Or in psychology [...] I think the only thing is to tell Sue the whole story and leave her to decide. (D, 2:97)

Whatever "story" White told her elder daughter, Susan Chitty did decide to publish her mother's diaries. Spanning the years 1926 to 1979 – White died in April 1980 – they appeared in two volumes in 1991 and 1992 respectively. The fact that White had contemplated publishing her diaries fifteen years before they were posthumously released to the public indicates that she was determined to keep up the pretence that her diaries were private documents. A consideration of her life reveals why this pretence was needed, while a close examination of the diaries proves that she had always intended they would one day be published.

Although the diaries are heavily edited – Chitty includes only one-quarter of the material – they offer a detailed record of a woman's life. White used her diary to document, among other things, her career as a writer of novels, translations, and commercial advertisements, her attempts as a single mother to raise two daughters, and her difficult Freudian analyses and troubled dreams. The diaries were also a space in which she confronted the haunting spectres of her father, her Catholic God, and her increasingly debilitating writer's block. The themes of analysis and religion, which permeate her diary, allow us to consider it in both Freudian and Joycean terms.

In addition to the diary proper, White kept other books for specific purposes. As Chitty makes clear, these include the "Analysis Diary," begun in 1935 for the purpose of documenting her Freudian analyses; the "Basil Nicholson Diary" of 1937, which records with explicit sexual detail White's relationship with this man; and the "Benedicta Diary," written in 1947 during another turbulent affair, this time with a woman.[2] These diaries are, to some degree, stylistically similar to the diary proper, and so Chitty has incorporated them into the chronological flow of the published text.

Of all the reviewers of the *Diaries*, it seems that Margaret Drabble alone has recognized that White's diaristic achievement is a literary one. Referring to the first volume, Drabble notes in her 1991 review that the diaries "have many striking qualities, and one of the most uncanny is their modernity." She finds the material in the journals "shocking, fighting, struggling stuff," and thinks that "Perhaps it is the explicitness of the sexual content that makes them appear so avant-garde."[3] In addition, White recorded her dreams in her diary: "Other people's dreams are notoriously boring, but, probably with the encouragement of her analyst, she had learnt to dream in a peculiarly revealing and fascinating manner, and many of her dreams are as good as short stories."[4] Freud himself argued that certain "rich" dreams "present whole novels," and this idea makes it even more appropriate to read White's diary as a literary accomplishment.[5]

In 1934 she began what would be the first of several periods of analysis, which impacted heavily on the way she wrote the diary.[6] Specifically, White presents a Freudian case study that documents herself and her life with both personal intensity and professional detachment. She noted of her journals: "I keep them to *clear my own mind* more than anything else" (D, 2:97). She used her diary to inscribe a psychoanalytic method for investigating the different levels of her consciousness, and in the process, she exploited psychoanalysis as a modernist literary aesthetic. As she acknowledged of Freud, "I owe very much to the technique he discovered" (HF, 123).

White's diary is an especially important text for women. As a child, she suffered from psychological and possibly sexual abuse by her father. As a young woman, she attempted suicide and was institutionalized for a year. Not long after this experience, she turned, like Woolf, to her diary as the only safe place in which her shattered self could be reconstructed. Though White had a neurotic personality, she took the time to make a text out of her neuroses. Casting herself as a character in a case study, she confronted the patriarchal forces that had dominated her, appropriating a Freudian discourse in order to explore and understand specifically female issues. Her neuroses became both her modernist text and her feminist stance. In laying herself bare, she utilized the material of her life as a woman for a text that could speak to other women.

To appreciate the significance of White's work, it is once again helpful to turn to Drabble. In a 1968 speech entitled "Women Novelists," she states that Doris Lessing's novel *The Golden Notebook* "is in many ways the textbook for the woman of our age, encompassing as it does most of the social and artistic doubts that beset her … She writes about life as a whole: the experimentation and fragmentation of the book add up to a new unity, an unprecedentedly complete synthesis."[7] Drabble finds Lessing's agenda in White's diary: "One of the more curious features of this volume is the way it prefigures the technique of Doris Lessing's seminal work, *The Golden Notebook* (1962), a novel which uses the device of dividing the fragmented personality of its narrator into [four] different-coloured 'notebooks.'" This is exactly the number of different-purpose diaries that White kept. (Nin similarly used several diary books in an attempt to reconcile her various selves.) Drabble concludes of White's diaries: "as with the *Golden Notebook* itself, the final effect is, oddly, not of fragmentation, but of a powerful urge towards synthesis. Here was a woman who longed to be made whole. She may have driven others mad in her quest, but … we are fortunate that she recorded it."[8] In 1968 Drabble had described Lessing's book as "the textbook for the woman of our age." From her 1991 review of White's diary for 1926–57, it is clear that the diary is "the textbook for the woman" of both the modernist and post-modernist ages, for White recognized, in the spirit of Neuman and Schenck, how her fragmented psyche afforded her a marginal position from which she could critique the male-dominated centre, while she refused to give up the quest for her own unified, authoritative selfhood.

Woolf is one of the most famous writers of the twentieth century, Smart has achieved a certain cult status because of her novel *By Grand Central Station*, and Nin has maintained her reputation as the guru of modern diarizing. In contrast, Antonia White has been only slightly remembered, if at all, as the author of a book about a convent (though the publication in 1998 of Jane Dunn's biography of her will likely stimulate interest in White's other works as well). Although she wrote four autobiographical novels, she is generally identified with the first, *Frost in May*, which was published in 1933. White's father, Cecil Botting, was a classics teacher at St Paul's School, London. In 1906 he suddenly converted from Protestantism to Catholicism, his wife and daughter necessarily following him in his faith. (Broe connects this forced conversion to an imposed state of exile, a point I will return to later.) By 1908, eager that his daughter be immersed in a Catholic environment, Botting sent the ten-year-old Antonia to the Convent of the Sacred Heart at Roehampton, a private Catholic boarding school for girls. Her experiences there are fictionalized in *Frost in May*.[9]

Frost established White as a critically acclaimed writer. She produced no more fiction, however, until the early fifties, when in a prolific outburst she wrote the sequel trilogy: *The Lost Traveller* (1950), *The Sugar House* (1952), and *Beyond the Glass* (1954). The year 1954 also saw the publication of a book of short stories, *Strangers*. Three years later *Minka and Curdy*, a children's book about cats appeared. Following it, White's output was meagre. Her novels went out of print and she was forgotten. She developed severe writer's block which she attributed to her father and to God, and which she ironically documented throughout hundreds of pages of her diary. In 1978 *Frost* was reissued as the first Virago Modern Classic, and all her works have since been reprinted by Virago. As Drabble states, White died "in the midst of a triumphant literary revival."[10] It likely fostered the audience which would be receptive to the publishing of the diaries in the early nineties.

In 1940 White had written to a friend: "You make me feel quite dashing when you call me a 'vile modern'. To the real 'moderns' I seem the dearest old-fashioned auntie. I stop somewhere about Proust, Joyce and T.S. Eliot" (*HF*, 31). It is the availability of her diaries that has made it possible to recognize that White is far more than an "old-fashioned auntie." She further commented on the moderns: "when it comes to serious artists like Joyce or Proust who have put their whole life into their work, I think one must at least be respectful and try to see, without prejudice, what they are trying to do. Sometimes things which are beautiful and wonderful seem to reach a point where one can no longer see them ... Then they usually go underground till someone rediscovers them and reinterprets them" (*HF*, 43). White's diary similarly went "underground," but now that it has been published, we may "reinterpret" it as the modernist work it is.

BOW COTTAGE

Less than an hour's drive north from Monk's House, Woolf's Sussex retreat, lies Binesfield, the cottage where White spent many childhood summers. A short drive east of this is Bow Cottage, the present home of White's older daughter, Susan Chitty, and her husband Thomas Chitty. Knowing that White's diary manuscripts were in the possession of the Chittys, I had tracked Susan Chitty down through the publishers of the diary and had written to her asking if I might visit her home to look at her mother's journals – a bold request to be sure, a stranger asking to see these most personal documents. I kept reminding myself, however, that Susan Chitty was the one who had ultimately decided to release the diaries to the world. To my surprise and delight, she responded with an invitation to Bow Cottage. After a transatlantic flight, my husband, Ian, once again acting as chauffeur, and I, as official navigator, found ourselves one August morning in a rented Fiat winding our tricky way through what is unquestionably one of the most verdant, voluptuous countrysides in the world.

Bow Cottage is lovely. Standing slightly crooked along the edge of the road, it is old but not tired, propped up by fresh hedgerows and flowers. Though it appears cramped from the street, its back extends into a sprawling field crowned with the sort of well-laid garden one would expect to find only in England. This is Thomas's garden, and at the end of a long day's work I was rewarded with a tour of it. But to return to my arrival: I was apprehensive as I banged the knocker on the door, for I was acutely aware of the fact that I was standing, not at the doors of a large, impersonal university library, but on the steps of a rustic, family home. I was also nervous because I had read about the unpleasant court battle waged between the Chittys and White's younger daughter, Lyndall Hopkinson, for the rights to the manuscripts. (The Chittys had won.)

My anxieties were quickly alleviated. Ian and I were instantly whisked into the kitchen for an introductory pot of coffee. While we were chatting, the ghost of Antonia White walked in through the patio door – or so I thought. I was greeted by a young woman with long red hair and a lovely face, who looked exactly like White in certain photographs in the published diary. Her name is Miranda, though, not Antonia: she is Antonia's granddaughter. Susan acknowledged that of all their children Miranda bears the closest resemblance to White. Miranda, who lived nearby, had come to check out "the Canadian" who had travelled so far just to see Grandmother's diary.

After a short while, Ian left to spend the day sightseeing, and I was ushered into the study, whose open window looked into a magnificent wall of hedgerows, scented and breezy. On an old wooden desk I saw a pile of notebooks, disordered, seemingly tossed there. These were the diaries, and I could only marvel at the difference between this archive and those such as the New York Public Library, where manuscripts are filed out of sight. As I began to sift through the disarray, Thomas brought me in a Turkish coffee and placed it beside one of the diary books. I simply could not believe the casualness of it all, and yet it was the disarray, and the coffee, that made me feel I had stumbled upon the diaries of one of my own relatives, caught them in their living form. I have returned to Bow Cottage several times since that initial visit, to continue my research and to continue drinking in the spirit of the place.

A WELL-WRITTEN MANUSCRIPT

It was just before her first marriage that White began to keep a diary, in 1921. She was twenty years old and unhappy, tied to an impotent alcoholic whom she did not love. While this early diary would prove a valuable record of her thoughts at the time, in 1947 White was encouraged by her lover Benedicta de Bezer to burn her first two diary books. The first extant volume is thus the one which briefly documents a trip that White made to Paris in 1926. There is nothing more until 1933, when the diary proper begins. It continues, at times sporadically, until the last year of White's life.

The diary is contained within thirty-nine notebooks of varying size and colour.[11] As with my analysis of Woolf's diaries, I will draw on the criteria proposed by Lawrence Rosenwald. In the process, it becomes obvious that White's diary, like Woolf's, was neither artless nor strictly private, but was composed with a great deal of "control and awareness."[12]

White chose ordinary notebooks, available from any stationery store. The books are in a variety of colours and are small to medium in size. They may be in hard or soft cover, spiral or ring bound. White stuck to one brand for a certain length of time. For instance, she bought two "Quartier Latin" notebooks while in Paris, and these constitute books 10 and 11. Books 23 and 24 were written in the same "Century Notebook," while books 25 to 33 were all contained in the brand-name "Pirilex" notebooks. These might or might not be lined, but either way they offered unconstricted space in which White wrote freely, profusely. Her entries are generally long, indicating the large amount of time she must have devoted to them. That she considered the diary a place to explore her literary sensibilities is evidenced by the fact that she often referred to it as her "notebook."

While the entries tend to be long, there are intermittent periods during which White did not record at all. She wrote fairly regularly from 1933 to 1939, but between the end of 1939 and early 1948, her diaries, though kept, are sparse. Book 15, for example, contains only twenty-one pages written in July 1941; book 17, only two entries for August 1945; and book 20, seven pages written in March 1948. It is not surprising that the diaries declined almost at the moment that World War II began. During this time, White struggled to support her two children while she worked with the BBC Overseas Department and then with SOE (Special Operations Europe). These jobs, coupled with the hardships of the period, would explain why she did not have time for her diary.

Moreover, White suffered from severe bouts of depression. Although she sometimes used the diary as a therapeutic release, and though she kept the "Analysis Diary" in which she recorded her attempts to deal professionally with her illness, like Woolf she often stopped writing altogether. This is apparently what happened in the early forties. In an entry made on 5 August 1944 she acknowledged: "Cannot find any entry since June 1943. Have not looked at notebooks for a very long time. Once again have had a prolonged bout of the usual state [...] Inertia, paralysis, depression, extreme sleepiness" (D, 1:181). This comment is contained in book 16, of which only eleven pages have been filled.

White's volumes begin to expand by the middle of 1949, a change that coincided with a creative outburst which allowed her to produce three novels in a row, in 1950, 1952, and 1954. By the end of the fifties, though, she was unable to write more fiction, and not only are her diaries once again only partially filled, but they tend to contain many financial calculations instead of prose passages. White was obsessed with her (always poor) financial situation – her "finsit," as she called it – and she constantly did her accounts within the diary. Her lack of entries could be explained by the fact that she was working as a translator of French novels and had neither the time nor the energy left over for her personal writing. Chitty remarks that in 1958 White "translated a quarter of a million words" (White, D, 2:15).

It is not until the mid-sixties that the diaries become really dense again, and this development can be attributed to the fact that White was becoming obsessed with her inability to write fiction. As her writer's block increased, so did her need to document it in the diary, perhaps as a consolation for writing not produced elsewhere. In particular, in 1965 she began her autobiography, a project that was doomed from the beginning by her "block" – by 1980 she had written her life only to age four. The very fact of this book drew her attention to her inability to write it. It also encouraged her to reflect on her past, which was then duly and prolifically recorded in the diary in the "present."

By the mid-seventies, whether or not White had writer's block, she was aging and often ill, and was unable physically to write. Her 1974 journal is a "dataday diary" with tiny spaces allotted for each entry, as is her 1975 book. These are virtually blank save for some financial calculations (books 37, 38). Her last diary, though, which was kept from August 1978 to the end of 1979, is a regular spiral notebook. The entries grow increasingly brief, and the handwriting, small and shaky, testifies to the winding down of the writer's life.

In response to Rosenwald's query of "how a volume of the diary is presented *qua* volume," we can observe that there are signs which suggest that White must have conceived each book as such. We can recognize this fact alongside a consideration of whether the text "is given a formal beginning or ending" and whether it "is immaculate or scribbled over with revisions."[13]

At the start of a new book, White occasionally announced that it was new, as in her entry for October 1935: "It is cheating, I know, to begin a new notebook – But the last one never felt right. And, as I have moved to a new room, I felt it might be excusable" (D, 1:57). And she provided a "formal ending," often commenting on coming to the end of a book; for example, "The end of this book will mark the end of a phase of my life." She then went on to explain why (D, 1:83). It should also be mentioned that, in her late December or early January entries, she almost always summed up the year, whether or not she was actually at the end of a volume. This practice suggests that she considered her life itself (as opposed to the book in question) a kind of text which deserved, at specific points, a certain formal closure. For example, on 30 December 1952, she took stock: "This year has not been so violent in happenings as last [...] The first five months ... I was in many ways happier ... This year ends in a kind of desolation" (D, 1:257).

White's diary was written almost entirely in what can only be called perfect handwriting, and there is virtually nothing crossed out, so that the text appears clean. She mentioned her handwriting in a diary entry for 1951: "nothing is more agreeable than a well-written M. S." (D, 1:232). It is not clear whether she was referring to the writing in her diary or a draft of a novel. But the fact that her writing was definitely "agreeable" in the diary, and that this is where the "agreeability" was noted, suggests that the diary itself was perceived as a kind of manuscript.

Its status as such is emphasized by White, who frequently subjected the text to revisions. She did not "scribble over" the text, but rather, she made discreet intrusions which resemble professional footnotes. For instance, describing a house she had once visited, she wrote on 26 January 1933: "'Rose Cottage' was a miserable tiny brick villa in a row of others, with a tiny garden." To this comment, she has added in a darker blue pen, and thus sometime later, an "x." Then at the bottom of the page she has produced a similar "x" and a correction: "1965. This is wrong. I have seen it recently and it is a very pretty old brown stone house" (book 2).

White's practice of revising her text is proof that she reread it. She constantly drew attention to this habit within the diary, as in her comment on 10 September 1936 regarding her entry for 31 August: "The last entry was written with a good deal of spleen and self pity" (book 5). Because she would sometimes go a few months between entries, she always went back to the most recent ones before beginning again. Having not written since 2 April 1964, she observed at the start of 14 June: "As usual found myself re-reading what I had written" (D, 2:95). Not only did she reread from entry to entry, but it was her habit to reread a whole volume, or year, at one sitting. In August 1952 she "just read through the year's entries" (D, 1:245). This remark proves that White was able to construct her entries thematically, relative to what had gone before. And it highlights the fact that she considered the diary to be like any book which one reads from beginning to "end."

These last points are supported by the fact that White, like Woolf, was conscious of the narratives within her diary and was determined to keep them woven together. One way she did so relates to the formal quality of the text, its status as "volume *qua* volume."[14] While White considered each volume a separate entity, at the same time she often drew attention to how each one was part of a whole. For instance, leaving book 21 in the middle of an entry for 10 May 1951, she opened book 22 with "May 10th contd." She also continued the narrative in a more localized way. On 4 June 1935 she promised, "I will finish the history of Sunday June 2 later on," and she picked up the thread on 14 June and continued the story (D, 1:49). Even within a specific entry she was determined to keep the narrative rolling, as this one for 28 July 1954 illustrates: she wrote in her diary in the morning; then she added, "Later," and updated the reader about her afternoon. But as she had more to say, she added, "Later still," and continued her account (D, 1:278).

Taken together, these points allow us to see how White's diary resembles Eliot's *The Waste Land*. On the one hand, her entries are fragments, recorded on separate days and often at scattered intervals. On the other, her consistent rereading of passages and connecting of narratives indicate how she fused those fragments into a unified whole, a story which reveals the careful patterning beneath its seemingly random form.

White composed her diary in a novelistic fashion, as a story for herself to read. But she also wrote it for others. There were several occasions on which she read it, or gave it, to certain people who were close to her. While involved with Ian Henderson, she "read one of the green volumes of notes to him (Sept to Nov 1937)" (D, 1:133). She "looked up [her] old notebooks and read them" to Eric Siepmann, an old friend (D, 1:308). Angry at her friends Geoffrey and Denyse because they had criticized her fiction, she recorded: "And yet they talk with such love etc. of the diaries (fool that I was to show 2 notebooks)" (D, 2:24). And she made two references to taking the diary to her analyst, Dr Galway (D, 2:132, 136).

This limited showing of the diary was a prelude to, or an indication of, writing it for a more general, public audience. Like Woolf, White was likely inspired to this end by an awareness of the diary as a publishable text. Rosenwald's suggestion that "Barbellion's 1919 coup gave precedent for living diarists' entering the literary marketplace"[15] reflects on White, for Chitty tells us that White "admired the work of published diarists, particularly Barbellion (*Journal of a Disappointed Man*) and Julien Green, whose journals she bought off the presses."[16]

Her friend, the British poet David Gascoyne, recorded in his own diary that he had borrowed Barbellion's journal from White's bookshelf.[17] Perhaps this book was what motivated him to publish a fragment of his own diary in the November 1937 issue of *Booster*. White would likely have read this piece; she was emotionally involved with Gascoyne, and some of her own poems would soon appear in the same magazine. She would similarly have read the journal *Seven*, which ran from 1938 to 1940, for many of her friends had work published there, as she herself did. In the first issue for summer 1938, she could have read another fragment of a diary, one by Anaïs Nin. These connections make it likely that White was well aware of the possibility of publishing her own diary some day. Chitty would agree, for in discussing the ethics of her decision to publish her mother's diaries, she stresses: "Some might question making public these private journals, but I am convinced Antonia wrote them with an eye to the public."[18]

White's own actions explicitly prove that at least parts of her diary were written that way. Some time in 1937 she typed up a revised portion of her 1935 diary, kept during her attendance at the summer school of the Group Theatre at Summerhill. While the details of this project are vague – White does not refer to it in the diary proper – Chitty affirms that White worked up the manuscript with the specific intention of sending it to a publisher. It was rejected, and apparently she did nothing more about it.[19] What is particularly crucial here is White's motivation. The fact that she considered her diary a creative piece which she tried to publish indicates that she was aligning herself with Barbellion and others like him. It is interesting that what she sent off was a fragment, just like the pieces she would read by Gascoyne and Nin.

This desire to have even a portion published probably coloured her attitude towards the rest of the diary. Once awareness of the possibility of publication set in, on some level she must have written her entries with a future audience in mind. There is evidence which strongly encourages this conclusion. From 1940 to 1941 White corresponded with "Peter" Thorp, a Jesuit novice.[20] Discussing her diary in one letter, she noted, "I may do something about it one day and transcribe parts of it – much is repetitive and dull – as I don't think I can write a straight novel" (HF, xvii). It is arguable, then, that she wrote the diary *as* a novel. For the same reason, when she told her diary, "It is always, for me, good to envisage a reader" (D, 2:59), she may have had in mind a reader not only for her fiction but for her diary.

White's letters to Thorp were published in 1965 as *The Hound and the Falcon*. Earlier, in 1950, she had published extracts from the letters under the title "Smoking Flax" in the magazine *The Month*. In a diary entry written on 8 September 1964, she recorded an evening with friends, including Neville Braybrooke and John Guest, a publisher who was interested in bringing the letters out as a book. It is here that she made the most telling revelation about her diary. They had been talking about the diary of Raïssa Maritain, which White was translating.[21] She then recounted: "Suddenly Neville said 'Antonia – what about *your* marvellous journal. The one you published extracts from in The Month?' Guest said he'd like to see *The Month*. Found the copy – 1950! – reread *Smoking Flax*. *Had forgotten it wasn't my diary*, but extracts from my correspondence with Thorp. Explained this when I sent it to Guest" (book 28; my emphasis).

White's confession that she "had forgotten it wasn't my diary" is highly loaded. It suggests that at least from a period some time after 1950 she was under the impression that extracts of her diary had been published. Everything she had written in the diary since then was arguably conceived as potential material for further publication. The comment also reveals a certain unabashedness, for White seemed to find it quite natural that her journal had been exposed to the public. She tried to publish some of the 1935 diary in 1937, and almost thirty years later, she admitted that she thought some other part of the diary had in fact been published. These thoughts frame a time span in which White could have written with "an eye to the public." The span extends to 1964, when, as we have seen, she contemplated the publication of the whole diary.

UNDERGROUND WRITING

The reason why Antonia White had to turn to this private space in the first place can be understood by considering two episodes from her childhood. When she was four years old, she decided to "scribble" on the dining-room walls. She tells us in *As Once in May*, her posthumously published (unfinished) autobiography, that when her dining-room "crime" was discovered, her father dragged her into his study and, grabbing a ruler, said, "I'm going to take down your knickers and beat you with it." White recalled: "The thought of these most secret and shameful areas being exposed bare to the person I most revered, and not even accidentally, but by his own hand, was so shocking that I felt I should never survive such shame." Although she admitted that he never did actually "carry out his dreadful threat," she also acknowledged, "I never scribbled on walls again."[22] White interpreted this incident to mean that she would be punished for trying her hand at art – her "scribbling," which she had considered "handiwork."

The second significant episode in her early "creative" life was equally traumatic. It was when the fifteen-year-old White was expelled from her convent school for writing an "illicit" novel. Because *Frost in May* is autobiographical, we can imagine how White felt as a child by looking at how she represented protagonist Nanda's situation; Nanda's punishment was White's own. This is more than mere speculation, for in her letters to Thorp, White referred to herself as "the grown-up 'Nanda'" and the "actual 'Nanda'" (*HF*, 15, 47). It is necessary to examine the end of *Frost* in some detail, because the consequences registered there were ones that would plague White for the rest of her life.

When an ill Nanda is sent to the infirmary, she takes the opportunity of being isolated to work on her novel. As a Catholic, she is painfully aware of having to reconcile art with religion: "she knew that religion must play a large part in it, but feared that too much piety would conflict with a really exciting plot. So she decided to describe a brilliant, wicked, worldly society, preferably composed of painters, musicians and peers, and to let all her characters be sensationally converted in the last chapter."[23] Nanda's/White's recognition that pious and exciting plots would have to be reconciled can be read in the context of DuPlessis's notion of how twentieth-century women try to write beyond patriarchally prescribed endings. White would, in fact, spend her life struggling to negotiate narratives which both conform to and reject traditional dictates of female behaviour.

From an artistic point of view, Nanda is pleased with the results of her work: "Surveying what she had written with as dispassionate an eye as possible, she decided that it really was rather good. Anyhow, it seemed to read remarkably like a real book."[24] Before the novel is finished – she has not had time to write the important conversion chapters – it is discovered by the nuns during a routine desk check. Nanda, who in an earlier mood of self-confidence had praised her work as "rather good," bows to the authoritarian judgment she knows is at hand and condemns it: "Where was the wretched book now?"[25] The anticipation of punishment leads her to devalue her own production, and it reinforces the tension between self-expression and self-repression that would bind the adult White.

Nanda is punished, but to a degree of humiliation she had never expected. On her birthday she is summoned by Mother Radcliffe to meet with her parents in the parlour. Her father's face is "stiff as a death-mask." When Nanda addresses him as "Daddy," he destroys her by saying, "I would rather you did not use that name." Confronted with her authorial crime, she tries to explain. Her father denies her the voice to speak, silencing a part of her forever: "Then I say that if a young girl's mind is such a sink of filth and impurity, I wish to God that I had never had a daughter." Nanda responds to her father's debasing of her in words which echo White's dining-room punishment: "If he had stripped her naked and beaten her, she would not have felt more utterly humiliated." She then comes to the greatest turning point in her young life: "Never, never, could things be the same."[26]

Nanda, like White, is sent into exile. In "My Art Belongs to Daddy," Broe states about the religious context of Frost: "Born a Protestant and middle class, Nanda is forced into the father's text of 'convert,' a term meaning exile in the midst of the 'old great Catholic families, the frontierless aristocracy of Europe.'"[27] By the end of the novel, Nanda, like White, as a Catholic exile is further alienated: she is exiled from the convent school; she is exiled from and within her family when her father disowns her; and she is exiled from her text when it is taken from her, and when she learns that writing, for a woman, is connected with shame, punishment, and paternal abandonment. These reverberations of exile would echo on White's later sense of belonging. Recall that Dedalus promised at the end of A Portrait of the Artist as a Young Man, "I will not serve that in which I no longer believe whether it call itself my home, my fatherland or my church." White, too, would challenge the institutions which had exiled her and from which she exiled herself. And like Joyce, who, as we shall later see, remained ambivalent about his home, fatherland, and church, White would grapple with her identity as one who was ensnared by patriarchy even as she managed to flee it.

Frost in May is significant because it reveals the dominant themes that run throughout White's diary and life. In her journal in October 1960 she affirmed: "One thing is sure, the two most important things in my life ... the Catholic religion and my father" (D, 2:38). She explicitly connected them to *Frost* in March 1962: "And how all the themes of my life are there – my father and religion" (D, 2:67). There are other themes which are constantly played out against these two, and they are sex and art. White's diaries document what can only be described as her tortuous attempts to come to terms with herself as an artistic, sexual, egoistic woman, living under the patriarchal control of her father and God, who have instilled in her the belief that art, sex, and self are essentially bad. The diary is therefore preoccupied with issues raised by several theorists whom we have encountered in chapter 2: how White struggles to negotiate self and text (Neuman; Brodzki and Schenck), how she accepts and rejects traditional female narratives (Smith), how she both conceals herself as object and and reveals herself as subject (DuPlessis), and how she plots a romance yet goes beyond its ending (DuPlessis).

It is likely that it was the convent novel coming up against the male authorities of father and God that motivated White to begin her diary. As we have seen, she burned her first journal, which had been started in 1921, around the time of her marriage to Reggie Green-Wilkinson. While we do not have White's immediate diaristic account of her decision to keep such a record, we do have her fictional one. Her protagonist Nanda, called Clara in the sequel, *The Sugar House*, illuminates White's thoughts at the time.[28] Just over half-way through the novel, Clara, like White, is on the verge of a breakdown. She has been trying unsuccessfully to write fiction, and she is feeling destroyed by her unfulfilling marriage. Desperate to assert her identity, "Clara bought herself a stout black notebook ... and began to keep a kind of diary. Writing in it gave her the illusion that she was at least producing something."[29]

Clara connects the diary to her convent novel. Sitting with her father on "the eighth anniversary of that incident," she hopes that he will finally allow her to explain her side of the story: "Suppose he were going to give her, after all these years, a chance to explain? Suppose he were actually to forgive her for what had outraged him in what she had written, in all innocence, at fourteen?"[30] That this "incident" and her father's response to it have negatively impacted on her self as a writer is made clear: "Might that relieve the appalling guilt and self-mistrust which overcame her every time she tried to write anything which was not merely confected? In the last two months, this guilt and impotence had spread to anything she wrote at all: to advertising copy, even to letters; to anything, in fact, designed to be read by others." Significantly, "Only the black notebook, though it contained much that might make her reasonably feel guilty, was exempt from the blight, simply because it was secret."[31]

This passage reveals that the writer's block experienced by Clara is directly attributable to her father, whom she mortified, and to God, whom she failed to serve when she wrote a novel about "wicked, worldly" characters. It also allows the argument that White's diary was conceived of as a subversive space in which she could do the writing that was most important to her. She was inhibited in her writing only when the space – or genre – she chose to use was a public one, "designed to be read by others." Clara makes it clear that the only reason she is able to write in a diary is "simply because it was secret." It is the freedom of being released from judgment by those who might read her words that allows her to produce work there and nowhere else. This does not necessarily mean, however, that Clara never intends her diary to be seen at some point later on. Her awareness of how texts are classified and perceived by others makes her choice of the diary a deliberate, subversive act. She will tell her story, but in the form that provides her with the greatest artistic autonomy possible.

White offers comparable revelations in her diary which serve to reinforce this interpretation. In an entry for June 1938 she acknowledged: "I did not begin to write notebooks until just before I married Reggie: my writing went underground as it were. The only form of writing I have persistently kept up [...]" (D, 1:140). Though Clara started her diary only during marriage, White and her fictional persona began a diary for the same reasons. If Clara used the journal to write freely, for the purpose of having her "real" story told, White implied the same thing about herself: "It is as if I kept my identity in these books. I become more anxious to show them to people" (D, 1:149). She later commented on her general desire to "show": "I woke up this morning suddenly realising something so obvious that it is amazing I never spotted it before: the need of an audience. I would never have been expelled from Roehampton if I hadn't yielded to the temptation of letting someone read my book" (D, 1:215). In 1939 she again recognized that she was writing for an audience – but she was also aware of the danger: "You may not want to write, but you want to tell someone something [...] You also want to display yourself to people. But you are afraid that this telling and displaying may expose you to contempt" (D, 1:168). In 1965 she affirmed, "I can only write if I think it is not going to be published" (D, 2:131). This last point goes a long way in explaining why White would be able to keep a diary while she was constantly blocked in her fiction.

Her description of her diary as a place in which she could go "under-ground" reminds us of her comment that works by modernists such as Joyce and Proust "usually go underground." It also suggests that the diary is the ideal space for revealing her unconscious thoughts, and thus it is a private forum for self-discussion similar to the analyst's office.[32] White implied as much when writing about the different lay-ers of the mind: "The conscious mind works in fits and starts; the unconscious *never stops* ... Perhaps the function of art is to reveal as much unbearable truth as possible in a bearable form." (*D*, 1:87). Her diary, a sustained work of psychoanalytical art, emerges as the only "bearable form" in which she could write.

ANTONIA: AN ANALYSIS OF A CASE OF DORA

In order to appreciate how the diary is such a work of art, it is neces-sary to consider how psychoanalysis may be associated with literature. In *Essential Papers on Literature and Psychoanalysis*, Emanuel Berman describes a symbiotic relationship: "Literature can be understood (fruitfully) in psychoanalytic terms, whereas psychoanalysis can be understood (no less fruitfully) as a form of literature."[33] In his intro-duction to Freud's *Dora: An Analysis of a Case of Hysteria*, Philip Rieff calls Freud's writing "literary as well as analytic talent of a high order; indeed, the fusing of these two talents was necessary to the case history as Freud developed that genre."[34] To understand just what kind of literary genre Freud developed, it is helpful to turn to Steven Mar-cus, whose article "Freud and Dora: Story, History, Case History" has been called by Berman "the most influential literary discussion of one of Freud's works."[35]

Dora is the case history of a young German woman, Ida Bauer, who was taken to Freud for treatment by her father in 1900. She was suici-dal and was labelled by Freud "neurotic" and "hysterical." She felt hostile towards her father. She accused him of having an affair with the married "Frau K." and of passing her (Dora) off in sexual compensa-tion to the cuckolded "Herr K." Though she complained of being sex-ually harassed by Herr K., Freud interpreted her revulsion to his advances to mean that she unconsciously desired him. Dora eventual-ly broke off analysis.

Like Rieff, Marcus considers the case history "a kind of genre of writing ... which in Freud's hands became something that it never was before."[36] Significantly, he observes that "Freud's chief precursors in this, as in so much else, are the great poets and novelists," a point acknowledged by Freud himself in his *Studies on Hysteria* (1895): "I have not always been a psychotherapist. Like other neuropathologists,

I was trained to employ local diagnosis and electro-prognosis, and it still strikes me myself as strange that the case histories I write should read like short stories and that, as one might say, they lack the serious stamp of science." He explained: "The fact is that local diagnosis and electrical reactions lead nowhere in the study of hysteria, whereas a detailed description of mental processes such as we are accustomed to find in the works of imaginative writers enables me, with the use of a few psychological formulas, to obtain at least some kind of insight into the course of that affection."37

Marcus believes that *Dora* "is a great work of literature – that is to say, it is both an outstanding creative and imaginative performance and an intellectual and cognitive achievement of the highest order." Freud presents Dora's situation by drawing on his "analytic, expository, and narrative talents."38 Specifically, Marcus argues that Freud's style resembles modern experimental novels, while his content reads like Henrik Ibsen's realist plays – plays which feature strong, often unconventional female leads.39 White's diary, like Ibsen's dramas, deals with the social and economic concerns of its protagonist, such as White's status as an (un)married mother raising two children and trying to hold down various jobs. And like Dora's story, it explores the often turbulent and unpleasant internal family dynamics among White, her parents, her lovers, and her children. The diary treats the kind of sociohistorical reality we have heard described by Woolf: "Fiction is like a spider's web" which is "attached to grossly material things, like health and money and the houses we live in."40

Freud is more than just the playwright, though, for Marcus points out that he is also a character in the play.41 We can consider his presence in his own text in terms of the narrative strategy outlined by Donald M. Kartiganer in "Freud's Reading Process: The Divided Protagonist Narrative and the Case of the Wolf-Man." Kartiganer fits Freud's case history of "The Wolf-Man" into the nineteenth- and twentieth-century literary sub-genre known as "the 'divided protagonist' narrative," which is "characterized by the division of the traditional central figure of narrative, the protagonist, into an actor and an observer: one to carry out the events of the narrative, the other to understand and articulate their meaning."42 Kartiganer links this narrative type to psychoanalysis in that the dynamic between actor and observer parallells that of patient and analyst.43

While Freud was the analyst writing about subjects such as "the wolf-man" and Dora, White could perform both roles in the divided-protagonist narrative. Though she underwent analysis with real doctors, it was White who recorded and examined each session in her diary after she returned home, a practice which paralleled Freud's, for he turned to his notebook only after Dora had left his office. And even in the periods of her life when she was not undergoing analysis, White never ceased to perform as an analyst, questioning herself and then documenting her responses in her diary. Kartiganer notes, "Like the observers in the divided protagonist narratives, the analyst studies the patient-text through the privilege of his own presence in it."[44] White's observing presence in her own narrative action is not so much a privilege as a given. Her diary is as much about White as analyst as it is composed by White as patient – just as *Dora* is as much about Freud as it is about Dora.

That Freud penned a divided-protagonist narrative is further supported by Marcus, who reads Freud's "Prefatory Remarks" as "a kind of novelistic framing action," whereby he reveals "his motives, reasons, and intentions." For instance, "exactly like a novelist," Freud informs his readers that they are being taken into confidence: "If it is true that the causes of hysterical disorders are to be found in the intimacies of the patients' psycho-sexual life, and that hysterical symptoms are the expression of their most secret and repressed wishes, then the complete exposition of a case of hysteria is bound to involve the revelation of those intimacies and the betrayal of those secrets."[45] Though not at the beginning of her journal, White informed her future readers of similar "intimacies," as in her admission about her diaries, "I know they are a rather horrible exposure of myself" (D, 2:97).

Another aspect of the novel that Marcus identifies in the "Prefatory Remarks" is Freud's insistence that he was writing science, not literature. Freud acknowledged: "I am aware that – in this town, at least – there are many physicians who ... choose to read a case history of this kind not as a contribution to the psychopathology of neuroses, but as a *roman à clef* designed for their private delectation.[46] Marcus counters that "nothing is more literary – and more modern – than the disavowal of all literary intentions." White often made such disavowals, as when she noted that her diaries "do not 'count'" for her as serious writing (D, 1:58). And yet the fact that she exhibited a lifelong interest in publishing her diaries proves that she considered them worthy of an audience.

Freud resembles the novelist in that, as far as Dora and her family are concerned, he has fictionalized names, places, and circumstances. Part of his strategy in maintaining this obscurity was to delay publication of the case.[47] Freud informed his readers in 1905: "I have waited for four whole years since the end of the treatment and have postponed publication till hearing that a change has taken place in the patient's life of such a character as allows me to suppose that her own interest in the occurrences and psychological events which are to be related here may now have grown faint." That he had to publish the case at all was due to his sense of professionalism: "But in my opinion the physician has taken upon himself duties not only towards the individual patient but towards science as well; and his duties towards science mean ultimately nothing else than his duties towards the many other patients who are suffering or will some day suffer from the same disorder. Thus it becomes the physician's duty to publish what he believes he knows."[48]

White, too, withheld the publication of her diaries until the time was right. She contemplated publishing them in 1964, when she, like Freud, considered the value which her story would have for others who had lived through similar experiences: "if anything of my writing survives, other writers might find things of interest to them in it." She continued: "Yet here and there in them I think there are things which are interesting and which I have not said anywhere else. And, if I ever do write a good novel, which might encourage other writers who have suffered the same agonies of impotence and self-distrust" (D, 2:97).

Freud's overall status in his case study is that of modernism's unreliable narrator,[49] a status conferred largely because he was working with a text he consistently referred to as, and actually titled, a "fragment": *Fragment of an Analysis of a Case of Hysteria*. Making much of the fact that Dora had broken off analysis early, Freud admitted: "In the face of the incompleteness of my analytic results, I had no choice but to follow the example of those discoverers whose good fortune it is to bring to light of day after their long burial the priceless though mutilated relics of antiquity." He revealed his strategy: "I have restored what is missing, taking the best models known to me from other analyses; but like a conscientious archaeologist I have not omitted to mention in each case where the authentic parts end and my constructions begin."[50] Writing about Dora's disgust at being kissed by Herr K., for instance, Freud noted with cavalier creativity: "I have formed in my own mind the following reconstruction of the scene."[51]

White was as much an unreliable narrator as Freud, and like him, she consistently mentioned "where the authentic parts end" and her "construction" began. She was unreliable to the extent that she did not always record facts accurately. In a 1933 entry she wrote of her daughters, "Susan and Lyndall for the last two months (they are 4 and 2 respectively) have been much interested in Death" (D, 1:24). In the original manuscript, White has added, "1978 odd mistake – in Sept. 1934 they were 3 & 5" (book 2). This comment reveals that she recognized that she might not always have recorded accurately. And it highlights how even her supposed "corrections" could be unreliable, for in fact White was right the first time – her entry was written not in 1934 but in 1933, when the children would indeed have been "4 and 2 respectively."

Further, her 31 March 1935 entry starts with this admission: "It is very difficult to write up last ten days" (D, 1:46). In one sense, her difficulty was due to the painful subject matter that White had to relive – she had left her husband ten days earlier. But in a different sense, she was drawing attention to the fact that the description to follow would be one that was reconstructed from memory and would therefore be prone to inaccuracies. Another time, she acknowledged the problem of writing in May about events that had happened in April: "I shall never be able to catch up with my shorthand notes on Spain. Even in the few recorded scraps I see how much I have consciously forgotten already" (book 5). This lament echoes Freud's confession, "The case history itself was only committed to writing from memory, after the treatment was at an end ... Thus the record is not absolutely – phonographically – exact."[52]

Likewise, in 1964 White was rereading her diaries to find information pertaining to her important decision to return to the Catholic Church in 1941. She noted with surprise: "I make no mention of it at all at the time [...] It only shows how people often don't record the most important things that happen to them in their private journals" (D, 2:100). This passage reflects Freud's text in terms of both him and Dora. Like Dora, White was highlighting the fact that she could never expose herself and her life fully to anyone. Like Freud, she was driving home the human inevitability of even the analyst's missing, or failing to register, something that was crucial to the case or experience at hand. White's recorded life remains a fragmented text made up of separate diary entries which in themselves are incomplete, but which are carefully strung together to form something whole. She negotiated not only her text in these terms but her self, for she used her diaristic space to negotiate art and life and to validate her fragmented selfhood while seeking autonomous unity. Along these lines, we can also consider that the actor and observer in the divided-protagonist narrative may in fact be the same character – split and thus a representative of the fractured modernist subject.

Freud's text in part presents a random narrative delivered through the stream-of-consciousness technique. As we have noted, this now-commonplace literary term was appropriately borrowed by May Sinclair from the psychologist William James. In 1920 Freud discussed his method of narrating case histories in these terms: "Linear presentation is not a very adequate means of describing complicated mental processes going on in different layers of the mind."[53] His anti-linear perspective contributed to the fracturing of the text, and it is this breaking down of "linear presentation" and the simultaneous rendering of "different layers of the mind," as practised by Freud, that mark the quintessential modernist works of writers such as Proust, Woolf, Joyce, Richardson, and White. This technique works as well for the analyst as for the analysand, for Freud's strategy was to "let the patient himself choose the subject of the day's work, and in that way I start out from whatever surface his unconscious happens to be presenting to his notice at the moment."[54]

It is in this way that White sat down to write both her fiction and her diary. Recounting a session with her analyst, she recorded: "We went this week into the work question. How do I do my work? [...] If by any chance working continuously as on *Frost* leave over a bit unfinished, so that I have an easy thread to pick up" (D, 1:46). She followed this thread in her personal examinations too, as another entry testifies: "Tired and depressed tonight. What things have made me happy lately? New hat ... Party. In feeling I looked as nice as I can. In coping with a person, not minding if I appeared stupid" (D, 1:33).

This stream is related to time, a quality captured by Freud through his Proustian use of past, present, and the connective memory. As Marcus observes, Freud "is never more of a historical virtuoso than when he reveals himself to us as moving with compelling ease back and forth between the complex group of sequential histories and narrative accounts with divergent sets of diction and at different levels of explanation that constitute the extraordinary fabric of his work." He was especially skilled in organizing Dora's multi-layered dreams,[55] a useful talent given that he claims any and every dream establishes a link between "the event during childhood and the event of the present day – and it endeavours to re-shape the present upon the model of the remote past."[56]

Freud's rendering of Dora's two dreams, which constitute the third and fourth sections of the text, is thus highly literary. Of the first dream, Marcus notes, "Part of it is cast in dramatic dialogue, part in indirect discourse, part in a shifting diversity of narrative and expository modes, each of which is summoned up by Freud with effortless mastery."[57] White's diaries are full of her dreams, recorded with equal "mastery." An example of one dream, discussed with her analyst, Dr Ployé, and recorded in her diary, illuminates her skill to this end. I will consider the passage in detail because it is so representative of White's psychoanalytic narrative drive.

On 1 August 1967 she wrote: "I go to Ployé today. As so often the night before a session I have an obviously 'psychological' dream":

I was with a party ... the hostess took us to an exhibition, one of the exhibits was a model submarine. It lay at the bottom of a kind of swimming bath and to get inside the submarine you had to go down a steep iron ladder. I went down rung by rung into the depths. At one point there was a gap in the rungs and nothing to tread on but a kind of handle, like a stop-cock. I called up to the man behind me about this. I said "It seems a kind of pump handle and I wonder what happens if you tread on it, perhaps it turns something on or off." I know one suggestion that either he or I made was that it cut off the air supply to the people in the submarine.

White returned to her diary the next day, offering both her doctor's and her own analyses: "Ployé certainly was interested in this dream ... I told him how extraordinarily the unconscious used actual happenings as a basis for a significant dream. We have no hot water because the tank on the roof went dry owing to a ball-cock jamming and the gas heater cracked the cylinder of its boiler as a result." She went on: "He interpreted the whole thing as a pre-natal trauma that at some time in the womb the supply to the foetus through the umbilical cord had been cut off – 'a matter of life and death' he said, which would cause acute anxiety." White then connected this interpretation to her writing: "this idea of a blockage or jamming is always how I describe my writing trouble and the accompanying anxiety is of course acute [...] On the way home I tried to think what could represent the 'ball-cock' that had got jammed. The first word that came into my head was religion" (D, 2:182–3).

At the end of the month, having returned to her doctor, White updated her diary on the interpretation: "Ployé agreed with my association of 'religion' with the jammed ball-cock in the 'tank' dream. Also pointed out what I'd obviously already noticed – the male sexual symbol. Suggested that the pre-natal shock might have been during sexual intercourse between my parents when my mother was pregnant." Once again, this interpretation was tied to White's career: "He asked quite a lot about the writing jam. I told him again, since it came up about the trouble with my first 'novel' and my father [...] Also association of writing with loss of love [...] and feeling something bad comes out in my writing wh. will alienate those I love." This led to an analysis of religion, as White admitted: "I said some of the obvious things about religion – that Catholicism was 'forced' on me at 7 by my father – also about the 'brain-washing' of a convent education [...] Also that I suffer, and always have, from constant anxiety. Obviously not always acute but even if things are going well I am never wholly free from it: even if I'm happy, I soon feel guilty" (D, 2:185–6).

187 The Diaries of Antonia White

In concluding his study of Freud's *Dora*, Marcus argues: "Freud's case histories are a new form of literature – they are creative narrative that include their own analysis and interpretation."[58] White's written dream proves how true this description is of her diaries as well. And not only her dreams but her daily thoughts and actions were also consistently subjected to scrutiny. At this point, a more thorough examination of White's recorded life is called for in order to drive home her diary's status as a psychoanalytic text and, in the spirit of Freud, a literary one as well. In examining this diary, we do well to keep in mind the general observation made by Marcus, that *Dora* was composed with "literary and novelistic devices or conventions," including "thematic analogies, double plots, reversals, inversions, variations, betrayals, etc."[59] White's diary employs many such devices, so that her life has become as compelling a narrative as any.

Before proceeding, however, I would like to consider Susan Friedman's "Hysteria, Dreams, and Modernity: A Reading of the Origins of Psychoanalysis in Freud's Early Corpus," for it provides us with a way of understanding how White both appropriated and challenged Freudian discourse in her construction of her life. Drawing on Freud's descriptions of Dora's story, Marcus suggests that the hysteric narrative is in fact the modernist one, since both are considered to be fragmented and incoherent, depicting the fractured subject and the breakdown of authority.[60] While Friedman finds Marcus's connections "compelling," she disagrees with the notion that modernism inscribes the discourse of the (female) hysteric.[61] Rather, she provocatively argues that his early corpus "can be read intertextually to reveal a textual unconscious of sexual politics in which the male subject displaces the female subject." She identifies a crucial split between Freud's two early works: "the hysterical symptom contains the story of trauma and its conversion whereas the dream represents the story of desire and its repression. In *Studies on Hysteria* [written between 1893 and 1895], the story of hysteria centers on the female subject; in *The Interpretation of Dreams* [written between 1897 and 1899], the story of dreams features the male subject, in the figure of Freud split between the dreamer and the interpreter of his own dreams." The transition from the first to the second text, and from his seduction theory to his theory of an Oedipus complex, is parallelled in a literary shift from realism to modernism, such that modernism privileges a male discourse of dream and desire.[62]

Friedman identifies *Dora* as the text which re-enacts the "dual origin of psychoanalysis," in that it invokes *Studies on Hysteria* in terms of Dora's being sexually harassed by Herr K., while it ultimately summons up *The Interpretations of Dreams* in terms of her supposedly unacknowledged desires not only for Herr K. but also for her father.[63] Friedman shows at great length how Freud appropriated and suppressed Dora's speech, and although Dora indicated her refusal to be co-opted by slamming the door on his analysis, Freud "has the last word" and it is his text.[64] Friedman concludes her detailed argument by emphasizing that within *The Interpretation of Dreams* and *Dora*, Freud has effectively denied women authority over their stories. But writers such as Gertrude Stein, Woolf, and H.D. refused, like Dora, to be thwarted, creating instead their own versions of modernism, through which they could register their central stories of female trauma, agency, and desire.[65] White is also one of these writers. Her diary, like *Dora*, inscribes the discourse of hysteria as she contemplates the likelihood that she was a victim of incest. And it inscribes the discourse of desire as she probes, especially through her dreams, her often-orgasmic responses to her father's image/memory.

I find the theories of Marcus and Friedman compelling, and both may be applied to White. Her "hysteric" narrative inscribes the modernist stylistics identified by Marcus, while her diary in general is testament not to the erasure of the female subject in modernity but to her presence. White eluded silencing because she played the parts of both Dora and Freud. It is White as both analysand and analyst who has the last word: it is *her* word, and it is delivered through *her* text – her diary.

A VERY QUEER SEXUAL RECORD

Antonia White's psychoanalytic narrative is an intricate one, at times tangled by its various threads. Despite the fact that she underwent analysis which led to expansion and greater awareness, in many ways she was not a developing figure. Most of the fears, anxieties, and preoccupations which are plaguing her when we first meet her are the same ones which will inform her middle and old age. For this reason, I will approach her life and text in a somewhat thematic manner, since it is only by disentangling the narratives that specific patterns can be appreciated. To this end, the subjects that will be treated are White's sexual relationships, her relationships with her father, God, and the church, and her sense of self as a woman, mother, and artist.

White's extant diary effectively begins in 1933, when she was nearly thirty-four years old. She had just published her first novel, was in her third marriage, and was the mother of Susan and Lyndall, aged four and two. What is most significant about this period is that White, having left the Catholic Church in 1925 and having buried her father four years later, appeared to have been released from the bonds of patriarchal authority. And yet from the moment the diary begins, it is clear that this was not the case.

The fact that she did not publish her first novel until after her father's death suggests she could only begin to take herself seriously as a public writer once the threat of his judgment was removed. It could be argued that with *Frost in May* White had freed herself from the fear of her father's "contempt." Unfortunately, she enjoyed no such liberation, for the publication of *Frost* led to a prolonged nervous breakdown, which in turn precipitated the end of her marriage in 1935. These crises may have been brought about by her guilt or distress in publicly treating the subject of her painful relationship with her father: although *Frost* traces White's upbringing at a convent, the underlying theme is the daughter trying to please the father and the devastating consequences that befall her when she fails.

She immediately began *The Lost Traveller*, another story about her father. That she wrote about him in all four of her novels indicates not only that he was a dominant force in her life but that he was a force which needed to be dealt with. At one point, discussing *The Lost Traveller*, she told her diary: "I believe the book should be about my father. If some of the trouble comes from having my father inside me, I should get him out" (D, 1:168). She recorded the development of this book in her diary, and her comments reveal the extent to which this second work would have contributed to the breakdown. Although the book was started in 1933, it was not completed until 1950. While White wanted to get her father "out" of herself, she suffered writer's block, which ironically forced her to keep him "in."

Driven to analysis by the breakdown, she did experience some relief, and this was documented in the diary. It should be emphasized that White consistently drew attention to her analysis, so that her diary is as much about psychoanalysis as it is a demonstration of it. Not long after beginning, she wrote: "I think I must accept analysis meekly since it is difficult for me to accept, to blot myself out, become a featureless, a 'case' ... Yet at intervals after these apparently pointless and painful arguments, these frustrated tears and irrational rages, the pressure is here and there relieved" (D, 1:58).

Psychoanalysis allowed White to confront the dominating personality of her father and to identify the traumatic psychological and possibly sexual abuse she had endured from this man as a child. Even before beginning psychoanalysis, she perceived the oedipal nature of the relationship: "The book: what is it *about*? The relation of a father and daughter." She boldly observed: "Possibly the first part should be entirely devoted to getting *him* [...] I want *him*. His life is finished: can be examined. I will *not* be afraid of him any more. It is a pure accident

that we were father and child. I have a *right* to look at him, yes, sexually too" (D, 1:34–5). Her determination not to feel "fear" and to
assert her "rights" suggests she was using the diary in a manner
described by Broe as a place in which she could empower herself by
reclaiming her body and her text. We can also read this passage in light
of Friedman's contention that modernist women created their own versions of agency and desire.

In 1935 White began analysis with Dr Carroll and created her
"Analysis Diary," where she made a great effort to record her sessions.
We might recall her good friend Djuna Barnes's comment, which was
in fact directed to White: "Keep writing. It's a woman's only hope."
White's "Analysis Diary" may have been one of her best hopes for
dealing with childhood abuses. During the "1st phase," she was
"noticing objects in room. Constipation [...] Sight of half-opened desk
brought up quite forgotten walnut desk of my father's" (D, 1:39). She
then turned to rooms: "Thought I had nothing to say, but ... a lot came
up. My father's study, the lavatory between it and my nursery (used
almost exclusively by my father and myself)" (D, 1:41). Soon after, she
had a powerful memory: "Most interesting emergencies: the linking up
of the click with my father's latchkey. Convulsive horror aroused by
C[arroll's] shaking his bunch of keys" (D, 1:51). Given that the first few
months of analysis triggered uncomfortable memories of her father, it
is not surprising that White's new novel would be particularly preoccupied with him.

As analysis progressed over the next few years, so her thoughts
about her father were clarified and intensified. She had been exploring
the possibility of a sexual relationship with him: "I suppose by this
time Carroll knows what I really want but I don't [...] Now if as it
seems clear from several indications I want my father's penis or a child
by him e.g. a work engendered with his loving approval. What am I
fussing about?" But she went on, "I can't have his loving approval
because he is DEAD," and "I couldn't have had intercourse with him
anyway because presumably apart from morals (a) he didn't want it (b)
I couldn't have endured it without mutilation" (D, 1:140).

While there is no proof that White's father sexually abused her, the
psyche she revealed throughout the diary very often seems "mutilated." She provided much material over the years which indicates that he
affected her in sexual terms. Not long after she wrote the above entry,
she told her diary that her father "treated his wife like a child, his
daughter like a wife" (D, 1:162). Another time, she recorded a dream
about him: "I saw a man like my father looking out of the window of
a friend's house. Then I went into the house and it *was* my father. We
embraced with such love and relief [...] I was so happy, so relieved. I

would not be lonely any more ... I longed for us to get home here and be quiet together. It was all so vivid." Eventually "things got dim and unreal and I began to wake up. As I did so, I was aware of a very faint sexual tremor" (D, 1:251–2). White's diary here inscribes the Freudian discourse of dream and desire.

Later in her life she documented "The Ritual Rape Dream": "I was to go through the ritual of symbolic rape by my own father. The setting was a mediaeval town, richly decorated [...] But my mood was one of great dread. I wore nothing under my rich robe. I was laid on a kind of stretcher, covered with a black cloth, and handed over the heads of the crowd up the steps to the cathedral porch [...] I seemed to be aware of an old knight [...] waiting. He was my father [...] I was carried inside the cathedral and laid in the darkness, in an ark, before the altar. Then I felt the gentle but firm pressure of a penis in the front part of the vagina, as of an experienced lover."[66] While this dream could be another example of Freudian desire, it could also be an inscription of that alternative, earlier discourse of hysteria. White's sexual preoccupation with her father could stem from early sexual abuse. The description of the "ritual rape dream" fits well with Broe's argument of how the daughter–incest–survivor is exiled "from the realm of childhood, where, as the child bride of the father, the mother's husband, she must now act as an adult woman."[67]

Chitty tells us that White "always pointed out" the fact that she shared a private bathroom with her father, concluding: "It is hard not to suspect that Cecil [Botting] may have, even if only to a small degree, sexually abused Antonia as a child."[68] White's younger daughter, Lyndall Hopkinson, offers corroborative evidence in her memoir. Visiting her ill mother in 1979, she describes being wakened one night by her mother's screams: "As I tried to soothe her, I asked her what she had dreamt. For the first time in her life she would not answer my question: 'It's too obscene to tell you,' she said; 'It was about my father.'"[69]

While White infused all of her novels with oedipal elements, one incident crystallizes her interpretation of her father. In *The Lost Traveller*, Clara's friend Patsy is alone with Clara's father in his study. We are told, "He fell on his knees and leant over her, his face close to hers." When Patsy begs, "Please don't – *please*," he replies, "You're not frightened of me now, are you, Patsy?" He then "pulled her fur coat open and kissed her neck, almost groaning: 'So white, so soft.'"[70] Referring to that episode, Chitty offers this insight: "But Antonia's neck was the one that was white and soft. She later admitted that the passage was pure invention, 'to explain things in Daddy.'"[71] Once again we can see how White used textual spaces to negotiate what Broe has described as "that paradoxical link between survival and exile, between bodily memory and repression of that memory."[72]

We can never know what happened, but we do know that White grew up consumed by troubling memories about her father, and these arguably impacted heavily on her sexual sensibilities. Her dreams were not only about her father but about herself as a kind of "fallen" or "bad" woman. In 1935 she recalled a dream: "I had forgotten that strange one months ago which ended (I was grown up) lying naked on the pavement, mad and knowing myself to be mad, yet peaceful and the little street boys looking at me and touching me, curious and rather frightened, saying 'She's a sleasy lady'" (D, 1:48). White mentioned that she had "Lately reverted to masturbation again, always with stripping fantasy [...] angry, ashamed and aggrieved that this shd. be so" (D, 1:68). And later she expanded on the fact that masturbation was "accompanied always by fantasies of cruelty, whipping, humiliation" (D, 1:75). These feelings may be explained by Judith Herman, who states in *Father-Daughter Incest* that the incest survivor often carries "a deviant and debased self-image" and demonstrates a "masochistic search for punishment."[73] If White was indeed such a survivor, then her diary can again be read as an hysterical text.

Her real sexual relations were often at best unhealthy, at worst traumatic. White used her diary to present the kind of modernist "sexualized identity" noted by Benstock, but we must keep in mind that this identity was born out of much pain and anxiety. Her first marriage was annulled for lack of consummation – her husband was impotent, and she was terrified of sex. After this, in 1923 she had an intense three-week romance with Robert Legg, an officer in the King's Own Scottish Borderers. The relationship was permanently interrupted when White suffered from what she, and others, crudely referred to as "insanity." She attempted suicide – a common practice among incest survivors[74] – and she was institutionalized in the Bethlem Asylum for nearly a year, during which time Legg married someone else. The consequence of White's incarceration was twofold: she was convinced that she was "abnormal," and she would live the rest of her life (much as Woolf did) in fear of the return of madness, which she called "the beast in the jungle."

Years later, White would briefly describe what happened in a letter to Thorp: "I had a sudden and completely unexpected mental smash and was put by my father into a public asylum. I was 23 and in those days no one attempted to discover the causes of insanity or tried to cure it. That, as you guess, was 'the beast.' There is no doubt about the insanity but it had causes and was neither mental deficiency nor a hereditary disease" (HF, 24–5). White's analysis of her circumstances takes on greater significance in light of a comment made in her diary in 1937. Discussing Legg, she referred to his desire for a sexual relationship and her inability to comply: "I was not ready for it and the shock drove me out of my mind" (D, 1:94). Her assertion that her "insanity" "had causes" is here clarified – she was terrified of sex. It is arguable that the trauma caused by even the idea of intercourse was related to an earlier crisis brought on by her father's advances – hence, for instance, her "terror" at the sound of his latchkey in the door announcing his arrival home, as well as the "Patsy" episode. Once again this interpretation is corroborated by Herman, who shows that "Women reporting sexual aggressions in childhood were 'more apt to say that they were disgusted by all sexual subjects.' The strongest emotional reactions were reported by women who had been molested by relatives, namely uncles, brothers, or fathers."[75]

In 1925 White married Eric Earnshaw Smith in what can only be called a safe move. He was much older than her, a senior civil servant, and gay. We might understand her choice in terms of Herman's research that shows that many incest survivors "had affairs with much older or married men," hoping to "fulfill their unsatisfied childhood longings for protection and care."[76] After two years of marriage, however, White's sexual drive asserted itself and she began a series of liaisons, another common tendency among incest victims.[77] Not surprisingly, this activity precipitated her official break with the Catholic Church (D, 1:176).

Silas Glossop, the most important of her lovers at this time, describes White as "a sexually maladjusted woman, who, after repeated attempts over a period of years, had failed to find any satisfaction in intercourse."[78] White became pregnant with Susan after only one night with him. Though they planned to marry for the child's sake, White fell in love with copywriter and aspiring novelist Tom Hopkinson and married him instead in 1930. Her persistent hatred of sex, however, contributed to their eventual breakup, as she realized: "I wasted physical love when I could have had it richly because it was a fear and a horror to me. I have lived all my life dominated by fear" (D, 1:41).

This fear was persistent, and it reinforces the likelihood that Herman's research applies to White as a subject. After leaving Hopkinson, she once again had affairs, and they were just as unsatisfactory as her previous relationships. She described a night with a lover: "Physically I was cold, terrified and in pain: immediately afterwards my fears came up, anxiety, sense of sin" (D, 1:49). This reference to sin emphasizes how her sexual inhibitions were as related to God as to her father. The fact that White was supposedly a lapsed Catholic underscores the degree to which she was morally indoctrinated in her youth.

By 1937 she had found a man with whom she was able to fulfill her longing for what Herman describes as masochistic punishment. His name was Basil Nicholson, and as Chitty summarizes the relationship, "During the summer of 1937 Antonia was Basil's slave."[79] Nicholson was a journalist whom White had met two years earlier, and when they got together in 1937, White devoted a separate diary to the relationship. Many of the entries are in French, presumably because she felt embarrassed by some of the material. White admitted in June, "I find myself more and more attracted to this curious, and perhaps perverted man [...] He says that he wants to know me, to possess me entirely. But he expresses this only in the flesh" (D, 1:89). She went on to relate that "everyone whom he dislikes MUST be punished," and that "I would guess that he was trying to revenge himself on some woman" (D, 1:96).

His treatment of White bore this out, for her "Basil Nicholson Diary" is full of entries in which she is left sitting by the phone hoping for a call from this lover who picked her up only to leave her again. He was psychologically cruel to her when they were together, evidenced by such comments as: "Usually if I talk at all about my own subjects he says rudely 'It all sounds very boring'" (D, 1:98). He told her that being with her "is rather like having an affair with a mermaid," the result being that her "old fear of being a monster came up" (1: 99). But White was obsessed with this man, for "life except for Basil seems utterly false and unnatural" (D, 1:95). Desperate to be with him, she officially filed for divorce from Hopkinson, at which point the elusive Nicholson left her forever. Thus abandoned, she nonetheless felt that "I would rather be an animal with Basil than have the most exquisite 'love' relation ... I do not regret at all that I was Basil's bitch" (D, 1:104). Herman shows that for many incest victims, "Never having learned to protect themselves, they seemed to have a predilection for men who were at best aloof and unreliable, and at worst frankly exploitative."[80] Perhaps this characteristic helps to explain White's destructive attraction to Nicholson.

She soon became simultaneously involved with two brothers, Ian and Nigel Henderson, twenty and twenty-one respectively. White once again selected not only young lovers but men with homosexual tendencies (D, 1:123–4). While the affair with Nigel was short-lived, the one with Ian continued, albeit with many problems, for over a year. Examining this latter relationship, she admitted, "I *know* Ian is very fond of me," but she recognized the limit of this fondness: "I suppose I must allow him to be very assertive at the moment and a bit of a bully but I don't a bit like his manner of asserting himself – cold and sneering – and I can't help asking myself 'Why put up with this?'" That she did so was the result of the nature of her attraction to men: "It's funny how I'll go on being obsessed by a person as long as they have any power to hurt me. I used when I was young to define love as giving someone the power to hurt me" (D, 1:142). Hers is a sentiment that recalls Herman's incest survivor, who exhibits a "masochistic search for punishment." The relationship with Ian Henderson petered out when he enlisted with the RAF at the start of the war and ended officially when White decided to return to the church. He would prove to be her last heterosexual lover.

White's pattern of sexual relationships with men was complex. She was at times cold, at others promiscuous. She chose men who were safe and comforting (the good father), domineering and controlling (the bad father), or impotent (the no-man), such that none of her relationships was particularly healthy or fulfilling. She confessed in 1951, "I can see that I am always after fathers or sons, not husbands" (D, 1:226). And tracing the history of her sexual life, she admitted in 1954, "It is a very queer sexual record, even in these days" (D, 1:274). Her "queer sexual record" reads to a large extent like Herman's case studies of incest survivors: many engaged in "a series of brief, unsatisfying sexual relationships," and "Many oscillated between periods of compulsive sexual activity and periods of asceticism and abstinence."[81] The fact that White took the time to document her experiences allows us to consider the diary not so much as a "queer sexual record" as a radical one. As a woman in psychic exile, she turned to the exilic space of her diary and made it into a modernist text, one in which she wrested her female subjectivity from a Freudian discourse that would have suppressed it, reinstating herself and her "hysteria" in a central, authoritative position.

White's "sexual record" reveals the degree to which she was dependent on men. She always needed at least one in her life, for it was through men that she defined much of herself, as a woman and an artist. In 1935, as she prepared to leave her husband, she noted with frustration: "I want a *man*, whatever I mean by that and I can't be a woman or happy as a woman until I have a man" (D, 1:36). Two years later she referred to herself as "being a woman without a husband – a mutilated woman as it were" (D, 1:115). And in 1939, "It is mainly as humiliation that I feel the divorce. That it rebounds on me. 'There goes a woman who couldn't keep her husband. Look at her'" (D, 1:168). Her self-judgment underscores how she had been conditioned by a society which demands that a woman, to be "normal," must have a husband; because she did not have one, there must be something wrong with her. White was defining herself in Stanton's terms as an "object, the inessential other to the same male subject," and for this reason she scripted herself into DuPlessis's "marriage plot."

Her need of men was largely based on wanting to be desired as a woman. To follow DuPlessis, we can see that White wanted to construct herself as an object in order to "please." Like Orlando, she was well aware that it is a particular kind of fashioned femininity that attracts, and she was willing to perform as required. Sick in bed one day, she mused: "Whenever I am ill I become morbidly conscious of my looks ... When I was seventeen I was afraid of marriage because I thought I should look so repulsive in the early morning that a lover would be disgusted." She wondered: "Powder and face-cream have come to acquire a value for me which I cannot explain – it is almost like a lust or a kleptomania. What would happen if I had never been introduced to them?" (D, 1:27).

But she had, at high school, under the tutelage of her more worldly friend, who became the fictionalized Patsy in The Lost Traveller. A passage from this novel illuminates the impact of cosmetics on the inexperienced Clara/White: "The two were always sending for free samples of face-creams and powders ... And they discussed endlessly and earnestly the appearance of every other girl they knew and the exact degree of her success with men as if they were trying to lay down basic principles for a philosophy of attractiveness."[82] It was at this time in her young life that White began to write advertising copy; her first job was to market Dearborn's beauty preparations. Thus not only did she enact in her life and diary DuPlessis's romance script and Smith's womanly-woman narrative, but she literally wrote them and sold them to other women.

Her job at Dearborn's initiated her into the workforce, and as she developed as a writer White began to associate a career with being unattractive as a woman. In a list of everything that would happen to her if she should get a particular freelance job, she included: "I shall lose any feminine charm; become harsh, dried up, ugly" (D, 1:116). Given that she would spend her whole life working, this prediction indicates that, on some level, she may have constantly felt unwomanly, so that the tension between wanting to serve herself as an independent career woman and wanting to serve others as a traditional female was a pressing, persistent one.

White consistently considered her writing in terms of men, and vice versa. She informs us in the "Basil Nicholson Diary" about how her analyst interpreted her "queer sexual record" to this end: "Carroll says my object in love affairs and in attempting to write is to *get myself disappointed*." And "C. says I treat work as a mistress or a tyrant, to be forced into unwilling submission or to be slavishly obeyed in unreasoning fear" (book 7). But however apt these descriptions may be, White was just as interested in being satisfied by men and work. Actually, she hoped to satisfy her men *through* her work, for she looked to them for approval of herself as a competent writer. She was beginning, or trying, to rewrite the romance narrative, for she was drawing on her "feminine charm" to win men over not to her body but to her body of work. She was hoping to negotiate, in DuPlessis's terms, the desire to conceal as object and to reveal as subject.

In 1938, for instance, she reflected on her method of composing *Frost*. Referring to her inability to complete another novel, she noted: "The only one I finished was *Frost* ... about 17 years after I had begun it and then because Tom told me to and it had all the feeling of a boring, disagreeable imposed task, the only pleasure being in reading it chapter by chapter to Tom and finding he approved of it" (D, 1:140). Another time, having shown Nicholson a poem she had been working on, White was pleased that "After we had been together for several hours he said 'I do not think your poem ["Epitaph"] was morbid' and that was all I needed him to say for reassurance" (D, 1:94).

With Ian Henderson, she described how she wrote for his sake: "The shock last night when Ian was cold and unenthusiastic about the first bit of the book which I'd managed to write. I burnt it. I ... hoped he would stop me [...] I wrote to please him and he wasn't pleased." Within this entry, White connected this need to please with her father. She had read some of her fiction to him, and he had not been impressed: "But obviously he judged me by too high standards and felt that if I weren't George Meredith full grown ... I was no good." She confessed, "I always feel that, unless I produce a good piece of writing I shall cease to be loved"(D, 1:161). White's father's rejection of her when her first, "bad" novel was discovered had left her with the notion that she must "produce a good piece of writing" if she was to be accepted. Her comment that she had not met her father's "too high standards" suggests that she continued to incur his disapproval, so that she grappled with her identity as a "bad" writer versus a "good" daughter.

It is precisely because White failed to win her father's love through writing that she suffered from writer's block. From the moment she started *The Lost Traveller*, she informed her diary of her inability to go on; for example, "I am completely paralysed on the new book" (D, 1:23). Though she wanted to write, she was aware of the fact that by doing so, she further destroyed any chances of being loved. She made this predicament clear in June 1938, when in a bid for artistic control she claimed, "When my father destroyed the beginning of my first silly novel he did not destroy my ability to write" (D, 1:136).

By the end of the month, however, White unconsciously revealed the truth that he had. I use the word "unconsciously" because in the entry in question, her small, always controlled handwriting breaks out into what her daughter so aptly describes as "a childish scrawl."[83] For me as a reader of the manuscript, coming upon this dramatic and hor- rific passage was almost chilling, for I realized that I was witnessing what Broe has described as the incest survivor's writing "out of that paradoxical link between survival and exile, between bodily memory and repression of that memory." White literally reverted to being a child as she uncharacteristically lashed out at her father in large, block letters: "Yes I will write backhand in spite of my father I WILL WILL WILL. Couldn't even write – filthy dirty beastly old man the way I WANTED TO – Well I will. You'll see. I spit on your corpse. You're dead and I'm alive. So I'm one up on you now. I hope you've been punished. You punished me enough [...] You've ruined my life [...] You never loved me for a second and I'm damned if I'm going to go on loving you. The letters you wrote me. I was hurt and wanted your approval. THAT would have hurt you all right to know your standards meant nothing to me" (D, 1:140). White's insistent "WILL WILL WILL" emphasizes how the diary was a space in which she would negotiate "memory and repression," and how in the process she would wrest from her father his control over her body and her text, reaffirming her authority over both.

Unfortunately for White, the impact of this one-sided confrontation was not sufficient to release her either from her block or from her father's control. Within a few years she confessed to her "Analysis Diary," "I think I must still want his approval" (D, 1:179). For this rea- son, she was unable to progress with her novel about their relationship: "My father is dead [...] Yet I feel too that he would never forgive me if I wrote about him – that it is the unforgivable sin to expose his naked- ness to the world" (D, 1:162). She repeated the sentiment in 1960, this time blocked on a new book: "I find I am still worrying about 'expos- ing' my father in this [book]" (D, 2:38). White's use of such physical terms to describe writing about her father – "expose," "nakedness," "exposing" – recalls the description in her autobiography of her pun- ishment for writing on walls: she was terrified of having her "secret" areas "exposed bare" to and by her father. This connection reinforces how her writer's block was likely related to early sexual abuse by him. Though she could not "expose" him in her fiction, she could in her diary, and once again it emerges as a space in which she empowered herself to expose whom and what she wanted, on her terms.

THAT MONSTER THE "WRITING WOMAN"

Antonia White's diary at times inscribes a Freudian discourse that is subversive, while at other times it inscribes one that is more traditional; but it is no less modern for that. It embodies, for instance, Freud's theory of "penis envy," which has been described thus: "The castration complex of girls is also started by the sight of the genitals of the other sex. They at once notice the difference and, it must be admitted, its significance too. They feel seriously wronged ... and fall victim to 'envy for the penis,' which will leave ineradicable traces on their development and the formation of their character."[84] And, "After a woman has become aware of the wound to her narcissism, she develops, like a scar, a sense of inferiority."[85]

We can see this "sense of inferiority" in White. It was probably initially instilled in her by her father, who clearly privileged the male. He was disappointed that she was a girl, and White perpetuated his preference for a son when she gave birth to Susan, commenting on "all the disappointment of her not being a boy." Susan was born out of wedlock, but White noted that "If Susan had been a boy," her father "would have found it far easier to overlook the circumstances of her birth" (D, 1:139). This privileging of the son became associated with the production of a text, as she admitted: "I suppose I want a book in some funny way to be a male child, something powerful, able to fertilise other people. I can understand the extraordinary satisfaction of producing a son. A woman has not a penis but she can produce a being with a real penis" (D, 1:139).

As perhaps the logical extension of this feeling, White privileged the artist as male and consistently denigrated herself as a woman writer. Unable to compose, she compared herself unfavourably with a male writer who sat at a neighbouring window: "Why can't I do it? The young man in the red shirt almost *afflicts* me [...] He is aware of me, I am pretty sure, but resents the intrusion of that monster the 'writing woman'" (D, 1:48). As a representative of her "underground" thoughts, the diary unconsciously connects her denigration of the female artist to her father. She told the diary that he "didn't think much of women writers. Had a horror of 'the new woman'" (D, 2:196) – his "horror" fuses with her image of herself as a "monster." In a more general sense, White (and her father) were capitulating to the pervasive imaging of women as monsters that had been going on for centuries, a trend made clear by Gilbert and Gubar throughout *The Madwoman in the Attic*. The "angel in the house" who aspired to a writing career was especially in danger of becoming the "monster in the house," or, in the spirit of Gilbert and Gubar, the monster in the attic.

It bears noting that in 1975, after reading the series of letters that her father had sent to a friend before he was married, White learned that he had actually wanted to be a writer himself (D, 2:248). His hostility towards any kind of writing produced by his daughter could be interpreted as envy or jealousy on his part, directed at the child who accomplished what he had not. In a different sense, the physical and psychological punishments that he inflicted on White as she tried to realize herself as a writer suggest that he was merely reinforcing the patriarchal imperative that writing, or the general act of creating, contradicts a daughter's prescribed feminine passivity.

White devalued not only herself but what she wrote. She had, as mentioned earlier, referred to her dining-room "handiwork" as "scribbling." Following her punishment, she never scribbled on walls again. More significantly, she would be condemned to spend a lifetime "scribbling" on paper, prevented by fear of punishment from actually "writing." The word "scribble" appears over and over again in descriptions of her writing as an adult. Struggling with a new novel, for instance, she noted, "Somehow I have got 17 pp. done – all mess and scribble"(D, 2:50). Another time, she "did NOT mean to sit scribbling" in her diary (D, 2:108).[86] Woolf, too, consistently called her work "scribble,"[87] a practice which indicates that the tendency for women to devalue what they produced was a common one.

White's negative self-image was probably associated with her conviction that as a female she was necessarily a flawed male. In 1937 she offered this startling confession: "it is very clear that a great part of my unconscious preoccupation is with the idea of myself as a mutilated man" (D, 1:115). Her diary is once again the site of her own psychoanalysis, presenting Freud's notion of the girl who, lacking a penis, feels necessarily "castrated" – or "mutilated," as White would have it. Given that she privileged the male artist, it is hardly surprising that she referred to her writer's block in terms of male sexual deficiency. She used the word "impotence" over and over again. It was early on in her "Analysis Diary" that she first recognized "the identifying of the jam on writing with impotence" (book 3). She used the term freely; for example, "It is still impossible to work. I tried on Saturday: total impotence" (D, 1:121).

If White wanted a penis, she also wanted to write. During her second week of analysis she recorded a dream in which she had said: "I wish I had *five* fountain pens like my father instead of only two" (D, 1:39). This dream aroused what would be (for White as for Woolf) a lifelong obsession with actual pens. She announced: "I have a new pen – always an important thing for me. And now, to my annoyance it turns out to be very intractable. Possibly it's the pale ink I don't like." She kept writing and then wondered, "Now let us see if that is better. Perhaps it always starts very faint at first and then dries darker. It seems very unsympathetic now" (book 8). White spent a paragraph writing about this pen, studying it from moment to moment. She continued to dwell on it in the next entry: "I can't break this pen in ... Does this old one of Daddy's write better? Can't do anything till I've settled this pen question" (D, 1:125).

It is understandable that a writer might remark upon her tool, but White's singular focus suggests that her concern was symbolic of deeper meanings. One such meaning was likely related to sexual performance, as she herself acknowledged: "complete jam in writing again after a tolerably steady period ... desire to eat, drink, smoke. Loss of fountain pen" (D, 1:180). Referring to an episode in which she had forgotten her umbrella with her analyst and was then given it back, she told herself, "I *hope* the unconscious grasps that this penis-symbol (writing power) is quite OK for me to have" (D, 2:137).

In one sense, White was writing a narrative of classic Freudian desire, caught in her oedipal complex of wanting her father's penis, which was translated by her unconscious into the more acceptable symbol of a pen. In a different sense, though, she was scripting her own narrative of desire. Gilbert and Gubar ask at the opening of *The Madwoman in the Attic*: "Is a pen a metaphorical penis?" They suggest that male sexuality "is not just analogically but actually the essence of literary power. The poet's pen is in some sense (even more than figuratively) a penis."[88] Smith has noted that the female autobiographer "would know and name herself, appropriating the self-creative power patriarchal culture has historically situated in the pens of man."[89] Though Gilbert and Gubar ask if "a pen is a metaphorical penis?" White might have answered, subversively, that "a penis is a metaphorical pen." Perhaps she was accommodating herself to what was expected of her in Freudian discourse – that she desire the penis – in order to take what she really wanted – "writing power," a pen in which to "know and name herself." The diary in which she revealed what her "unconscious" was "grasping" sets up at once a traditional and a revisionary psychoanalytic model.

White's distress over her writer's block can be attributed to her real social and economic circumstances, which often denied her the time to write. In 1925 she began work as a full-time copywriter at W.S. Crawford's advertising agency. (*Frost* was written at the end of days and on weekends.) Wanting to be a serious writer, she felt that this job was "silly" (D, 1:249), and she became so uninterested in it that she was fired in 1933. During the next four years, the period of her breakdown and first analysis, she was unable to hold a regular job, but she did contribute to household finances by doing freelance journalism and copywriting.[90] In 1937, somewhat restored by treatment, she accepted a high-paying position at J. Walter Thompson, an American advertising agency.

These various jobs were all related in some way to the marketing of beauty and fashion. We have seen how important physical appearance was to White, but she nonetheless struggled to reconcile this side of her nature with her desire to be taken seriously as an artist. She criticized herself as "a useless frivolous creature" (D, 1:157). And upon accepting the job at Thompson's, she lamented: "I have sworn never to go back to advertising but I am going back to full-time and real drudgery [...] I feel as if I were renouncing the life of an artist" (D, 1:83). Six months later, she despaired "of ever being a writer" (D, 1:88). By September she told of her frustration with having to do unstimulating work for the sake of her children: "I am resentful that I am to be left with the children – that all my life now I am to be tied, committed to making money" (D, 1:112).

This last comment is an appropriate place at which to pause to consider White's attitude towards motherhood. If she was willing to perform as the made-up womanly woman, she was unwilling to sacrifice her career for her children. Just as the ideology of femininity and its spokeswoman the "angel in the house" took hold of society during the eighteenth and nineteenth centuries, as we have seen, so too, according to Chodorow, did the "ideology of the moral mother" and its representative, the angelic mother who lovingly devoted her existence to her children.[91] White, however, refused the latter role, challenging traditional dictates that women were "naturally" or "instinctually" maternal. She wrote well beyond the marriage plot as she scripted her more radical story of a woman who did not really want her children, the products of her feminine destiny within the patriarchal family. In her summary in her diary at the end of December 1934, for instance, she made a list of her "Hates." Included here were "Being pregnant"; "People who automatically ask first 'How are the children?'" (D, 1:33); and "People thinking a woman's only function is to have children" (book 2). Demythifying the "ideology of the moral mother," she admitted, "I wish I loved my children more" (D, 1:43).

While there is no doubt that economic and maternal circumstances were disabling to her artistic career, White was often unable to produce serious writing because of other factors revealed only unconsciously. Through analysis, and through the recording of that analysis in the diary, these were brought to consciousness in an enactment of Freud's "talking cure."

In 1936 she revealed how the subject of money impacted on her writing: "I want the certain consciousness of unlimited talent without the necessity of having to give evidence of any money at all. Now that was quite unconscious – I meant to write 'talent' ... I am just as anxious and embarrassed when anyone asks 'are you writing anything now?' as when my mother or anyone in authority asked if I had been to the lavatory." She wondered: "How can I have got writing, money, defaecation all mixed up? ... I can only now write freely if I do not get paid at all" (D, 1:75).

White could only "write" if she did not anticipate remuneration, a fact that testifies to just how ideal and subversive a text the diary was for her, for she would not expect to be paid for her private thoughts and thus could "write freely" there. But that she was debilitated by the idea of earning money needs to be explored. To do so, we can turn to her autobiography, for it is here that White documented receiving her first monetary reward.

When she was four years old, she went looking for her father in his study. Though he was not there, one of his pupils was, having arrived early for his tutorial. To pass the time, this young man asked White "a great many questions and seemed interested and amused by" her answers. She admitted: "Soon I was indulging in the intoxicating pleasure of showing off as I recited my other bits of knowledge – the names of the gods and goddesses of Olympus and some of their history. Finally the young man laughed, said I was such a good pupil that I deserved a reward." He gave her "a half-sovereign," adding, "You've earned your prize." When her father came in and discovered the money, he forced her to give it back. White related the impact of this event: "After seventy-two years I have not forgotten that breathless moment ... I wonder if that pupil ... ever realised that, unintentionally, he had sown the seed" of "as pretty a complex about money as any psychologist could be called on to resolve."[92]

In White's version, Botting never explained just what "principle" it was that made it inappropriate for his daughter to be financially rewarded for her knowledge. As Ellen Cronan Rose argues, however, "The most obvious implication" of this event "for White's identity as a writer is that it is an early instance of the father's denying her the earning power of her talent, a prohibition many Victorian daughters encountered." White was a girl, and as such, she could not be valued for her "labour" within a capitalist patriarchy.[93] Rather, it was her job to remain passive, to consume rather than to produce.

It is likely that her later feeling of being able to produce only if she did *not* get paid was a direct outgrowth of the "seed" which this episode had "sown." She described her anxieties connected to some freelance work she was doing: "Impotence, fear of failure, also very likely guilt that I am asking too much money for it" (D, 1:145). These feelings help to explain White's need for the diary. She had learned that going public, as it were, was inappropriate for a girl. The diary was a place in which she could "indulge" in "showing off" her writing without fear of recrimination.

The notion that as a child she had been "indulging in" "intoxicating pleasure" is connected to her adult obsession with feces. The first things that she wrote about her initial analytical session were "Constipation" and "Great deal about faeces " (D, 1:39). She expounded on this preoccupation in her "Analysis Diary" for April 1938:

C[arroll] says I put very high value on faeces. From my dream says "35,000 dollars for them" (because I heard someone offering this sum for some information from me to my literary agent while I was giving birth to a bag of faeces) ...

... The act of defaecation is important, pleasurable and highly satisfying to me [...]

Now, if I really think of my work as faeces, why does the act of writing cause me such distress and misery? ...

Obviously if I really thought writing was shitting, I should be ashamed to admit I enjoyed it, even to myself. I don't of course always "disenjoy" it: often quite enjoy it [...] Must SOMEHOW get my own permission about writing and making money ... (D, 1:129–30)

This passage exemplifies how White used the diary to register her unconscious thoughts and to try to make sense of them through analysis. Her preoccupation with feces was likely leading her doctor and herself as analyst to Freud's theories about the anal zone. On the one hand, White enjoyed defecation, a fact that suggests the tension reduction which comes from successful elimination. On the other hand, she was constipated, which suggests the retention brought about in a child whose toilet training was particularly strict.[94] White was perhaps unconsciously associating her writing with "shitting" as a means of explaining why she was suffering from writer's block: she wanted to write and be intellectually released, but her early educational (as opposed to toilet) training had been punitive, forcing her to retain her words.

White's comment "if I really thought writing was shitting, I should be ashamed to admit I enjoyed it" is borne out by the fact that she *was* ashamed to admit it, because once she did, she would be taking pleasure in her own production, something her father discouraged "On principle." The diary is therefore full of entries to this end; for example, "The real ... thing is the having no pleasure in writing. Because one ought to enjoy using a talent" (D, 1:217). Precisely, "one ought to," but White had been taught not to. Between the two volumes of her published diaries, there are over sixty passages devoted to discussing her writer's block and how it was connected to her father. She admitted: "It is an awful pity that I don't *like* writing. That is my curse. My poor Papa destroyed my natural pleasure in it. . . ."(D, 1:300). At another point, she wrote about a session with her analyst: "He asked quite a lot about the writing jam. I told him again, since it came up about the trouble with my first 'novel' and my father" (D, 2:186).

In destroying her pleasure, her father had instilled in her the patriarchal notion that not only female production but female ambition to produce was to be discouraged and devalued. White's childhood eagerness to display her talent could be considered a kind of ambitiousness. She wrote that when the pupil "asked me if I was learning Greek yet, I said proudly that I knew the first line of the *Iliad* and proceeded to recite,"[95] clearly taking the initiative to flaunt and challenge her abilities.

But the adult White had difficulty accepting her ambitious nature. Recall that with regard to the dining-room crime, which happened just before the half-sovereign episode, she described her artistic attempts thus: "After making a few tentative squiggles and finding it a most delectable surface to draw on, I decided to do something more ambitious."[96] This was precisely how she described Nanda's intentions in writing a full-length novel in *Frost*: "For the most part, she wrote laboured little lyrics ... But now she was projecting something far more ambitious."[97] Each of these three events entailed some form of punishment for the young girl. White received the message that it was inappropriate for her to have ambitious drives, as she acknowledged in a 1941 letter to Thorp: "I shall probably always be a failure which is probably my punishment for having once so desperately wanted to succeed" (HF, 107). And in her diary in 1953 she wondered, "but what *is* my weakness? ... I myself would say ambition ... to excel and above all to be *recognised*" (D, 1:261). White struggled with the desire to reveal herself as a subject while giving in to the more expected desire, which was to conceal herself as object.

With this conflict in mind, we can comprehend the full import of her need expressed at the end of her discussion of feces: "Must SOMEHOW get my own permission about writing and making money." White ostensibly spent her whole life worrying about how other people would perceive her, what kind of woman they would judge her to be. As she stressed, "Oh this fear, fear, fear, fear, fear [...] fear of other people's opinions" (D, 1:157). And clearly, her reflected self-image was a negative one, for it is a "bad" woman who is ambitious and expects to be paid for her intellect. White repressed her desires for production and reward, with writer's block and an inability to work for money as the result.

The purpose of analysis and her diary, however, was, as she put it, to "get [her] own permission about writing and making money," and she granted herself "permission" through subversive strategies. In writing *Frost* for Hopkinson's approval, she had stressed that the work "had all the feeling of a boring, disagreeable task." Just as Woolf conceived her work in terms of a duty, so White was able to deny that she was engaging in something pleasurable by transforming it into a task that must be done. In this way, her writing was legitimized as something necessary, and she was able to negotiate traditional and modern behavioural codes, challenging while heeding Smith's womanly-woman narrative. Her subversive conception of her writing was further encoded in her tendency to feel guilty for not doing it. Though she suffered from debilitating blocks, she presented herself as a conscientious worker who resented having to call in sick, as it were. The diary is full of passages to this end, such as, "Guilt, of course, at NOT working" (D, 1:252). White appropriated Chodorow's notion of women having fluid ego boundaries and thus seeing themselves in relational terms: she was determined to sacrifice herself, but to her work rather than to other people.

But White was and remained a true "grappler" in Smith's sense of the term. She explained her predicament in 1935: "This guilt about my writing: distaste for it: guilt at not doing it: fearful anxiety connected with it" (D, 1:56). Her difficulties, both practically and psychologically, stemmed from the fact that she spent her life wrestling with the paradox of simultaneously wanting to write and not wanting to write. She wanted to please others, but she also wanted to please herself. She wanted to conform to what was expected of her, but she wanted to rebel against these prescriptives. She wrote a romance plot, but she consistently tried to go beyond it to a modernist one. These seemingly irreconcilable differences were tied to her father and, as we shall see, to God.

PORTRAIT OF THE ARTIST AS A CATHOLIC

From the opening of her diary we discover that concomitant with her analysis of her father, White was preoccupied with the other Father whom she had forsaken almost ten years before. If her account of her father is Freudian, her treatment of her father-God is Joycean. Both Joyce and White were preoccupied with their f/Fathers. Just as we have heard White affirm, "One thing is sure, the two most important things in my life ... the Catholic religion and my father" (D, 2:38), so in his autobiography *My Brother's Keeper*, Joyce's brother Stanislaus Joyce states: "The two dominant passions of my brother's life were to be love of father and of fatherland ... Both passions stemmed, I believe, from his ancient love of God."[98]

Joyce offers, especially in *Portrait of the Artist* and *Ulysses*, the most canonized version of how Catholicism has been translated into modernist art. But his version is one-sidedly male. White, in *Frost in May* and in her diaries, presents the necessary correlative of a female version. She made it clear that with *Frost* she was reworking Joyce's fiction to tell how a Catholic upbringing impacted on a girl's becoming the artist as a young woman. Immediate comparisons between *Frost* and *Portrait* are obvious, since both Stephen Dedalus and Nanda Grey (personae for Joyce and White) are raised by Catholic families and educated at Catholic schools, and both struggle to develop their artistic selves against hostile figures and institutions of authority.

In the opening pages of *Frost*, White alludes to *Ulysses*. On the way to the convent, Nanda and her father share a horse-bus with an Irish woman named Bridget Mulligan, who invokes the Buck Mulligan appearing at the start of *Ulysses*. Whereas Buck accuses Stephen of torturing his dying mother by refusing to pray with her – "You could have knelt down, damn it"[99] – Bridget urges Nanda to avoid such cruelty to her father: "I'll say five decades for you this very night that you may grow up a good Catholic and a comfort to your father."[100]

The first night at the convent, Nanda attends prayers and asks God to make her a "proper Catholic like the others." But during the litany, "She was flooded with a feeling that was half ... delight in the beauty of the words, pronounced, not in her father's harsh English accent, but with an Italian softness."[101] Similarly, while a young boy at Clongowes Wood, Stephen associates the tolling of a bell with the words of a nursery rhyme: "A tremor passed over his body. How sad and how beautiful! He wanted to cry quietly but not for himself: for the words"[102] Their attraction to aesthetics here is significant, for even from this early moment both Nanda and Stephen are unconsciously struggling with something beyond God, something which suggests the artistic direction they will intuitively follow.

Joyce's call to art is reflected in Stephen, who has no trouble choosing between art and God. He heeds "the call of life to his soul not the dull gross voice of the world of duties and despair, not the inhuman voice that had called him to the pale service of the altar. An instant of wild flight had delivered him and the cry of triumph which his lips withheld cleft his brain."[103] Stephen's artistic calling comes from the vision of a pagan bird-girl he has on a beach, one that he accepts "in an outburst of profane joy."[104] And at the end of *Portrait*, as he goes off to create, he asks for artistic direction from his mythological father, Daedalus: "Old father, old artificer, stand me now and ever in good stead."[105]

In contrast, we have seen through the example of Nanda how a young White tried unsuccessfully to reconcile art with religion. Not only was her book taken away from her before it was finished, but she enjoyed no support from her father, who in fact disowned her. Rose, in "Antonia White: Portrait of the Artist as a Dutiful Daughter," concludes that Stephen and Joyce succeeded in the bid for artistic freedom while Nanda and White failed "to achieve artistic maturity and authority."[106] If on the surface this appears the case, on a deeper level we can see how both artists maintained attachments to the father and to God, and both achieved varying degrees of artistic and personal freedom.

White recounted in an article that she wrote for *Born Catholics* how she had been led into the Catholic faith when her father converted in 1906: "I was instructed for several months before I was received ... I learnt eagerly and conscientiously. My father said it was true and that was all that mattered."[107] White was forced as a child to follow her father's orders and exile herself from her Protestant background. As an adult, however, she claimed the autonomy to choose her own state of spiritual exile: "I continued up to the age of 22 to be a fervent Catholic, often finding the Church's discipline galling, but never questioning the fundamental truths of the faith ... It was not till I had married and left home that I began to be worried and to question the Church's claims to be the one infallible repository of truth." This questioning was inspired by art: "The general climate of the 1920's, the scepticism, the almost idolatrous devotion to art got under my skin" (HF, 155). By 1925 she had decided to stop practising: "All that I can say here is that I reached a stage where I was convinced it was intellectually dishonest to believe in God." If Nanda's childhood struggles had been over the impossibility of reconciling religion and art, White's adult renunciation of the church was due to the fact that "art was beginning to appear the highest and purest of human activities."[108] Consequently, "the artists came to replace the saints" in her "private pantheon" (HF, 155).

Her motives echo Joyce's. Stanislaus Joyce tells us that his brother's "breakaway from Catholicism" was based on his "imperative that he should save his real spiritual life from being overlaid and crushed by a false one that he had outgrown. He believed that poets ... were the repositories of the genuine spiritual life of their race."[109] White's and Joyce's rejections were specifically modernist gestures, for as White indicated, she was influenced by the "scepticism" of the times to conclude that God was "dead." She would later acknowledge, "There can never have been so much unrest in the Church since the days of Modernism" (D, 2:177).

In leaving the church for art, White was finally able to respond to the "wild flight" that symbolized Stephen's artistic calling on the beach. And not only did he dream of creating "a living thing, new and soaring," but he himself was determined to take to the wind in the spirit of the modernist in exile, as he informs his friend Davin: "When the soul of a man is born in this country there are nets flung at it to hold it back from flight. You talk to me of nationality, language, religion. I shall try to fly by those nets."[110] At the end of *Portrait*, Stephen, like Joyce himself, supposedly leaves everyone and everything behind as he flies away. He had earlier announced to Cranly: "I will not serve that in which I no longer believe whether it call itself my home, my fatherland or my church: and I will try to express myself in some mode of life or art as freely as I can and as wholly as I can, using for my defence the only arms I allow myself to use – silence, exile, and cunning."[111] Though White would never leave her English homeland, she did for a time "fly by" the net of religion which her father had "flung" at her as a child.

And yet, despite all appearances of successful escape, neither Joyce nor White was able to fly high or far. For one thing, just as White was unable to escape her dead father, so she was haunted by the presence of her "dead" God. Though "the artists came to replace the saints," she had not sufficiently laid God to rest to become an artist herself; her writer's block was as connected to him as to her father. One of her earliest diary entries supports this view: "Last week an intermittent headache and malaise, probably psychogenic in origin, made excellent 'reasons' [for not writing]. Again I feel 'if only' ... if only I could make up my mind once and for all about religion" (D, 1:24).

She made up her mind in 1940, when she returned to the church in a move likely motivated by the threat of World War II and the end of her three-year analysis. In September 1938 she noted with startling self-absorption: "The beginning of the last week of analysis [...] War suspense everywhere. Irony if just as I am through with analysis, war breaks out." She had hoped her doctor would marry her – "Have decided that the best Dennis [Carroll] can do for me is – *literally* – to 'make an honest woman of me'" (D, 1:154) – but of course he did not, and analysis ended. The fact that she would no longer have this man to guide her may have inspired her to look in the direction of God, for surely no one would be more qualified to "make an honest woman" of her than he.

On 22 July, in what would be her last diary entry before the war, White described having "a great many blank spaces" in her life (D, 1:165). After returning to this book in November, on 31 December she summarized the year 1939: "Today last day of year. It has been full of 'events.' A severe operation, the war, my mother's death on Dec 17th. One can only plan one's life in a very general way for next year"

(D, 1:171). This is the first that reference White made to her mother's death. That it affected her deeply will be discussed later on; for it was only later that she herself realized its impact. Recall White's acknowledgment that "people often don't record the most important things that happen to them in their private journals," a sign here that she was the unreliable modernist narrator.

Her diary entries for 1940, between January and June, discuss her writing, but are largely taken up with information about the war. White also summed up her life at this time in a letter to Thorp, but in contrast to her negative tone, cited above (again the unreliable narrator), she implied that she had been living in a state of optimism: "The war broke out just when I'd pieced my life together again, had arrived at some mental stability and was doing very well as a free-lance journalist. Home, jobs, money went literally overnight" (HF, 27). Taken together, these factors suggest that, psychologically, White would have been receptive to the idea of being comforted, supported, or renewed by the religion which had been thrust upon her younger self.

Her ambivalent need for this God came to a head in 1940, when she embarked on what would become her road to reconversion by way of her letters to Thorp. He was a former Jesuit novice who had written to White in November in admiration of *Frost in May*. The two continued to correspond, and within only two months, White was inspired to return to the church. Her diary remained virtually untouched during this time, Thorp proving a particular drain on her time and energy. Her letters to him served as a kind of surrogate diary, being as intimate and meditative in tone and content. White would later remark in her foreword to *The Hound and the Falcon*: "Reading over my journals for that time, I found disappointingly little about what had been my most intense preoccupation. Everything vital, I realised, had gone into my correspondence with 'Peter'" (HF, xviii). Surely it was this focus that made her later exclaim over the published extracts, "Had forgotten it wasn't my diary." And it is what makes these diary-letters worthy of examination.

The published correspondence is one-sidedly White's. Beginning with her first response to Thorp, she explained that Catholicism informed her secular sensibilities. Earlier, in 1936 she had admitted, "All my life I shall see things in the Catholic idiom though I shall probably never again be a practising Catholic" (D, 1:74). This sentiment was reiterated to Thorp: though she had given up practising, she still found herself "automatically taking the Catholic point of view and defending the Catholic position and instinctively using Catholic imagery and terms in thought and speech. Yet it is very much a case of *Odi et Amo*" (HF, 1). She mentioned the influence of George Santayana

(1863–1952), the philosopher who argues that the church is poetically rather than literally true (*HF*, 2). Joyce was similarly intrigued by the poetic, ritualistic elements of the church, rather than its literal aspects. Stanislaus Joyce quotes his brother to this end: "The Mass on Good Friday seems to me a very great drama." He stresses, "The chant and words of Judas or Peter on Palm Sunday, '*Etsi omnes scandalizati fuerint in te, ego numquam scandalizabor*', moved him profoundly."[112]

When White returned to the church at the end of 1940, it was a Santayanan hand that initially guided her back. She recalled the Christmas of 1940: "I thought I would go to Midnight Mass, for the first time since I had given up my religion. I wanted to go simply for its beauty, as I might have gone to a performance of Verdi's *Requiem*."[113] White, however, found more than just beauty on this return trip: "Several people were waiting their turn for Confession. Suddenly, as if some invisible person were pushing me, I found myself, quite against my will, taking my place in the line. I ordered my body to get up and walk out of the church; it simply refused to obey. When my turn came, I automatically went into the confessional."[114] She went back on Christmas morning and took Communion, and by January she had "tentatively begun to practise again"(*HF*, 44).

Although White asserted that there was "some invisible person" pushing her into the confessional, it is likely that this "person" was the conflated spirit of her father and Thorp. She explicitly associated them: "But it is true that, if my father were still alive, he would be only three years older than you are" (*HF*, 88). She recognized the degree to which Thorp contributed to her reconversion: "As to my return, yes, I am sure you were very much an instrument of it. I can't say the only one, though of course I can't know!" (*HF*, 60). While her father brought her into Catholicism as a child, Thorp, a father figure, encouraged her to return as an adult – but note the distinction that White's reconversion, unlike her conversion, was something that she had decided for herself.

If White associated Thorp with her father, it can further be seen how she associated her father with God. In particular, her anxiety about disappointing her father was manifested in her certainty that she would disappoint God as well. Immediately after her reconversion, she told Thorp: "Oh, I know I shall have endless doubts, reserves, difficulties and rebellions. But I think you will know the extraordinary pleasure of simply being able to say, when people ask you what you are: 'I am a Catholic'" (*HF*, 46). She was able to define herself according to the image that her father had constructed for her in childhood, but again it must be emphasized that White was this time complicit in the image; she was deliberately fashioning her present identity out of the fragments of her past one. As always, this identity was not fixed, so that the first part of her statement was proven true when her "doubts, reserves, difficulties and rebellions" began almost immediately. Though she reconverted early on in the correspondence, the dialectic tone of her subsequent letters makes it clear that her faith was not yet fully decided upon. She wrote as much about her past problems with religion as her present and future ones. They are registered in terms of the church's attitudes towards sex, art, and authority.

Writing in her diary in the early sixties, she explained how her father and God were fused in her conception of male authority. This realization was brought about by the analysis she had undergone in the thirties: "Analysis had done one great thing for me by showing that my attitude to the Catholic Church was deeply bound up with my attitude to my father, who, far more than my instructors, had been the 'authority' on whose word I had accepted it as true."[115] Her father had inspired her not only to accept the religion as "true" but to accept it with fear. As has been seen, despite the fact that he was dead, she continued to feel threatened by his authority.

White's return to the church meant that she once again had this other Father to appease as well. For she had always associated the two fathers as one, conflating familial and religious authority in her conception of male domination. Referring to her father, she "felt that he only loved me when he was pleased with me." Similarly, "The way God is 'put over' to me in the Christian religion is so much the idea of an omnipotent being who only loves you when you please him and is exceedingly angry with you when you don't and, if you are not careful, will punish you not only in this world but eternally in the next" (D, 2:159). Contemplating her father's power over her, she wondered, "Is that because a father can become such an idol, such a representative of God on earth?" (D, 1:216).

White linked her writer's block to her father, but God was also an obstacle: "I would say the two 'physical' causes of my alienation from the Church were (1) its attitude towards sex [...] and (2) the fear that, as a writer, I should have to write nothing but 'safe' books" (HF, 58). After discussing her religious doubts with Father Hugh, she reiterated, "I told him God the Father was my great stumbling block" (HF, 102). Still, many years later she submitted to this force: "For a fortnight I have not attempted to work on my book [...] If God does not wish me to, that is that. The old problem – is it wrong to write my kind of book at all?" (D, 2:94). God's "wish" and her father's became the same wish of deterrence. White, however, could also reconcile her art with religion, conceding: "I can in my heart renounce neither religion nor art: I can only try and combine the two in some mixture that suits a mixed nature" (HF, 118). For this reason, then, she was able to assert in 1943: "Any art I have is inextricably rooted in Catholicism" (*D*, 1:180).

So, too, was Joyce's art. White believed that Joyce was never free of his God, and that the mode of art he chose to express himself in was a Catholic one. Discussing him in a letter to Thorp, she concurred: "I too was profoundly disturbed and influenced by *Portrait of the Artist* [...] [H]e has transformed all his torments, physical and mental, into art." But this art was grounded in religion, as she emphasized: "What I think is interesting is the way that, for all his efforts, he never can get away from Catholicism and that all his work could be interpreted as the friction between the odi and amo" (*HF*, 115). Recall that in her first letter, White had described how she had used "Catholic imagery and terms in thought and speech," and that this was a "case of *Odi et Amo*."

Joyce was ambivalent about God and his father in both his art and his life. Richard Ellmann in his biography tells us that in 1902 Joyce's impoverished father, John Joyce, had "urged" James "to seek a clerkship in Guinness's brewery" so that he could be "supported by his gifted son".[116] James ignored this plea and two years later eloped with Nora Barnacle to Zurich, where his destiny as a writer slowly began to unfold. This elopement proved to be one of the most painful episodes in John Joyce's life, as he made clear in a letter to his son: "I need not tell *you* how your miserable mistake [the elopement] affected my already well crushed feelings ... You know I did all in my power to forward your every wish ... So you can well understand *my feelings* when I discovered my dream so ruthlessly dispelled, my hopes – proud hopes – shattered."[117]

Like White's father, Joyce's "kicked up blue hell" about his son's writing, complaining that James was "an out and out ruffian without the spark of a gentleman about him."[118] And like White, Joyce remained preoccupied with his father's opinion of him and constantly sought his approval, especially of his writing. When *Portrait* was to be released in 1916, for instance, Joyce sent Harriet Shaw Weaver a list of eleven people to receive first copies. John Joyce's name appeared at the top.[119] Joyce's attachment to religion remained equally strong, even though he had long ago forsaken it. In 1905 he wrote to Stanislaus from Trieste that an English teacher "says I will die a Catholic because I am always moping in and out of the Greek Churches and am a believer at heart."[120]

It was a state of *odi et amo* that informed White's sense of self when she was in exile from God and helped to bring her back "home" to him. Though we have heard Stephen say he wanted to fly by the nets of "nationality, language, and religion," White drew attention to how all three are interconnected, making Stephen's – and Joyce's – escape something of an impossible dream. She made it clear, for instance, that for Catholics, the church and the state are one. In *Frost*, Nanda's best friend, Leonie, remarks that "Catholicism isn't a religion, it's a nationality."[121] Not surprisingly, then, when White's faith was gone, she, like Stephen, felt homeless. But her status as a modernist in exile was, like Joyce's, an ambiguous one, as White wrote of her faith: "It is like one's native language and, though one may have become denationalised, one cannot help reverting to it and even thinking in its terms" (*HF*, 1). She admitted soon after: "Of course I long to be part of something as one may long for a language and a fatherland," and she described her return to the Church in patriotic terms: "I cling to the faith because it is old, organised, tested and my natural language" (*HF*, 9, 99–100).

The idea that Catholicism is a nationality is reflected in Joyce to the extent that he experienced not only *odi and amo* towards his religion but towards his homeland. His inability to get away from his religion was equalled by his preoccupation with the social and political climate of Ireland. And though he wrote from the position of exile, Dublin served as the setting for most of his fiction. Further, it is possible to understand why Joyce infused his oeuvre with the subject and language of Catholicism: in White's opinion, one's faith is "like" one's "native language," and so it would follow that Joyce's faith – however ambivalent – was grounded in his nationality and would be expressed in this "native language."

White used her native Catholic language to artistic ends, offering in her diary the concepts of epiphany and impersonality that inform so much of Joyce's work. Ellmann tells us that as Joyce's "faith in Catholicism tottered, a counter-process began: his faith in art … grew great." While Joyce was a student at university, "It was becoming clearer to him that, of the two ways of leaving the Church that were open to him, denial and transmutation, he would choose the second. He would retain faith, but with different objects."[122] This process is most obviously realized in his secularization of the epiphany, initially outlined by a "young" Stephen in *Stephen Hero*: "By an epiphany he meant a sudden spiritual manifestation, whether in the vulgarity of speech or of gesture or in a memorable phase of the mind itself." It is the function of the artist rather than the priest to deliver, or interpret, such messages.[123] These epiphanies are a significant structural device in Joyce's work, a succession of holy moments on which the lives and thoughts of his characters turn. Joyce never actually rejected religion; rather, he adapted it to meet his artistic ends.

White's version of epiphany can be detected in her letter to Thorp in which she affirmed: "I do believe that, once one gets a taste for the 'Moment of Truth,' you find it has a quality far more exciting than any romanticism, however fervent and charming" (*HF*, 139). Like Joyce's, her "moment" involves a "sudden" awareness or an instant of profound psychological insight. Her diary, in its inscription of the analytic process, is necessarily replete with epiphanies in that they are the logical outcome of concentrated explorations of "moments of truth."

A good example is found in her diary-letters when she tried to discover the moment of truth about her reconversion from a psychological perspective: "The psychologists would presumably say that Catholicism was one of the factors in my life with which I had failed to come to terms ... Obviously the Catholic Church would be very mixed up for me with my father, who was directly responsible for my becoming a Catholic in the first place. Analysis convinced me without any shadow of a doubt that my ambivalent attitude of unconscious love and hate towards him was one of the prime factors of my neurosis. Therefore I would naturally project into my attitude towards the Church, particularly such a very authoritative Church, the same mixture of love and hate, submissiveness and rebellion." White went on to note that having supposedly reconciled herself to her father, "reconciliation with the Church became a possibility." In true Freudian fashion, she admitted that her return might be "a regression in face of a conflict too difficult to sustain alone or it might be yet another stage in the cure" (HF, 160–1). In this way, analysis contributed to her spiritual and psychological enlightenment.

In addition to epiphany, both Joyce and White advocated a detached position for the artist. Stephen Dedalus's credo that the successful artist should remain detached, "invisible, refined out of existence, indifferent, paring his fingernails,"[124] is echoed by White when she asserts: "Of course we must try to get rid of our egotism [...] I want to love God and not to hate myself but gradually become detached from and indifferent to myself"(HF, 66); and "Humility, detachment, recollection and discipline are extremely necessary for the artist – as necessary as for the saint" (HF, 118).

It is this shared sensibility of detachment which has been noticed by the few critics who observe a similarity at all between the two writers. In her introduction to Frost, Elizabeth Bowen considers that the only analogy to White's passages "is to be found in Joyce's Portrait." It is specifically because of stylistic detachment that this analogy applies, for "We are shown the school only through Nanda's eyes – there is no scene from which she is off stage. At the same time there is no impressionistic blurring, none of the distortions of subjectivity: Lippington is presented with cool exactness."[125] Likewise, in a 1969 article for the Times Literary Supplement, Samuel Hynes refers to the "cold objectivity" and the "aloofness that prevails" in White's fiction.[126] And in her introduction to the section on the novelist in The Gender of Modernism, Jane Marcus discusses White's use of the third-person "she" to narrate her four autobiographical novels: "White's narrative suppression of the 'I,' inside the very discourses in which subjectivity and I-narratives are the accepted form, is a splendid subversion of the trap that catches the woman writer in narcissism or complaint and then renders her discourse trivial." White "enacts Stephen Dedalus's aesthetic, remaining indifferent and above her story."[127]

Dedalus's aesthetic informs not only White's fiction but also her diary. She used this journal as a space in which to construct such an aesthetic, and to enact it as well. Although she wrote her diary in the first person, I have already suggested that her use of the psychoanalytic method enabled her to present her psyche in an objective way, for she filtered her thoughts through her own and her analysts' detached "scientific" interpretations. In a different sense, she suppressed the "I" within her diary during her relationship with Benedicta de Bezer, who was, according to Chitty, "a notorious Lesbian" and religious maniac (D, 1:183–4).

For this relationship, White kept a separate diary entitled "1947 Benedicta." It is a small book in which she made uncharacteristically brief entries in point form. In testimony to her religious zealousness, she tended to write the name of the saint's day at the beginning of each entry; for example, "Fri 7 March St Thomas Aquinas" (D, 1:185). This and other entries were dedicated to the saints in question rather than to White herself, so that she seems distanced from her own text. The diary is also impersonal to the extent that, unlike her candour in other volumes, White was reticent in discussing the physical nature of her relationship with de Bezer. The only comment she offered is a cryptic one: "Sex and the fingernail" (D, 1:185).

White's detached narrative is further evidenced by de Bezer's seeming takeover of the diary. A few examples of White's one-to-two-line entries illuminate this dominance: "She has a terrible day"; "She sends me her Gethsemane picture"; "She has *Adoro Te*"; "She arrives here in a terrible state. She gives me the Samurai sword" (D, 1:184–5). Though White used the first-person "I" to refer to herself, it is the third-person "she," Benedicta, who emerges as the main subject of the diary. White's "I" becomes the object, not the subject, of the discourse, confirming DuPlessis's notion that the diarist often writes a concealing narrative in her desire to please.

Throughout her recording of her other relationships, White had maintained a firm sense of narrative "I." With de Bezer, however, she became subsumed not only by "she" but by "we"; for example, "We stay here: it is raining. She brings Pommard '37 and daffodils. We are very happy. We talk again of the hesychast prayer. We talk about her family." Within this entry, for 21 March, White went on to state, simply and with no explanation: "I burn my notebooks" (D, 1:186). These were the early diaries previously mentioned. Just as remarkable is this entry for 21 March 1948: "A year ago today, at B[enedicta]'s instigation I burnt my first two notebooks" (D, 1:202). It is incredible that, as a writer who had been preserving these notebooks for years, White would not offer any explanation of why she had suddenly burned two such documents.

One reason why she destroyed them, though, might have had to do with the "we." Perhaps de Bezer wanted some kind of symbolic ritual to prove that they were now a unit, a "we."[128] This interpretation draws attention to Chodorow's concept that women have fluid ego boundaries. Even within the supposedly egocentric space of the diary, White was exhibiting her interdependent nature. Within a short time, though, this "we" became too threatening for her, and she extricated herself from the liaison. Although women are relational, it is imperative that they erect some boundaries around their selves in order to prevent a total collapse of independent selfhood.

"ANTONIA WHITE" REALIZED

After leaving de Bezer, White began her second period of analysis, with the untrained Dorothy Kingsmill. During this time, her diaries were neglected: the book she kept between June 1947 and February 1948 is less than one-quarter full (book 19), and her next book contains only seven written pages (book 20). Just as her letters to Thorp replaced the diary in 1940–41, so White's letters to Kingsmill did here. Because Kingsmill specialized in interpreting dreams, White became a prolific recorder of her nightly dreams, often mailing them to her analyst the next day. Those that were not posted were kept in a special "dream book" for Kingsmill.[129]

Dorothy Kingsmill helped to release the writer's block that White had struggled against – it was this possibility that had inspired her to re-enter analysis (D, 1:213). During the autumn of 1948 she finally finished the novel she that had begun fifteen years earlier. Her daughter Lyndall notes of this time: "She had decided, with Dorothy's help, that her creative side was her feminine side, not the masculine as she had always imagined, which was instead the side trying to block her writing."[130] Referring in her diary to the novel, White acknowledged: "Where D. *did* help, was in making me see my relation to my mother" (D, 1:214). White was able to trace her writing self through her maternal lineage, detaching herself from her father and reclaiming control of her previously exiled body/text.

Before we turn to this development, it bears noting that the issue of paternity also preoccupied Joyce. When he wrote to Stanislaus in 1905 announcing the birth of his son, he stated, "I think a child should be allowed to take his father's or mother's name at will on coming of age." He followed this observation with what has become one of the most famous comments elicited by Stephen Dedalus in *Ulysses*: "Paternity is a legal fiction."[131] Despite this claim, towards the end of his life Joyce, who had eloped with Nora Barnacle to the horror of his father, married her in what was surely a symbolic gesture to him. The ceremony was held on 4 July 1931, his late father's birthday, a choice that Ellmann appropriately suggests was made for purposes of atonement.[132] Joyce explicitly added his personal signature to the law of paternity when he told his solicitor: "I cannot explain very clearly why I wish my son and grandson to bear my name. Nevertheless I do wish it."[133]

If Joyce came to believe that paternity is not so much a "legal fiction" as a "legal reality," White went on to prove just how much of a myth it really is. In her autobiography she tells us: "My mother wanted me to be called Cynthia. My father pointed out that such a romantic name would sound absurd with such a prosaic surname as Botting." Not surprisingly, her father won, and "In the end I was given a name which at that time was universally spelt Irene but which my father insisted on being spelt, as in Greek, Eirene."[134] White grew up despising this name: "I rejected my first name – Eirene Botting – it is the first time for years that I have dared to write it – because it felt so terrible to me, so degrading."

Both first and last names were attributable to her father, so in rejecting his names, she in effect rejected identification with him. She went on to wonder: "It is odd that I take 'Tony,' the name by which all my friends know me, from my mother's nickname for me as a child and her own name of White, since all through my childhood and after I hated, despised and rejected all of my mother and would like to have been only my father's child" (*D*, 1:59).

She realized, of course, that she could not possibly have "rejected all" of her mother, for she deliberately chose to define her adult self, and specifically her writing self, by the two names directly associated with her mother. Years later she recorded of her analyst: "He suggested that my writing side may really come from her [my mother], and I am inclined to agree ... her imaginative, intuitive side [...] quite different from my father's" (*D*, 2:159). White's first creative piece to appear in print was published in 1928 under the pseudonym Antonia White. She rejected what Alice Jardine has called the patriarchal system of "naming, controlling," asserting her right to self-determination.

White slid from paternal to maternal identification in other ways as well. Although she did return to Catholicism and thus to her father's faith, the church she went back to was associated more with her mother than her father. She felt that it was "probably significant" that her reconversion happened "in the Carmelite church to which I had gone so often as a child and had a special affection for. It occurs to me now that this church was one to which I went more often with my mother than with my father." When her father was there, she was "always painfully aware of his presence," whereas her mother's "much looser attitude towards religion" "was a great relief" to her. White goes on: "When she was alive her vagueness and her irritating ways made it very difficult for me to be with her. But now she is dead, I can see what a lot of remarkable qualities she had ... real sweetness of disposition, an extraordinary capacity for forgiveness, a kind of independence in judging [...] She made absolutely no demands on me"(D, 1:174).

With these thoughts in her mind, and with some help from Kingsmill, White was able to appreciate both her mother and her writing self in a positive way, and finish the book. And in addition to coming to terms with her biological mother, she confronted her biblical mother, Eve. In 1941, she had expressed a basic acceptance of Catholic ideology: "It is a profound truth that makes Eve the *Channel* of the fall" (HF, 86). It seems that White had identified herself with this original mother by accepting some inherited responsibility for "the fall." More specifically, she seems to have been connecting Eve's sin with the sin of her writing.

But by 1949 White was slowly coming to reject these implications. Still in contact with de Bezer, she recorded a conversation that they had about her convent novel: "Now B. comes out with the very interesting idea that, in the famous book episode ... part of me thought my father judged rightly. Therefore, since he pronounced me guilty, I must remain under sentence for ever ... What B. is trying to convince me of is that I am NOT GUILTY." White returned to Eve: "To be 'NOT GUILTY' in Benedicta's sense doesn't mean I have a beautiful nature or am not liable at any moment to behave disgracefully. It simply means that I am not responsible for the Fall of Man [...] Somehow the unconscious has to accept the 'NOT GUILTY' verdict" (D, 1:215–6). White was here writing beyond the ending of perhaps the greatest patriarchal narrative in history, replacing it with a modernist ending in which women may empower themselves to "name and control," as Jardine would have it, their own presence in religious and cultural discourses.

In early 1950 White received a grant from the Royal Literary Fund, and her response to this award makes it clear that she was, if only for a while, able to "accept the 'NOT GUILTY' verdict": "The extraordinary change that has come over me [...] Among other things it [the grant] must have symbolised a pardon of some kind: an official permission from Society to go on writing" (D, 1:218). And this was precisely what she did. In an unprecedented bout of productivity, having finished her second novel she went on to write and publish two more in 1952 and 1954 respectively and a collection of short stories in the latter year.

And yet in a July entry she returned to the issue of the grant: "Now, gradually, society is forgiving me and encouraging me to write. But can I accept forgiveness or – as so often – does something in me prefer to sulk and grieve and say 'No. It's too late – You see what you've done to me'" (D, 1:220). Though she enjoyed a few years of productivity, White rescinded her own "pardon" in testament to her lifelong "grappling" with her identity. Following the three novels, her guilt towards her father and her preoccupation with God's will returned with a vengeance. These forces were likely reawakened by the novels in question, for within them White had confronted painful memories of her past, especially concerning her father, God, and sexuality. The fourth, *Beyond the Glass*, takes Clara/White up to and through her incarceration in Bethlem. The novel she began after this one was supposed to deal with her father's death, but it was never completed. The re-emerging power of father and God necessarily brought with it the return of White's writer's block. She would begin several manuscripts, all of which remained unfinished at her death.

White's diaries became virtually clogged with entries documenting her frustration and agony at not being able to produce more fiction. In compensation, she busied herself with crossword puzzles and over-spending on home decorating, described meticulously in her journal, a practice that underscores its modernist status as the site of the mundane as well as the profound. There was, however, one kind of work she could do. It was during these later years that she worked diligently as a translator. In June 1955 she justified not working on a novel with "the excuse that in the next three months I have undertaken to translate some 90,000 words" (D, 1:286). While this figure is daunting, White seems not to have had to translate; rather, she could not write her own material – her use of the word "excuse" implies that she turned to translations as a strategy of procrastination.

She could do translations because they did not require invention. Throughout her diary, she has made it clear that her writer's block was due to the fact that her material was personal, and that she was unable to write anything else: "I feel the only bearable way to write would be never again to write about myself. But in both my projected things I have no alternative but to introduce myself" (D, 1:95). "About writing this book [*The Lost Traveller*], what I *think* I am worrying about is this question of using my own life as material. It seems too good not to use, I don't feel the power to create something new, yet when I come to try and use it, I find it very hampering" (D, 1:136–7). She lamented: "I think I tried rather feebly to *invent* a subject. Then with relief, also with guilt, fell back on the old autobiographical subject" (D, 1:161). The reason she needed to "fall back" on this material was that "I know writing too is a way of 'putting myself across.' I *want* to do that" (D, 1:162). White needed to communicate the story of herself. She wanted to take the fragments that made up this story, especially those fragments of diary in which it was captured, and fuse them into a unified pattern of selfhood. She wanted to articulate who she was in a narrative that would reveal herself as a subject, claiming the authority to speak from her social and diaristic margins.

By 1965, admitting to herself that she was unable to produce any more fiction, but needing to "put herself across," White decided to write her autobiography instead. Not surprisingly, just as her novels had brought on writer's block, so did the autobiography. In an effort to release herself from it, in 1966 she began another three years of analysis, first with Dr Galway and then with Dr Ployé. As she had with her other analysts, White discussed and recorded in her diary her dreams and her thoughts about her father and God. But added to these was the depression that she felt as an aging woman and an unrecognized writer. From the moment she contemplated writing the autobiography, she felt a "Terror of failure" (D, 2:121). A year later, sixty-five years old, she mourned: "Oh, my life, my life. What a mess. What a failure" (D, 2:152).

Like Woolf, White connected these negative feelings to her sense of failure as a novelist. She wanted to be part of a tradition even as her diary testifies how she was trying to rewrite it. She became increasingly bitter at what she perceived to be her unfair neglect as a writer. While *Frost in May* had been a tremendous success early in her life, *The Lost Traveller* was received with mixed reviews (D, 1:219). Worse still, the reception of *The Sugar House* was "the coldest and most hostile" that White had ever experienced (D, 1:245). Though *Beyond the Glass* received "some amazingly good reviews" (D, 1:283), they were not enough to bring White the recognition – and financial rewards – she had been hoping for. She informed her diary in 1954: "But I'm 55 now and would like a status ... to be mentioned when other novelists are being discussed in articles etc." (D, 1:276). She reiterated: "All I can do is try and fight against my 'evil inclinations' – the usual one of resenting I never get even a mention among modern novelists. It is all Iris Murdoch, Muriel Spark, Kingsley Amis, Lawrence Durrell etc. etc." White's anger stemmed from the fact that she believed she was deserving of a place in literary history, feeling that she was "as good as" the modern novelists listed above (D, 2:91). And yet her sense of self as "evil" for having ambitious "inclinations" recalls her earlier denigration of herself as "ambitious" and thus doomed to failure as punishment. Once again we can see how she struggled to accept and reject traditional definitions of women and her desires to reveal and conceal.

In addition to the psychological difficulties of aging, White documented the physical ones. In 1968 she underwent a cataract operation, which affected her ability to write. And a year later she recorded from a hospital bed: "Shall have been here a fortnight tomorrow with pleurisy and pneumonia [...] It's an unexpected blow" (D, 2:207). In January 1979 she had an operation which proved that she had cancer of the rectum (D, 2:303); it was this illness that would kill her just over a year later.

As White aged, so did her friends, and she was saddened at their deaths: "In my own small world, one's friends dying [...] One thinks all the time 'who next?'" (D, 2:246). That she might be "next" was one of her main preoccupations. She became "Increasingly conscious of there not being many more years left and wondering when, where and how it will end" (D, 2:240). In 1979 she "had to think seriously about what's left of my future and of my death. It cannot be more than a very few years before I die." In fact, it would be less than one. She accepted death: "Only thing is to leave it all in God's hands (D, 2:309).

White seems to have been very little reconciled by the end of her life. Her relationship with both her daughters had improved considerably over the years, but this change was arguably more because she became dependent on them than because she became a "better" mother. And she spent the last part of her life feeling unhappy where her children were concerned. Hopkinson closes her memoir by mentioning some letters that her mother had written to two friends: "But those letters said she felt abandoned by her daughters, which saddens me."[135] In the last year of her life, White stated, "I am more and more conscious of my own sinfulness. How selfish, how cowardly, how self-indulgent, how unloving I have always been" (D, 2:308). She was thus capitulating to the ideologies of the "angel in the house" and the "moral mother." Her last diary entry, written some time in late December 1979, refers to the physical pain that she was suffering; given her remark above, however, it is likely that her agony was emotional as well as physical: "Oh, I want my family close and some sign of painkillers. None after all these hours [...] If only someone could come in and offer a crumb of consolation! But they don't" (D, 2:319).

Perhaps, though, the book in which this passage is written can offer White a posthumous "crumb of consolation." Throughout her life she often lamented the fact that she was able to work productively on the diary but not on novels: "The last 2 of these books have been filled between June 13 and Sept 3 – a period of only 7 weeks [...] If I could turn this on to outside work, I could get quite a lot done [...] This represents roughly ... 21,000 words ... say between [one quarter] and [one third] of a full length novel" (D, 1:153–4).

Though White was here distinguishing between the diary and a novel, she proved how arbitrary this distinction really was: "Take the word 'novel.' – Various things are written, all called 'novels' which in itself means no more than 'something new.' Then critics invent an imaginary abstraction called 'THE NOVEL' and every 'something new' is then dissected to prove that it is or is not 'a novel.' There can never be 'THE NOVEL' because there is no such thing" (book 10). Here, in 1938, White was ahead of the critical times, for she was anticipating the many life-writing scholars of the eighties and nineties, such as Kadar, Mudge, Lensink, and Schenck, who draw attention to the arbitrary, constructed nature of literary genres.

By 1965, reflecting on the idea of writing the autobiography, she realized that it was a good one, because "I don't think I AM a novelist. All my novels are autobiographical" (D, 2:123). While this remark seems to reinscribe the distinction that White had earlier dismissed, within a few months she had returned to the problem of genre specificity. Discussing her difficulties in writing about her parents in the autobiography, she recognized, "It is difficult at this stage not to turn my parents into *fictional characters*, or to *invent* things about my grandparents in Storrington: autobiography I see now is as difficult in its way as a novel" (D, 2:126). Having admitted that her "novels are autobiographical," White then had to contend with the converse fact that her autobiography was becoming "*fictional*." Given this observation, one can see how her diary would be a site on which she fused the fictional and historical, trying, in Schenck's terms, to negotiate "the tension between life and literature ... selfhood and textuality."

White enacts a (post)modernist agenda. She originally set out to be a novelist but was forced to admit that every novel was really autobiographical, so she should just write a "proper" autobiography. But then, just as she was unable to write "proper" novels, so she could not write a "proper" autobiography. Though she wrote her life up to the age of four, the rest of the autobiography is embedded in the diary. She was constantly breaking down the barriers between genres, fusing elements of one into another and thereby creating out of the diary a text that ascribes to Joyce's – and Eliot's – notion of impersonality while it undermines them with notions of female personality.

In 1969 Dr Ployé, White's last analyst, was forced to end her treatment early because of his increasing load of patients. She recorded the impact of this decision: "I said I was quite willing to try and manage on my own. I said it was a shock, but not too bad a shock. He made it obvious that he didn't feel that the treatment was finished – when I said 'It is like an unfinished story' he agreed" (D, 2:203). Though for clearly different reasons, White's ending of analysis resembles Dora's; Freud commented of Dora's case, "The treatment was not carried through to its appointed end."[136] Marcus rightly perceives that by breaking off analysis, Dora "refused to be a character in the story that Freud was composing for her, and wanted to finish it herself." Like Dora, White wanted to finish her story herself. Her lifelong recording of her investigation into her psyche proves that, even after her visits to a doctor's office stopped, her own analysis continued. The story that was left unfinished with one analyst was continued by another, herself, and in this way White claimed the final authority and subject position for her narrative.

Acknowledging that Freud's text is a "fragment," Marcus emphasizes: "It nevertheless remains at the same time a whole in itself and has to stand by itself in its own idiosyncratic way – which is to be simultaneously fragmentary and complete."[137] This comment echoes Drabble's affirmation of White's diary: "the final effect is, oddly, not of fragmentation, but of a powerful urge towards synthesis." Recall that Woolf too had wanted to "achieve in the end, some kind of whole made of shivering fragments." Like *The Waste Land*, White's diary is a text that weaves a pattern out of its fragments, and that affords White the ability to celebrate her fragmentary selfhood while striving for a unified one in the terms suggested by Neuman and Schenck.

White's diary testifies to the life that has been lived, both inside and outside the text. The diary had always been there to console her, to absorb her neuroses, and to reconcile her fractured selves. But above all, it emerges as her most important work, for it alone was sustained for a period of more than fifty years and without inhibition. Its very existence testifies to White's ability to subvert patriarchal and religious domination, for despite her problems with writer's block, she filled forty diary books. She wrote unabashedly about subjects generally considered taboo, including intercourse, masturbation, and sadomasochism. She examined her inability to love her children, recorded her dreams, documented her Freudian analyses, and of course, confronted her parents and God. Antonia White is surely the successful female version of a Stephen Dedalus who wanted to express himself "in some mode of life or art as freely as I can and as wholly as I can."

In 1938 White was trying to write an autobiographical story detailing the breakdown of her third marriage. In her diary she wondered: "What is necessary for this story to turn it from the private case into the universal one? The shadow of madness is, I think necessary, since it is part of the woman's nature. Yet let us eliminate actual case-history madness and see what we have left" (D, 1:124). In eliminating "actual case-history madness" from White's diary, what *we* have left is a major literary achievement.

6 "Keep out / Keep out / Your snooting snout"[1] The Irresistible Diaries of Elizabeth Smart

"Bill said write all the time keep a diary – so here it is" (NS, 5). And here it was that on 6 March 1933 Elizabeth Smart introduced her diary to an as-yet-unidentified audience. Seven years later, on 1 March 1940, she revealed just what this diary had come to represent: "But this my book I carry everywhere, and its blank unwritten pages and shabby cover – its menial use for dancing notes, addresses, and accounts deglamourize it. I must not forget it is my heavenly key – my work – my purpose" (NS, 239–40). Just as White used her diary as a "key to unlock" her life, so Smart similarly used hers.

Elizabeth Smart's "purpose" – her diary – was one that sustained her throughout her adult life. It was so clearly her "work" that towards the end of her life she set about having its extensive volumes published. In 1982 she was working as writer-in-residence at the University of Alberta, and her colleague Alice Van Wart tells us, "While visiting her in her office one day, I noticed on her desk formidable piles of paper, which she informed me were the transcripts of her journals" (NS introd.). After Van Wart expressed an interest in these papers, Smart phoned her a few months later and asked her to edit them. She accepted the proposal, and in 1986 *Necessary Secrets: The Journals of Elizabeth Smart* appeared. Though Smart died in March that year, just before this work was published, Rosemary Sullivan confirms in her biography *By Heart* that Smart had "proofread the manuscript" and "was pleased with it."[2]

Smart's diaries were only the last of many creative projects to be published. Her work first saw the public eye when she was ten years old, an occasion she recalled in a 1984 interview: "First, there was this silly poem. A teacher at school liked it. She was one of those people who inspire you, and I sent it off to an American magazine for children and it was accepted and printed and I got a dollar for it. And then I got inspirations where I'd sit and write quite a few at a time. I produced a whole volume."3 The volume in question, entitled "The Second Edition of The Complete Works of Betty Smart," though not "technically" published, was painstakingly printed by hand by "The Betty Publishing Co. Ltd." in 1929 – Smart was only sixteen. (Many of the pieces in this volume have been included in the posthumously published *Juvenilia*). Smart's "Complete Works," consisting of stories, poems, satires, and drama, is significant because it registers the inception and development of her literary talents and interests. Van Wart, also the editor of *Juvenilia*, describes it as "varied in form, content, and tone; sometimes it is earnest and sometimes playful. It displays a lively imagination, a strong sense of humour, a romantic sensibility and a satiric eye."4 These qualities would inform not only Smart's later fiction but her diaries as well.

Concomitant with her juvenilia, Elizabeth and her sister Jane were keeping journals, private books they called their "Personal Pronouns,"5 which unfortunately have not survived. Nonetheless, it is important to note that Smart was writing a diary from the beginning of her literary career, for it highlights how the boundaries between supposedly private jottings and more finished pieces of art could be blurred. This conclusion is encouraged by the fact that she consistently dated the stories and poems in her juvenilia – dated them in the way a diary entry would be, that is, at the time of composition. In the section she titled "Part Two," from February to March 1928, each story was recorded with the date at the top of the page as if she were making a diary entry for that day; for example "The Birth of a Genius" "Feb. 18th 1928 14 yrs" or "The Little House" "Feb. 22nd 1928 14 yrs"(ESF box 2, f. 2). While the "entries" may be stories she had worked on and revised, their presentation is diaristic. They recall the essays that Woolf dated in her early journals.

The earliest diary preserved, and the volume that opens *Necessary Secrets*, is one that was started primarily to coincide with her new artistic and literary life in London. After finishing high school in 1931, Smart had left her native Ottawa and gone to London with her mother for the purpose of studying music. Home in Canada the following summer, she returned to London in the fall of 1932, without her mother but in the company of her sister Jane and chaperone Susan Somerset. However, Smart's ambition to be a concert pianist was slowly being overtaken by a stronger passion to be a writer. By the end of her second year in London, she had given up music and committed herself to a literary life.

Out of this life would emerge several pieces of fiction, all of them autobiographical. "My Lover John" is a satiric story about male impotency based on an early relationship with Lord John Pentland; "Dig a Grave and Let Us Bury Our Mother" recounts the intensity of her brief affair with Alice Paalen; *By Grand Central Station I Sat Down and Wept* translates her obsession with George Barker into one of the most metaphorically searing works of the twentieth century; and *The Assumption of the Rogues & Rascals* describes her experiences working in and around London while single-handedly raising four children. If her fiction is autobiographical, the corollary is that her life writing is fictional. Or, as Van Wart states, "All her writing was life writing."[6] Referring to Smart's accomplishment in *Rogues & Rascals*, Sullivan suggests that Smart shattered "the safely constructed boundaries between fiction and reality."[7] I would argue that from the beginning of her career – marked by her juvenilia and "Personal Pronouns" – she was learning how to shatter these boundaries.

Within these blurred spaces, Smart was living and writing a modernist life. Drabble, in her "Women Novelists" lecture in 1968, pays tribute to her as an innovative writer. Drabble acknowledges that in novels "today" "there is a vast increase in what one can only call gynaecological literature – the literature of childbirth, breast-feeding, contraception, abortion, and copulation. The voice of the emancipated woman is raising itself." While "Men have always written about sex ... [Women] have been modest and reticent." Focusing on the difficulty of rendering the subject of love in language, Drabble uses Smart's *By Grand Central Station* as an example of a work that has radically and powerfully combined the lyric with the erotic.[8] Smart's novel consequently stands as a work that was ahead of its time.

And so too was her diary. An examination of these journals will reveal how they have been constructed as a literary work that is neither "modest" nor "reticent," and how they have thus inscribed the "*sexualized* writing" which Benstock finds in so many modernist expatriate women's works. My analysis will also explain why the journals were necessary. Unlike the title of Smart's published diaries, which emphasizes that "Secrets" were "Necessary," I believe that communication was the motive behind them.

THIS BELONGS TO BETTY SMART

Smart's archive is housed at the National Library of Canada in Ottawa, and because this is so close to my home in Toronto, I travelled to see her diary manuscripts before I went further afield to examine those of Woolf, White, and Nin. A trip to Ottawa is not a particularly exciting venture for a native Canadian who has already made the requisite pilgrimage to her capital city. But I had never seen Elizabeth Smart's diaries; in fact, I had never examined an archive before. And so Ottawa, Smart's hometown, was transformed in my mind into something of an exotic destination.

Arriving on a Monday morning at the National Library, I was confronted by a security guard who gave me a key to a locker, in which I had to leave everything but paper, pencil, and wallet. I was given a special week's pass and then ushered through a barrier and up to the next floor. I had arranged my research trip through Lorna Knight, the curator of the collection, and after we had introduced ourselves, she led me to a trolley brought out for my benefit, which was lined with the grey corrugated boxes that constituted the filed life of Elizabeth Smart. I was then left alone to work at a large table by a broad window overlooking the Ottawa River.

As I have said, I had never handled archival material, much less the personal diaries of a writer I had admired only through the more impersonal pages of her printed books. Opening the first volume from the first box, I felt waves of excitement and awe. This is her diary, I was thinking; this is one of the books she really held, trusted, loved – "this my book I carry everywhere"; "IT is my heavenly key" – and here was I carrying it to the window, "IT" the "key" to my research. An image of her face came between me and her book, her absolutely gorgeous young face as pictured in one of the photographs in Rosemary Sullivan's biography, a face that is looking away from the camera, seductive but shy. And my wave of euphoria was soon crashing into a rising tide of guilt, for I felt intrusive. If she could not look me in the eye, how could I look her in the diary?

Turning to the river for relief, I was reminded of Andrew Hassam, who explains in "Reading Other People's Diaries" why reading a published diary is an acceptable act while reading the original is not. He contends that diary manuscripts carry with them an inherent "secrecy clause" which tells any potential readers that they have no moral or legal rights to enter the private life.[9] In contrast, the most significant "effect of publication is to alter the status of the reader to that of authorized reader. I feel free to pick up the published diary precisely because it has been published ... For I am guaranteed that I am not the first person other than the addressee to read the diary. In other words, the violation of the secrecy clause has been performed for me by an editor, a person licensed to examine the work prior to its release to the public. The editor thus not only makes the diary more comprehensible to me but certifies that the work can now be read without scruple."[10]

As I unscrupulously turned back to the manuscript (I was, after all, there to do a "job"), my heart began to sink deeper into a pool of ethical violation when it became apparent that Smart was warning me about the "secrecy clause." The first diary I opened presented me with a title page that read: "This Belongs to Betty Smart [...] Of no Spying Interest" (ESF box 2, f.3). The title page of another diary named "Book of Discipline II" offered an entire poem to this effect:

> Keep out
> Keep out
> Your snooting snout
> As any honest man would do.
> In case you're not a man
> Resist it if you can
> Its [sic] Despicable, and low, and mean
> Its [sic] the fault of the vilest epicene
> Leave it alone
> And I'll atone
> *Are* you as willless as plasticene [sic]?"

Smart then begged:

> Oh God be good
> As you know you should
> If not
> *Beware*!!
> For I really care –
> I Honestly, Absolutely Care
> For you to keep out of
> This book. (ESF, box 2, f.5)

In another volume, Smart printed a "*Notice*" on the cover waging a moral war with her reader, who in this instance happened to be a trembling me: "If you can persuade yourself that it is *not* wrong and immoral and criminal to read this book you are guilty of the worst crime of all – dishonesty with yourself [...] This will be a test of your character [...] Such a thing once done is done – It cannot be undone! Don't ruin your chance of success. Now is your hour of trial. B.S." (VWC, box 1, f.10) The consequences I was facing should I fail this test were announced in the "Notes" at the start of another volume:

My wrath is terrible to behold
I will spare no abuse
I will utterly revenge
I can – for large in me are the powers of destruction and evil.

She then added insult to injury, telling me, "You smell" (ESF, Box 3, f.2).

As I was reading these wrathful warnings (clearly failing her test), a part of me expected Smart to jump out from behind the diary trolley and exact her "revenge." But another part of me realized that she had constructed her diary in terms of some other, some "you" who could not help but be driven by curiosity to want to read what was proclaimed as forbidden. She was playing games with me, subtly luring me into the diary while testing and rewarding the resistance that she knew I would be incapable of. I suddenly imagined that she had turned away in the photograph so as to give me this opportunity to peek.

Though her notices might be full of sound and fury, I understood that they signified an adolescent's heightened sense of self-importance, full of humour and exaggeration. They also present a more sophisticated, though equally playful, challenge to genre specificity. The most dramatic evidence undermining Smart's dire threats to her "immoral" audience can be found on the title page to volume 3 of her "Details of a Detour." Here, at the bottom of the page, the "immoral" reader will find in small print: "The Betty Publishing Company Ltd., 1937" (ESF, box 2, f.9). The private diary, the text that was ordering me to "keep out" and to "beware," was now revealing its public orientation by flaunting its status as a "published" work. It was because of her sense of humour that I found Smart's manuscript diaries so utterly engaging to read, and it was because of her "Betty Publishing Company" imprint that I felt justified in reading them at all.

Released from guilt, I proceeded to examine the multitude of journals that Smart kept throughout her adult life. At the risk of oversimplifying, I noted that she used versions of only two kinds of books: a lined notebook and a pocket appointment book. While this observation in itself is not illuminating, it is her choice of one over the other at a particular time that sheds light on her art and emotions. From 1933 – the period from which her diaries are first preserved – through to 1945, Smart was a prolific and consistent diarist. She wrote in books that are more often called notebooks – the lined, softcover, medium-sized books that any student might use. She also wrote in lined, plain, hardcover books of similar size. These are the journals of a writer, an artist searching for her voice and style, honing her craft as she goes along. Not surprisingly, these years were arguably Smart's most productive as an artist; for it was during this time that she drafted and published *By Grand Central Station* and worked on the novellas "My Lover John" and "Dig a Grave and Let Us Bury Our Mother," material that she would return to over and over again in later life (the latter being published in *In the Meantime* in 1984).

Between 1945 and 1970 there is a dramatic and clearly extensive break in her writer's diary. During this period she kept appointment books, pocket-sized agendas that allot about a quarter-inch of space per day. These books, unlike the kind discussed above, with their blank and limitless pages, are prescriptive and constraining. Manufactured by companies capitalizing on such record-keeping, they bear titles – often in italicized and gold-coloured lettering – such as "Collins Compact Diary," "Letts Diary," "King's Own Diary," and "Pepys Lady's Diary." Smart also used lined notebooks, but the entries, as in the daily agendas, are almost entirely composed of appointments, addresses, shopping lists, notes for commercial writing, bills, and the like.

There may be several reasons that account for the sharp contrast between the writer's diary and the appointment book; I can offer two here. Emotionally, the discrepancy could signal a crisis in Smart's confidence as a writer. Up to the publication of her first novel, the diaries reflect the energy, excitement, and discipline of any young writer struggling to produce a work of art. *By Grand Central Station* was not, however, the success that she had hoped for. As Sullivan relates, "The book was discussed among friends, admired in small circles and disappeared." Closer to home, Smart's mother, offended by her daughter's "illicit" subject matter and what she considered a cruel depiction of the family, bought the six copies in an Ottawa dry-goods store and burned them.[11]

A more practical explanation for Smart's neglect of diary writing is simply lack of time. She gave birth to Rose, her fourth child, in May 1946. In addition to having to raise four children single-handed, she eventually began writing copy and commercial articles for magazines such as *House and Garden* and *Queen*. Domestic and economic factors kept Smart from pursuing what she considered serious writing – that is, novels and poems – and this fact was reflected in the kind of diary she maintained. It is crucial to note that in keeping a diary at all, she was registering her need to document her life, preserve some sort of record that proved she was here.

In 1970, after twenty-five years of squeezing her life into a pocketbook, Smart seemed to break out – liberate herself as she once again took up her writer's diary. Having retired from *Queen* at the end of 1966, she took a trip to Canada in February 1970 in order to write. She was back in London by the end of the year, but returned as writer-in-residence at the University of Alberta in Edmonton for the 1982–83 semesters. She kept up this diary, with a few gaps, until 1982 and then sporadically until 1984. She then wholly returned to the small calendar agenda, keeping such books until her death in 1986.

These later diaries are preoccupied with several themes, most notably aging and writer's block. But that she persevered is again arguably connected to her literary life. The seventies saw a revival of Smart the writer: *By Grand Central Station* was reprinted in 1966 and 1970; a collection of poems, *A Bonus*, came out in 1977; and her second novel, *Rogues & Rascals*, appeared in 1978. Her rejuvenated literary status provided her with the encouragement to rouse her dormant potential, and this renewed sense of herself as a writer in turn may have driven her back to her journal. Tragically, her daughter Rose died of a drug overdose in March 1982, and it is at this point that her diary drops off again. Smart never really recovered, either professionally or personally, from the loss. Editor Van Wart similarly sees the death of Rose as a breaking point in both Smart's life and her diary, for she closes the second volume of her journal, *On the Side of the Angels*, with a poem that Smart wrote for her daughter entitled "Rose Died."

LADY PEPYS

Addressing the issue of "how a volume of the diary is presented *qua* volume," which includes "whether it is given a formal beginning or ending,"[12] we can see how Elizabeth Smart constructed her diary volumes as individual, literary wholes. Using a variety of techniques traditionally reserved for the novel, she framed her diary entries with fictional self-consciousness, ultimately frustrating the distinction between public and private.

Perhaps the most obvious sign that she presented whole diary volumes as books is her employment of provocative title pages. Examples of titles include "The Adolescent Outlook Alone and Abroad," "Lubricational Day Book," "Betty Smart's Book of Agony," "Journal from Magnanimous Despair Alone," and "The Stifled Moment or, the Story of my Life By Belinda Blue, a girl without humour" – this latter title is clearly ironic, given her penchant for game playing discussed earlier.

To a diary kept during a cruise to Sweden and Norway with her father in July 1935, she gave the title "The True Account Of A Trip" (*NS*, 66). This is noteworthy, for it is generally taken for granted that the diarist tells the "truth" as best she can. By drawing attention to truth here, Smart, like later autobiography theorists, underscored that telling the "truth" may be an impossible goal, and she forces us to question the veracity of other entries. Does the fact that they were not labelled "true" mean that they should be suspected as fiction? The title brings to mind a line from the preface to *Robinson Crusoe*, provided by author Daniel Defoe: "The editor believes the thing to be a just history of fact; neither is there any appearance of fiction in it."[13] The irony of this disclaimer might equally be applied to Smart's tales of adventure. I am not suggesting that she was lying, but rather that she conceived her life in novelistic terms.

Smart also titled specific entries, such as "The Music and Sappho's Girl" (NS, 203) and "Perennial Day of Tears" (NS, 223). Her titles may come from a quotation, such as "Look Homeward Angel Now and Melt with Ruth," from Milton's "Lycidas" (NS, 251), or "They've Severed all the Wires," from an untitled W.H. Auden poem (NS, 261). These make the diary's association with literature explicit. Moreover, her entry for 4 April 1940 contains the heading "Ten Days in Vancouver by E.S." (NS, 264). The "by" is crucial. Smart's diary was obviously written by her, yet here she seems to extract herself from her own text and then re-enter as the author of only this particular passage. These examples show how individual entries may be conceived as completed pieces, little works in themselves. Further, "by E.S.," coupled with her use of fictional names such as "Belinda," shows how she was negotiating what Brodzki and Schenck call the "tension between life and literature ... selfhood and textuality."

Following the title page, Smart often provided a preface to introduce a volume. In this, she was undoubtedly aware of employing a well-worn literary convention. The question that obtains is why, if the text was presumably private, she would have to introduce it at all. The most appropriate answer is that Smart was deliberately invoking a correlation between her diary and a literary work written for an audience. But once again, as with her title pages, the invocation to literature was a comic and playful one.

For example, in "The Stifled Moment," the diary written by pseudonymous Belinda Blue, not only did Smart offer a preface, but she further confused the notion of what a diary is when she wrote: "ANYone reading this book damns themself irrevocably. It is private personal and Untrue." She went on: "You betray your soul when you read my PRIVATEness." Here she undermined the notion of private, and the damage caused by reading what was private, by the disclaimer that the diary was after all "untrue." This statement confuses her earlier proclamation that her account in the volume "The True Account Of A Trip" was "true". She played games on the opposite page too when she provided a "Post Preface": "But why protest, my dear Belinda, why protest? B.S." (ESF, box 2, f.6).

In her "Details of a Detour," volume 3, Smart offered a nonsensical preface: "Preface to the 2nd Edition just in case there *isn't* a 2nd

Edition" (ESF, box 2, f.9). And in the "Lubricational Day-Book" she confessed in the preface: "I feel in order to save my face I have to write a pre-face" (ESF, box 3, f.8). Just as she did with her title-page warnings, Smart seems to be having a good time here, with herself and with her audience. On the one hand, she utilized the literary tradition of the preface in order to signal her diary as a literary text. On the other, her parodic use of the preface serves to confuse not only what it means to be private but what it means to be literary.

There are other indications that Smart's diaries were given, in Rosenwald's terms, "a formal beginning or ending." The last word in a 1933 diary is "Finis," announcing that her text has come to an end – a practice not usually associated with the endless flow of diarizing (esf, box 2, f.4). In another journal she wrote the final entries under the heading "Epilogue" (ESF, box 2, f.5). And she drew volumes to a close with reflective conclusions such as "This was a very sad year for ES" (ESF, box 4, f.7).

Wondering "whether the text is immaculate or scribbled over with revisions," I found that Smart's diaries are, for the most part, messy. She submitted her entries, either in whole or in part, to editing, such that individual words, lines, paragraphs, or entire passages were scratched out, revised, or clarified. Like Woolf, she added detail – as a second, artistically conscious thought – either at the time of writing or at a later date. For instance, she wrote: "The sun in the grass made me think of places that are all that – where you can wallow in them." She then expanded her description to include "and the shining sky," inserted between "grass" and "made" (ESF, box 2, f.4). And to her initial description of "a large open air restaurant," she added "partly" after "large" to qualify its sense of space (ESF, box 2, f.4). Examples such as these abound. Though perhaps seeming trivial in themselves, they indicate the care that Smart took in writing, the subtle concern for each word as she formulated images and experimented with language.

Passages have often been revised at a later date, a fact signified by the change in writing instrument. The entry for 18 December 1933 was written in black ink. It has been altered in pencil. Thus to "No more joy" she has pencilled "There was no more joy," and "ever since Daddy left" has been changed to "Especially after Daddy left" (ESF, box 2, f.5). Many revisions were grammatical: "there is a walks" is corrected to "there are gravel walks," "are" and "gravel" being written in a different colour (ESF, box 2, f.4). These kinds of revisions have profound implications for the text as constructed artistically and intended for an audience. The diarist who rereads her entries is able to shape future ones according to the themes, subjects, images, and the like which have come before. And the very fact of correcting sentences and improving structure and grammar indicates a professional – and hence public – concern for how the diary will be read and judged by others.

Smart had a habit of going back over a particular word that was apparently unclear or faint and writing over it, making it clear and bold. She thus reveals her concern for the readability of her handwriting and her determination that, when she was read, she would be understood; remember that Huff has noted that this was also the habit of nineteenth-century women diarists. As well, Smart constantly scratched out entire passages. Because she used her journals to experiment with poetry as well as prose, and because any kind of writing could be subjected to scratches – that is, both poems and diary entries – once again we can appreciate how her distinction between literary pieces and raw outpourings – what they are, whom they are for – was blurred.

One thing that remains clear is that Smart was writing for an audience. Her diary was being read by others as it was being written. She recorded of her friend: "Graham [Spry] gave me back my red journal of the Scotland trip, and I looked at it and then decided that he might as well see it so returned it. Then I felt no – he shouldn't see it, it's too personal" (NS, 25).[14] This passage is rather ambiguous. As there is no reference to this red journal in an earlier entry, it is not clear when Smart actually gave it to Spry. But it is evident that at some time she did, so that the perception of her diary as a solely private text has been undermined. She would later share it with her boyfriend John Pentland in London: "I read him my diaries and he said he thought they were good" (NS, 156). The adjective "good" emphasizes how the diary was admired as a piece of literature.

Smart revealed that she inevitably wrote with an awareness of writing, and that this consciousness impacted on how and what she released into her book. Anticipating the public's response, she feared that her diary would be judged "before" she had "finished it complete and satisfactory." Contemplating how to make it "satisfactory," then, she urged herself to write with discipline; she qualified this exhortation: "Oh give me more willpower and less self-consciousness – no that's misleading – less shirking – and less distrust of adolescence, which, after all, may not be so shame-worthy" (NS, 54). Though Smart was quick to shift from "self-consciousness" to "shirking," the meaning has changed very little. For in urging herself to be "less shirking," she was simply asking that she not neglect her duty of recording things pertaining to "adolescence." But it was this very awareness of what she should be recording that made the diary self-conscious. In an earlier entry she had complained: "The reason I don't like this diary is because it is so conscientious." Even without her, as it were, the diary was aware of how it must perform, self-conscious of its prescribed function to "describe any and everything" (NS, 21).

Like Woolf, Smart acknowledged that diary writing is an art: "What *is* writing? Isn't it just getting things on paper? What things? Just putting them down? But there is an art. Yes" (NS, 30). Another time, she wrote: "Everything in the day can be equally valuable if you spend energy on it." She has added in the margin at the top of the page: "Everything can be equally valuable *artistically*" (ESF, box 2, f.10). Given that the diary is a record of days and that "everything in the day" can be "valuable artistically," then the diary itself is of artistic value.

DETAILS OF A DIARY

Smart considered her diary a work: more specifically, one that could be published. The prospect of publication was in her mind certainly from the period of her adult diaries. During the summer of 1936 Smart, acting as secretary, accompanied Margaret Rose Watt as she travelled around the world giving lectures to the Associated Country Women of the World. One of Smart's first efforts to make her diary a professional book centred on the travel diary she kept during this trip. Her artistic intentions for it are especially interesting when we recall how Francis Bacon, in his essay "On Travel," urged travellers to put their journals to good use.

Once again beginning the journal with a "Preface," Smart explained in August 1936: "I call this [the trip] a detour because it was only an excuse to put off for a little while longer the settling of my future. It is my long-winded excuse for never having done anything. An alibi, in fact" (NS, 86). The trip did help her find some direction, and specifically, it came through and by the diary itself. Lamenting that she had "never" "done anything," she came to recognize that she might "do something" with her journal.

Sullivan notes that while at the King David Hotel in Jerusalem, Smart encountered I.J. Hermann, "editor and business manager of the *Palestine Review* ... To him she gave the diaries she had been keeping and asked him how to turn them into a book."[15] She made these revealing entries: "Then Hermann coffee and this book. (I *will* make it into a book, for discipline and for publication)" (ESF, box 2, f.10); and "As I am not an expert at anything at all, I think the best thing to do is to tell you [the diary] of my life – in a few [illegible] in facts which are suitable for publication" (ESF, box 2, f.11). Smart had likely been considering the possibility of publishing her journals for some time, and if so, they must have been written with the self-conscious and crafted intentions that inform any public work.

Upon her return to London in 1937, she proceeded to shape her diary into a text for publication, charting her work pace as she went along. For instance, on 3 March she "did a bit of 'Details'" (NS, 155). A few days later she "awoke alive and worked all day. Lunch on a tray. Up to chapter twenty-eight of 'Details'" (NS, 158). These one-line accounts emphasize the notion of duty, as she was eager to register her writing in regimented terms, taking stock, as it were, of her daily output. They reinforce the argument that women need to legitimize their writing, especially when that writing is diaristic.

Within "Details of a Detour" we can see how Smart elaborated on the fact that work is necessary for any production: "Whatever meaning, search. Never any rest. Blake felt and spoke. Follow the days with accepted organised work? Today ten pages – on, on." She considered the quality of her work and how it might be improved: "It is getting dull. It is all flippant and vain. I could make it better [...] WORK MORE Each bit could be so much better, if I sat and thought and turned over before I wrote. But it is a diary. It is preparation" (NS, 166). This passage reminds us of what Nicholls says of modernism: "the true work of aesthetic modernity depends on the assiduous cultivation of style, on that 'atrocious labour' of which Flaubert was to become an exemplary practitioner ('Last week I spent 5 days writing one page')."[16] Smart and her diary were thus in good, hard-working modernist company. Though she apparently conceived her diary-cum-manuscript as simply a "preparation," I believe that the diary here *is* this work for which she was preparing.

As far as "Details" goes, Smart never fulfilled her original intention of publishing it. Sullivan relates the fate of this project. Hermann corresponded with Smart over the book, offering a detailed criticism of the manuscript: "Part of the problem, he felt, was that while she as narrator was interesting and vital, the people she met were of little value." Sullivan concludes: "It is unclear how much of Jay's advice Elizabeth used. She eventually abandoned her manuscript, perhaps finding it too unwieldy. She would need to invent a new prose form to contain her vision."[17] This last comment, that Smart "would need to invent a new prose form," is best understood through Lawrence Durrell. For it was through him that Smart was able to conceive what this "new prose form" might be. And it is here that my argument, that Smart's diary was not a preparation but the work prepared, can be fully appreciated.

Living in Mexico in 1939, Smart was inspired by the authors she was reading to articulate her technical needs: "A Poem, a note, a diary. These are the raw moments, the raw thoughts. I do not want, I am irritated with the devious method and hidden indirectness of the novel, for instance, or even the short story, or a play. Poems, notes, diaries, letters, or prose such as '*The House of Incest*,' in *The Black Book*, only meet my need" (NS, 201–2). While there are many reasons to account

for Smart's fascination with Durrell's *The Black Book*, the one most
relevant here is that the form of this novel is diaristic. The narrator,
Lawrence Lucifer, tells us about his present-day life in a London room-
ing house. Having found the diary – the "Black Book" – of a former
boarder named Gregory, he intersperses this text throughout his own
narrative. Within his journal, Gregory underscores the self-consciousness of his diary, claiming: "(It is artifice which dictates this form to
me.) ... All diaries have been written for an audience.[18] As a diarist,
Smart must have found this statement fascinating, and perhaps, to
some degree, confirming. Gregory's comments fuse with Smart's celebration of the diary form as an innovative alternative to the "hidden
indirectness of the novel, for instance." Given that she documented all
of this within her own diary, the self-reflexivity becomes overt, making
it impossible to separate her journal as a private text from those other
more public ones: "Poems, notes, diaries, letters, or prose."

Smart's frustration with traditional genres such as the poem was further registered in a confession from Hollywood in 1940: "I cannot
write poems now. Other things are rumbling pregnantly in my brain
but cannot emerge yet, want *rumination*, and encourage the mouth to
cover the earth with a kiss. This is TODAY, this is where all words strive
to lead, all feet to attain. If I write one page, part of its radiance might
slip by me untasted." She was also unable to write fiction: "I cannot
write a novel – the form needs padding, the form needs to be filled up
with air – for no nugget of truth can last so long or be so boringly consistent. I want each word to be essence, irreplaceably and authentically the only only note." Smart wanted to "rend the Now, the Now is
only important – I can't reconstruct the past, and if I could I'm afraid
of missing the present" (NS, 236). She thus understood well the theorists of autobiography who contend that the past is not recoverable
and is instead always shaped by creative, fictionalizing forces.

Smart vividly summons the diary to mind in her invocation to the
"Now," for the diary is the quintessential book of the moment, the present, the day. While she admitted the impossibility of recording all
things, she nonetheless recognized the potential benefits of the diary
form. These are the same benefits identified by Woolf. Describing "the
rapid haphazard gallop at which" her diary "swings along," Woolf valued this method because "it sweeps up accidentally several stray matters which I should exclude if I hesitated, but which are the diamonds
of the dustheap" (D, 1:233–4) Similarly, Smart contended: "The important juice-drops are small, but worth a million of the garrulous chaff
that the will forces out when it says do this or that" (NS, 236). Woolf's
"diamonds" become Smart's "juice-drops," Woolf's "dustheap"
Smart's "chaff." Both valued the diary's potential to sift out those

moments that make each day particularly symbolic and epiphanic, and hence modernistic.

Smart acknowledged that she could write neither novel nor poem, and in so doing, she privileged the form of the diary. That she did so reinforces the notion that the diary, contrary to her earlier statement, was much more than a "preparation." For not only was it the new form that met her needs, but it was the form that she had been using all along. Further, given my thesis that the diary resembles modern fiction and poetry, then Smart's "I cannot write a novel" and "I cannot write a poem" are subtly undermined. Her diary stands as a testament to her creative ability to fuse genres, and the intentions that go with them.

Smart called her diary a "preparation," but it is possible she saw it as much more than that. She habitually recorded in her diary the books she was reading, and many of these were published diaries. Like Woolf, White, and Nin, she was clearly aware of the diary's potential to be published, and this awareness may have informed her conception of her own journal as just such a public work.

She was inspired, for instance, by the journals of Katherine Mansfield. From Stockholm in 1933 she quoted: "'Life with other people becomes a blur: it does with J.[ohn Middleton Murry], but it's enormously valuable and marvellous when I'm alone, the detail of life, the *life* of a life.' (Katherine Mansfield)." Smart then applied this journal entry to her own: "It was a blur all day. I tried to write – then in desperation I turned to K.M. She says the truth – I know the truth. Work. Work. She was sick. I'm not. Why can't I work? This blur, this apathy, haze – I don't know. She gave me some new life suddenly, at last a gleam of life. When I read that I knew. It is *not* only my vacant soul – it is *that,* what she says. I *will* do it and I *can.* I will go for a walk and see things and *note* things" (NS, 30).

In an entry for 9 February 1934, Smart transcribed an excerpt of Dorothy Wordsworth's journal from the *Canadian Forum* into her own diary (ESF, box 2, f.5). On the last page of a volume kept from August to December 1938, she listed, among the books she wanted, the *Journals of Dorothy Wordsworth* and Rilke's *Journal* (ESF, box 3, f.5). It is her awareness of diaries as publishable texts that is important, for this surely impinged on the construction of her diary as a work which might negotiate private and public spaces. An entry made in 1934 highlights this probability: "What a lot of autobiographical writing there has been lately! Tonight I picked up *The Atlantic Monthly* and it was all diaries and records and autobiography – perhaps in the wake of *Testament of Youth*" (NS, 61). Vera Brittain wrote *Testament of Youth* as an autobiographical account of her experiences during World War I, relying heavily on quotations from her own diary. *Testament*'s fusion of private and public would serve as a model not only for Smart's diary but for her incorporation of diary material into *By Grand Central Station* and *Rogues & Rascals*.

Perhaps the diary that had the greatest impact on Smart was James Agate's. Born in Lancashire in 1877, Agate was a failed shopkeeper who turned to the theatre, becoming chief drama critic at the London *Sunday Times* in 1923. However, he is largely remembered (when he is remembered at all) as the author of an extensive, nine-volume diary entitled *Ego*, which he produced and published from 1935 until his death in 1947 – volume 9 appeared posthumously. As Ivor Brown describes him in *The Dictionary of National Biography*, "He set out accordingly to be the diarist of his epoch," and he "never lost his sense of himself as a character bestriding his own stage."[19] Agate thus surely takes his place beside Barbellion and Marie Bashkirtseff, two other diarists who wrote journals solely for the purpose of publishing them. Particularly interesting is the first line of *Ego 1*. Writing on 2 June 1932, Agate introduced what would become his life work with the statement: "To-day is the day on which my review of Arnold Bennett's *Journals* ought to have appeared." A few lines down he admitted, "It is A.B.'s diaries which have prompted this one."[20] Agate situated himself in the tradition of public and publishable journals.

Smart's comments about Agate thus become more meaningful. In a diary entry for 2 March 1937 she wrote: "Tonight I have been reading James Agate's 'Ego 2,' his diary. *He seems to have done what I'm trying to do* except that his is full of famous names and definitely aims at being topical and a running commentary on what's happening" (my emphasis). Making the fact that she was writing for an audience explicit, she worried: "They'll think I'm just copying him. It's mean of him. Or perhaps a precedent is good" (ESF, box 2, f.9). Agate confirmed and inspired her project, so that Smart became another link in this diaristic chain.

If diarists turned to the public, Smart understood how fiction writers turned to the private. In Australia in 1936 she praised Hemingway: "Nothing seemed new or exciting or worth the effort. But I found Hemingway good, and sane and his diary-style encouraging and easy to read, which is a sign of good writing. Hurray for Hemingway!" (NS, 109). By virtue of the fact that she recorded this comment in her own diary, in her own "diary-style," she was by extension calling her own writing "good." A few days later she "Read *Farewell to Arms*. It's winning. It's all right. His diary style is stimulating" (NS, 110). It was no doubt feelings such as these that led her to celebrate the diary style of Durrell's *The Black Book*. And when the passage is recalled in which Durrell's narrator asserts, "All diaries have been written for an audience," then the connection between diaries, novels, and publication becomes explicit.

PARING HER FINGERNAILS

Elizabeth Smart was educated at private high schools, and although she wanted to earn a university degree, she was not allowed to. But she was permitted to go to London to study music – because doing so was in keeping with her mother's social agenda. As she described it in an autobiographical fragment, "My Life," "When I was seventeen, I wanted to go on being educated and my Father thought this was a good idea, but my Mother wanted me to be 'finished.' She believed that England was entirely filled with aristocratic families all with noblesse oblige and New England Puritan consciences" (A, 129). As noted earlier, Smart's passion for music soon gave way to one for literature, and during her first few years in London she took extension courses at Gresham College and then at King's College, University of London, studying, among other subjects, English literature.[21] Though her attendance was sporadic because she was constantly forced to socialize for the sake of her "finishing" education, she did continue to read voraciously on her own. Like Woolf, Smart set up her own "survey of literature" course, reading the gamut of greats from Shakespeare, Donne, Milton, and Wordsworth to Proust, Joyce, Woolf, and Eliot. What she studied, in other words, was the Western tradition.

Not only did Smart read this tradition, but she wanted to live it. She desperately wanted to be part of a writing community, as she told her diary: "O that I knew as my comfortable friends Yeats, McNeice, Roger Fry, Virginia Woolf, A. Huxley, Spender, Auden, McLeish, G.B. Shaw, etc!" And it was in this state of longing to belong that she acknowledged, "O that I were a poet" (NS, 165). Smart wanted to produce an art that would simultaneously embrace the new and accommodate itself to the monuments of the past. And she used her diary to that end.

Specifically, and perhaps not surprisingly, in wanting to join the Tradition as outlined by Eliot, Smart used her diary to enact the intertextual and impersonal agendas of his poetry. Just as within "Prufrock" and *The Waste Land* he made reference to such sources as the Bible and the Upanishads, Homer, Dante, Shakespeare, the metaphysical poets, the French symbolists, folklore, fables, and popular songs, so Smart did within her diary. Her text is a fusion of high and mass culture, for she frequently interrupted her more literary observations with recipes and laundry and shopping lists, which, as we have heard her say, "deglamourize" the diary. Many of her journals also contain lists of the books that she has been reading. These lists effectively direct potential readers to Smart's sources for her countless literary references and quotations, and thus they may be equated with the explanatory footnotes that Eliot penned for *The Waste Land*.[22]

Though there are copious examples of her intertextuality, I will offer only a few here to make my point. In Ottawa in 1934 Smart was courted by D'Arcy McGee,[23] and she responded in the Romantic tradition: "D'Arcy has presented me with himself. Therefore, in me, he has subsided. And he does not trouble me any more. Now I am free again but oh, how dull. He is pleasant in me now, but he cannot disturb me." Smart went on to quote:

> Never pain to tell thy love
> Love that never told can be
> For the gentle wind does move
> Silently invisibly

At the end of the poem, Smart wrote, "William Blake" (NS, 59).[24]

She could be more subtle, weaving quotations within her own sentences and thus calling for a reader trained in literature to recognize them. Drawing on the metaphysical poets, she invoked John Donne's "The Sun Rising." His narrator begins with an accusation: "Busy old fool, unruly sun, / Why dost thou thus, / Through windows and through curtains call on us?"[25] In Smart's version, it is not the sun but herself who is chided: "Unruly self. Unyielding, ungrateful, unlovely self" (A, 186). Waiting hopelessly for her lover George Barker in Vancouver, she brooded: "But tomorrow and tomorrow and tomorrow lie as locked and uncharted as the other face of the moon" (NS, 262), echoing Shakespeare's desperate Macbeth: "Tomorrow, and tomorrow, and tomorrow, / Creeps in this petty pace from day to day."[26] Another allusion to this play was made later in life when she reflected on the tension between serving others and serving herself: "Still, a melting heart makes the purpose infirm. Give me the dagger!" (A, 157). This exhortation echoes the words of Lady Macbeth, who, sensing the sudden weakness in her husband after he has murdered Duncan and his men, realizes that she must take control: "Infirm of purpose! / Give me the daggers."[27]

Smart alluded to modern poets as well. In Australia in 1936 she subtly invoked "Prufrock." Where he mourns, "I grow old … I grow old," she emphasized, "I grow old – too old" (NS, 123). And in Cassis in 1938 she returned to this soulmate. Where Prufrock informs us, "I have heard the mermaids singing, each to each. / I do not think that they will sing to me,"[28] Smart wondered: "I hear the tickling song of the nightingales – not sad. Do they sing for me? Do I think they sing for me?" (NS, 190). In September 1940, contemplating her relationship with Barker, she asked: "Is there no other channel of deliverance? At first my reporter eyes gave no communication. By severing all the wires I functioned severally" (NS, 248). Smart was here alluding to an untitled poem by W.H. Auden:

> In my spine there was a base,
> And I knew the general's face:
> But they've severed all the wires
> And I can't tell what the general desires. (NS 284).

Fantasizing about Barker through his words, she recorded from his "Narcissus I," "my tired lips received that morning first kiss"; and "Him I mourn from morn to morning," from "Daedalus" (NS, 206, 233).

References to modern novelists abound as well. From the beginning Smart imagined her diary in literary terms: "of course when I started it I meant to be Proustian in my meticulous recordings" (ESF, box 2, f.9). Her diary was – and should be – valued as a modernist, Proustian autobiography. She was also inspired by D.H. Lawrence. She "Read six and a half hours of *Lady Chatterley's Lover*. Read till 1 o'clock. Good. Very good. The last letter from Oliver Mellors the gamekeeper, is *great*. And pure" (NS, 44). She quoted a long passage from Mellors's letter and then immediately launched into an examination of her diary: "Well, now this great bulky waste of paper is finished and it is not anything but a wind that bloweth nowhere. Oh! It should be better. And it could" (NS, 46). The fact that she contemplated the merits of her diary immediately after discussing Lawrence's novel indicates how she conceived this diary as a literary text, one that, given his "great" example, "should be better."

In addition to Lawrence, Woolf was one of Smart's favourite authors. She read *The Waves* and *To the Lighthouse* during her 1933 trip to Sweden and Germany (NS, 37, 39), and she admired them so much that she wanted to appropriate them: "I read The Waves and I loved V. Woolf and I want the Waves to be my book and I fingered it and made it mine" (ESF, box 2, f.4). It was in discussing Woolf that Smart profoundly analyzed how she, Smart, constructed her diary in imitation of the writers she respected: "I looked at the queer lake and thought it is like something. What is it like? Oh! It's like a wet olive. That's good I said. It will go well in my diary. It is like a wet olive. It will be impressive. Then thought: I am copying Virginia Woolf. I am being influenced and 'making phrases.' I am cheating. I am not being myself." Smart went on to justify herself: "But then I thought [...] isn't it permissible to be stimulated by people honourably, to be made more alert and alive and noting of things by others? To be shown and taught [...] Yes, why not?" (NS, 38).

One of the things that she learned from these influences was precisely the strategy of postmodern feminist theorists of autobiography: the negotiation of history and art, reality and fiction. Smart's systematic reading and subsequent referencing made it possible for her to transform her daily life into a literary adventure and herself into an entire cast of literary characters. This world of words instinctively framed her way of seeing both herself and life. As Van Wart describes it, Smart "created a romantic ethos by which to live and out of which she wrote, an ethos that ironically shaped the course of her life."[29]

Her use of intertextuality was motivated even further, I believe, by her desire to negotiate what was expected of her as a woman and what she wanted as an artist. Specifically, she was trying to reconcile the limiting conception that women are personal, men impersonal. She wrote in the traditional diary because it is a female, personal space and because she wanted and needed to write about things relevant to herself. But she also resisted being branded a "typical" relational female, and so she used the diary to inscribe a detached, impersonal narrative. As Patricia Waugh has suggested, "'impersonality' has much to offer, aesthetically and ultimately politically, to women writers."[30] By borrowing from other writers, Smart was mediating expressions of personal thought and feeling through these other voices, so that her self became textualized, linguistically referential like Prufrock's, for instance. And Elizabeth Smart the author was left standing back, indifferent, paring her fingernails in the company of Joyce and Eliot. In order to understand why she would have felt the need for such negotiations, we should consider her status as a Canadian and as a woman, at home and abroad.

Like many women, Smart had difficulty finding the right cultural context in which to secure her ego as a writer. She certainly believed that her native Canada lacked such a context. In a 1939 letter she sarcastically responded to Lawrence Durrell's queries about Canada: "there are no people in it, no poets but inarticulate ones [...] All the people who might have been poets go into External Affairs and never speak again.[31] And in an undated fragment entitled "A Transatlantic Pursuit (My Affair With England)," she compared her country unfavourably with England: "The Boredom of Canada," was "So great you'd worship anyone who'd heard of Stephen Spender" (A, 141).

She may have worshipped foreign writers, but people like Mrs Watt, to whom Smart was secretary, did not. Recall that Smart had praised in her diary Lawrence's *Lady Chatterley's Lover*, which she read while on tour with Watt. Within that passage, she recorded that she had read to Watt Frieda Lawrence's letters about the banning of the book and that Watt had reacted with moral outrage: "I think it's perfectly disgusting to want to read a book my country won't allow." Smart responded: "How people can contaminate things! She almost made it unclean for me. But no. There it was and I was swept on its great tide. She had made me feel as though I should read it in a corner secretly and then hide it. But when I finished that great declaration of D.H.L.'s faith in the last letter, I was conquered, and not ashamed of the book and not influenced by small minds [...] The book is good and essentially *clean*. Why on earth are sensual joys supposed to be so low?" (NS, 44-5). Watt embodied a puritan ethic that Smart believed was stunting the growth of an artistic Canada. And Watt was not the only one. Worried about "contamination," with her "small mind," Smart's mother bought and burned the six copies of her daughter's novel *By Grand Central Station*.

The irony of Mrs Smart's actions was that although she was disgusted that her daughter had written a book about adultery and thus had shamed the family, she encouraged that daughter to flaunt her beauty with the aim of securing social prestige. Elizabeth Smart, born in 1913 to upper-middle-class parents, had a conservative and "proper" upbringing in Ottawa. Her father, Russell Smart, was a successful patent lawyer; her mother, Louie Emma Parr, was a prominent hostess who, as we have seen, refused to let Elizabeth earn a university degree, preferring that her debutante daughter be "finished." The impact of such an upbringing on her artistic development was registered in a fragment that Smart called "Social Canada": "Having to camouflage books, read poetry secretly, pass ashtrays gracefully, be a Blonde" (A, 140).

Smart's Canada was clearly parochial, and it is not surprising that she expatriated herself to London. She was not alone. Judith Kegan Gardiner tells us in "The Exhilaration of Exile" that Jean Rhys, Christina Stead, and Doris Lessing were, around the same time as Smart, "born at the periphery of the British Empire," and that "As young women, each of the three left a home that practiced traditional sex roles for England, which provided a freer personal life and the chance to be an artist."[32] Exile was, however, ambiguous, because if one was from a colony, "home" meant, on one hand, one's native country and, on the other, "Mother" England.

Gardiner elaborates on the experiences of these three writers: "They grew up with adults who thought of home as elsewhere, and their own family homes were places of confinement and restraint for them; they were expected to grow up as ladylike participants in white English culture." Consequently, home was "a trap from which they had to escape as well as an implied goal. Like the conventional hero of the *bildungsroman*, each woman traveled from her provincial backwater to the more appreciative, more cosmopolitan, more diverse center – to London. To be exiled from the periphery to the center of one's culture is not the traditional meaning of exile, yet these writers do not define this center as home either: neither place is home; each is alternately desirable and oppressive." In terms of their artistic expression, Gardiner emphasizes, "As admiring and resentful foreigners, as colonials, they see English culture as a dominating discourse imposed upon their creativity, at the same time that it enables that creativity by freeing them from the psychological foreclosure of entrapment within home as the family of origin." In consequence, then, "For all three, the English literary tradition is both mother tongue and somewhat alien, shadowy, and duplicitous."[33]

Like Rhys, Stead, and Lessing, Smart found exile an ambiguous state because it continued to privilege the gendered roles that had forced her to "be a Blonde" in Ottawa. Though the world of literature may have opened up before her in London, she would find that this world was largely a male-centred one. During the 1984 interview she reminisced about the London art scene of the thirties, and she offered at least one reason why it was difficult for her to feel confident as a writer. She recalled: "The London pubs were great places for literary activity. Everyone gathered at the various places to talk and drink. Women sort of kept back on the edge of the crowd as the men discussed all the exciting things that were happening."[34] In another piece, from her notebook entitled "A Woman of Thirty," though she made the entry personal and specific, Smart similarly spoke on behalf of many women: "The circumstances in which I find myself are marginal notes, never the text" (A, 116). Whether hanging back from the crowd of men at a pub or feeling marginal, she revealed the sentiments of women who were rarely offered or afforded the positions of authority from which they might produce their own central and valued-as-central texts and selves. She emphasized this dilemma when discussing her second novel: "'Writing about the difficulties of writing,' one said. It wasn't that. It was about the almost impossibility of making works of art if you're a woman" (A, 183). In either "home," then, she spent her life grappling with her identity.

If she felt on the edge, however, we should remember that Smith and Nussbaum have shown how the margin may be a place of critical distance and empowerment. Smart used the marginal space of her diary to enact a critique of the centre in which too many men had positioned themselves. Gardiner's argument that colonial women both embraced and rejected the domineering discourse of the English literary tradition echoes my response to Benstock's query of whether women embraced modernist aesthetics for miming or undermining purposes. From the edge of her diary, Smart mined the impersonal aesthetic of Eliot in order to undermine its edict against the personal, for she held the unpopular belief that "poetry and the abstract must be personal" (NS, 103).

And in a different way, she appropriated the detached narrative position within her diary in order to allow herself the freedom, as Eliot would have it for the poet, "of talking about himself without giving himself away." By inscribing, among other things, a radical sexual politics through an intertextual strategy, Smart could distance herself from moral and social censure. As she once noted of her desire for self-expression, "Surely I'm sane enough to plot it into acceptable channels" (NS, 133). She would "plot" her desires into the "acceptable channel" of a high-modernist narrative that would deny or limit reference beyond the text.

Whole portions of *By Grand Central Station* came directly from the diary. Smart wrote only one other novel, also culled from her diary, and this one much later in life. Her output of two novels for her entire artistic life is really minimal. When she sat down to write, what she wrote was more often the diary; it was her major form of writing, a form that allowed her to experiment artistically while speaking honestly about herself. We might also note how the diary negotiates the ambiguities associated with colonial exile posited by Gardiner. It inscribes a parochial sensibility in that Smart, hoping to publish the diary, wrote in an aside in 1983, "and this would be a Canadian book – whatever else it was as well" (ESF, box 12, f.3). "Whatever else it was as well," it was, and is, the kind of international text associated with Eliot and Pound, grounded in the experience of expatriation.

THE TWO WAYS PULL

The very idea of "female" – what it means to be a woman, how to be one – was a problematic and preoccupying one for Elizabeth Smart. Her personal and artistic ends seemed to exist in direct opposition to what might be called public and practical ones, and she spent her lifetime trying to reconcile them. Louie Smart was one of the most powerful figures in her daughter's world, and Elizabeth would have to contend with this force throughout her life. As she conceded when making notes for her autobiography in 1978, "Dichotomy of pleasing mother and being self" (A, 147). While "being self" would surely include pursuit of an artistic, bohemian life and disregard for social conventions such as marriage, "pleasing mother" would entail behaving in a "ladylike" fashion and censoring her literary subject matter to reflect this behaviour – just as "Having to camouflage books, read poetry secretly" would constitute "being self," while having to "pass ashtrays gracefully, be a Blonde," would reflect her mother's aspirations for her.

On the one hand, having said of herself in her diary, "I am a rebel" (NS, 130), Smart went on to prove that she was. Forsaking her parents and their world of "loyalty and decency and common standards of behaviour,"[35] she became a writer in exile, involving herself in passionate and tempestuous relationships with artists who fuelled her heart and flamed her words, and travelling to places such as France, Mexico, and California in the name of love and poetry, until she settled down to the most unstable, unpredictable, obsessive relationship of her life, the one with poet George Barker. Although they never married, they had a relationship that lasted nineteen years, produced four children, and provided much subject matter for their writing.

In contrast to this life of poetry and romantic mythmaking, Smart spent years – in fact, the major part of her career – writing advertising copy and articles for magazines, struggling single-handedly to support four children, and living alone in very unromantic circumstances in and around London. Like White, at times bitter and resentful that she was forced to forsake poetry for child care, Smart nonetheless devoted her life to her children. It is startling that the woman who pursued love and art with unmitigated zeal and had four children out of wedlock is the same woman who contended: "I don't really think I've been all that rebellious [...] I was always trying to conform as much as I could"; and who suggested, "you'd be amazed at how practical my life really is."[36]

Rebellion and conformity, desire and duty, serving an artist and serving her own art – these are the contradictions which informed Smart's sense of self and purpose, and which she recorded and tried to cope with in her diary. Thus it is a classic woman's autobiography, exemplifying the textual and historical tensions identified in the studies by Blodgett, Benstock, DuPlessis, Schenck, Smith, and others.

Smart recognized how social and psychic divisions threatened her autonomy throughout her life, fracturing her into opposing roles: "The 2 ways pull at the moment [...] a going towards love, understanding, giving of sympathy and a need for retreat, solitude, a rejection of distraction, a need for a ruthless bashing on regardless." She "always said, saw, thought that goodness & art were not connected, were parallel. Yet I want so much to be good [...] But an aspiration to art has to be mean, selfish, oblivious of other people's screams, sufferings" (A, 183). In analyzing this dichotomy, she acknowledged what Chodorow would later describe as women having relational, permeable ego boundaries. Smart pitted this conception of women against Eliot's call for the artist (generally male) to write with an emotion "which has its life in the poem and not in the history of the poet." She was a woman who devoted herself to her lovers and who would eventually be a mother of four children. However much she wanted or tried to detach her emotions from "history," she would surely have been called back to reality by her lovers and her children.

Smart resisted the qualities required of the artist – "to be mean, selfish, oblivious" – while she unequivocally accepted them as inevitable ones. Feelings of selfishness are registered throughout the diary and are intricately connected to it. She once explained that it was "sort of petering out. It is fear, I think." What she feared was "being too egotistical. It is fear that it shall be seen and the final, damning, judgement pronounced," this judgment being that she was self-absorbed (NS, 54). Another time, Smart chastized herself for writing about herself: "Why all this continual talk and thought about yourself?" (NS, 66). Even though she was writing a text that was supposed to be private and strictly for herself, she brought to it assumptions from the outside, assumptions about how a woman should view herself; that is, women should be thinking only of others. Smart complied with the stereotypes of society and made the subject of herself taboo, thus constructing a womanly-woman narrative. We can also appreciate why she would find Eliot's impersonality a welcoming strategy, giving her a way to talk about herself without giving herself away.

In the above passage we can see that Smart was revealing the public, and hence subversive, nature of her diary, offering implications that it was meant to be read at some future date. For when she wrote that her "fear" was that the diary "shall be seen," she went on to suggest that this was her intention as long as the time was right: "I hate anything to be known or judged before I have finished it complete and satisfactory" (NS, 54). Thus did she negotiate what DuPlessis calls the desire to conceal, which would make her an object, and the desire to reveal, which would make her a subject.

Indeed, in contrast to shunning the subject of herself, other entries celebrate their potential for self-expression with unabashed, though clearly novel, confidence. Smart discussed the function of the diary in her Ottawa journal of 1933: "And I am not going to mind the cryptic criticisms of self-analysis and introspection – it is childish and dishonest to deny it. I shall say what I feel and I shall talk about myself unto the last page, and I shall make no apologies. You can't squash everything. Besides, points must be cleared up, discussed, sifted, concluded" (NS, 48). This last line emphasizes that the diary was a means of communication, a way of explaining herself to those who will read it. It further suggests that the diary was the site of Smart's Freudian quest for self-knowledge, for she used "self-analysis and introspection" as a method of sorting the fragments of herself into a unified, present-to-itself whole.

She ended this entry as she had begun it, with a resolution to assert her wants and needs not only in the diary but in the world, refusing to see anything inappropriate in this decision: "Why be ashamed? Surely it is more adolescent to be ashamed if you look at it largely ... like Sholto and the ice-cream and milk in the Savoy [...] I thought to myself: 'I want milk and ice-cream. It's the convention-al thing to take tea and sandwiches [...] But surely [...] it would be childish to take what I did not want because I thought it was the thing to do. The really mature thing then would be to take what I want.' And I did" (NS, 49). Though the subject of snack time may seem trivial in itself, what is significant is that she confronted the possibility of self-determination. Nevertheless the subject *is* trivial. The passage concomitantly reveals Smart as naive, a seeming ado-lescent despite the fact that she was twenty years old, for she cele-brated her "maturity" with a glass of milk, viewing this decision as a triumph. It illuminates the upper-middle-class society in which she was raised: so constraining was this world that her rebellion was to reject tea for ice cream at the Savoy.

At the time of this decision, Smart was casually involved with Meredith Frampton, a portrait painter she had met in London dur-ing the early months of 1933. Sullivan describes him as "older, a father figure," who had been elected to the Royal Academy. In addi-tion to milk and ice cream, Smart wanted an artistic life, and she took it upon herself to create one. However, because she was a woman – and women have traditionally been the muse rather than the maker, the inspiration rather than the inspired – she seemed per-ceptive to the reality that the fastest way into the world of poetry was through a man.

Exploring the genesis of Smart's literary campaign, Sullivan writes: "Desperate to get started as a writer, Elizabeth chose the route most easily available to women. She fell in love with an artist. It was a familiar history lived by most creative women before her. A young man wishing to write finds a circle, and often becomes the protégé of the famous writer. George Barker, at about this time, was being taken under the wing of T.S. Eliot. A young woman finds an artist/lover – a more dangerous strategy. Nurturing her writing is not always the dominant concern, and whose ego survives intact is not often in ques-tion."[37] It is interesting to note that not only was Barker Eliot's cho-sen one, but he would become Smart's long-time lover. Perhaps she adopted Eliot's agenda in order to show that she too was worthy of "protégé" status.

Although there are no surviving diaries from the beginning of her rela-tionship with Frampton, a letter from Smart to her father reveals that the basis of her attraction to him was artistic: "On Saturday I am going out with Meredith Frampton – that will be a 'golden moment.' He is so comforting and stimulating – why? Because he has ideas of his own – not educational ideas & he is a real artist all the way through." But while celebrating the "rare gift" of Frampton's presence, she felt it necessary to denigrate herself. Having described how happy he made her, she added, "But of course I may be a foolish female carried away by imagination."[38] This is the first indication of a phenomenon common to women writers and one that pervaded Smart's artistic consciousness: the assumption that what she imagined and expressed was somehow valueless, "foolish." This opinion is directly connected to her claims to artistic talent, evidenced in a poem she wrote in her diary shortly after the Frampton letter:

> Fool. I am a fool.
> [. . .]
> Silly mutterings and vain words
> Asking to be a poet!
> Futile and stupid.
> Just like adolescence. (ESF, box 2, f.4)

Smart had clearly internalized the denigration used to put down nineteenth-century women novelists. As Dale Spender remarks, the prevailing notion was that "silly women" wrote "silly novels."

The relationship with Frampton petered out when Smart returned to Canada for the summer. But she did not lose her ambivalent claims to art. Her diary for this period documents the tension between a spoiled, frivolous debutante and a serious, aspiring writer. Back home with her parents, she enjoyed a social life filled with parties and dates: "These are the sensuous days with the bang, now pushed back on high curls. Nothing but sensuousness seducing me, cajoling me, muffling me up in lazy luxury. That will to work is a faint idea, not an urgent immediate one." But she ended the entry with a subtle invocation to a muse: "Oh direct the sensual force into some more creating channel" (NS, 57–8). We can see how divided Smart was here, fractured into social and artistic halves that seemed destined to keep her from a sense of wholeness and hence well-being.

Within a few months, the invocation – to herself – was explicit: "Work is the only only only remedy for life: for happiness, for interest, for stability, for security. Hard, *willed* work. Oh *work*!" (NS, 62). By the end of the year had she composed a poem in her diary which made it clear that her frustration with her lack of productivity was tied to her conception of herself as a woman:

I'm going to be a poet, I said
[. . .]
But before I could chisel the first word of a concrete poem
My breast fell voluptuously into my hand
And I remembered I was a woman. (NS, 66)

Back in London in 1935, Smart was still remembering she was a woman and hoping that Lord John Pentland would realize it as well. She began a relationship with him that fall, but Pentland, the conservative grandson of Lord and Lady Aberdeen of Aberdeenshire, was an even more unlikely candidate than the older Frampton for fulfilling her poetic passions. Sullivan remarks that Smart's attempts to woo him with poems were generally met with Pentland's response to the tune of "I don't like being troubled."[39] Not only was he "troubled" by Smart's poetic overtures, but he resisted her sexual advances, or needs. Feeling rejected, she articulated the significance of love in universal terms, announcing that "All women must be loved," for "Women are only made whole by physical love" NS, 79). Her conception of a unified selfhood is ironic, for in wanting to be made "whole" by a man, she was in effect asking to be fractured into the multiple roles she was expected to play as a feminine woman in patriarchy: mistress, mother, muse, and so on. On the other hand, her admission that she wanted "physical love" shows how she was beginning to rewrite the romance narrative and go beyond the ending to scenes of explicit sexual gratification.

Smart did not have to worry about how her selfhood would be thwarted by Pentland, though, for at a time when she was trying to come to terms with her own sexuality and understand her burgeoning desires, he was failing to confront his own. In reaction to his reticence, she went so far as to subtitle her story "My Lover John" "a story of impotence."

Pentland's apparently repressed views on sex echoed the sentiments of Smart's parents. It was her upbringing as a "proper" girl that led her, as a young adult, to be obsessed about her virginity. Her diary is preoccupied with both losing and preserving this "valued" condition. There can be no doubt that the mores of conservative Ottawa, upheld and enhanced by Smart's well-stationed family, would have instilled in her a belief that sex was simply bad. And yet she experienced healthy sexual drives. A conflict necessarily ensued from this opposition: "the fight against the powerful, the irresistible, the compelling monster Sex" (NS, 57). Smart acknowledged desire but had to denigrate this desire according to how she had been taught to understand sex: it was something ugly, unnatural, a "monster." She later admitted to buying into this construct for the sake of appearances. Criticizing her relationship with Pentland, she noted: "Sex was to him a shame. *That* is a shame, a great shame. I don't, though I pretend I do" (NS, 82). His impotence was matched by her inability to negotiate private desire and social performance.

In this same entry, Smart returned to the subject of herself, and the diarizing of it. In March 1936, on her way home to Canada, she exposed Pentland as a man who preferred women to be unobtrusive: "And he said that my poems – or whatever other name better fits them – should be written and then destroyed – either destroyed or sent as a letter to a friend – to him!" She resisted this advice and instead argued for her right to self-expression in her diary. After wondering of Pentland, "Doesn't he keep a diary?" she asserted: "Mayn't I, without too much conceit or death-dealing self-love, arrange in order the heavy moments of my life? Set my life out for myself without shame, without the strategic self-depredation? – unnatural most unnatural idea that I am bowing to I!" (NS, 82–3).

The entry explicitly reveals Smart's awareness of what was expected of her as a "proper" woman in a patriarchy, and it shows how she conceived the diary as a space where these expectations may be undermined, where the "strategies" she employed outside the text to convince the world of her femininity could be put aside. The fact that she referred to her desire as an "unnatural most unnatural idea" drives home how much her femininity had been constructed according to what was deemed "natural." But as we shall see, in the spirit of Eliot's Fisher King, she would use her diary to try to set in order her "unnatural" fragments of self-determination.

Smart was generally unclear about what was appropriate behaviour for a woman and how to reconcile her desire with this behaviour. During her hiatus from Pentland, and while touring the South Pacific with Mrs Watt, she met Hall, a young man she diaristically dubbed "Velvet Eyes." She described the effect he had on her: "He can cause me violent overpowering moods and tears or utter happiness in a minute. What a fire, this sex!" She went on to contemplate the labour of love: "Is this business worth its trouble? Here I am sulking in my cabin for no apparent reason. What a destructive force until satisfied! What a consuming monster! Its thoroughness, insidiousness and subtlety astound me every time I suddenly see my puppet-like obedience to it" (NS, 106). Having earlier stated that she only "pretended" to be ashamed of sex, Smart now reverted to describing it as a "monster," a description that indicates how deeply her moral conditioning had penetrated and how consistently she grappled with identity.

Though she was aroused by Velvet Eyes, she also retained the opinion that sex was somehow "monstrous." Or rather, she learned through his attempts at seduction how wide the emotional gap was between having a desire and acting on it. She recounted the seductive efforts of her fellow traveller: "I did a few things for Mrs. Watt and again joined Velvet Eyes. We walked on deck, but then his old ploy came out. 'I'm going down to have a sleep.' I didn't like that. It was so defeatist." "[D]isgruntled" as she was with this "ploy" to get her to his room, Smart nonetheless went to lengths to present herself as a desirable object that evening: "Finally I went down and pressed my grey organdy dress and bathed [...] and put on unusual artificial things like mascara and cheek rouge and diamonds and whisked down to dinner" (NS, 107). She preferred concealing herself as object to revealing herself as subject, but she knew that this behaviour was what was expected of her, and so she complied with the womanly-woman script.

When her efforts at attraction were (not surprisingly) successful, she once again uncomfortably found herself confronted with the sexual demands of Hall: "So Velvet Eyes enfolded me in a soft embrace and we danced to old tunes like 'Dinah' and 'Darktown Strutters' Ball.' But he began to get difficult and not want to dance but to leave and spoil it all. So I went out on deck with him and we walked round to the back of the boat. But I began to freeze with the cold wind so we went in, but then V.E. got more morose and said, 'I'm going to bed,' and I like a fool told him not to instead of making him not by subtle means [...] What would be the use? I wasn't sure I want to anyway. I wasn't sure I want to anyway."

Alone on the deck, she examined what had happened and wondered what had been expected of her. Revived by the fresh air, she felt, "Surely, it isn't necessary to decide at once whether you are going to sleep with a man or avoid him altogether, the minute you see him, to be practical?" (NS, 108–9). Though she came to this conclusion, it should be noted that Smart seems to have been intrigued with her capacity to manipulate: "and I like a fool told him not to instead of making him not by subtle means." She was recognizing her potential powers as a woman – powers that she would need as she was forced to battle the "monster sex" within a patriarchy which preferred women to be weak.

The encounter with Hall was a confusing one for Smart. She had always been taught to flaunt her appearance and her femininity – as she put it, "pass ashtrays gracefully, be a Blonde" (A, 140). Coming out as a debutante, she had learned how to fashion herself as an object of desire. But the Hall episode raised a question perhaps rarely asked before: the question "why?" It was one thing to know how to construct one's femininity, but here Smart confronted the greater issue of why construct it, for whom, and to what ends it would lead.

As Smart struggled with the stereotypes that had conditioned how she perceived herself as a woman, her behaviour was surely complicated by a seeming uncertainty as to who exactly she thought she was and who she wanted to be. She faced this dilemma in her diary, as on the occasion when Mrs Watt accused her of being selfish. At first quick to agree, she was nonetheless perceptive to the dangers of *not* being selfish to some degree: "It is living, night and day, month in month out, with her. If I did utterly sympathize with her, I should *be* her. I should be swamped and submerged. I can't have one thing on top to be in control and have my strong personal secret life going on below and in odd moments" (NS, 129). Smart recognized that autonomy, and artistic creation, depended on her establishing some kind of border between self and other, inner and outer worlds. If she lived only as a relational female with her permeable ego, she would run the risk of being "swamped and submerged," drowned by her own limitless fluidity.

But it was in this "swamped and submerged" state that she continued to play out her sense of self not only as a traditional woman but as a daughter. When she was chastized for selfishness by Mrs Watt, Smart was concerned that she had let her father down: "But all these things I knew before I left home and I prayed often [...] that I would have the courage and the strength and the endurance to come through this with a noble character. Well, I haven't. I've failed. (Poor Daddy! I've disappointed him again!)" (NS, 129). At the same time, she admitted that she had been deceptive: "Think even of the dishonest, dull, subterfugic letters I write home to my parents. Why can't I be honest and clean-shafted, and direct to Daddy at least?" (NS, 132).

On the one hand, Smart wanted to be a good daughter, dutifully upholding the conventions in which she was raised. And to do so, it was necessary to deceive herself: "You see the things there. You've *got* to learn and follow [...] I suppose I must follow – what excuse is there for not following? The world does it like this. The world will point at you and call you eccentric if you don't do it like this. Why don't you do it like this? Appease the world" (NS, 133).

On the other hand, she resisted these deceptive tactics, as she went on to experience a burst of self-assertion: "But why have I been abasing myself lately? Denying my ego? Saying, 'I must stop talking about myself. People will think I am conceited, or too introspective.' What if they do? I am going against my own principles to deny my ego and its right of cockiness. I am trying to convince myself that I am nothing wonderful or mysterious or potentially great, when secretly I still hope and perhaps even believe I am. Ye Gods! I *should* believe I am" (NS, 133). In an about-face, turning to face herself, she revelled in this newly attained subject position.

MIGHTY POETS SOMETHING HAPPENING

It was in the spirit of subjectivity that Smart returned to the issue of poetry, determined to deny her artistic ego no more. Her self-assertion was still limited in that she planned to satisfy her creative self not so much by herself but through a man; but this may be regarded as a strategy to get to the centre more quickly. Having been frustrated by the likes of Pentland and "Velvet Eyes," she instructed herself: "From now on I must be *mental* until I find myself a proper mate. However, may that be soon!" (NS, 112).

The "proper mate" that Smart was longing for was a poet. Just before her world tour, she made the crucial declaration that she "must marry a poet. It's the only thing." But she went on to lament, "Why don't I know any?" (NS, 80). This was still her predicament almost a year later, towards the end of the trip. Resuming her quest for a man with laurel leaves, she wondered in Colombo, "How could I even consider linking up my life forever to John or Jimmy or any of the ones who are not even related to my species?" She was frustrated that her artistic life was being delayed: "What puzzles me is why I never meet those ones [poets] [...] I'm twenty-three. It's too late to be a question mark. I'm still still a question mark. Let me get back to London quickly and meet the ones who know" (NS, 132). Smart's "question mark" signified her questionable status on the margins of the literary centre, and she longed for London because it was just such a centre.

Back in London, though she briefly resumed the relationship with Pentland, she soon turned to "the ones who know." And her pursuit of these artists lead her to France. In the spring of 1938 she travelled with a group of friends to Cassis, to the home of collagist Jean Varda. (Cassis was a fashionable artists' colony, one which Virginia Woolf and her Bloomsbury cronies frequented throughout the nineteen twenties.) In Cassis, Smart worked on her own writing, developed friendships with artists such as surrealists Alice and Wolfgang Paalen, and became involved with Varda himself. This was one of the most liberating periods in her life to date. Professionally, she was finally immersed in creative surroundings, revelling, "At last [...] Mighty Poets something happening" (A, 147). Personally, what was "happening" was that with Varda, she had intercourse for the first time. There is a dramatic change in her diary here as it becomes more intense and metaphoric in its internal examining. Poetry and passion exploded simultaneously, highlighting how the two were interchangeable for Smart, and how she would translate her experiences into Benstock's notion of a sexualized writing identity. This fusion also marks a beginning of Smart's living as innovatively as she wrote, a trademark of modernist women, according to Hanscombe and Smyers.

Varda proved "a proper mate" because, as an artist who was sexually explicit, he satisfied her yearning for a union of body and soul (likely inspired by her reading of Lawrence). He drew out, however, the same problematic issues that Smart had been forced to face with Hall; namely, what does a woman want when she flirts with a man? Varda charged her with "being a 'vamp'": "He said I had been flirting all evening," a reproach that confused her. "He accused me because I refused him my body. It is true that when the heart expands the hand reached out to follow: the gesture towards wants an outward sign as well. I want to flow to everyone. But if I give my body as the natural accompaniment to my flow towards, what is to prevent me from giving my body to every sympathetic man I meet? And nearly every man I meet is sympathetic. I cannot think that would be right" (NS, 187–8). Smart's "I want to flow to everyone" once again indicates the dangerous consequences of a permeable ego whose floodgates are not held in check, for as she was suggesting, it could lead her into trouble with men.

Whether "right" or not, Smart did give her body to Varda. Actually, according to her description, it seems more accurate to say that Varda took her body. Smart's conception of passion was problematized by violence; her involvement with men was infused with elements of domination and subordination. An early sign of this characteristic was registered in her account of an afternoon with Pentland: "At the inn, after tea, I was unaccountably overcome by a longing. Such an overpowering feeling, numbing all else [.. .] I was afraid at what I saw – cruelty in the eyes, love on the mouth. I was aghast. I have never been so physically compelled to love" (NS, 77). Smart's sensations resound with masochistic intent: "John disturbed me for at least eight hours after I talked to him. What *is* that magical tragical power anyway? I am drawn to him, compelled to be miserable, chastened, subdued, humbled, curtailed, bound" (NS, 155). It is not surprising that she described Pentland, when the relationship ended, as "my tyrant John" (NS, 159). Her list of qualities that she was "compelled" to be was perhaps inspired by social conditioning which fashioned men as active and powerful and women as passive and weak – after all, she had been trained to "be a Blonde," her physical prowess limited to "passing ashtrays."

The dichotomy of wanting and resisting a man's power over-whelmed her when she dealt with Varda. At one point, "He terrified me and yet I knew he was good. He was like an element [...] I knew no conventions would restrain him. Virginity to him was a fruit to be eaten, to be taken in his chaotic stride. But I believed still nothing could happen to me" (NS, 186–7). If society had taught Smart that for "good" girls sex was a "monster," she easily presented herself as one attacked by it – and its name here was Varda. Her comment "But I believed still nothing could happen to me" exposes her as naive, yet this naïveté is revealed as a pose of innocence when it is placed beside her earlier diary entry: "But my wish is only that he love me and want me so much willy nilly that he can do nothing else. He *must* devour me. Minute by minute pouncing on it ravenously" (NS, 182).

Her wish was granted shortly after, when Varda literally jumped her. In a section of her France diary entitled "For the Little Cassis Book," she documented the experience:

Varda, the first day alone, attacked me in my room. I bit and fought like a wild animal and we scuffled around on the dusty floor [...]

Face fear. I faced fear. Ah well. Flowers must fruit.

"Come for a walk," he said that night.

We walked up the road, up the hill, up a path to the haunted house, up to a stone altar among the pines. The nightingales warbled, the moon shone – the mountains of rock were bulwarks. We sat on the cold stone of the altar, all the time the nightingales trilled around. (NS, 191)

The "fear" that Smart had to face was the fear of losing her virginity. After being attacked, she still went off with him, "up the hill" to her first sexual encounter, confirming that she found men who were threatening attractive. It must be emphasized that she wrote this entry after the event had taken place, and after she had had time to dwell on it. This passage is not raw, but a description that has been worked over by her literary imagination. Smart deliberately constructed herself as a woman who sacrifices herself to a man in fulfillment of her feminine destiny. Her double reference to the "stone altar" makes it obvious that she was presenting herself as a pagan offering to Varda. On the other hand, her preoccupation with sex here and elsewhere implies that she wanted to have it, and so she plotted a narrative in which she *could* have it; but because she was "taken," she could not be blamed for her participation. She concealed and revealed her desire, becoming both object (sacrificial victim) and subject (subversive agent of self-determination).

Another entry, for 14 May 1938, provides a detailed examination of the emotional, spiritual, and creative impact the sexual experience had on her:

From the beating of the heart O! like a pulse of the sea, uncontrollable, for a vision upwards through the thorns.

Should I have expected these tearings of the flesh by the way? For the *toiling* I had set my teeth against. Rip! Rip! The disobedient flesh and on top at last a soiled remnant gasping its goodbye. For me, these visions are a consummation worth the world beside [...]

This this is enough, and the upward mingling of the sun [...]

Out of these rocks comes the saving essence [...] an overwhelming force of spirit that may be fierce wanting, by an uncondensed and unadulterated throe of upward desire, enter, enter the body and purge. O glorifying! [...]

Entering daily and nightly into the body of God [...]

Yet the rocks tower above. Yet there are elements unfaced. My death to dare before I reach those green top trees, I attain the world, to drink in forever my overflowing metaphors. (NS, 175–6)

Once again, things secular and spiritual, glorious and hideous, combine to round out Smart's vision and experience of love. Sex was painful and veritably assaulting, suggested by her images of "thorns," the "tearings of the flesh," setting her "teeth against," and the exclamatory "Rip! Rip!" But this attack also yielded a religious transcendence, evidenced by her "visions" which "are a consummation worth the world beside." While the "consummation" was sexual, it was mystical as well, allowing her to "mingle" with the sun, to find comfort in Earth's breast, and ultimately to have access "into the body of God." Smart harnessed these effects in order to release not only her body but her writing as well – her "overflowing metaphors." She recognized how love could empower her heart and art simultaneously, symbiotically. The writing as practised and honed in the diary testifies to this empowerment, and to how she was constructing, in the words of Benstock, a "sexualized" writing identity in expatriation and thus changing "the history of modern women's writing, charting the terrain of female sexuality from female perspectives."[40]

With Varda, Smart matured as a woman and as a writer, but she still struggled with who she was and how she could and should behave. As Smith has noted of early-twentieth-century autobiographers, coming to terms with identity was difficult and involved much "grappling." Inspired by her affair with Varda, Smart nurtured a dramatic sense of herself as one consumed by love. In New York with him in October 1939, she explained how she lived through love: " I can only live, in its warm envelope, expanding, breathing, like a live, blind thing, more blessed than the embryo for it *knows* its own bliss. Be my surrounding cloak" (NS, 181). Just as earlier she had asserted that "Women are only made whole by physical love," so she was here reiterating in Chodorow's terms that women are relational, their egos dependent upon surrounding love and the men who embody it.

This romantic narrative of herself blinded by love gave way to a modernist one as Smart textualized how sex could be used to manipulate. When she was in Mexico with Varda in 1939, she tried to make him as jealous as he had been making her: "I began to flirt, to assert my womanly powers. (O well, if *that's* what you want, it's easy to seduce and enslave.)" (NS, 214). No longer the inspiration of poetic expression, sex was now an instrument of power. Earlier, as an inexperienced lover with Hall, she had just begun to understand how a man might be manipulated. Now she had obviously come to recognize fully the force she had as a woman. She inverted traditional roles by making herself, as aggressor, the subject of her own sexual story and by relegating Varda, as the enslaved, to the position of object.

And yet beyond the sexual, Smart had great difficulty expressing herself with any kind of force. Returning to the theme of self-determination in her New York diary, she challenged herself to "*Think, Trouble* to arrange the threads, *Dare* to be honest" (NS, 183). But days later she admitted defeat, retreating into her performance as the self-effacing female, that "dishonest" and "subterfugic" self she had earlier chastized herself for being. Examining her behaviour with Varda, she confessed: "I am not honest enough [...] I cringe. I acquiesce; I am a coward to hurt people's feelings. I haven't the dignity to speak out, to dare to be myself even if it offends. But I don't want to offend" (NS, 185). And so she continued to struggle with accepting and rejecting traditional roles for women.

Smart was in Mexico with Varda at the end of 1939: he had joined her during her visit there with the Paalens. If the sensual surroundings of Cassis – sun, sea, sex, and art – had allowed her to bloom as a lover and writer, the equally languorous climate of Mexico allowed her to ripen. Once there, she became infatuated with Alice Paalen, and had a brief relationship with her. Smart's celebration of women, and the power that obtained from their union, was directly connected to creation. For it was in Mexico that she searched for a new style of writing. I discussed earlier how she was inspired by the works of Nin[41] and Durrell, but it was specifically in maternal tones that she expressed her need for a new form: "But what form? Infinite pains for a poem. But I need a new form even for a poem. I have used up my ones [...] Each word must rip virgin ground. No past effort must ease the new birth. Rather than that, the haphazard note, the unborn child, the bottled embryo." Smart's work was not the only thing to be delivered. She herself felt reborn, as the entry announces: "LIFE BEGINS HERE" (NS, 202). Note that her description of her new form – "Each word must rip virgin ground" – echoes her earlier account of losing her virginity: "Rip! Rip!" Her sexualized identity as a woman was directly related to her sexualized identity as a writer.

Her response to Nin's novella *Winter of Artifice* was similarly conceived in erotic terms: "ALL ALL ALL. And a WOMAN, a real woman, only by or from a woman, ALL. It fertilizes" (NS, 205). In being "fertilized" by a woman, Smart was likely responding to a generic bond which transcended her sense of individual self and was manifested in women being relational, interconnected. She was also being "fertilized" by Paalen, and in announcing that she felt reborn, she was able to fertilize not only her passion for Paalen but the writing of it. The language in which she related their intimacy is particularly sexualized.

Smart, for instance, narrates: "The moon draws me like a magnet [...] Or it charges me and I leap like a shorn sheep. The moon forced my mouth open and my teeth and entered me as I lay shaking on the brittle beige grass. Like a baby forcing the womb open its electric globe forced open my mouth. It was in me" (NS, 216). She went on to celebrate: "I can never realize the *strangeness* of the moon, the *potency*, the *gloriousness* [. . . .] If anybody else has ever seen the moon why don't they go around talking, raving, being astonished about it? So exciting. So mysterious. So appallingly beautiful." Smart then criticized the surrealists: "And they (who despise all religion), the surrealists seek the *marvellous*. Surrealism then is only a religion, a measly simpering substitute. And they've *used up* the moon (they think) so they get their marvels out of (e.g.) a melting watch. (When I look at the moon not only my flesh, but my eyes, my hair, my bones melt melt melt into the reverberating rays.)" (NS, 217).

In his first "Manifesto of Surrealism" (1924), André Breton had defined the term as involving a "resolution" of the "two states, dream and reality, which are seemingly so contradictory, into a kind of absolute reality, a *surreality*." He explained that surrealists celebrate the "marvellous": "Let us not mince words: the marvelous is always beautiful, anything marvelous is beautiful, in fact only the marvelous is beautiful."[42] According to Smart, though, surrealists had become bored with the moon and so had moved on to other marvels. She, on the other hand, found the moon the perfect symbol by which to register her passion for Paalen, for it is associated with the feminine: "When patriarchy superseded matriarchy, a feminine character came to be attributed to the moon and a masculine to the sun. The *hieros gamos*, generally understood as the marriage of heaven and earth, may also be taken as the union of the sun and the moon."[43] By turning to the feminine moon at the same time as she turned to her first lesbian experience, Smart was reworking surrealism to satisfy her female desires, and she was participating in a new "marriage," one not between sun and moon but between moon and moon, or woman and woman.

She continued to write sexually about the sea: "O the well-being, the well-being, the freedom. Sun Sea Sand Foam. Waves that break that really break. That *joy*. The enormous sea's rhythm quivers like a jelly [...] Oh the boiling over, the curdling cuddle of the sea's burst!" (NS, 229). This "burst" gave way to surreal intercourse:

Then her smiling face bending over me with the falling hair. (I listening, listening, waiting, gathering this rare essence, waiting for the full revelation.) Her eyes – though – she was all women – womanhood – [...] her eyes like this, naked [...] but all the time her smiling dream mouth, smiling, smiling. "Have you ever been with another woman as you have been with me?" "No." "Never?" "Never." "And it seems natural to you to be like this with me?" "Yes" [...] In the night she entered the enormous caves. We are in the caves, warm, damp, fold upon fold, the caves bigger than the mind can hold, they hug the mind [...] Or with my mouth I swallow myself and her. (NS, 230).

These passages echo Smart's description of intercourse with Varda. In terms of style, she continues to register her sexual experiences in a powerfully imagaic and surrealistic language. She has constructed both herself and Paalen as the protagonists in a sensual, fantastic narrative. That she has done so is particularly relevant in terms of modernism and Schenck's discussion of what it means to be experimental. For here Smart delivers a vivid, unabashed celebration of her sexuality in what is considered a traditional form, the diary. She is doubly the modernist: she is experimenting in a classic high-modernist way with surreal prose, and she uses it to inscribe a radical sexual/textual politics.

GEORGE BARKER, THE "OO THE A – A – A!"

If Elizabeth Smart was briefly in love with Alice Paalen, she would be for a good part of her life in love with George Barker. He had many partners and admirers in addition to her, and so we should pause here to consider just what it was about this man that turned so many women on.

Only a few years before Smart met him, in 1936 Antonia White had become involved with a group of surrealist poets that included Barker.

She and Barker spent several evenings together, and she devoted many pages in her diary to him (book 5). Around the same time, White's close friend, American poet and novelist Emily Coleman (who was living in England), grew as obsessed with him as Smart would be, though for a much shorter period of time. Coleman's diary is filled with longing for him, with comments such as "for five months now – I have been suffering agonies because of you."[44] Anaïs Nin, too, in the early forties would bring Barker into her erotica-writing venture in New York, and she apparently slept with him as well. What did he have that so many intelligent, literary, diary-keeping women wanted?

Photographs taken in the nineteen thirties and forties show him to be a tall, lean man with a dark, receding hairline and glasses. He looks, I suppose, poetic in an arty, sensitive sort of way, a good candidate for the "new age man" of our nineteen nineties. White described him thus: "His face is more various than any face I know. It can be quite blank – a mere neat arrangement of features – often quite mean and common – or quite remarkably beautiful" (D, 1: 80). It is likely, though, that women did not fall in love (only) with his physical appearance. I think it more probable that they fell in love with the man *as* poet and for his poetry. Smart is the greatest proof of this aspect of his appeal, for she decided that she wanted to marry him long before she had ever seen him; she fell in love with poems of his that she picked up in a bookstore. His poetry could certainly inspire and provoke, for it is infused with themes of mad passion and passionate madness – homosexual, heterosexual, and incestual – themes that were preoccupying many modernists.

Another very different point that may help us understand his magnetism is that Barker had a "Christ complex." Coleman describes a night when she and Barker made love, and how he confessed that he did not enjoy the sex (he was at this point predominantly homosexual). "'Then why did you do it?' He went into a long explanation which I don't understand, saying he has a religious complex and thinks he must help people."[45] Perhaps Barker responded to women in ways they needed. He helped them to attain sexual satisfaction, but more importantly, he encouraged their writing and so conferred legitimacy on their artistic identities. White affirmed, "As regards work he gives me more hope and stimulus than anyone I know" (book 5). Perhaps, too, the fact that Barker was Eliot's protégé added to his appeal not only as a poet but as a poet who might be in a position to further their own literary careers. And we must keep in mind that however predisposed to relational and self-sacrificing behaviour White, Smart, Nin, and Coleman were, they were ambitious in their desires for artistic success.

Smart had first mentioned Barker's work at the back of a 1937 diary, in a list recording all the books read during this year – *Janus* was finished on 31 August (ESF, box 2, f.10).[46] More than a year later she referred to him in a letter she wrote to Durrell. She had begun a correspondence with Durrell after she returned from Europe to Canada in 1938. Writing for the *Ottawa Journal*, she was also sending her poems to magazines, including Durrell's *Booster,* which he was printing out of Paris.[47] Durrell not only accepted some of these poems, but continued to correspond with this new young poet. In her only extant letter to him, in addition to asking Durrell for technical advice, she told him: "About my favourite younger poet is George Barker. He excites me most, even when immature."[48]

Durrell quickly capitalized on Smart's enthusiasm for his friend, seeing her as a means of helping Barker's troubled finances. According to Sullivan, Durrell "had concluded Elizabeth was wealthy and gave her Barker's address, suggesting that he would be willing to sell manuscripts. With twenty-five dollars Louie [Smart's mother] had given her for clothes, Elizabeth bought her first Barker manuscript, a poem 'O Who will Speak from a Womb or a Cloud?'"[49]

At the same time as Durrell was encouraging Smart to assist Barker, she herself was becoming more and more obsessed with him. Although he does not appear in her diary until December 1939, when he does, it is with a vengeance. It was while visiting the Paalens in Mexico that Smart confessed, "George Barker's approach is in my mind always" (NS, 204). A few days later, "George Barker grows into a long dangerous image and is woven among the undertones." She was both sexually and linguistically aroused, quoting from his poems: "But O the excitement is in for instance: 'Wondering one, wandering on.' 'I penetrate the valleys bringing correct direction.' It is the complete juicy *sound* that runs bubbles over, that intoxicates till I can hardly follow (and the recurring lines in 'Daedalus'; 'the moist palm of my hand like handled fear like fear cramping my hand.' OO the a – a – a!)" (NS, 206–7).

Barker had a good sense of Smart's preoccupation with him, for even though they had never met, he wrote to her on 2 February 1940, asking her to help him and his wife, Jessica, get out of Japan.[50] Though this was the first time that Smart had heard about a wife, she was undismayed. Barker's request fuelled her passion, for by 1 March she felt that "If George Barker should appear now I would eat him up with eagerness. I can feel the flushed glow of minds functioning in divine understanding and communication" (NS, 240). Smart's diary entries, charting the advent of Barker, reinforce her conception of love as a paradox, earlier exhibited with Pentland and Varda: it was both mystical and masochistic. I have already touched on her association of religion and worship with love, and it is reinforced here by her naive certainty that contact with Barker would result in "minds functioning in divine understanding and communication." Her obsession was also rendered in images which threatened her physical and emotional autonomy, for Barker was perceived as "a long dangerous image." That she wanted to "eat him up with eagerness," however, once again suggests she would invert sex roles so that she could take control. She would become the subject to Barker's object in this sexually charged narrative.

It was in this frame of emotion that Smart wrote, "All day and all night I wrangle ways to rescue Barker from Japan" (NS, 243). She was so determined to help him that at one point she actually accepted a job as a maid in order to make enough money to buy the requested plane tickets. Sullivan's comment – "Nurturing her writing is not always the dominant concern" – proves accurate here, for by 29 April 1940 there was "No poem. I am engaged as a maid with Mrs. Kennedy. All for George Barker. But I am gleeful" (NS, 244). Although Smart was soon fired, she eventually raised the necessary funds, and thus, thanks to her, the Barkers arrived in California on 19 July. By August Smart was having her much-longed-for and carefully orchestrated affair with George.

As it had been with the Paalens, her selection of Barker had everything to do with the fact that he was artistic. In a letter written but never sent to him, Smart confirmed the grounds on which the relationship was based: "There are (for me) two things on which it was all founded: (a) I love you; & (b) you are a poet" (A, 105). As I indicated earlier, it is likely that the reason she loved him was because he was a poet. In another entry she asserted: "But if I don't believe in love, if I don't believe I was made only for you, if I don't believe you are a poet, if I don't believe poetry is all there is, I don't believe anything" (NS, 261). While this assertion implies that love and work slipped easily into symbiosis, in fact her relationship with Barker accentuated the dichotomies not only between "pleasing mother and being self" but between being a woman and being a writer.

Given Smart's previous worries that she had failed her father simply because she was behaving selfishly, it is not surprising that she examined her liaison in light of her parents' response, as she commented: "Passion and reason produced these children and reason was even the tenderer. But now my father has three prodigal daughters perenially and periodically supplicating for the fatted calf" (NS, 251).[51] Smart's allusion to herself (as well as to her sisters) as the biblical prodigal son reminds us how she transformed her historical "I" into a cultural artifact, one that was textually (re)produced within her diary. She was doubly undutiful, for not only did she leave Ottawa, but she forsook her parents and their propriety by having an affair with Barker. She registered the impact of her wayward behaviour on her family, depicting their disappointment in universal terms: "Parents' imaginations build a foundation out of their hopes and regrets into which children seldom grow, but contrary as a tree, lean sideways out of the architecture, blown by a fatal wind their parents never envisaged" (NS, 251).

The affair with Barker threatened to blow Smart away from herself too, specifically from the part that would be a poet. Shortly before the Barkers' arrival in California, she privileged her desire to write: "I knew love would never be enough [...] I am an artist first. *Pan*, not man, my lover" (NS, 242). Explaining to her diary how she should compose poetry, she instructed herself to "Sit and brood till it arrives and don't compromise and don't sit waiting for another to fertilize you" (NS, 245). But like White, Smart's celebration of her creativity was immediately dampened by a need to denigrate it: "Barker's new poems arrived and I say O how ashamed I am to have thought *mine* were poetry, for he alone says *exactly* what I wanted to say [...] His are all true. Mine limp and labour" (NS, 245). She returned to this theme, but with a new sense of injustice that Barker, now her lover, should be judged better. In Ottawa, "Gene discomposes me with telling me that I should not want to be a poet because George is and I can never be so great a one as he" (NS, 254).[52]

Smart's sense of self as artist and as woman was a fractured one. On the one hand, she seemed to buy into Pound's pronouncement that women could not invent "anything in the arts,"[53] and she thus provided her own justification for the fact that they were expected to "keep back on the edge" of the male-centred crowd of men who were doing all the inventing. On the other hand, she resisted her positioning as marginal and was "discomposed" because a friend had the audacity to tell her that as a woman she could never equal Barker's skill.

She went on to explain how motherhood necessarily problematizes creativity for women: "But though unable to articulate my protest I feel that the thing I want to say is the thing never said but always done, the saying invariably abandoned for the being. Which is, in truth, the simple fact of being a woman overpowered by voices of blood each time she rises to speak her piece. And love that gives, compels her to adore being devoured surrendering to a destruction that of course causes her to be born again, but obliterates all private ambition and blinds her eyes and her heart with images of unborn babies" (NS, 254). As I have shown, Smart had encouraged herself to become "fertilized" in order to create, and she referred to her work as "labour" in contrast to Barker's "true" verses. Though she may have given birth to a poem, the work more befiting a woman was the labour that yielded babies. She suggested as much when she contemplated the female artist: "And is not her true creativity (ie. having babies) the most creative thing possible anyhow?" (A, 183).

The tension between giving birth to a baby and a poem was not a new one for Smart. During her 1937 world tour, at the same time as she was fascinated by poetry and poets, she admitted, "It's coming over me again – this hungry passion for children" (NS, 125). And when she was in Cassis, though she was discovering herself as a writer, she was simultaneously fantasizing about marrying Barker and having babies. From an interview with Simonette Strachey, Varda's girlfriend at the outset of the 1938 Cassis trip, Sullivan quotes Strachey as remembering Smart's determination to have Barker's children: "Betty hadn't yet met him but she felt that, no matter what Barker was like, the children would all be wonderful poets."[54] Once again, we see how Smart approached art vicariously. Rather than producing the poetry, she preferred to produce the poets. This attitude also underscores the naïveté of a young writer in love with the idea of loving a poet, for it did not seem to occur to her that these children might not be – much less, might not want to be – poets.

These maternal yearnings can be appreciated through reading Chodorow, whose psychoanalytic explorations of gender formation is driven by her interest in, as her title informs us, *The Reproduction of Mothering*. Beginning her book with the truism "Women mother," she states that "the reproduction of mothering" is "a central and constituting element in the social organization and reproduction of gender."[55] She grounds her work in "the psychoanalytic account of female and male personality development" and she shows how "women's mothering reproduces itself cyclically. Women, as mothers, produce daughters with mothering capacities and the desire to mother," whereas "women as mothers ... produce sons whose nurturant capacities and needs have been systematically curtailed and repressed." It is this "division of psychological capacities which leads" daughters and sons to perpetuate the capitalist division between mother as nurturer in the private home and father as labourer in the public workforce.[56] The division fosters, as we have seen, the permeable ego boundaries of women and the bordered ego boundaries of men. It is just such a theory that illuminates Smart's psychologically driven desire for children – one that "compels her to adore being devoured" – and that explains how this desire, which is necessarily relational, "obliterates all private ambition."

But if Smart was a product of reproduced mothering, she was also a subverter of it. She appropriated the notion that women are mothers to legitimize her writing, for she described her artistic process in maternal terms. Recall that while in Mexico searching for a new literary form, she asserted, "No past effort must ease the new birth." And whereas she noted that the desire to have children "of course causes her to be born again," she made this desire metaphoric, for it was the thought of producing a new literary form that caused her to feel "LIFE BEGINS HERE."

THE LOVE OBJECT

Elizabeth Smart approached on a subversive level not only mothering but also romantic love. She acknowledged of Barker, "He is the one I picked out from the world. It was cold deliberation." She emphasized: "But the passion was not cold. No it kindled me. I begat." She then wrote in her next paragraph: "I can feel the small hard head jutting out near my bladder. That's our child" (NS, 266). While Smart was referring to her real pregnancy, she was just as likely alluding to her artistic production, for from the moment when she met Barker, she had been busily adapting the details of their relationship in a manuscript she had begun the previous spring. She had "picked" Barker to fulfill herself not only emotionally but also creatively. This selection would lead to the birth of their other "child": the plethora of diary entries in which she artistically documented the relationship, as well as her novel *By Grand Central Station I Sat Down and Wept*, culled largely from these diaries. This output overturns Sullivan's comment noted earlier: "Nurturing her writing" *was* clearly one of Smart's "dominant concerns."

Concurrent with subverting the womanly-woman narrative in which women are scripted to produce only babies, Smart reworked the romance narrative in which they fall in love with a man. She would fall in love, but in fulfillment not only of her feminine destiny but of her writerly one. Van Wart asserts in her introduction to *Necessary Secrets* that by the time Smart began *By Grand Central Station*, she "had already found a voice and a style; the relationship with Barker provided her with the subject she wanted – finally, subject and voice coincided." Smart corroborated this observation in an interview with Sullivan in 1979, when she admitted that the male figure in the book is not Barker per se: "he is faceless; the *he* is a love object."[57] Smart inverted the traditional dictates that the woman is the muse, the man the inspired. Barker himself recognized the extent to which he was made muse; in 1984 Smart spoke for him: "The fact that I was madly in love with the English language and with poetry may have given vent to my feelings. George Barker has said that *By Grand Central Station* had nothing to do with him but was more a description of my love affair with the English language."[58]

Though the novel is about poetic language, it is also undeniably about the poetry of human love – passionate, erotic, spiritual, agonizing, liberating, transforming, obsessive human love. And it is in this condition of heightened sensibility that Smart wanted to live always; she announced: "I want an ecstasy – not a comfort" (NS, 79). Perhaps it was for this reason, then, that concomitant with empowering herself with a muse, she ascribed to the stereotype that the artist must suffer. Wolfgang Paalen drove this stereotype home, as Smart related: "He said [...] if I wanted to accomplish something, the facility was dangerous – I must be unhappy to create" (NS, 214). In Hollywood in 1940 she wondered, "Why is it so hard to write, now that I have benevolent peace?" (NS, 235). Although she seemed not to have connected this query to her previous comments, she was likely unable to write because she was at "peace." She was not suffering enough and thus not facilitating that "dangerous" element of which Paalen spoke and through which art must come.

With the advent of Barker, not only did Smart suffer, but she completed her first novel based on the relationship and the suffering she had endured. It must be stressed that whole portions of this novel came directly from diary passages. The relationship of the two texts thus reveals that Smart's literary agenda included the breaking of boundaries, and it suggests how her conception of herself as a real woman experiencing this real relationship was literarily inspired. She produced a powerful, personal testimony of a woman suffering alongside an impersonal, allusive text of a modernist creating.

Smart drew on classical and Christian themes to personify herself in love, casting herself as the women in Ovid's *Heroides* and as Christ. It is this self-inflation, or mythomania, that directed her life and the narration of it. While she experienced dramatic bursts of ecstasy, she seems to have spent a greater amount of time, at least as it is recorded in her diary and fiction, in a state of agony and despair. This stemmed from Barker's habit of abandoning her.

One of the greatest accounts in literature of betrayal is Ovid's *Heroides*, a collection of letters written by mythical women at the zenith of their ecstasy and the nadir of their despair to their faithless and absent lovers. Smart was probably familiar with this book, for characters from the *Heroides* inhabit both her diary and her fiction. When Barker failed to join the pregnant Smart in Vancouver in 1941, she rendered her feelings in such mythical terms in her diary.

She became, for instance, a disillusioned Helen abandoned by her Paris: "He is not here. He is all gone [...] I contemplate vaguely the instruments of love and say with cold wonder, was this the face that launched a thousand ships? The breast that once caught fire from far away lies colder, and less ignitable than Everest" (NS, 262). And she was Penelope, left by Ulysses to spend her nights in domestic agony, preserving her sanity by weaving. Having admitted that "to say he will not and never come is to throw myself into the whirlpool and to deliver my mind into madness," she tried to find distraction in work: "I will not think of the thing now. I have no time. When I have washed these stockings I will. When I have written these letters of thanks, or sewn on a button, I will. O – meticulousness showers me with the skill of Penelope" (NS, 263–4). Decades later, Smart recalled her identification with these classical women, announcing in 1977: "On comes Dido [...] She is forever remembered. Her cry was heard. Over & over again. By Purcell. By me in 1941. O sister I feel your pain" (A, 169).[59]

The diary entries for the 1941 period are relatively sparse, but it is helpful to consider the letters she wrote to Barker at this time, for while she associated her situation with that of the women of the *Heroides*, she furthered this connection by making allusions to them in her own letters of loss and abandonment. Echoing any one of those mythical women, she poured out her anguish and desperation. For example, where Dido wrote: "I / am burning with love: all day long and all night, / I desire nothing but Aeneas,"[60] so Smart pleaded: "You must come back & get me. There's nothing, nothing at all in the world but this. You can't destroy me like this." She went on to admit: "George I am going crazy [...] I can't get to sleep & if I do I dream of corpses hidden in ice. I didn't think you would really leave me like that how could you? [...] O God really I am dying I am truly dying" (A, 40). In another letter she made Barker her Theseus, telling him, "Yesterday & today before I got your wire I was as desolate as Ariadne" (A, 43). In a fragment kept in her notebook in August entitled "A Little Note For Sebastian Barker Or, In His Absence, For Georgina Elizabeth Barker," she said of her as yet unborn child, "It was Dido's lament he heard in the womb" (A, 44).

Smart wrote through the image of herself as a woman abandoned, appropriating as she did so the poetic and emotional intensity of her mythical predecessors. That she was writing through a specific narrative is suggested by her diary entry for 24 May, in which she registered full knowledge of such a narrative. Contemplating Barker's fickle nature, fluctuating as he did between Smart and his wife, Jessica, she wondered: "For even if he intends wholly to return to her, he still turns from my tears with doubts and not willingly gives me up when he holds me in his arms – or does he?" She was horrified at these implications: "I could slit my throat from ear to ear better than know he stayed for melodramatic reasons concerning the world's favourite story of the too-well too-lightly loved and left with child" (NS, 267). Whatever Barker was doing, Smart was negotiating her life and her text. She was revealing the personal pain that she felt at being abandoned while concealing this pain through an impersonal melodrama already played out by someone else – the "world's favorite story."

If she identified with certain characters from classical times, she also associated herself with the most powerful figure of Christian times – Christ. While Dido and others suffered for the love of men, Christ suffered for the love of all people; just as these women were abandoned by the men they idolized, so Christ felt abandoned by his God: "O Father why hast thou forsaken me?" Smart's association with Christ is appropriate given that she fused secular and spiritual worship in her conception of love.

She became a Christ suffering for love and for her god, Barker, at the height of what might be considered his first abandoning – the period between the end of 1940 and mid-1941, when she was pregnant with their first child. She thought of him on 17 December: "I can't feel him- and silence writes more terrible things than he can ever deny. Is there a suspicion the battle is lost? Certainly he killed me fourteen nights in succession. To rise again from such slaughter Messiah must indeed 'become a woman'" (NS, 254–5). A few days later, Smart said of herself: "I don't bleed. The pin stuck in my flesh leaves only the hole that proves I am dead" (NS, 256). This image of the pierced Christ was repeated in the next entry, when she made her identification even more explicit. Referring to a comment apparently made earlier by Barker, she responded: "Why does he say minor martyrdoms? Didn't the crucifixion only last three days? [...] How can anything so total not be major? He has martyred me but for no cause nor has he any idea of the size or consequence of my wounds" (NS, 256).

Having established her death, she went on to suggest how Barker might bring her back to life: "I shall say nothing but perhaps he will notice that my heart has ceased to beat. Or he may with one glance restore me and flood me with so much new love that every scar will have a satin covering and be new glitter to attack and sing." If Smart was the crucified Christ (an ironic persona given his own "religious complex"), Barker was cast in the role of God, imbued with the power to resurrect her at the magical stroke of his will. She realized that this miracle depended on him. That he may not have been willing to save her filled her with despair: "What should happen if there is no instantaneous resurrection I don't know. Blackness more than death's blackest premonitions [...] But of one thing I feel too sure, too deadly a foreboding" (NS, 256).

It is likely that on some level Smart the writer was aware of her rhetorical stance, and thus the implications of sentiments such as this "deadly foreboding" must be taken with a grain of literary salt. Like the earlier passages describing her relationships with Varda and Alice Paalen, those which chart her affair with Barker are rendered in prose that has been carefully considered, filtered from the raw moment of experience through her reflective and literary imagination. This is not to imply that the intensity is not real, but rather that it has benefited from aesthetic attention. By aligning herself with figures such as Christ and women from the *Heroides*, Smart could confer cultural legitimacy and literary value upon her experiences, while simultaneously detaching herself from them and hence from the pain they brought her. Her text is grounded in history and in literature, in love and in modernism.

As an older woman looking back on the relationship as it was rendered first in her diary and then in *By Grand Central Station*, Smart not only acknowledged but blatantly parodied the self-inflation that had guided her narratives. In 1978 she composed a poem entitled "Grand Central Station Blues." Her humour is in top form, with stanzas such as:

> By Grand Central Station I sat down and wept
> Because of the date that you never kept
> By Grand Central Station I sat down and said
> Being in love is worse than being dead.

The refrain then blurts out its jazzy rhythm:

> Boohoo hoo hoo
> Choo choo choo choo
> Wish I could lose
> These Grand Central Station blues. (ESF, box 53, f.54)

Smart's poem reveals how truly carried away by love she was, and also that she was aware of how deliberately positioned her stance had been. It is therefore possible that even at the time she was documenting the relationship, she was doing so with some humour, making fun of herself and other women who become so obsessed with love. Her constructions may have been intended as a parody of the romance narrative, taking to extremes her feminine destiny as a woman who sacrifices herself for a man and giving it the subversive twist that she was no ordinary domestic daughter but the divine child of God who lays herself down. We can appreciate this potential for parody when we recall the younger Smart who was so sarcastic and self-important in her juvenilia and in the title pages, prefaces, and notices of many journals.

In a different sense, Smart may have been constructing herself as a victim for the sake of appearances. There is no doubt that on some level she comes across as being victimized: she is a woman abandoned by a faithless lover, and she is a Christ who suffers for others. Perhaps she felt guilty about her unconventional behaviour and tried to assuage this guilt by refusing to be seen as responsible for it. Instead, she received her fate passively, as something that was done to her. This is precisely how she presented sex with Varda, imaging herself as a sacrifice who gave herself up on the stone altar, like Christ on his cross, to be pierced. Of course, Smart revealed that she was well aware of what was going to happen with Varda. And later she had to admit to her full participation in – in fact, to her single-handed orchestration of – the affair with Barker: "He is the one I picked out from the world. It was cold deliberation" (NS, 266).

In addition to casting herself as mythical women and as Christ, Smart flirted with the idea of being, or playing the role of, a wife. This part, which was called "Mrs Barker," was played out against the character of "Elizabeth Smart." These roles can be considered an enactment of the dichotomy that plagued her – that of "pleasing mother and being self" (A, 147) – and they underscore how the diary was a suitable place for her to hone the skills required for such performances. Though Smart never married Barker, she did assume a married and thus conventional identity, which was what her mother wanted for her. She was Barker's wife both emotionally and imaginatively. And when she played the part of Elizabeth Smart, she was "being self" in more than just a nominal sense; she was "being" the artist she longed to be and very genuinely was. The dichotomy between Mrs Barker and Elizabeth Smart is best evidenced by the fact that she variously, and concomitantly, went by both names. For instance, once in 1944, when she was living outside London, "a woman on a bicycle stopped & said 'Can you tell me where College farm is?' & she had two telegrams one for Mrs Barker & one for Elizabeth Smart & I said 'They're both for me'" (A, 108).

Smart likely adopted her married pseudonym because it would have provided social respectability for her children and because she was conditioned, as most young women were, to believe that her most important goal in life was to find a husband and live out the romance plot described by DuPlessis. Her journals reveal that the issue of marriage had been a preoccupying one. Travelling in New Zealand, she confessed: "On awakening: this terrible problem of matrimony! I don't want to get married any more" – the "any more" signifying that before this "awakening," she had wanted to marry. She had this change of heart because "How can I possibly marry and sign away my life?" (NS, 115), an indication that she would write "beyond the ending."

But within a month her resolve had vanished, and she wrote: "I played everything on a lovely piano and it sounded well – oh yes really well – and I thought perhaps when I get married I shall take from Katharine Goodson again and write a play in earnest" (NS, 120).[61] Smart's "when I get married" implies that the event was predetermined; it was no longer a question of "if" but of "when." Her marriage thus seems a *fait accompli*, based on years of feminine conditioning.

And yet, unlike in the earlier entry in which marriage was imaged as a self-sacrifice, Smart viewed her "impending" marriage as a means to artistic fulfillment, for it was only "when" she got married that she would take piano lessons again and try to write a play. Thus it is important to note Smart's query: "Men, careers, one excludes all others for ever. Where is an occupation that embraces all things? And where a *man*?" NS, 115). By substituting "poetry" for "occupation" and "Barker" for "man," we can understand why Smart never married, but why she went by the married pseudonym "Mrs Barker." Fearing that marriage would be a "signing away" of her life, but feeling that a union with a man would inspire artistic production, she may have found in Barker the perfect "husband." On the one hand, he was a man for whom she could make beds and play the role she had been raised to perform. Awaiting his return to her in Pender Harbour, for instance, she "bustled about like a housewife, putting flowers in bowls" (NS, 265). On the other hand, he was a man who could lay no legal claim on her and who instead could serve as her muse, which he did, providing her with material for her diary and novel. She preferred

Barker in this latter capacity, for when he finally proposed to her in 1957, she turned him down.[62]

Smart strategically negotiated romance and modernist narratives by using her diary to inscribe endings that were at once traditional and radical. We can also appreciate how she empowered herself along the post-structural lines suggested by Neuman: in cultivating a fractured selfhood (Mrs Barker/Elizabeth Smart), she was positioning herself within the gaps left by the decentring of the universal (male) subject, in which women's experiences could finally find a legitimized home. "At the same time," as Neuman writes, women "have refused to relinquish the possibility of a unified self," and we shall see how Smart struggled to integrate her selves into just such an authoritative and authorized whole.

The most obvious way she went about these negotiations was in gathering the fragments of herself into the unity of her texts – both her diary and her novel. *By Grand Central Station* ends at the height of despair, with the protagonist arriving in New York. Unmet by her lover, she can only sit down and weep. Smart capitalized on this moment from her own life, and on her Heroidean personae, to create a dramatic ending to her novel. *Necessary Secrets* similarly ends at a point of abandonment, with Smart waiting desperately for Barker to return to her in Pender Harbour. Editor Van Wart capitalized on Smart's pain to effect a wrenching conclusion to the diary.

She has commented that the reason she ended the book where she did was that Smart's life changed from this point, and so it was a natural place to break.[63] This statement, however, is misleading. Barker eventually arrived in Pender Harbour, and though he left again, the relationship continued to be played out between Washington and New York. And though Smart moved to London in 1942, Barker came in and out of her life and was never absent from her diary. It is not until around 1945 that her writer's journal begins to peter out. It seems more probable that Van Wart made an editorial decision based on dramatic impact. Her ending does much to perpetuate the stereotypes of the suffering artist and the forsaken woman. Although Van Wart independently made the decision of where to end the book, the edited manuscript had been read and endorsed by Smart.[64] These points reinforce the notion that Smart was guided by a literary vision of herself and life, and that the boundaries between life and art were inextricably blurred for her.

When *Necessary Secrets* appeared, several critics recognized this blurring. Brent Ledger, writing in *Quill and Quire,* stated: "*Necessary Secrets* documents the evolution of both Smart's inner self and her literary persona. Thanks to the careful editing of Alice Van Wart, the book has, despite some dull patches, the shape of a novel."[65] Heather Henderson, reviewing the book for *Maclean's*, appreciated that although Smart may have written through feelings of depression, it was passion for language and literary expression that drove her: "As the diaries suggest, poetry was, for Smart, stronger even than sorrow."[66] And in her review for *Books in Canada*, Audrey Thomas, judging that Smart had wasted her talent as a writer by too much devotion to Barker, concluded: "I put these journals down thinking, 'What a waste. What a terrible waste.' The best of her writing is in here."[67]

Elizabeth Smart the writer was able to turn the pain of her life into a narrative about Mrs Barker, and Mrs Barker the woman was able to subvert her role as wife to play the role of writer. In this way they/she was able to reconcile the dichotomies of convention and rebellion, serving others and serving oneself, and documenting the historical self and constructing the textual self.

I AM I

In 1994 Alice Van Wart brought out a slim second volume of Smart's diaries entitled *On the Side of the Angels*.[68] The fact that this volume includes entries from the early forties, beyond the date of 1940, at which *Necessary Secrets* ends, underscores the likelihood that by concluding the first volume where she did, Van Wart was arbitrarily shaping a good story. The most interesting entries in the second volume are, however, the much later ones, written in the seventies and eighties. Smart essentially stopped writing her creative journal for roughly twenty-five years, taking it up again in early 1970 at the age of fifty-six. And it is to these later entries that I would like finally to turn.

While the earlier diaries are highly literary, these later ones are less so. There is far less editing in terms of scratching out and additions to the margins, and there are far fewer intrusions with different coloured pens. The younger Smart was determined to be a writer, and she wrote with the energy and promise of all that lay ahead. In contrast, the older Smart often lacked enthusiasm, and her diaries are full of reflections of what was and might have been. They also document her debilitating writer's block, in entries that are forced rather than poetically inspired. More than anything, these diaries really speak *as* diaries, revealing their self-consciousness as texts that were produced by Smart as her ultimate means of communication.

As an older woman looking back on her life, she attempted to reconcile her ambivalent feelings towards her parents, in particular her mother. She raised this issue in 1977: "About parents. Shall I ever be able to write about my mother? The crunch. The painful ambiguities, dichotomies, would touch some terrible nerves" (A, 163). She admitted, "Writing this, I can't seem to find anything to base my love on. Guilt riddles me. How she would suffer if she could read what I have written. The tears. The hysterics. She wouldn't want a true portrait of herself." Smart remembered how her mother had tried to control her life, "how she wanted By Grand Central Station completely destroyed & forgotten because of the things in it (very few) that she thought were about *her* [...] How she used any & every weapon she could command to get her way – about George, about the book, about my movements."

Smart was forced to recognize that she "went on loving her – if this is love. If what a child feels for the mother is love. If it isn't love, what is it?" (A, 164). She wondered: "Is it mother I need to speak about? (If I still cry out at night, aged 63, heard throughout the house, through several walls, still wrestling with infantile anguish & anxieties?)" (A, 168). Soon after, she picked up this thread, "So the past is still with me, battering to get out [...] An unresolvement." She compared her relationship with Barker to that with her mother, noting: "Love (i. e. George) was worked out, done, resolved, to the last painful echo dying away, a metamorphosis into an impersonal unpossessive love. I never cry out in my sleep for *him*" (A, 170).

If Smart was ambivalent as a daughter, she was torn as a mother, for she loved her children but had been forced to give up her artistic career for them. She acknowledged: "I was 63 before these things became resolved, before I began to be free and the womb subsided quietly, and the cries of children (left out in the rain) grew faint enough to let me hear that muse-ical calling, that animus rising So it's not too late at 68" (vwc, box 1, f.6). Having devoted, or sacrificed, so many years of her writing life for her children, she was now recalling her muse. Unfortunately, it failed to respond, and Smart struggled alone with writer's block. Her situation was a common one for women who devote their energies to their families. It goes a long way in explaining why, on the one hand, she could never write an "emotion which has its life in the poem and not in the history of the poet," as Eliot would have it; and why, on the other, she would appropriate his dictum of impersonality so as to detach herself from "cries of children," since doing so was necessary if she were to write.

Smart's attempts to reconcile these relationships can be seen in the broader terms of trying to understand her life, something she did via a modernist discourse which advocates that anything is potentially celebratory, everything is equally valued and considered valid subject matter for a work of art. She acknowledged, "It takes years for the pattern to appear" (A, 159); and she asked, "Can you see a pattern now?" (A, 171). One way that the pattern could appear was through a perpetual stream-of-consciousness narrative. As she commented in the earlier entry, "there might even be some nucleis [sic] in the scribbling, a starting-off place for the next crippled sortie" (A, 160). In a 1979 diary she connected the stream-of-consciousness method and the meaning that obtains from its use: "If only, every day, day after day, a little scribbling could take place, the obscure design the larger purpose would emerge" (ITM, 137). And she reiterated this sentiment, noting: "This stuff is too loose to make any bricks of. Is it any use at all? We'll see. The thing is to keep the hand moving" (ITM, 151).

Smart wanted a pattern to appear so that all the fragments which made up her life would be gathered and herself made whole, understood – just as Eliot had clarified the pattern of his fragmented narrative with explanatory notes. She was specifically weaving these fragments into a pattern for the benefit of an audience that would come to look at it and her. She wondered, "Why am I explaining to myself so many things I know?" (ITM, 140). Perhaps she was really "explaining" things to her audience, which could not "know," a common strategy of publicly oriented diarists, as Thomas Mallon, Gail Godwin, and others have noted. In this same entry, "Old age, aging, growing old, is what [she] must mention, and the severing of the ties, the divesting oneself of the love of created objects" (ITM, 144). Smart "must" mention certain things because she wanted to explain herself to us. This purpose is even more explicit when she ended the entry with a promise: "But, there are many compensations, even improvements, in old age. I'll tell you about these later" (ITM, 145). She is engaged in an ongoing dialogue with an audience which participates in her words by reading her text. In this way the diary becomes an important feminine site, for in its status as a shared document, it enacts the fluid and relational flow of women's egos.

One of the things that Smart tells us about later is in fact her desire to be heard. On 6 April 1979 she asks incredulously, "It is *possible* there are people hearing me? There are tiny signs, but it seems too good to be true." She contemplates the consequences: "Would this be a help to me? Or too much of a responsibility? O a help, I think, a help to know one was not a totally mistaken person, piling up a small heap of old rubbish. It's a heady thrilling thought to think that things *do* get through, might, *have* " (ITM, 145).

On the surface, Smart may have been referring to the communication made possible through the channels of her fiction and poetry. Since the publication of *By Grand Central Station* in 1945, she had distanced herself from the literary marketplace for thirty-two years. Then between 1977 and 1978 she published two works that substantially revived her reputation: a volume of poetry entitled *A Bonus* and a prose poem, *The Assumption of the Rogues & Rascals*. And in 1979 plans were made in Canada for the first hardcover edition of *By Grand Central Station*. These, then, could be some of the "tiny signs" that Smart was being heard.

Perhaps too, it was in and through the very diary she inscribed her desire to be heard that she hoped to be heard. In September 1977 she stated: "I don't care what form, which form. I have not ambitions to *be*, only to *say*, somehow. By hook or crook. What thunders & threatens inside me. Low down, beneath the acceptable carefully-tended surface" (A, 168). Her indifference to "form" here and yet her privileging of the need to "*say*" – that is, explain herself – imply that the diary was a form she would more likely use than the poem or novel. In addition to questioning whether "It is *possible* there are people hearing me?" a month later she asked, "There are a few people who *hear* me. Want to hear more? Yes" (A, 173). Here the "people" are directly implicated as the readers of her diary, the audience she was speaking to, and it is by reading this text that they listen and she is heard, underscoring the diary's relational, permeable ego. In 1978 Smart discussed the importance of art: "A sacred duty is not too strong a way to put it. I've said all this, tightly if elliptically, in R & R. But wasn't heard perhaps" (A, 183). The fact that she was saying this in her diary suggests that if she was not heard in her novel, at least she could make certain she was heard here.

Towards the end of her life Smart tried to write an autobiography. A fragment of this unfinished work reveals not only why she could not complete it, but why it was nonetheless necessary to explain herself. Affirming that "The secret life is the real," she confessed, "I can't write an autobiography." Given that the diary is a text which presumably preserves this "secret life," then the life within the diary is her "real" one. Perhaps she could not write an autobiography because it is too explicitly a prescriptive and public text. Like White, she preferred to continue freely expressing her self and her life in a text which announces itself as private, and thus for her a more appropriate register of what is "real." We must understand that Smart's life as documented in the diary is at once historically grounded and textually constructed. "Real" in the latter case would apply to the notion put forward by Timothy Dow Adams, that in autobiography the "narrative truth" is "real." Thus we must appreciate that Smart was offering her version of this "truth."

All the time that she was blocked in the writing of her autobiography, she continued to keep a diary. She provided an explanation for this fact when she mused, "Sometimes you catch a glimpse of someone else's idea of you – way off centre – far from where you are" (A, 149). This description of being "way off centre" underscores how women are relegated to the margins, but Smart makes it clear that the margins are "far from where she" was – that is, she was at the centre. Though she may have cultivated a multiple selfhood for strategic reasons, she also refused to give up a position of central authority. Her diary registered this centred self, making certain that she can now be "glimpsed" in the way she wanted to be. Or as she put it much earlier, the diary allows "points" to be "cleared up, discussed, sifted, concluded" (NS, 48).

If the "secret life is the real," it is also the most comforting, for "Silence is safe. Silence is sympathetic. Silence breaks no bones" (A, 152). The diary, as a genre assumed to be silent, would be the "safest" place for Smart to reveal herself. The notion of bone-breaking could be applied to her fear of expressing herself genuinely in public – that "unsafe" place. Recalling some of her earlier comments – "I try to make everyone like me" (NS, 132) and "I haven't the dignity to speak out, to dare to be myself even if it offends" (NS, 185) – we can associate her fear of offending people with metaphorically breaking their bones. The diary is a place where she could feel more liberated to "speak out, to dare to be" herself, "even if it offends," because the diary was safe and sympathetic to her feelings. Since, as I am arguing, her diary was in fact meant to be read, it becomes the perfect medium for communicating without her having to worry about the immediate, offensive impact it would have.

Smart explained just how indirect the diary allowed her to be. Contemplating her old age, she asked: "Have I said I was here? Did you know I loved you? and you? and you? One does communicate with people after they are gone. Small murmured words take on their meaning, half gestures become quite clear, hidden things behind masks, masking behaviour, contrary attitudes, float slowly to the surface long after graves are overgrown, ashes scattered, letters lost" (ITM, 150). Her reference to masks recalls those personae she so carefully constructed and narrated in her diary, in the spirit of Prufrock, who was always preparing "a face to meet the faces that you meet."

It is therefore possible that in this passage Smart was alluding to her diary and how, after she died, she could communicate through it.

While "ashes" may be "scattered" and "letters lost," a diary preserved and published would certainly allow us to know that she "was here" and what meanings she intended behind those "small murmured words" and "masks." Since Smart set about having her diaries published while she was still alive, perhaps she did not want to wait quite so long for her message to be delivered. She suggested as much when she wrote: "I've crawled out of the dark waiting place [...] I remember where I'd got to when the long underground sentence began" (vwc, box 1, f.6). This "long underground sentence" is the diary itself, and it is exactly the image that White used to describe her own diary: "my writing went underground as it were." Smart, like White, was determined to bring this writing to light and to strip off the masks that had kept her "true" selves covered.

She went on to reinforce why the diary is an appropriate method of communication:

Regret – mostly for the slow too stately way of words spoken. (Written, they go off on their own life, find their right time, like seeds, whirling, floating, snapping, bursting, lying low for generations till conditions are right [...])

I tried too hard to cut through the gooey casing, knew it had better be oblique, except at special moments, but what a long long waste of time. Necessary? It seems so, but why is it not yet clear? [...]

Still, there's nothing to tell, except what this breathing (still) nugget, this going-on person, this me, can tell you. (*ITM*, 150–1)

Once again it would seem that Smart had her diary in mind here, for it is made up of words not "spoken" but "written." These words are the ones that "find their right time [...] lying low for generations till conditions are right." The diary could release communications after the author and the people written about "are gone." She privileged the written over the spoken word: "Try not to be tempted to explain yourself, your work, your past actions. Why? Because it diminishes the pressure of speaking on paper, I think. Explain here, if necessary" (A, 162).

Smart's question "Have I said I was here?" coupled with her declaration that "there's nothing to tell, except what [...] this me, can tell you," emphasizes that the diary is a site not only of communication but also of self-assertion, for "Somebody's got to say I am I, not hold back simpering on the sidelines, bashfully self-effacive" (A, 171). From what she has revealed throughout her diary, Smart has indeed been one to stand back – as she described it, "The circumstances in which I find myself are marginal notes, never the text" (A, 116). But with the fragments of her diary she could become "the text" and the centre. It is here that she was able to step forward and "say I am I," fulfilling her vision of an independent, unified selfhood. She claimed the voice and the authority to speak for herself, and to offer the most relevant version of herself: her own. No wonder she insisted of her diary: "it is my heavenly key – my work – my purpose" (NS, 240).

7 "I was born to hear applause"[1] Self-Promotion and Performance in the Diaries of Anaïs Nin

"Volume 1 of the Diary is published!" (*D*, 6:396). So exclaimed Anaïs Nin in the spring of 1966, in what would be volume 6 of *The Diary of Anaïs Nin*. Volume 1 was only the beginning. She would publish five more in her lifetime; volume 6 (1980), four *Early Diaries* (1978–85), and the unexpurgated supplements *Henry and June* (1986), *Incest* (1992), *Fire* (1995), and *Nearer the Moon* (1996) were published posthumously. The result is perhaps the most comprehensive self-record of a person's life known to date. The diaries begin in 1914, when Nin is eleven years old, and end in the summer of 1974, two and a half years before her death in January 1977.

While this sustained documentation is extraordinary, perhaps even more remarkable is the fact that from its inception Nin's diary was written to be read and published. She is located at the farthest end of a spectrum of publicly oriented diarists. Fothergill has commented that "the major achievements in diary-writing ... have been produced out of a conscious respect for the diary as a literary form,"[2] and it is arguable that no diarist draws more attention to conscious intention than Anaïs Nin. Her lifelong work is clearly one of, if not the, "major achievements in diary-writing" in the history of English letters. And within the twentieth-century in particular, she is the quintessential modernist diarist, as her biographer Deirdre Bair makes clear: "She was a shining examplar of the modernist dictum 'Make it new,' for she was prescient enough to poise herself directly in the path of all that was fresh, exciting, and frequently controversial." Nin set herself "among the pioneers who explored three of the most important" concepts of the century: "sex, the self, and psycho-analysis."³

The fact that the *Early Diaries* exist alongside the initially published series is a significant advantage for scholarship, for it makes it possible for us to draw connections between the young, inexperienced girl and the older, more calculating woman. The *Early Diaries* reveal the same themes and preoccupations as the later ones. The child who began a diary at age eleven and the experienced writer who finally published her diary at age sixty-three shared the same vision and agenda for this work: it was to be a text written for an audience and for publication, as a means of securing a literary reputation and as a way of communi-cating with the world.

This general statement must be qualified in that the actual diary – that is, the book that was written at any given moment – did change in status and purpose over time. There is a gradual shift in the journal as it moved from being a letter to Nin's father to a letter to the world, from a romantic document to a modernist text, and from a work that was written in order to be published to a work that was written because it was being published. These shifts have everything to do with the way that Nin's self-conception evolved. Because she used it to con-struct an identity, or identities, the development of her character unavoidably impacted on the diary as a form. As she informed her diary, "You are still alone and unsurpassed in that you are the most intimate, if not the most complete, of the reflections of my changing self" (ED, 3:13).

The division of the diary into its three "stages" – the initial *Diary*, the *Early* series, and the unexpurgated supplements – is purely arbi-trary, reflecting publishing conveniences and editorial mandates rather than Nin's actual diaristic breaks. But the decision of where to begin and end each volume for publication (with the exception of the unex-purgated ones) was made by Nin, and it thus offers helpful parameters for critical discussion. We shall see that, in terms of both the diary's form and Nin's identity, there were indeed dramatic changes taking place between the last *Early Diary* and the first *Diary*, and thus her division here was appropriate.

At the beginning of her biography of Nin, Noël Riley Fitch asks and answers this crucial question: "Why does a writer who kept a diary all her life need a biographer? *Because her diary is itself a work of fiction,* an act of self-invention."⁴ Nin's diary is "an act of self-invention," but this is a fact often registered by Nin herself. At the start, she used the diary the way that children often use private spaces: to create, by means of the imagination, a world of her own. Reflecting on the past, she wrote in a later diary: "The paradise of my childhood was an invented one, because my childhood was unhappy. It was by acting, pretending, inventing, that I enjoyed myself" (D, 2:161). The diary was the place in which the majority of Nin's inventions were made real. And when she told this early diary, "I created you," it is likely that she was also referring to her self, created by herself in and through the diary (ED, 1:410).

Nin admitted that she used the diary to perpetuate an admirable self-portrait. Telling her diary, "You see, I am really a very plain and ordinary person, wicked, moody, selfish, thoughtless," she went on to inform it of its function in light of all this: "I have dreams, dreams which are finer than anything I have ever done or said, and I do not want them to die. It is my better self, the self of my ideals and resolutions struggling against the dreamless self with its faults and defilings, and they struggle in your pages [...] You are the strongest help I have to fulfill my vision to achieve womanhood" (ED, 2:165). Nin's need to invent a happy childhood was conflated with her desire to create an ideal self, both of which were realized in the diary. There is nothing particularly unusual about this motive. The writer of any life text necessarily creates herself in the process of self-documentation. Moreover, Nin was a child from a broken home, and her sense of self was understandably informed by a need to compensate for an unhappy reality.

The area in which the diary becomes problematic is in her editing of carefully selected portions of the later *Diary* for publication, and in her revising and manipulating of "characters" and events for such a purpose. While the four *Early Diaries* have been published with few alterations, thus remaining true to the originals, the diaries from late 1931 through to 1966 have been heavily excised, edited, and rewritten.[5] A thorough comparison of how and what Nin rewrote over the course of her life would require a text as long as the diaries themselves, as Bair's massive biography proves. Length notwithstanding, it is not the purpose of this chapter to show that Nin fabricated portions of her journal, nor is it my purpose to criticize her for doing so. Rather, the intention is to explore how and why she constructed herself in the plethora of ways she did.

Even though a consummate liar, Nin often indicated that "truth" was elusive and that, as readers, we shoud be wary of taking her text as fact. She told her diary: "You and I are waging our great battle for truth, secretly and quietly, but our purpose is not to describe Anaïs Nin; indeed not – what a waste of time that would be. We are here practicing in order to be able to write someone's life, someone who would be a character, a hero, for the edification and despair of the world" (ED, 2:394). She admitted that within the diary she had become the "character" Nin, a persona. Just as she stressed that her job "is not to describe Anaïs Nin," so it is not our job as readers to track down her lies accusingly, for she is presenting the life of a "character" – not surprisingly given modernist and postmodernist arguments that the self has no referent beyond its textual and linguistic configurations.

Henry and June and *Incest* are preoccupied with the theme of lying. Nin admitted that she lied "To make life more interesting. To imitate literature, which is a hoax" (*HJ*, 206). Although she was referring to lies she told people outside of the diary, the reader must surely be put on guard, especially given that the diary itself approaches "literature." And when she asked, "Why not live literarily – why not, when it is an improvement on the reality?" her question could similarly be posed in terms of the diary, which documents her living (*I*, 235). Her conception of truth can be considered in light of her confession that she suffered from a "vice for embellishment" (*HJ*, 208); her assertion that "there are always two truths" (*I*, 304), and her acknowledgment "I will always invent my life" (*I*, 333).

Nin was a compulsive liar both inside and outside the diary. While the unexpurgated supplements serve as a kind of running check on the expurgated volumes, they too must be considered in terms of a Nin who admitted to inevitable inconsistencies, double truths, and necessary inventions. Editor Gunther Stuhlmann has conceded that "Nin's truth, as we have seen, is psychological" (*D*, 1:xi). Bair cautions against positing "truth" as the barometer of diaristic integrity.[6] So too do many theorists of autobiography. Nin's "psychological truth" is legitimized, for instance, by Timothy Dow Adams, who asserts that autobiographies "partake of narrative truth." Let us admit, then, as Nin was wont to do, that her diaries are not factually genuine. But let us also admit that they are a genuine self-portrait. Each diary is a version of self that Nin believed in.

She began the diary for the purpose of communication. Born in a suburb of Paris in 1903, Anaïs Nin had a nomadic childhood because of the career of her father, the concert pianist Joaquin Nin y Castellanos. She enjoyed some stability between the ages of seven and ten, when her parents settled in Brussels.[7] In her tenth year, however, her father abandoned his family, including his wife, the concert singer Rosa Culmell, his sons Joaquin and Thorvald, and his daughter, Anaïs. Bidding them farewell in the French resort town of Arcachon, he went off to pursue his relationship with a young woman only six years older than Anaïs.[8] Rosa took her children to Barcelona and then in July 1914 to New York, where Nin would spend the next ten years. Devastated by the loss of her father, Nin started a diary on the ship to New York as a means of maintaining contact with him, in the form of a diary-letter. Though she never sent him the actual diary – her mother "explained that it might be lost" – she nonetheless "copied a few paragraphs" from it to send to him (ED, 1:48). She made this her regular practice, as she told him in a letter: "You know that I write everything in my diary, so I would rather just copy here the description of it all from beginning to end" (ED, 1:177). Recall that Fanny Burney similarly began her diary as a letter to her sister.

Nin wrote her diary for an audience more extensive than her father though, as evidenced by the frequency with which she read and showed her diary to people close to her. From the moment she began the journal aboard ship, she intended it for others. On 4 August she noted: "The second mate invited us to his cabin. He has a typewriter and I would have liked to type my diary on it because no one in the family will be able to decipher my horrible handwriting" (ED, 1:11). While her mother stepped in to discourage her from doing so, the passage foreshadows Nin's later practice of preparing typescripts of her diary.

She drew attention to her artistic sensibilities from the beginning of her diary. In February 1915, at the age of twelve, she had a dream in which her vocation as a writer was revealed to her: "[A] great lady" presented her with a piano, an easel, and a pen, and said 'Choose.'" At the end of the dream Nin "picked up" her pen "and began to write without stopping" (ED, 1:50–1). The fact that she documented this dream in the diary is significant, for, of course, in reality Nin wrote her diary for the rest of her life "without stopping." The incident also helps to explain her early conception of the diary as a book which she, in the literary sense, was writing. As a child, she kept her diary displayed on the mantelpiece with her other books (ED, 2:4). Even when married, she placed it with other books, establishing its literary kinship: "I wanted my favorite books on one shelf with my journals (ED, 3:163).

AT HOME WITH NIN

Nin's conception of the diary as a public, literary work is best understood by first considering it in its material dimensions. Her journals were purchased by the University of California at Los Angeles in 1977, and nearly two decades later I found myself at this archive. One of the first things that I did upon my arrival in Los Angeles was to telephone Rupert Pole, Nin's executor and companion for the last half of her life. I had written him a letter asking for permission to see the manuscripts, and in addition to granting my request, he encouraged me to look him up when I arrived. On the morning of the day we had arranged to meet, he picked me up at the run-down guest house that he had recommended – it was close to the university, and as he informed me, it was where "all the scholars stayed."

He drove me to the home that his stepfather, Lloyd Wright, had designed for Nin in the late nineteen fifties, a bungalow hugging the hills above Silver Lake. I was especially fascinated with her study, a low room at the back of the house built into the shrubbery, an inverted tree house planted underground. It was quite dark despite the row of windows, but it was tranquil, a kind of chamber of the unconscious, mouldy and cool, a space for telling secrets. After giving me a tour of the house, Pole took me to a French restaurant, where he talked incessantly and adoringly about Nin – Anaïs – and then we went back to the house, where his practical side emerged. He asked me what books by Anaïs I did not have, and I casually mentioned a few, only to realize that he had made his way over to his bookshelf and was selecting them for me, pressing me for more titles until I had a stack of hard-to-get books, which he gave me as a gift. After more reminiscing, he drove me back to my hotel. Gallantly, he got out of the car, kissed my hand, and was off, no doubt ready to receive the next eager scholar with his equal supply of charm and support. My day with Rupert brought Nin to life, transformed her from "Nin," the subject of my academic study, to "Anaïs," a woman who really lived and who was loved by this man.

The first day of my research I stopped for a coffee near the library, and I remembered Elizabeth Smart writing in her diary in Mexico: "When I woke up I thought what is causing that rich warm undertone? Coffee? Mail? Alice? the Sun? No. It was Anaïs Nin. She has poured things into the world" (NS, 205–6). When the library opened, I was led downstairs to the special collections room. Because the librarian, Octavio Olivera, knew of my visit, he had already brought up the diaries. There against the wall was a trolley loaded with the boxed life of Nin, unearthed from stack-tombs, lifeless. I went over to the trolley and selected the first item, carefully took it out of its protective plastic bag, and carried it to the table, the carcass stiff in my outstretched hands. I laid it down on the velvet book-support, and then, removed from its confines of classification and preservation, the diary breathed. And I thought of Nin asking herself decades earlier, "Why has the diary come to life again?" (D, 1:340).

The journals are generally of two kinds: either blank, lined notebooks with decorative marbled cardboard covers and bound with leather or leather date books. Nin regularly commented on the physical quality of the book in which she wrote. Her entry for June 1919 is a typical example: "Maman bought me a new diary, a very beautiful book bound in black leather, and I am eager to begin writing in it as soon as possible" (ED, 1:248) – just as I was eager to begin examining this and other diaries.

Rosenwald's query about "how a volume of the diary is presented *qua* volume"[9] can be satisfied with the overall comment that Nin took great and consistent pains to present each volume as such. Her first, from July 1914 to May 1915, is an imaginatively constructed work, reflecting her childlike sensibilities in its collage-like design. Begun on board the ship that was taking her away from her beloved father, the book opens with a photograph of him pasted onto the first page, opposite which are two postcards of Arcachon, the town in which he had abandoned her. They are followed on the next page with the invitation to Nin's baptism, and opposite this is a postcard of the ship she wrote from, the *Monserrat*. Throughout the book, Nin wove poems, sketches, coloured drawings, and other photographs of her family among her diary entries. The book closes with another photograph of her father, so that his image is a framing presence, which is appropriate given that this volume was begun for his sake.[10]

By the third volume Nin had started providing title pages for the diary, a practice she would continue throughout her life. The information she gave here would be included in every diary after: a title, the dates covered in the volume, her name, and her address or, in many cases, addresses. This first volume was titled simply "Mon Journal." Every volume would be titled thus until book 9 (July to September 1920), at which point Nin began writing in English; henceforth the diary became "My Diary." In book 18 (June 1922 to February 1923) she started to offer descriptive titles, beginning with "Journal d'une Fiancée." By the next one she had expanded her generic title to "Journal and Note-Book." It is within this volume that she got married, and in the middle of the book she made a new title page, "Journal d'une Épouse." Every diary from this point on would thus be titled "Journal and Note-Book," usually with the addition of something more thematic, such as "The Woman who Died," "June," "Incest," and "Flow" (books 31, 32, 42, 46).

Coupled with this use of titles was Nin's penchant, begun with the first volume, of providing a photograph of the person who most significantly embodied or represented the theme or content of a particular volume. Following her father's, a picture of Nin's fiancé and then husband, Hugo Guiler, appears on the opening pages of books 15, 17, and 18. Three photographs of Nin's dancing instructor, Paco Miralles, decorate the title page of book 25. D.H. Lawrence appears at the start of book 29; June Miller, book 32; and Henry Miller, books 33, 35, and 37. Nin also often provided a quotation at the start of a diary, either on the title page or opposite it. For example, she introduced book 16 with "'To act is easy, to think is hard; to act according to our thought is troublesome ...' Goethe." This practice illuminates the extent to which she set each book up as a volume unto itself.

Starting with book 18, Nin began to keep a "Calendar of Frivolities or Journal of a Society Girl" at the back of the diary. It became "Calendar of Engagements" in book 20, and by book 21, "Journal of Facts," and would be included in almost every volume thereafter. Under this heading, Nin listed virtually every social event she gave or attended throughout the period contained in the diary. Another practice started, in book 7 (October 1919 to January 1920), was the listing of "Ma Librairie" or "Books Read," also at the back. Most significantly, at the back of book 13 (April and May 1921), she offered a "Table of Contents" page for which she had gone through the entire diary and indexed it; for example, "[page] 55 – Friendship"; "313 – Illness humorously described." While the diary book she used here came with pagination, at other times she was forced to number the pages herself, which she dutifully did for every volume necessary. In book 24 (July 1927) she adopted the term "Index." She became a more experienced and professional indexer, as proven by the complex lists she made in book 30. Nin paginated, for instance, every reference made to D.H. Lawrence: "Lawrence 55-102-108-114-120-153-215-240-244-247-260."

Rosenwald's query of whether the diary "is given a formal beginning or ending" is thus partially answered by this consideration of Nin's diary as a volume. The "formal" qualities of "beginning or ending" are also evidenced in the actual entries. Nin welcomed almost every new diary and bid farewell to each one that ended. On 30 September 1920 she announced, "The last day of a month and the last pages of a diary!" (ED, 2:54–5).

If each diary was an independent volume, each volume was concomitantly part of an extended or progressive whole, underscoring both the fragmented and the unified nature of this modernist text. It is Nin's greetings and farewells that make this clear. She informed her diary, "I go to a new book, but they are always a part of You" (book 12). She drew explicit attention to the narrative continuity which she strove to preserve, as in the opening of her diary on 18 July 1926: "(continued from other Journal)" (book 23). The diary contained in book 37 ends in mid-sentence; book 38 begins "(continued)" and carries on to complete the sentence.

Another feature indicating Nin's literary sensibilities is the care with which she penned her entries. Rosenwald asks us to consider "whether the text is immaculate or scribbled over with revisions," and Nin's diary, like White's, leans towards the "immaculate" side. While I have argued that Smart's diaries reveal literary aspirations because they have been "scribbled over," it is equally possible to make the same claim for a more "immaculate" text. Nin's appreciation of the physical book, such as its beautiful leather cover, extended to its pages as well, so that ever conscious of producing a text, she took great pains to make it presentable. This concern is evidenced by her insistence that all entries should be written in black ink. In some cases, having had to write in pencil, like Smart, she later traced over those entries in pen (books 1, 2) – a practice, we recall, that Huff has identified as a common one for nineteenth-century diarists as well.

Nin made some intrusions into the text, correcting spelling mistakes and adding a word or two in the margin, but in general her diaries are clean. There are a few crossed out passages, either wholly blackened or crossed out with a large "X," but these appear, for the most part, in her earliest volumes (books 1, 2). There are several occasions on which she has torn out one, two, or three pages (books 14, 15, 16, 17, 18); their deletion suggests a desire to edit writing she was ashamed of or content she considered too revealing, and it also reinforces the notion that she considered the text a literary space and was determined to keep it as aesthetically pleasing and "professional" looking as possible.

One final aspect that bears mentioning is in response to Rosenwald's interest in "such matters as how long the average entry is, and how frequently and regularly entries are made." From the start of diarizing, Nin established herself as a prolific recorder, all the more remarkably given that she was only eleven years old. From July 1914 to October 1931, the period of the four *Early Diaries*, Nin filled thirty-one volumes. Between October 1931 and November 1934, the period during which she was coming into her own as a modernist writer, she filled fifteen books. While she did skip days, the entries that were made, from volume one on, were generally quite long, amounting to developed prose pieces. It is not an exaggeration to say that she lived obsessively in and for the diary.

Rosenwald's criteria allow us to recognize the extent to which Nin constructed her diary as a work in itself, as a text which she treated with respect and crafted with diligence. That she did so surely stems from the fact that when she was young, she became aware of a very long and literary tradition of diary writing. Some of the earliest books she read were published diaries. In July 1919 she noted: "I have just read a thin little book that contains the diary of a little Japanese girl. It's like a storybook." That Nin likened this, apparently the first, diary she had read to a "storybook" is prophetic and underscores her conception of the genre. She also connected herself to the girl: "There is a tiny little resemblance between her thoughts and mine" (*ED*, 1:275). And she personalized a relationship with Washington Irving's diary. In a letter to her cousin Eduardo Sanchez, she wrote: "I visited again

Washington Irving's nook in the public library, the display of his letters, his diary [...] And people gaze at those relics reverently [...] Can
you ever fancy your letters, your diary, your poems thus displayed – or
mine?"(ED, 2:27–8).

From its inception, Nin "fancied" her diary not only "displayed"
but also published. Reinforcing the idea that the diary is a mode of
communication, she asserted that the reason she wrote was "to let
those who want to understand my heart know it" (ED, 1:64). Of
course, the only way for "those" to "know" anything was by reading
her diary. More emphatically, she affirmed: "I would like all my papers
to be burned except my diary and such of my stories and my poems as
you [the diary] think deserve to be read" (ED, 1:72). Nin was only
twelve years old here, yet she was fully conscious of the possible interest that her diary would have for future readers.

SO THEN, WHAT AM I?

Nin wrote her diary not only so that others might know her but so that
she could know herself. Her early sense of self was based on several
binaries, including being a good girl or a bad girl; serving others or
serving herself; being American or French, pretty or ugly, a conformist
or a rebel, and a woman or a writer. She constructed these dichotomous selves in romantic, overwritten tones suggestive of any adolescent's self-perception – especially when that adolescent has literary
aspirations. Though young writers such as Nin easily take themselves
too seriously, she never really relinquished this quality. Whereas we
have seen that Smart balanced intensity with a good degree of humour
and self-parody, Nin was, and remained, for the most part incapable of
these characteristics.

Her sense of self as it was initially recorded was informed by the loss
of her father. As is typical of children of separated parents, she blamed
herself, wondering, "Could the parting be my fault?" She certainly
thought so, for she went on: "Oh, my confidant, what it costs me to
admit that! To tell the truth, if I haven't opened your pages for a long
time, it was because I knew I had to make this painful confession"
(D, 1:85). The result was that she considered herself bad: "It's true that
I consider myself the worst of all" (ED, 1:240).

Like earlier Puritan diaries of moral censure and spiritual improvement, Nin's journal served the purpose of absorbing these self-criti-
cisms, and it also functioned as a space where she could document her
rise to goodness. She literally drew a chart: "I am going to make a
drawing here of a staircase. On the left I shall put my failures, on the
right my victories, and that way my diary will be able to follow the

rocky road on which I am going to walk and see whether in a year I acquire a speck of kindness" (ED, 1:159).

Because the diary was ostensibly for her father, and because she thought he might be angry with her for her "bad" behaviour, she began a furious campaign to be good for his sake. She hoped that if he were pleased, he would return. Fitch draws attention to the fact that writing for Nin was a means of seducing her father, and her motivation for writing about being good is certainly early proof of this interpretation.[11] Shortly after arriving in New York, she determined: "I shall correct myself and try to be better and to behave. I shall do this in thinking always of Papa and I shall say, if I do that, will Papa be pleased? No? Well then, I won't do it, and so on" (ED, 1:24).

Not only was the diary *for* her father, but often it *became* her father. She spoke to it and feared it just as she would her father, asking it "to pardon me for writing in pencil but I am in bed" (ED, 1:24); and she worried that "My dear diary will scold me and judge me severely" (ED, 1:68). Words such as "pardon," "scold," and "judge" are associated more with a figure of authority than with the secret "confidant" that the diary also served as.

Like White's, Nin's diary inscribed the authority of that other, more exacting father, God. Raised by her Catholic mother, Nin devoted herself to religion with a fervour, again for the purpose of strengthening her character. She spent a great deal of time writing about the church, offering long descriptive passages on subjects such as "The Nuns"; for instance, "let us love them, respect them, and above all try to be like them, let us try to be devoted, good, as tender as they. If we can't do that on the battlefield, let us do it in our homes. If we have no family, let us serve the poor. Let us not merely admire those heroic women, but let us imitate them" (ED, 1:46). This is a typical example of how Nin was naively carried away by her desperate desire to be good, and it shows how she wrote through traditional conceptions of women as self-sacrificing nurturers.

Another time, she recounted her overwhelming response to being in church: "I wept because I had a great desire to be consumed in love for our savior. I wept because I am too small and I would like to suffer greatly, like the martyrs" (ED, 1:123). Her early desire to be a martyr established one side of the dichotomy that would plague her and many women throughout their lives: how to reconcile the "selfish" demands of being an artist with wanting only to serve others. This longing to be a martyr also highlights how her concept of being good was connected to both her father and the Father. That she perceived these two fathers as one is suggested thus: "At the moment of Communion, it seems more as though I am kissing and hugging Papa, rather than receiving the body of Christ" (ED, 1:27). White's conception of her father as God is identical to Nin's here.

The association expands so that Nin's merging of her father and religion was intricately connected to feelings of patriotism. Taking Communion one morning, she "murmured, *God, France, Papa!*" (D, 1:58). From the moment that she arrived in New York, she was determined to preserve her French heritage. She initially wrote the diary in French so that her father, who did not know English, could "read" it. (She continued to use French until 9 July 1920, when it became more important for her to communicate with boys who spoke English, as we shall see.)

A few months earlier, Nin had been at a social gathering, and she recorded what a "gentleman" there had told her: "if one knows two languages, one is two people. If one knows three, one is three people. So then, what am I?" (ED, 1:41). As a Spanish-French child transported to the United States, Nin understandably suffered from a confused identity, a problem that would concern her throughout her life. At one point, for instance, she felt: "There is no unity in me, I am not whole. It is amusing to be composed of fragments" (ED, 3:9). But at other times she lamented, "I suffer most of all from a breaking up of myself, from a lack of wholeness" (ED, 4:77). An entry made in 1932 underscores the impact of her childhood division: "I have always been tormented by the image of multiplicity of selves. Some days I call it richness, and other days I see it as a disease, a proliferation as dangerous as cancer. My first concept about people around me was that all of them were coordinated into a WHOLE, whereas I was made up of a multitude of selves, of fragments" (ED, 1:47).

Nin's conception of her multiplied selfhood as being, on the one hand, a "richness" and, on the other, a "cancer" presciently articulates the agenda of postmodern autobiographers and theorists such as Neuman: a decentred subject position is a "richness" in that it bestows a new authority on women's traditionally marginalized selves; it is a "cancer" in that women, traditionally not socially constructed as independent, autonomous beings, cannot afford to give up new-found positions of unity and centrality. Like Eliot's Fisher King, Nin would shore up the diary "fragments" of her fragemented self, working them into a coherent narrative to protect her from psychic ruin.

Her geographical displacement led her to wonder, "what am I?" and she was equally concerend with the issue of "where am I?" Against her passion for France was this sentiment: "I now hate school and everything American" (ED, 1:42). In 1920, though, she evened things out: "The other day we talked about patriotism. Like the true Artist's children that we are, we realize that we aren't really attached to any country. I discovered that my love for France existed purely in my imagination, not in my heart. I would like to explain to you the confusion that reigns between those two kingdoms, for each considers itself the All-Powerful Ruler, but in truth, imagination is the real victor, a thousand to one!" (ED, 1:407).

Nin was an exile not only in the physical sense but also in the spiritual one. Living then in New York (already in a state of exile from her native France), she would move back and forth to and from France several times before settling permanently in the United States. And yet, as she here attests and as she would later reiterate, she consistently believed she belonged nowhere, was an artist like Stephen Dedalus who transcended place – "imagination is the real victor." Living in the world of the imagination, she was in the modernist company of the likes of Pound, who had "world citizenship," and Eliot who was an "international hero."[12]

If imagination was victorious, it was also perpetually forced to do battle with "femininity." Having decided to be a writer, the child Nin was immediately confronted with the dilemma faced by women throughout history – the difficulty of reconciling the solitary time required to produce a work of art with the self-sacrificing hours of domestic labour traditionally expected of women. It was the diary that seemed to suffer as Nin pitted her desire to write in it against her heavy load of domestic duties; her two brothers were typically not expected to help run the house. The diary is full of passages illustrating this dichotomy, such as in her confession "The effort I am making to make myself useful, not to dream, not to be idle a single minute, has been very difficult for me. My diary has seemed like a forbidden country that I didn't have the right to enter until I could say to myself: the work is all done" (ED, 1:179).

This sentiment problematizes the status of the diary, for it suggests that the diary was the site of pleasure and hence a frivolous place. Nin later recorded, "Too many things to do today to waste my time writing" (ED, 1:297–8). She clung to this notion, so that she was proud to announce: "Before, one of the most difficult things, perhaps, was not to pick up my diary until all the stockings were darned and all the other work done. Now it's a habit. And it's with all my heart that I want to stay this way, my brothers loving me more, Maman loving me more, and what would I live for if it weren't just for my little family's happiness?" (ED, 1:335). She considered her writing at odds with her "family's happiness" because this happiness depended, to some extent, on her performing as a selfless caretaker. Nin was thus accepting traditional female roles, writing the autobiography of the womanly woman, "that ideal script" described by Smith.

At one point, Nin went so far as to proclaim: "I have lost my literary ambitions, and I write only for the pure pleasure of writing. My ambition is to be a little woman of whom Maman can be proud" (ED, 1:479). Presumably, it was the diary that was for "pure pleasure," for it was the writing that she had consistently kept up. This comment goes a long way to explain how the diary early on became the site of Nin's "literary ambitions," a book she could convince herself and others was for "pure pleasure," but which would unobtrusively encode its own artistic status and agenda. We can here appreciate DuPlessis's argument that Nin used her journal as a space in which to negotiate her object and subject positions, manifested by her "desire to please" and her "desire to reveal."

Because the diary was conceived in terms of pleasure, it is not surprising to find Nin consistently denigrating the writing that went on there. She referred to her diarizing as "wasting ink" (ED, 2:277), she associated herself with "all the young people with the scribbling mania" (ED, 2:339), and she called herself "the scribbler" (ED, 2:397). Remember that Woolf and White similarly devalued their writings with the word "scribble."

In direct opposition, and perhaps in response to this attitude, Nin also described her journal as a place of discipline. Like Woolf, White, and Smart, she was a diarist who needed to legitimize her private and hence devalued writing as work. She consistently described her writing in terms of household chores, so that like the chores, it had to be done. Nin was able to convince herself that she was fulfilling her female duties while simultaneously subverting them, as evidenced in her habit of apologizing to her diary for neglecting it and her promises to be more diligent. In January 1915 she "made a resolution to keep my diary all year long" (ED, 1:39). By March she had slipped, and she offered a lengthy excuse, complete with a doctor's note which proved that her absence was legitimate: "If I haven't written, I have had good reasons. First I caught pleurisy that lasted four days," so that "the doctor ordered me to stay home from school for a week to rest" (ED, 1:51). When she was healthy, her diary became her "daily self-discipline" (ED, 2:308). Once again we can see how Nin appropriated the "disciplined" regimen expected of Puritan and female diarists, in order to permit herself the sinful "pleasure" that the writing gave her.

Her sense of the diary as discipline was also connected to her father. In apologizing to the diary for neglecting it, Nin was arguably at times addressing him. That she did so can be explained as follows. The diary was her best friend, her "faithful confidant" (ED, 1:23). Initially, this friend was only the replacement for the father who had abandoned her and made her feel unloved, without a friend. At one point, in describing her appearance, she dared "not admit that I am a monster because my diary wouldn't love me any more"(ED, 1:106), and she later confessed, "When I was little, I heard Papa say that I was ugly and the idea never left me" (ED, 1:414).

Therefore Nin's fear that her diary would not love her if she was ugly is likely an allusion to her father. And when she insisted that "no one will love me," she made it clear that the diary had become the father she wished she had, as when she wrote, "my diary will be doubly dear because it will not desert me" (ED, 1:90). Earlier, when she apologized to the diary for not writing more often, she put herself in the position of her father, who did the abandoning: "I wonder, when I let so many days go by without writing, if my diary thinks I have abandoned it! Oh, no, never." Though the diary is the father who had abandoned her, Nin determined never to treat the diary, her only true friend, the way her father had treated her: "I promise my diary never to give it up, oh, no, never" (ED, 1:63). True to her words, Nin would never "give it up."

Her diary was indeed her best friend, and she constantly reminded it of its status as such: "How and to whom could I say everything that goes through my mind? When I am angry, I write and my anger cools; when I am sad, I write and my melancholy wears off; when I am happy, I write, and I am happy every time I reread what I write; when I have no friends, I write, and you are there; when everyone calls me an ignoramus, I write and am consoled; when I bungle a poem, I write and am comforted" (ED, 1:228. This friendship can be considered in the sociological terms posited by Friedman and Chodorow, in that Nin saw herself in relation not only to those outside the diary but also to her "friend" inside.

ROMANCING THE DIARY

Functioning as such a multi-purpose friend, Anaïs Nin's diary satisfied her powerful longing to be cared for. We have seen how she equated being ugly with being unloved, and it is not surprising that, as she grew up, she became more and more preoccupied with her appearance, wanting and needing to see herself as pretty in order to feel deserving of love, a quality typically associated with women and women diarists, as Blodgett has noted. As Nin reached puberty and began to develop a sexual identity, she turned to boys as a source of attention and acceptance: "Lately I have read romances, seen them at the cinema, in the theatre, in the street [...] I would like so much, oh, so much, to be worthy of receiving their golden rays! [. . .] What must I do to make my dream come true? No doubt: be beautiful!" (ED, 1:385).

This sixteen-year-old was influenced by romance genres, and they impacted on the diary in two ways. First, they coloured how she wrote: her language is heightened and flowery, full of overwritten passages. Secondly, they inspired Nin to create in the diary a world in which romantic characters really exist. In this way the young Nin was scripting the limiting romance plot identified by DuPlessis. Her preoccupation with romance led her to conceive love as ideal, and boys as princes and knights.

Her first crush was on John O'Connell, a boy in her class. "Is it possible! A girl of 14? Yes, my little diary, it's true! Your crazy little confidante has found her knight" (ED, 1:171). Her response was one of socialized domesticity: "I went to the public library and took out a book on housekeeping [...] I put down my books, made myself an apron, and shut myself in the kitchen: I made biscuits and they were successful" (ED, 1:171). Just as her mother's insistence that she perform domestic duties interfered with her writing, so boys would arouse stereotypical feminine sensibilities in Nin that were at odds with the pursuit of so self-absorbed a career. Two years later she further recognized that boys were "princes as in the fairy tales, and they are all looking for princesses because their father, the king, wants them to marry [...] The world is full, too, of princesses who are waiting"' (ED, 1:215). Nin would certainly have considered herself one of these available "princesses," for she was longing to be rescued.

Her adolescent perception expanded, and men were not only "princes" but "shadows," as she stressed, "I will only be the wife of my Shadow, my Ideal" (ED, 1:437). Before she met and married the shadow named Hugh (Hugo) Guiler, she was infatuated with several boys. She met Marcus Anderson at a dance in December 1919 and kept her diary informed of the progress of their relationship: "Dearest diary! Dearest diary! My Romance has come! Seeing my little Love sorrowing in front of the closed door, someone sent him to me with his precious message and I am the one who forbids him to enter. But I can open the door when I want to." The message was a letter in which "He says that he loves me, O little diary! And his letter is so beautiful, like a poem." Nin was impressed with Anderson's attention and his artistic expression: "Marcus is going to become a poet later on, he says [...] He is just a boy, perhaps, but what sweetness in those words: 'I love you, Anaïs'" (ED, 1:423). Though she accepted his tribute, she could not reciprocate. Referring to how difficult it was to get Anderson to stop loving her, she admitted, "I suppose at the root of it all is my power as a coquette" (ED, 2:57). Thus Nin, like Smart, came to appreciate her power as a woman over men. But "at the root" of her future problematic relationships would be her trying to reconcile this "power" with the dictates that she should be a weak woman.

Though Anderson was her boyfriend, the boy who most influenced Nin in terms of her diary was her cousin Eduardo Sanchez. It was for him that she gave up writing in French and began to write in English, as she noted in July 1920: "Eduardo does not read French as freely as I read English, and we wish to show each other parts of our diaries" (ED, 2:5). This linguistic turning point may have helped Nin answer her question "who am I?" as she began to construct herself as an English writer. Moreover, as she had been growing up, and especially since she began dating, there had been fewer and fewer passages devoted to her father. Here Nin made a symbolic break with him. While she began the diary to communicate with him, it was now of less concern to her that he would not be able to read the English because the diary was no longer for him. It should be clarified that in a letter to her father she did tell him, "You should learn English, that's all there is to it" (ED, 2:16). Nin was perhaps using the diary's "power as a coquette" to lure her father into this English text. She may also have been using it to seduce other men as well, such as Sanchez and Guiler.

In this second volume of the *Early Diary*, the first one in English, there are at least twelve references to her showing the diary to others, primarily to Sanchez and her boyfriend-cum-fiancé Guiler, and to her reading their diaries in turn. She told her diary that Sanchez "read some of your pages" (ED, 2:36), and she described how "Hugo and Eugene opened their journals, and we discussed and read, compared experiences" (ED, 2:258).[13] Besides men, she trusted the diary to her school friend Frances Schiff (ED, 2:355) and to her mother (ED, 2:375).

Any seductions of men at this point, though, were likely subconscious. Nin dreaded things physical, even an innocent kiss. Horrified, she recounted of Anderson: "The boy I once idealized enough through his letters, his poetry, to call a Prince [. . .] asked me to kiss him good-bye! I believe he saw the surprise, the *pain*, the anger, in my eyes." Anderson had been demoted to a "poor shattered idol." Nin's conception of love was romantic rather than sexual: "It seems as if I am always climbing the dangerous ladder to reach romance and always slipping down again" (ED, 2:9). Healthy young men have sexual drives, but Nin had been so absorbed in her imaging of them as "princes," "idols," and "shadows" that their true and natural physicality shocked her. Her exaggerated response to Anderson's seemingly harmless request also raises the possibility that Nin was controlling her behaviour according to preconceived romance plots of how "good girls" should react.

On a very different note, there is evidence to suggest that she had been the victim of childhood sexual abuse by her father. That she felt "*pain*" at the thought of a kiss or that she could wonder, "Why am I repulsed by talk of sex and mention of whatever is animal in us?" (ED, 2:471), reinforces the idea that she may have been such a victim. For according to Herman, "Women reporting sexual aggressions in childhood were 'more apt to say that they were disgusted by all sexual subjects,'" and the most intense disgust was articulated by women who had been abused by male relatives, such as fathers.[14] I will return to this issue later on.

On 13 March 1921, having been invited to a party by his sister Edith, Nin met Hugo Guiler. What impressed her most about this man was that he wrote poetry (ED, 2:155) – just as she had been interested in Anderson, whose letter was "like a poem." Nin cast Guiler in the same romantic, unreal roles as her previous boyfriends. In addition to the fact that he was the "shadow" for whom she had longed, she would at different times refer to him as her "Magician of Happiness," her "Healer," her "Deliverer," and her "Prince Charming" (ED, 2:414, 427, 453, 456), reinforcing how she bought into romance narratives in which men are given active roles and women passive ones.

Nin would eventually marry Guiler. Just over a month before she met him she had confided: "I want passionately to marry an artist" (ED, 2:144). This desire echoes Smart's: "I must marry a poet. It's the only thing" (NS, 80). From the moment that Nin had put down her books to bake cookies for John O'Connell, she had been torn between her desires to write and to serve men. Her indication that she wanted to "marry an artist" suggests that she would live her creative life vicariously, approaching art through the man she served. This was, as we have seen with Smart, the most viable means for a woman to access male-centred literary sites. Nin's desire may have been one of the first steps that she took to rewriting the romance plot: if women must be defined by love and marriage, she would take a husband; but in partnering herself with a poet, she could claim for herself an artistic identity, out of which she would produce her own art that would go "beyond the ending" of a "happily ever after" union. Volume 2 of the *Early Diary* is understandably preoccupied with art and marriage, for it is within those pages that Nin became engaged to Guiler and realistically confronted her future as a woman. She pitted being a wife against being a writer. She felt that she had to choose one role or the other; she could not be both.

Before examining this dilemma, we should note that, prior to meeting Guiler, Nin had divided herself into two characters: "Mlle Linotte" and "Miss Nin." When she was twelve, she had dubbed herself "Linotte," "a little bird, I say, who has neither strength nor energy" (ED, 1:68). She explained the difference between this self and "Miss

Nin": "It is true that Mlle. Linotte belongs to herself and to you, but Miss Nin must concentrate on her tasks and be useful. Only it is so much easier to be Mlle. Linotte" (ED, 2:34). Within this entry, Nin copied a letter to her friend Frances, in which she furthered the distinctions: "You know Miss Nin is the sensible side of me, Frances, the little housekeeper and sister and obedient (ahem) daughter. Linotte is the side which is always in a state of confusion and alarm [. . .] the moody and cranky individual and also the verse scribbler, etc."(ED, 2:35). From here it is easy to see how Miss Nin, the dutiful and obedient, would evolve into Nin the wife, and Linotte, the "individual," the "verse scribbler," would come to represent Nin the writer.

This division underscores the idea, as put forward by Franklin, that the diary is a kind of stage upon which women may practise various roles. It also supports Smith's argument that women "grapple" with identity as they struggle to negotiate acceptance and rejection of traditional roles. And it opens the door to Nussbaum, who contends that the diaristic self "lacks an obvious centre." As Nin matured she would play more and more roles, increasinlgy destabilizing her diaristic presence.

By the time she met Guiler, she had convinced herself that she had to select one self over the other: "I can dream now, but it is only in preparation for the future. Perhaps soon I will face a great dawn, the day of revelation and decision. I shall take my first faltering steps toward my Achievement, whether it be Authorship or Wifehood" (ED, 2:244). But Nin was soon angry that she had to choose and vowed not to: "Why should a woman cease to be feminine because she cultivates her mind as well as her heart? No, I do not believe a word of it. It is possible, this ideal of mine" (ED, 2:328). This "ideal" was at the centre of Nin's critique of the romance plot, a critique she would spend her life writing and living.

Anaïs Nin was a modern woman who wanted a "home life" as well as a career. At this point, however, she priviliged tradition, wanting to "please" Hugo as subject and relegating herself to object. In deciding whether or not to marry him, she had one question: "would my marriage to Hugo mean happiness for him?" She continued in the selfless tone of the martyr she sometimes wanted to be: "If it did, at least my life would not have been in vain, as it otherwise would be if I chose rather to live only for myself and my writing" (ED, 2:475). It is in this self-sacrificial spirit that she married Guiler on 3 March 1923, shortly after her twentieth birthday.

The diary which Nin titled "Journal of a Wife" preserves the naive and romantic qualities more appropriate to an adolescent. In this context, her comment quoted earlier – "The paradise of my childhood was an invented one, because my childhood was unhappy" (D, 2:161) – can be further understood. Marriage, like her childhood, made her unhappy. The diary was used, with all its linguistic and imaginative possibilities, to convince herself and any possible readers of just the opposite: that she was happy and the marriage plot successful. But other, less-guarded passages reveal how unsatisfied she was, as a woman and as an artist, and in her later diaries she began to rewrite the blissful ending. This revision was, however, psychologically taxing. She would spend her life doing editorial battle with herself as she tried to integrate romance and modernist narratives.

Nin and Guiler initially lived in Richmond Hill, New York, with her mother and brother Joaquin. At the end of the year they moved to a house of their own in Queens. Nin lived the conventional life of a housewife while her husband worked in a bank. She revealed, "I want to make my home so beautiful and my Love so happy" (ED, 3:27), and she affirmed, "I am above all preoccupied with the making of a home" (ED, 3:85). Success was registered thus: "[Hugh] took me in his arms and said: 'How happy we are together, my darling, what a perfect marriage!' And he repeated once or twice that our marriage was without a flaw. And I believe him" (ED, 3:101–2).

Yet Nin became increasingly full of doubt. After two years of marriage, she confessed: "Today, returning from the park I felt a wave of rebellion against all my little duties; I wished I had no dinner to cook, no dishes to wash afterwards, none of that eternal, vicious circle of housework." Significantly, though, she considered herself a failure for these thoughts, saying, "How weak I am" (ED, 3:130), and thus pitting her rebellions against her conformities.

Castigating herself, she echoed the critical tone of her childhood. In another entry, she alluded to her adolescent dichotomy of Mlle Linotte and Miss Nin: "My very real self is not wifely, not good. It is wayward, moody, desperately active and hungry" (ED, 3:208). Clearly, this was Mlle Linotte, the "verse scribbler," speaking. Much of Nin's frustration with her married life had to do with how her writing had been compromised. She constantly tried to convince herself, "I am Hugh's wife, first of all." In this position, she became a writer "because this is the only outside occupation which does not conflict with his happiness and his comfort" (ED, 3:185). This is precisely the sentiment expressed by Woolf in "Professions for Women": "Writing was a reputable and harmless occupation. The family peace was not broken by the scratching of a pen."[15]

Just as Nin's mother wanted her daughter to sacrifice her literary ambitions, so Guiler had certain expectations of his wife. Nin tells how "He did confess that he was distressed by his unmended socks [. . .]

and that a wife, from a practical point of view, was a very necessary object" (ED, 3:138). This attitude related to her writing: "The Cat [Guiler] is home. It is his holiday. He is here to be petted, fed and taken out for walks. When I write, he frowns. I can only do so when he reads" (ED, 3:185).

Despite her efforts at compliance, Nin often resented having to forsake her writing: "The machinery of our home does demand a great deal of attention, but it has no right to submerge me. I hate to see that it has brought my mind down to the level of the most ordinary woman. Today I resolved to push it all out of my mind [...] To write every day – that will be the first rule of my life from now on" (ED, 3:175). She recalled their days of courtship: "Marrying him seemed then just as fantastic a dream as flying from him does today, if I dared" (ED, 3:208). This thought – "if I dared" – suggests that Nin had been contemplating leaving Guiler, but that she was afraid to, primarily because she feared being alone financially.

Though she presents Guiler in an unflattering and repressive light, he deserves his due, for as Leonard did with Virginia Woolf, Guiler encouraged his wife to write. Nin acknowledged that, "following a second raise," he hired a full-time housekeeper so that she would have the time to write: "due to the thoughtfulness of my Pussy, I am going to be free" (ED, 3:170). Her situation was relatively unique. In heterosexual relationships where the writer is the man, it is the woman who traditionally works hard around the house, so that the writer is "free." When the writer is the woman, as has been seen from Nin's early experiences, her writing takes a back seat to domestic chores. But while she began her marriage as a traditional wife, Guiler's increasing financial success made it possible for her no longer to have to perform those household tasks that made her life so traditional. And it is for this reason that Nin did not "dare" to leave him.

Guiler's bounty extended to her mother and brother as well. In December 1924 he got a promotion, and they all moved to Paris, where they were supported by his salary. Life in France would profoundly affect Nin: there she would develop as a writer and as a sexual being. In the diary kept before she moved, her persistent "repulsion" of sexual subjects accounts for the fact that, although sex is one of the most integral parts of marriage, she neither had it nor mentioned it when she discussed her early married life.

Whereas Anderson had horrified her by kissing her, Nin's new husband kept his distance. In recounting their honeymoon – fifteen months after the event – she described a Guiler who "read me poetry on our first night and who knelt at my knees and hid his face in his hands before turning off the light, the Hugh whose delicacy and sensitiveness every day keeps me from the things I had feared of life" (ED, 3:45–6). Their second anniversary reads like a repeat non-performance: "We had a reminiscent and tender evening, like the most sentimental of couples. Finally, we went to bed with our books and our journals" (ED, 3:113). That the journal went to bed with them illuminates its function and status at this point in Nin's life. Her reading of her diary to Guiler became a favorite pastime and a special way of sharing her life with him. Entries such as this abound: "Last night my Love was happy, for I read him of our life together, as my journal writing has pictured it. Fired by my example, he again wrote in his own journal" (ED, 3:22). Rather than being a secret document, the diary became a kind of romantic – even erotic – symbol which united and stimulated the married couple. But of course it functioned as the substitute for sex, for what it stimulated was writing.

When the Guilers arrived in Paris, then, we can appreciate that Nin was disturbed by the city's lack of sexual restraint: "I hate Paris for the importance of sensuality in its literary and human life" (ED, 3:115). Despite her reaction, it is surely not coincidental that her first sexual experience, in 1925, took place within three months of her arrival in this city – although she did not reveal this fact until volume 1 of the *Diary*. In an entry for May 1932 she suggested how the reading of certain books precipitated intercourse with Guiler. She recalled their first days in Paris, living in the rented apartment of a Mr Hansen. While cleaning the cupboards one day, Nin found a stack of pornographic books: "One by one, I read these books, which were completely new to me [...] They overwhelmed me. I was innocent before I read them, but by the time I had read them all, there was nothing I did not know about sexual exploits." She went on to connect this experience with Paris itself: "These books affected my vision of Paris, until now a purely literary one. They opened my eyes and my senses" (D, 1:96).

In addition to surprising her with sexual discoveries, to which we will return later, Paris fulfilled her literary expectations. Before she left New York, she had confessed how "deeply thrilled I am at the thought of going there – to the Paris of Balzac, Flaubert and Anatole France, to the Paris of the poets, of Dumas and Victor Hugo" (ED, 3:43). And once in the city, her mind expanded: "With more time, new and exciting scenery, new people, new literature, new atmospheres, it is not strange that I should think more" (ED, 3:119). In particular, as an expatriate in a modernist mecca, she appropriately thought about her diary and how she could "make it new."

A MANIFESTO FOR DIARISM

To appreciate the diary's status as a modernist "ism," we must go back a bit to see how Nin was formulating its aesthetic. Her English journal documents her attempts to trace a tradition within which her own journal could be situated. By the second *Early* volume she was following an extensive diary-reading program. In September 1920 she exclaimed, "Eureka! Eureka! Would to heaven you could read the book I am reveling in. It is the journal of Eugénie de Guérin [...] Many of the things I have wanted to express, or have expressed so diffidently, Eugenie has in her diary" (*ED*, 2:48). Nin was learning from this diarist, absorbing her techniques of expression and self-awareness: "things that I never say, because I am not able to and yet which I have thought and vaguely explained, Eugénie expresses so charmingly [. . .] I read her journal each day" (*ED*, 2:61). This last comment appropriately suggests that daily diarizing requires daily effort.

Nin was also fully absorbed by the journal of Marie Bashkirtseff. Referring to Nin's discovery of this text, Nancy Scholar rightly perceives that she found "a confirmation of her life-work perhaps unavailable elsewhere."[16] Nin recognized these similarities: "I understand her [Bashkirtseff] so well that sometimes I wonder if I am like her" (*ED*, 2:291). It is likely that she was highly influenced by Bashkirtseff's self-conscious and publication-directed project.

Another diary that inspired her was the *Journal Intime* of nineteenth-century Swiss author Henri Frédéric Amiel. Between January and August 1922 Nin referred to it ten times. An August entry outlines an artistic philosophy she would spend her lifetime developing: "Like Amiel, sometimes I feel more each day that 'I am becoming more purely spirit [...] All personal events, all particular experiences, are to me text for meditation [...] Life is only a document to be interpreted [...]'"(*ED*, 2:467). If life is a document, it follows that a document may become the life. Nin's diary would become an autonomous modernist work in which the "life" and the "I" who experienced it would be constructed within the text.

The result of reading so many diaries was that Nin began to consider them critically. In January 1926 she met Hélène Boussinescq, "a middle-aged French teacher of English literature" (*ED*, 3:172). She became Nin's "teacher" in Paris, introducing her to early modern works by writers such as Waldo Frank, René Lalou, Thomas Mann, Heinrich Mann, and Sherwood Anderson (*ED*, 3:178–9).

At this point, it should be mentioned that when Nin was sixteen, she had dropped out of high school. Bair believes that Nin's mother made a terrible mistake in permitting her to leave: "It was tantamount to giving the already otherworldly girl permission to live in a totally unstructured manner."[17] On the one hand, Nin would be somewhat debilitated as a writer in that, without a formal education, she would lack knowledge of and the skill to adhere to formal principles of writing (a fact that has led many to dismiss her work and that caused her to dismiss all negative critics). On the other hand, Nin was well positioned to be a feminist modernist in linguistic exile. In discussing Gertrude Stein, Shari Benstock writes, "her presumed inability to master the basic rules of grammar and syntax made her question the logic and operations of those rules." Benstock reads Stein as a modernist who rejected a patriarchal "logic" and who created her own lesbian one.[18] Nin may be considered in similar terms: she fashioned her own mode of expression, prefiguring, as we shall see, the French feminist notion of writing with the female body.

Another consequence of her leaving school was that Nin learned early not to dismiss the generally devalued diary from aesthetic discourse, and in this way she was heralding the recent theorists of autobiography who recognize that the diary belongs within the literary canon. Nin's tutor Boussinescq helped her to develop her critical faculties, and Nin immediately – and presciently – applied them to her diary reading. Just after she had begun studying with Boussinescq, she wrote: "I have been reading a most uninteresting Journal, that of Josephine Peabody, an American poetess who died in 1922. The writing was exclamatory and very young throughout the book"; her "style is more often banal than anything else" (ED, 3:206).

Nin had previously summed up her interest in life writing: "I want to know the inner self [...] That is why I am fascinated by journals and biographies. Nothing holds so great an interest for me now than the study of a human heart seeking to express itself in life" (ED, 2:340). She later stressed: "The purity of biographies is going to turn me away definitely from novels. I have read few things as impressive and lasting as [. . .] the journal of Marie Bashkirtsev and Katherine Mansfield, and others of the same kind" (ED, 4:151). Nin was inspired by the many literary diaries that she had read as a child and as a young woman. They facilitated her own artistic and critical "logic" as a diarist.

Over the years, she thought a great deal about diary writing – about appropriate content, language, and style. On the eve of going to Paris, she decided to collect her ideas of what constitutes a well-written diary: "Someday I want to write about this, as a tribute to a much despised form of literature, as an answer to those who have shrugged their shoulders when they saw me bending over a mere diary. I shall try to give diary writing a definite character and a definite place in life, and for the sake of the practical people who have wept over the wasted hours, I shall demonstrate the uses, the purpose, the visibly beneficial effects, of the much deplored habit" (ED, 3:32–3). Words such as "mere," "wasted," and "habit" emphasize the devaluation of the diary that Nin had experienced in childhood from people such as her mother, and they were in fact the words she herself used as she bought into those judgments. It has also been seen, however, that even as Nin was denigrating her diary, she was simultaneously elevating it to a disciplined and serious art – "making it new."

Just after her arrival in Paris, inspired by the literary atmosphere, she mentioned making plans for "a book on 'Journals and Journal Writing'" (ED, 3:92), and she was soon referring to this "booklet" as "my Bible" or as "my Commandments." These "Commandments" dictate that a diary must be, among other things, a "self-confession, self-criticism," "a following and unveiling of ideas, a development of philosophies," and "a reminder of the clearer and higher moments in the intellectual life" (ED, 3:123). Like Baskhirtseff's preface, Nin's "Commandments" were nothing less than her manifesto, delivered most appropriately in Paris, a "political" arena in which many modernist "isms" were decreed.

Having spent over five years working through diary-writing techniques, Nin must have been applying them to her own diary. Only months after conceiving the journal essay, she wrote, "I have a feverish desire to invent a form for myself" (ED, 3:143). This new form was, I believe, the diary itself. This correlation may be understood through an exploration of her relationship with John Erskine, an American novelist and Guiler's former English professor, whom Nin had met in New York. While a banking career had deterred Guiler from realizing himself as a poet, Erskine, as a published novelist, fulfilled Nin's need for a creative lover. She was thrilled when he appeared in Paris. She was desperate for him to notice her, and he did, paying particular attention to her diary. Like Nin, Erskine saw the diary's potential, evaluating it according to its literary merits. Although Nin had been struggling to be a novelist, Erskine considered that of all her work her essay on journal writing was "the most interesting thing" she had done; he called her writing in it "exquisite" (ED, 3:173).

The fact that Nin had been writing fiction needs to be elaborated, for her failures and anxieties in this area impacted upon the journal as a work. She had brought with her to Paris the manuscript of her first novel, *Aline's Choice* (ED, 3:13), but found herself incapable of finishing it, as she was overwhelmed by her sense of "immaturity." She explained: "How I came to feel my immaturity is through the 'critics.' I can visualize what they would say about my book [...] I could not hope to convince a critic [of her maturity], and unfortunately they have power for good or evil, such as was granted to ancient kings." Nin then confessed: "In short, I am afraid. I have no faith in myself. Which does not mean that I will stop writing, but which means that I can never look at writing as a profession, as a *'public'* work. I think I am doomed to loving and practicing it in *secret*, in short, to possessing it as a vice, as a useless and blamable waste of time"(ED, 3:159; my emphasis).

The words that Nin chose to describe the kind of writing to which she was doomed – "vice," "useless," "waste of time" – were precisely those she had used to castigate her diary during her childhood. And as they did then, so they here belie her subversive strategy. Just as Benstock has explored how Stein critiqued patriarchal language, so we can see how Nin recognized the exclusionary agenda of an Eliotesque tradition, one which was ruled by powerful critical fathers – "ancient kings." In the spirit of Joyce's Stephen Dedalus, she turned to the silent, exilic space of her diary, where she could cunningly practise her art without immediate fear of censor by those "ancient kings." For this reason, then, the diary was the "form" that she had been "inventing" all along.

It is easy to see why Nin was so carried away by Erskine's praise of her essay on diary writing, for the diary was to be her form. The effect of his compliments was that she suddenly realized that she was not a failure, for "Erskine did approve my life and my writing" (ED, 3:177). She acknowledged: "It is having received encouragement from Erskine which I consider the 'vita nuova'" (ED, 3:173). And by the next day she had seemingly altered the course of her life: "My whole life is clear now. I work every day towards that development which is to bring me nearer to Erskine and all that he represents." She had "been too much the woman" and not enough the writer, and she resolved to change (ED, 3:174–5). If Nin's epiphany is too drastic to be entirely convincing, it does emphasize the degree to which she had felt suffocated and unfulfilled. The writer remained intricately connected to the woman, for Nin's identity continued to be relational, flowing without boundary between herself and Erskine's approval of this self. More subversively, her writing became intricately connected to her performance as a woman; she used it to seduce, and thus to gain satisfaction as both a woman and a writer.

Nin and Guiler went to the United States in June 1927, but had returned to Paris by July, at which point volume 3 of the *Early Diary* closes. The fourth volume opens with Nin taking stock of herself and her life, and her tone suggests that the themes raised above will be preoccupying ones: "Our trip to New York has given me confidence, courage, worship of life and a clear vision of what we have here. I don't know what has given me the strength I lacked before, this clarity and self-confidence. My imagination, which only teased me before, supports me now. I should be able to do the great things of which I have dreamed" (ED, 4:2).

This new "supportive" imagination directly coloured her diary. Between February and December 1928 Nin created the diary of a character she named Imagy, specifically to accommodate her increasing desire to fictionalize. She introduced this other diary: "I was tempted today to keep a double journal, one for things which do happen, and one for imaginary incidents which pass through my head [...] I live *doubly*. I'll write *doubly*." She explained that she felt "split into two women – one, kind, loyal, pure, thoughtful; the other, restless and impure, acting strangely, loosened, wandering, seeking life and tasting all of it without fear." This "other" was named "'Imagy,' after the origin of its curse, imagination." Nin wanted "to follow her doings because they are the ones which haunt my writing" (ED, 4:56).

Once again, it can be seen that these two selves are the Miss Nin and Linotte that had divided her since childhood, and they underscore how the diary was a site of role playing for Nin. By April she could not "live within reality" – she "must live *within stories*." Her plan was to "*fuse both* [reality and Imagy] and surrender the real me and Imagy to the world as One" (ED, 4:87). Ultimately, though, Imagy petered out, since Nin wrote Imagy's diary "in another book. She was getting troublesome and occupying too much space, considering her unreality" (ED, 4:118). There is, however, no evidence of this other book. The journal of Imagy had been composed within the "regular" diary, distinguished only by the simple heading "Imagy"(book 25). This pattern encourages the notion that Nin's sense of reality and imagination existed side by side, were in fact fused. Imagy did not really disappear. Nin continued, as would always be her practice, to write through a modernist sense of the self as fractured. And in drawing on both her "real" and her "imaginary" selves, she was negotiating what Brodzki and Schenck have described as the postmodern "tension between life and literature ... selfhood and textuality."[19]

Part of Imagy's function was to record Nin's growing sexual restlessness and her anticipation of Erskine's return to Paris. He had gone to the United States, but when he came back Nin lost no time in turning her diary over to him to arouse him. She described this day in December 1928: "John came to see me alone, and I became his confidante and he my friend. *A day I have long desired.* I read to him from my Journal about himself." Erskine's flattery was literary: "when I read him from my Journal, merely to nourish our conversation, his

attention was more taken with style, and he said: 'beautiful, beautiful'"
(ED, 4:143).

Nin and Erskine progressed from reading the diary to kissing (ED,
4:184) and from there to unconsummated sex (ED, 4:190). His indifference and his return to New York sent her into a depression. Perhaps
not unconnected to this experience is the fact that she began to doubt
the diary and herself as a writer: "I opened my Journal. Am I just making scales, too, studying for a real work? And when will I do this real
work? Already, the praises I received are wearing off and I look at my
Journal uncharitably" (ED, 4:196).

Her ever-present and faithful knight Guiler came to the rescue, offering unprecedented appreciation of the diary, so that shortly after the
expression of these doubts she recovered: "Hugh says: 'Your story is
good, but nothing compared to your Journal. I really believe you have
reached perfection in that form and that you will never do anything
else. That will be your whole life's work'" (ED, 4:199). Her confidence
regained, Nin became preoccupied with publishing the diary, as she
noted: "I might get my Journal published" (ED, 4:221). But by the next
year she was wondering about the ethics of publishing it (ED, 4:342–3).
She had in fact been concerned with this much earlier, as there were
times when she was certain that she would destroy her diary because
the material was specifically private (ED, 3:151).

By March 1931 Nin was planning a way to publish the diary "in
disguise," thinking that she could bring it out as someone else's diary
in which she would provide critical commentary: "Opposition of two
characters, with my signature under the 'other' character and 'myself'
denied!" (ED, 4:399). In June, she talked about a slightly different project: "I began my life's real work, the transposition of my Journal into
a printable form: use of 'she,' of continuous inward consciousness, a
kind of Proustian tapestry" (ED, 4:433). In transferring subjectivity
from "I" to "she," Nin was removing herself as an autobiographical
referent, once again negotiating the division between art and life.

She made many references to Marcel Proust and his great life work,
Remembrance of Things Past. She constantly compared her writing to
his and her diary to his "continuous novel," pointing to her equation
of her diary with autobiographical fiction. In terms of describing
people, she asserted, "Like Proust, I don't look at people; 'Je les radio-
graphie' [I x-ray them]" (ED, 4:80). In general, Nin wanted to "weave
all [her] stories together like a Proustian epopée [epic]" (E IV: 359). She
did distinguish her work from his – "Proust's work was a 'journal
intime,' a journal of memories. Mine is a journal of consciousness"
(E IV: 363) – but the comparison nonetheless locates her work on the
publishable, literary level of his modernist masterpiece.

From the start, Nin conceived the diary to some extent as fiction and her "I" as a textual construct. In childhood she related her life to fiction: "I live the books that I am reading at present" (ED, 1:390); and she described "how I love to sit alone thus, adding a chapter to the story of my great adventure" (ED, 2:74). Her life is a story and all the people in it merely players, and thus "Some day I may write a chapter in which all the characters meet" (ED, 2:523). Just as a good book contains a plot and characters, so it must have a theme. Nin's diary had "swallowed up every theme" she had "created during the years" (ED, 4:14). And as has already been shown, she began to title her diary volumes early on. Her conception of the diary as fiction and her interest in publishing it may have had a lot to do with the fact that her fiction and articles were being rejected by publishers, for by January 1931 it was "an accepted fact" that she wrote "unsalable stuff" (ED, 4:372). If she could not successfully translate her life into a novel, she would translate the diary into one.

MY MODERNISM, SO SINCERELY ARRIVED AT

Another factor that influenced the development of Nin the writer and hence Nin the character was her discovery of Freud and D.H. Lawrence. Together with Proust, they brought her into a consciousness of twentieth-century modernism.

Nin's absorption of Freud's theories rendered her a modernist who was preoccupied with analysis as a scientific mode of inquiry and as a literary technique. She was intuitively in touch with psychoanalysis, in that she was writing and thinking along its lines long before she had heard of the process as such. As a child, she had turned to her diary because she needed "to describe my state of mind" (ED, 1:109). Not only did she spend a lifetime doing so, but from the beginning she was her first analyst. At twelve years old she was already commenting, "When I analyze my impressions in these pages [. . .]" (ED, 1:91). And she later affirmed, "My idea is to first train myself by introspection, by analysis" (ED, 2:262).

By the end of 1927 Nin was celebrating her talent as an analyst, telling her diary that "no woman ever looked down into herself with as much cold criticism, no woman ever analyzed her ideas and actions more carefully, none was ever more doubtful of herself, more self-depreciating, more fearful of hypocrisy, more terrified of lies, more eager for truth, than I" (ED, 4:42). Though the veracity of these statements may certainly be called into question, what is significant here is that Nin was constructing a persona for herself that would soon be identified with Freud. Her sense of self is an embodiment of his theories of a neurotic, fragmented psyche, which informed so much of modernism. His division of the mind into the conscious and the unconscious and later into the ego, superego, and id, would be reflected in her own sense of self as fractured and in her Freudian drive to recover by means of analysis full self-knowledge – the "truth" which she was "eager" to seek out.

According to Nin, she first heard of psychoanalysis through her cousin Sanchez. On a trip to New York in May 1928, she had lunch with him, and he informed her that he was gay and was in analysis. Nin's curiosity was such that she asked him, "Please tell me as much as you can about it, what this knowledge has done to you, what it means." She then re-evaluated the diary: "I owe to it what some people owe to psychology: knowledge of myself, extreme consciousness of what in others is vague and unconscious, a knowledge of my desires, of my weaknesses, of my dreams, of my talents" (ED, 4:95). Nin honoured psychoanalysis as a "science" and related it to the diary when she wrote: "Praised be the Journal, the scientific basis to my creative fantasy"(book 30). She thus conferred legitimacy upon the traditionally feminine (irrational) diaristic enterprise by aligning it with masculine (rational) scientific inquiry.

Nin's lunch with Sanchez was eye-opening. From here on, her interest in and knowledge of "scientific" self-study began to expand. In January 1930, after Guiler told her that he liked to make other men jealous by flaunting his wife, Nin remarked: "'My, my,' I said, 'a case for Freud [whom I haven't read yet], a real complex'" (ED, 4:269). Of course, this was more a case for Nin than for Freud, and it hints at the later Nin who was unable to resist analyzing anyone. Though she made further references to Freud, it was apparently not until January 1931 that she finally read him: "I read murky Freud, for the first time. What a mind! His 'cases' fascinate me" (ED, 4:372). By July she was wanting to become a psychoanalyst: "I am absolutely determined. I am studying here, stubbornly." She added, "A strange thing happened which ought to augur well for my future work. I discovered my own illness and am taking care of myself." Going through various "symptoms" which had been attacking her, she concluded: "All this is duly described by Freud and is called anxiety neurosis. Cause? Sexual." She admitted that her suffering had been because of John Erskine, "the one thing I wanted and was deprived of" (ED, 4:437). But this was just the beginning. Nin – like White – went on to produce several pages of self-analysis, transforming the diary into a case study in which she was both the subject and the object of the investigation.

Nin was studying Freud's *History of Psychology*, and she remarked, "I can see the future psychoanalyst taking shape. My mind takes so easily to this young science." In the next entry her "admiration of Freud is confirmed" by her reading of *Beyond the Pleasure Principle* (ED, 4:440). From this reading she discovered: "I have not told my Journal the whole truth. Whatever I have left out, however, has been justified in two manners: the things that happened to me which I did not realize or face, which frightened or bewildered me; and the things that made no sense in my life" (ED, 4:441).

She explored the former mysteries. Although she had had sexual feelings as an adolescent, she unfortunately inspired men to love her only spiritually, ideally. She provided a detailed account of Guiler's own troubled childhood, during which he was punished for playing with his penis (ED, 4:444-5). Focusing on the lack of sex in their marriage, Nin admitted: "I had obscurely begun to blame Hugh for my neurosis." That he proved impotent on their wedding night had shocked and disappointed her. She described how "He used to fondle me and lose his strength between my legs, and thought this was coitus [...] My virgin's natural recoil from the final surrender and his timidity and gentleness lasted for a year, during which we played at coming together [. . .] until one day he was strong enough and violent enough to break through" (ED, 4:447).

Nin further understood that she had "mistress sensibilities," wanting to be treated not as a wife but as a lover. As she explained, "This is a new phase, which began only in 1931 and which may save our marriage." Her fantasy of being a mistress was summed up thus: "If a wife cannot include the prostitute, who is the woman who knows how to play, she is only a half-wife" (ED, 4:442-3). Nin's awakened sexual and psychological desires herald the woman who would be presented in the diaries that follow the *Early* series. Benstock notes that women "discovered sexualized writing identities in expatriation" in Paris, and this was clearly the case with Nin, whose linguistic release would make possible not only the graphic sexual descriptions in the unexpurgated volumes of her diary but also what would become her best-selling erotica, much of which was culled from the diary.

Given Nin's sexual and psychological awakenings, it is not surprising that the novelist who influenced her most during these years was D.H. Lawrence or that she explicitly linked him to psychoanalysis: "Lawrence's descriptions of the undercurrents of body and mind were but means of bringing to the surface many feelings that we do not sincerely acknowledge in ourselves. Freud and Jung have also done this."[20] Nin first read Lawrence on 24 December 1929, and what she appreciated in him was a reflection of her own personal and artistic growth: "Evening: I read a strange and wonderful book (*Women in Love* by D.H. Lawrence), concerned only with the description of feelings, sensations, conscious and unconscious, with ideas, and with the physical only as a transcription of spirit" (ED, 4:266). By April 1930 she was "planning a study of Lawrence's writing – reading all his books. Crudely entitled, for the moment, 'When D.H. Lawrence Found Himself'" (ED, 4:291). Nin's working title is ironic given that she was writing her essay during the period in which she was "finding" her own self. She was proud to announce: "my article on Lawrence is to be published in *Canadian Forum*. How fitting a beginning – praising my Lawrence" (ED, 4:326).

Within six months, Nin was developing this essay into a book. She lied to her agent, Edward Titus, telling him that she had a manuscript on Lawrence; when he asked to see it, she went home and wrote it in two weeks. She said of that time: "At certain moments I feared that I lacked maturity, but then I relied on my instinct. I even wrote the book with my body, as Lawrence would have it – not always intellectually" (E IV: 379). Nin was here a precursor of the French writers, such as Hélène Cixous, Luce Irigaray, and Julia Kristeva, who advocate "*l'écriture féminine*," or writing with the body.

It was the incorporation of the body into her intellectual and artistic agenda that would set Nin up as a modernist. To affirm the value and pleasure derived from physical experience was a radical move, especially for women. Nin took it to extremes, hailing herself as a "feminine" woman who thrived on cultivating her appearance with seductive clothes and makeup, and on sleeping with countless men to satisfy herself – and the men – sexually. It was this emphasis on the woman's body and its traditional function as a "servicer" of sex that would cost Nin feminist votes later on: many women who might have supported her as a modern woman staking out her claims to artistic autonomy were repelled by her continued playing of sex-object roles. Bair tells us that while Nin was speaking to a group of young women at Smith College in 1969, she was "hooted and hissed."[21]

Nin had written of Lawrence's detractors: "many have dreaded having to acknowledge this power of their physical sensations, as well as to face in plain words, the real meaning of their fantasies. Lawrence was reviled for going so far."[22] She, too, had gone "so far," at least by the standards of those Smith women who "reviled" her. But she may be, as she hoped, celebrated for daring to "face" her physical desires and fantasies, and to enact certain roles to realize those feelings. As she implied during a self-analysis, "the woman who knows how to play" is the whole woman. Nin used her diary to imagine certain experiences and document others, transgressing linguistic boundaries as she constructed a sexualized identity. Her followers today might include the small but assertive number of feminists, such as Nancy Friday, who favour a female-controlled and female-directed pornography.

In addition to Proust, Freud, and Lawrence, Nin had been reading other modernists. Most notably, in October 1930 she read *transition* for the first time, and it was this magazine that would open wide the doors of literary modernism for her. Launched in 1927 in Paris by Eugène and Maria Jolas, *transition* published writers such as James Joyce, Gertrude Stein, André Gide, Franz Kafka, Carl Jung, Samuel Beckett, Kay Boyle, and H.D. While it was an international magazine, it was simultaneously the mouthpiece of expatriate modernism, as it announced: "Transition wishes to offer American writers an opportunity to express themselves freely, to experiment, if they are so minded, and to avail themselves of a ready, alert and critical audience."[23] It is no wonder that the expatriate Nin noted: "But how I peek out, alive and excited [. . .] to devour *transition*" (ED, 4:353). She was soon considering her own work in its experimental context: "Reading the last number of *transition* has been tremendous for me. I read all these things after I have done my work and then find an affinity with modernism which elates me" (ED, 4:358). Only days earlier, Nin had received a letter from Erskine, who wrote: "I am hoping that the diary continues and that it is going to be turned into a novel before long. I am backing you as a real modern novelist" (ED, 4:366). His conflation of the diary with the modern novel underscores Nin's own conception of the diary as a means to a modernist end.

It was after much reading of psychoanalysis, Lawrence, and *transition* that Nin began her first serious novel, later called *House of Incest*, and it had a clear affinity to these sources: "I wrote fifteen little pieces like bits of prose-poems [...] They would fit in *transition*" (ED, 4:424). So too would the diary, for its preoccupation with modernist themes and styles rendered it her new form as well. In this way, Nin parallels Smart. It will be remembered that Smart considered her diary as a "preparation" (NS, 166). Likewise, Nin addressed her diary: "You may ask me what I am doing meanwhile if I am only preparing myself now. Why all this writing, these scattered thoughts, these descriptions? It is still the preparation" (ED, 2:262).

Just as I have argued that Smart's craving for a new form in fiction was in fact already being realized with the diary, so Nin's arrival at her new form had been suggested in the diary all along. Indeed, in the entry in which she first mentioned what would become *House of Incest*, she was "entering a new phase" in her writing (ED, 4:425). Within a month, she began her "life's real work, the transposition of [her] Journal into a printable form" (ED, 4:433). Her new phase in writing coincided with the journal becoming a public text. And when she mused,

"My modernism, so sincerely arrived at," she could just as likely be referring to the diary as to her fiction, for her ideas about psychology and sexuality had first been explored in the diary (*ED*, 4:464).

Volume 4 of the *Early Diary* closes with Nin exclaiming: "I'm dancing inside myself with a new bliss" (*ED*, 4:489). She had put Erskine behind her, she claimed to have been sensually reawakened by Guiler, she had begun her first modernist novel, Titus had promised to find a publisher for her Lawrence book, and she was continuing to work on the diary. Decades later Nin would decide to publish, as the first volume of the *Diary*, the story of her life as it unfolded immediately after this point – the point at which she began to live and to write modernism as a mature young woman.

It must be stressed that there are two kinds of later diaries: the expurgated and the unexpurgated ones. In the introduction to volume 1 of the *Diary*, editor Stuhlmann informs us that certain people did not want to appear in the published diary, and thus for legal and ethical reasons Nin removed them. These included Guiler and other members of her family (*D*, 1:xi). Guiler, however, is fully present in *Henry and June*, *Incest*, *Fire*, and *Nearer the Moon*. These volumes can be appreciated as the natural extension of the *Early Diaries* for several reasons. We leave Nin at the end of the fourth volume on the threshold of a new life, inspired by sexual and psychological awakenings. Although the *Diary* deals with the theme of psychology, it touches on sex in only a spiritual way, emphasizing the sensuous and poetic. In contrast, *Henry and June* explodes with physical and linguistic passion, the logical continuation from the fourth *Early Diary* volume. The explicit treatment of sex continues in *Incest*, in which Nin presents taboo subjects such as incest and abortion. *Fire* and *Nearer the Moon* expose Nin's affairs with her analyst Otto Rank and the Peruvian Marxist Gonzalo More, set against the backdrop of her ongoing liaison with Henry Miller and her relationship with her husband.

The *Diary* (volumes 1–7) must be considered the intermediary phase of a work which is only now being fully realized with the unexpurgated series, collectively entitled "A Journal of Love." After all, it was Nin's intention to publish the whole work. She told a reader in 1973, "Someday the entire Diary will be published" (*D*, 7:252). In his introduction to *Incest*, Rupert Pole stresses: "Now that virtually all of the people referred to in *Incest* have died, there is no cause to hold back on publishing the diary as Anaïs wished: in unexpurgated form" (*I*, ix). He makes it clear that this is her life's work: "When the 'Journal of Love' series of Anaïs Nin's unexpurgated diaries is complete, we will have an extraordinary lifetime record of the emotional growth of a creative artist, a writer with the technique to describe her deepest emotions and the courage to give this to the world" (*I*, x). As I have indicated earlier, my analysis focuses on only the first two of these supplements, as they are the volumes corresponding to the archival material that I was permitted to see.

I RULE BY SEDUCTION

Volume 1 of the *Diary* and *Henry and June* open on to the Paris suburb of Louveciennes in the winter of 1931, on the eve of the publication of Nin's first book, her study of Lawrence. By this time she had met the American novelist Henry Miller, who would prove to be one of the most important people in her life. He liberated her sexually from an unfulfilling marriage and remained one of her lovers for fifteen years. And he became one of her greatest champions, inspiring and encouraging her fiction writing, but more significantly, recognizing that the diary was her most crucial work. He would devote much time and energy in helping to get it published.

In December 1931 Nin began an affair with Miller. The language and content of her diary were dramatically coloured by his crude vocabulary and sexual experience. It is not surprising that Miller was depicted as a real and fleshly embodiment of Lawrence's fictional lovers: "Henry has done something to me, Henry the man. I can only compare what I feel to Lady Chatterley's feelings about Mellors. I cannot even think about Henry's work or Henry himself without a stirring in my womb" (*HJ*, 162). Given this association and given that Miller loved Nin, it is highly appropriate that he told her: "If Lawrence had lived and known you, he would have loved you" (*D*, 1:78).

What she specifically inherited from Lawrence and Miller was the ability to address issues which had historically been taboo as literary subject matter, such as sex itself, orgasm, and masturbation, so that, to quote Benstock, she "changed the history of modern women's writing, charting the terrain of female sexuality from female perspectives."[24] Nin, for example, described Miller: "Hands, fingering, ejaculations. I learn from Henry how to play with a man's body, how to arouse him, how to express my own desire" (*HJ*, 192). Her words are important because they deal with the reality that women have and need physical pleasure.

Against Nin's recognition and documentation of her "desire" was the bold confession that she did not have orgasms (*HJ*, 130). She confronted the issue with Dr René Allendy, a psychoanalyst whom she began seeing in April 1932. "I feel an imperative need to tell him my biggest secret: In the sexual act I do not always experience orgasm." When asked, she did admit that she knew what it was: "Oh, very

well, from the times I did experience it, and particularly from masturbation." She recounted that she masturbated often, but had always
been "ashamed afterwards." In the passage Nin continued to discuss
the subject until she realized that what she had been doing was natural and healthy (*HJ*, 172–3). Though her writing style is rather conventional here, her modernism can be appreciated by recalling Schenck's
argument that non-experimental forms are often used to present radical content.

In addition to heterosexuality, Nin documented her increasing lesbian desires: "The love between women" appeared "possible" to her,
"a mixture of fraternity and curiosity and perversity" (*ED*, 4:432). By
1932 she had found a woman to love, and this was Miller's estranged
American wife, June. Visiting Henry Miller in Paris, June went to Nin's
house in Louveciennes, and Nin recalled how in bed "We kissed each
other passionately. I fitted my body against every curve of June's body,
as if melted into her. She moaned. Her embrace was around me like a
multitude of arms [...] We rolled and heaved together. I under June, and
June under me" (*I*, 39). The moment was ruined, though, when June
became "self-conscious," and the encounter ended. Nin later problematized her desire when, in an argument with June, she admitted that
she "had intended to 'pull a lesbian act' to discover whether June loved
Henry" (*I*, 41).

Nin's experiences with Henry and June Miller led her to confront the
differences between men's and women's sexual roles. While she noted
that it is "bad for a woman to feel masculine" (*ED*, 4:432), she also
yearned for the power implicit in such a position. Thinking of Henry,
she admitted: "Often, though, the passivity of the woman's role weighs
on me, suffocates me. Rather than wait for his pleasure, I would like
to take it, to run wild" (*HJ*, 101). And she acknowledged "that a freer
life would be possible to me as a lesbian because I would choose a
woman, protect her, work for her, love her for her beauty while she
could love me as one loves a man, for his talent, his achievements, his
character." Performing as a man "would eliminate all concern with my
beauty, health, or sexual potency. It would make me confident because
everything would depend on my talent, inventiveness, artistry, in which
I believe" (*HJ*, 133).

These sentiments reveal Nin's full awareness of how "masculine"
and "feminine," as terms for thought and behaviour, have been constructed, and how men and women have been guided by the dictates of
society to perform roles. Recognizing what society expected from a
woman, she wanted to behave as one in order to fulfill those expectations, to which she had been conditioned. But Nin also wanted to be
independent and to be a writer, and thus she was forced to adopt a

kind of masculine sensibility as well. She would struggle with this dichotomy for her whole life, trying to reconcile her masculine and feminine assumptions and desires. In so doing, she played many roles, a fact she freely and consistently acknowledged in comments such as "Always imagining another role. Never static" (*HJ*, 119), and "Playing a million roles" (*F*, 24). Like Woolf's Orlando, she equated role-playing with gender: "Woman always has to act a role, for the sake of the love" (*F*, 349). Nin proves Blodgett's assertion that too often women accommodate themselves to the roles that men expect them to play. But her recognition of this expectation made her actions subversive: she was playing a role to get what *she* wanted.

One of the things Nin most wanted was revenge, and thus she appropriated the role that would empower her to this end: that of the femme fatale. She inverted traditional gender relations by positioning herself as subject and men as (sex) objects. She was proud to announce: "Quite definitely, today I felt classified, categorized as a species of seductress not often encountered. I play not only with sex but with souls, imaginations [...] I am a new kind of enchantress" (*I*, 185). She stated, "I rule by seduction" (*F*, 345), elaborating: "The *frisson* I feel now is power – power to enslave and to torture" (*F*, 346).

Nin's desire not only to seduce and enchant but also to enslave and torture had a lot to do with her father, who may have violated her as a child before abandoning her. Fitch based her biography on the assumption that Nin's father sexually abused her as a child, and Bair reinforces this view. Both draw attention to the fact that Joaquin Nin physically beat Anaïs and that this treatment probably led to sexual abuse. Bair, for instance, quotes a seventeen-year-old Nin recalling: "He was a strict father to us [...] I would do anything to keep him from lifting my dress and beating me" (*ED*, 2:86). (This was eerily the experience, and the dread, described by White: "What horrified me was not the idea of being beaten ... but those dreadful words, 'I'm going to take down your knickers.'")[25] Bair follows the quotation with a passage from the unpublished diary recounted years after an alleged attack against a nine-year-old Anaïs: "He begins to hit me with the palm of his hand. I feel his hand on me. But he stops hitting me and he caresses me. Then he sticks his penis into me, pretending to be beating me."[26] As Fitch comments, "A psychoanalyst today with [. . .] a description of a violent, patriarchal father, a lifetime of seductive behavior, and dreams of prostitution in a patient who is nonorgasmic, passive, masochistic yet fearful of pain, and sickened by her own sexual aggressiveness – would look for childhood sexual experience in the patient."[27]

Fitch's analysis matches Herman's groundbreaking description of many incest survivors. Of especial interest here is Herman's observation "Some women even embraced their identity as sinners with a kind of defiance and pride. As initiates into forbidden sexual knowledge, they felt themselves to possess magical powers, particularly the power to attract men."[28] This is exactly what we witness in Nin's pride: "I am a new kind of enchantress"; "The *frisson* I feel now is power" (*I*, 185; *F*, 345).

With this power, Nin recognized "I am becoming aware that I am wreaking a kind of revenge upon men, that I am impelled by a satanic force to win and abandon them" (*I*, 196). She specifically wanted to win her father and then abandon him, forcing him to suffer as he had made her suffer. According to the diary, this revenge took the form of adult consensual sex between parent and child. It must be emphasized that beyond Nin's own testimony, there is no proof of such an act. Bair, for instance, qualifies her account by saying: "If Anaïs Nin the diarist is to be believed ..."[29] On this point, two things must be kept in mind. First, as Adams argues, what matters or what should concern us in studies of autobiography is "narrative truth," and my treatment of the incest narrative is grounded in this assumption.

Secondly, evidence gathered by Bair and Fitch does suggest that Nin fits the profile of an incest survivor, and if she does, we can more plausibly accept that she later engaged in sexual relations with her father. Karin C. Meiselman, in *Resolving the Trauma of Incest*, aids us in appreciating this behaviour. Discussing "repetition compulsion," a common phenomenon of incest survivors, she describes it thus: "Victims of trauma of many varieties have been known to repeat the traumatic situation in a compulsive, unconsciously symbolic way, possibly as an attempt at mastery. The unconscious goal is to replay the scene in such a manner that she maintains control."[30] In similar spirit, writing about incest survivors who turn their experiences into the stuff of their fiction, Broe argues: "At stake is the writer's authority over two texts: the survival story and the incest story, both of which require control to break the denial of the subject position that has described the women's lives. Transgressions or transformation of enclosures in dreams or dramas manifest a peculiar spatial logic that testifies to the women's new-found authority."[31]

Nin possibly engaged in adult incest as a "repetition compulsion" in an effort at "mastery" – "the *frisson* I feel now is power" – in order to rewrite the "incest story" and inscribe her own "survival story," thus making herself the subject of both narratives so as to (re)gain control of her bodily text and her textual body. That her "repetition" was carried out in symbolic terms is manifested in the manner in which she drew on psychoanalysis, symbolism, and surrealism, as well as the dream and the drama, to document her trauma.

Though Nin revealed her fascination with psychoanalysis in the late twenties, it was not until April 1932 that she actually began analysis, with Allendy. She would be his patient for about one year and in November 1933 would take up with her next doctor, Otto Rank. With him, Nin would realize her long-held dream of being an analyst when she travelled at the end of 1934 to New York to practise. But after five months she returned to Paris and her writing. She would remain a patient of analysis, however, for most of her life. The impact of all of this on the diary was profound.

As a child, Nin had recorded her dreams in her diary and sought to understand them. In adulthood her fascination only intensified. She titled a section at the back of her diary for June to October 1931 "Dreams" and offered several pages of her dreams and interpretations (book 31). The next diary volume opens with her statement that Guiler's and her main interest of late had been "Freud on 'Dreams'" (book 32). Once she entered analysis, her documentation of dreams became more frequent and her interpretations more professional. Nin's diary, like White's, became a textual embodiment of Freud's work; it reads like an extended supplement to his case studies.

Her psychoanalysis affected the form and content of the diary. It also encouraged her to explore herself and her relationships, which further impacted on what and how she wrote. Psychoanalysis helped to guide Nin through the depths of her unconscious to the surface of her writing. After working on certain prose poems, she wrote: "And immediately I made a note on the psychoanalysis of the creator: 'creation by undirected imagining – a state of being like a trance – produces subconscious poetry'" (ED, 4:424). She adopted Jung's dictum "To proceed from the dream outward" as her personal modus operandi (D, 1:132). In 1941 she would comment: "All effort to make the transmutation required of poetry, which is an alchemy of ordinary natural events into heightened myth, is taboo. Yet the very role of the poet is to exalt whatever he touches, it is to take ordinary reality and give it a fiery incandescence [...] Without this alchemy all writing remains dead" (D, 3:175). Nin's diary remained alive, though, for it was her "drug" and her "vice." She described recording in it: "This is the moment when I take up the mysterious pipe and indulge in deviations. Instead of writing a book, I lie back and I dream and I talk to myself. A drug. I turn away from reality into the refracted, I turn events into vapor, into languid dreams [...] I must relive my life in the dream. The dream is my only life" (I, 366).

As Bair notes, one of the reasons Nin entered psychoanalysis was that she was concerned about the fact that she was able unable to write fiction[32] – this was why her diary was here and elsewhere imaged as a "vice." Ironically, though, Nin, like White, would pen thousands of pages of diary while trying to work through her writer-of-fiction block. Her comment above – "Instead of writing a book" – becomes even more ironic when we realize that in the act of writing the dream, Nin was writing her diary, and it was a surrealistic one that would have made André Breton proud.

Breton was the French proponent of surrealism who in 1920 published (with Philippe Soupault) *The Magnetic Fields* and in 1924 the first of his surrealist manifestos. He argued for an automatic writing that could tap into the creative sources of the unconscious or into the dream state of the psyche. As Nicholls shows, "Breton familiarised himself with Freudian concepts of the unconscious, repression, complexes and sexuality, and, above all, with the analytic technique of free association." Though "Surrealism would be the only modernist avant-garde to welcome Freud's ideas," Nicholls does distinguish the various ways in which the surrealists differed from Freud, one of the most significant being that if Freud viewed the unconscious as the repository for illness and fragmentation, Breton and colleagues saw it as the site of "prophecy" heralding a self newly integrated with unreal (dream) and real states of being. Surrealist automatic writing thus invoked Jung's dictum to "proceed from the dream outward," privileging a life in which there is no distinction between dream and reality, a life that is "surreal."[33] Given that the diary is where Nin simultaneously lived and wrote the dream – her "only life" – then it is her quintessential surrealistic text.

THE THEATRE OF INCEST

Nin embraced surrealism, and for this reason, we can place her in the context of those modernist women, identified by Hanscombe and Smyers, who were as innovative in how they lived as how they wrote. Nin lived and wrote in the spirit of Breton, and she also constructed text and life in the spirit of another surrealist, the avant-garde poet and playwright Antonin Artaud. Through Artaud, Nin learned how to dramatize her psyche.

It was through Allendy that she first met Artaud, famous for his 1932 manifesto "The Theatre Of Cruelty." It is my contention that she enacted this "Theatre" both in her life and in her diary, and so a brief overview of Artaud's aesthetic is necessary. Though his ideas are complex and they evolved throughout his career, it is possible to touch on some of his theories propounded during the early thirties. Artaud was convinced that people had become too removed from cosmic life forces, had become deadened as the result of privileging the mind and reason over the body and instinct. He advocated a theatre of cruelty which would shock the spectators into an awareness and hence a liberation of their repressed emotions and sensibilities, so that the audience could be rejuvenated, redeemed. Artaud was influenced by Freud, whose theory of repression was grounded in the notion that people were privileging "civilization" over their natural drives and instincts. A closer look at Artaud's "First Manifesto" of "The Theatre Of Cruelty" explains these points further.

In describing the "Technique" of his proposed theatre, Artaud wrote: "The problem is to turn theatre into a function in the proper sense of the word, something as exactly localised as the circulation of our blood through our veins, or the apparently chaotic evolution of dream images in the mind, by an effective mix, truly enslaving our attention." He argued that in order to be "truly illusive," the theatre must provide the audience "with truthful distillations of dreams where its taste for crime, its erotic obsessions, its savageness, its fantasies, its utopian sense of life and objects, even its cannibalism" must "gush out" "on an inner level." Artaud elucidated how this theatre was to realize its intentions in terms of scenery, costuming, and the like. In general, he privileged gesture, action, lighting, and sound over words. Artaud addressed his specific concept of cruelty thus: "There can be no spectacle without an element of cruelty as the basis of every show. In our present degenerative state, metaphysics must be made to enter the mind through the body."[34]

In "Theatre and the Plague," first presented as a lecture in April 1933, Artaud posited, "A real stage play disturbs our peace of mind, releases our repressed subconscious." He offered an example of this kind of "real play": "As soon as the curtain goes up on [John] Ford's 'Tis Pity She's a Whore, to our great surprise we see before us a man launched on a most arrogant defence of incest, exerting all his youthful, conscious strength both in proclaiming and justifying it." Indeed, "He does not hesitate or waver for one instant, thereby demonstrating just how little all the barriers mean that might be set up against him." This desire is directed at and shared by his sister Annabella: "the strength of his tumultuous passion" "evokes a correspondingly rebellious and heroic passion in Annabella." Artaud generalized: "If fundamental theatre is like the plague, this is not because it is contagious, but because like the plague it is a revelation, urging forward the exteriorisation of a latent undercurrent of cruelty through which all the perversity of which the mind is capable [...] becomes localised." As Nin interpreted, Artaud's theatre "is a place to shout pain, anger, hatred, to enact the violence in us" (D, 1:187). Artaud drew attention to the purgatorial possibilities of the theatre: "The plague is a superior disease because it is an absolute crisis after which there is nothing left except death or drastic purification." Likewise, theatre "urges the mind on to delirium which intensifies its energy."[35] This "energy" is ultimately channelled into artistic creation.

Nin recorded first meeting Artaud on 12 March 1933: "At the Allendys': Artaud – the face of my hallucinations. The hallucinated eyes. The sharpness, the pain-carved features. The man-dreamer, diabolical and innocent, frail, nervous, potent [...] He is veritably haunted and haunting [...] I did not expect that face. '*Je suis le plus malade de tous les surréalistes.*'" She described him as "a broken, quivering decadent, another 'lusty decadent' – opium, perhaps [...] The burned-up face, the malice, the passion, the violence." She was pleased, for "His eyes following all my gestures. I forgot everyone else in my absorption. Our eyes were constantly converging" (I, 118–19). As the "sickest of all surrealists," Artaud was the classic tortured artist, in exile from self and society. It was for this reason that Nin was so drawn to him, and that she saw herself akin to him: "What a demon there is in me" (I, 133), she wrote; "I'm a neurotic – in the sense that I live in *my* world. I will not adjust myself to the world. I am adjusted to myself" (I, 134). Like Artaud, she would live her life in exile, in the dream.

By June, Nin was discussing her attraction to Artaud as one of repulsion. Though she wrote, "As I looked at his mouth, whose edges were blackened by laudanum, a mouth I did not want to kiss," she went on to admit: "I knew I was drawn toward death again, always drawn to death, to the end, to culminations, to insanities. To be kissed by Artaud was to be poisoned" (I, 186). It is important to note that the eroticism of death is a function of the Theatre of Cruelty.

A few days later Nin documented an unsuccessful sexual encounter with Artaud. She made her entrance into the scene dramatic, since she was in costume: "Madness. When I arrive before Artaud he stands nobly, proudly, with eyes mad with joy ... I have come in black, red, and steel, as Mars, at war, warring not to be touched by Artaud. I feel his taut desire, oppressive, obsessive." She recounted: "He knelt before me and he talked violently, holding me with his eyes, and I forget his words. All I remember is that he drew me out of myself, out of my resistance. I sat there magnetized and my blood obeyed him. He kissed me devouringly, fiercely, and I yielded" (I, 191–2). But Artaud became impotent, blaming it on too much opium. At this point, Nin performed the greatest gesture she could think of – "I knew that I must save him immediately from his humiliation" – releasing him between her hands and producing a "futile outpour of honey." She acknowledged: "His humiliation was appeased. He stood up and made a gesture of despair" (I, 192). Although Nin had come "warring not to be touched by Artaud," she wound up touching him, performing gestures; and it was through the "gesture of despair" that Artaud took his leave of the scene. As we have noted, "gestures" are an intergral component of absurdist theatre.

Nin's performances with Artaud prefigured the incestuous direction that her relationship with her father would take. To recall her interpretation, the Theatre of Cruelty "is a place to shout pain, anger, hatred, to enact the violence in us." Specifically, I believe Nin was recreating as an adult the sexual abuse that she may have suffered as a child. We have heard Broe explain that "Transgressions or transformation of enclosures in dreams or drama manifest a peculiar spatial logic that testifies to the women's new-found authority."[36] In telling her own survival story, Nin drew on both the dream (via Freud, Jung, and Breton) and the drama (via Artaud).

After many years apart from him, Nin was reunited with her father in Paris in 1933. On 5 May, when she saw him, he did "not seem to be my Father [...] We flirt like lovers" (I, 156). After this meeting, Nin had a dream in which "my Father caressed me like a lover[. . .]" (I, 157) – a dream that she would soon realize in a surreal reality when she travelled to the resort town of Valescure to be alone with this man. She began her entry dated 23 June 1933 with "First Day," and then "King Father arrives." The nine-day period that follows, however, was actually written after the fact, as the entire portion is contained within an entry that Nin dated "Chamonix, 8 Juillet 1933" (book 42).

Earlier, in May, she told us: "Father, too, is jealous of the journal. 'My only rival,' he says'" (I, 164). In June she ceased writing in the diary – she wrote it up later. What is so significant is that this "Father story" is Nin's account of her incestuous relations with her father; that the father considered the diary his "rival" reinforces my earlier argument that it was the personification of a lover, an instrument of seduction. Another time, referring to all the men in her life, Nin added: "(All of them would slay the journal if they could.)" (I: 215). By ceasing the diary at the moment she had sex with him, Nin pleased her father by choosing him over her textual lover.

In describing the events that unfolded, Nin created a drama of incest. It is important to recall that Artaud had used Ford's play about incest as an example of a "real stage play" that "disturbs our peace of mind, releases our repressed subconscious." Nin could have been releasing repressed memories of childhood abuse which she then appropriated to empower herself. According to Nin, her father treated her "as his fiancée" (I, 205). They spent much of their time in his bedroom, with him recounting the story of his life while Nin sat listening in her "satin negligee" (I, 207). They confessed to each other: "I don't feel toward you as if you were my daughter" and "I don't feel as if you were my

Father." Thereupon he demanded, "Bring Freud here, and all the psychologists. What could they say about this?"(I, 208). Nin's father as speaker and Nin as writer deliberately place their taboo acknowledgments within a Freudian context, fashioning their own case study.

At this point, in the spirit of the Theatre, words became subordinate to action, and Nin's father kissed her: "He put his arms around me. I hesitated. I was tortured by a complexity of feelings, wanting his mouth, yet afraid, feeling I was to kiss a brother, yet tempted – terrified and desirous. I was taut." She continued: "We kissed, and that kiss unleashed a wave of desire. I was lying across his body and with my breast I felt his desire, hard, palpitating. Another kiss. More terror than joy. The joy of something unnameable, obscure." His advances were threatening; though her body responded to his touch, "all the while some part of me was hard and terrified." Nonetheless, "With a strange violence, I lifted my negligee and I lay over him." Though he "emptied all of himself in me," Nin was unable to have an orgasm because of the "core of fear" that prevented it. After sex, she admitted that she felt "revulsion [...] I wanted to run away." She felt "poisoned by this union," and she repeated "poison" three times (I, 209–10). In this passage, she figures as both the performer and the spectator, an appropriate role for the participant in the Theatre of Cruelty; she shocks herself, and her readers, into an awareness of her father's cruelty.

It is here that the connection with Artaud is manifest. Nin's description of this night with her father echoes the supposed sexual encounter with Artaud; taken together, they enact the Theatre of Cruelty. It should be stressed that Nin had a tendency to perform, through actions and gestures, the contents of her psyche. This inclination is implied in February 1933: "My need of gestures [...] My need, my need of gestures." She emphasized, "I am an unusually expressive, demonstrative being, that I exteriorize constantly, that every feeling I have has instantaneously a form, an expression" (I, 104). This can be contemplated alongside Artaud's comment that the theatre, like the plague, urges "the exteriorisation of a latent undercurrent of cruelty." Most tellingly, Nin had said of the diary, "Very often it is nothing but a gesture" (book 16).

Her assertion that "To be kissed by Artaud was to be poisoned" is matched by her feelings of being "poisoned" by her father. Her costuming as Mars so as to be "warring not to be touched by Artaud" echoes her ambiguous feelings of having to resist her father. The notion that the Theatre of Cruelty allows us to "enact the violence in us" is borne out not only by the persona of Mars but more significantly by Nin's mounting of her father: "With a strange violence, I lifted my negligee." In this way the adult Nin was displaying the "mastery" associated with the repetition compulsion. Moreover, while Artaud was "taut," so Nin is "taut" here. Words used with Artaud, such as "oppressive," "obsessive," "resistance," "magnetized," "obeyed," "devouringly," and "yielded," similarly colour her encounter with her father. That Nin confronted "pain, anger, hatred" with him is made explicit in words such as "afraid," "tortured," "terrified," "terror," "fear," and "revulsion."

Artaud's fascination with incest was registered in his attraction to Lucas van Leyden's painting *The Daughters of Lot*. In her diary entry for 13 June 1933, which discusses Artaud, Nin has added at the top of the margin: "Antonin took me to the Louvre to see 'Lot and his Daughters'" (book 42). Her reaction to the picture matched Artaud's in intensity, as he implied in a letter to her shortly after: "I have brought many people, men and women, to see this marvellous painting, but this is the first time I have seen an artistic emotion touch someone and make her throb with love." He went on: "Your senses trembled and I suddenly realized that inside of you the body and the spirit are deeply linked, since a purely spiritual impression could unleash in your body such a powerful storm."[37]

Of course, this painting depicts incest, and the fact that Nin responded to the "artistic emotion" suggests that it was this emotion – "artistic" – which she would harness in her experience and depiction of her own incest. To be sure, Artaud's "unleash" is precisely the word that Nin used to describe the impact of her father: "that kiss unleashed a wave of desire." In this case, her desire was to control her body/text. She herself connected her own experience and the work of art when she wrote about the "fourth night" with her father: "I told him about the painting of Lot and his daughters" (I, 212).

It is interesting to note that Herman identifies what she calls the "Seductive Daughter" as being one of the major "culprits in the incest romance," and that among the earlist examples are the daughters of Lot.[38] The "seductive daughter" is the girl who relentlessly pursues and seduces the older male figure, usually her father, so that the man cannot be held responsible for his actions because he did not initiate sex, and because in giving in to sex, he simply "couldn't help himself." Herman cites Vladimir Nabokov's *Lolita* as a modern-day version of such a plot. I do not believe, however, that Nin was writing herself into a role that in effect confers subjectivity, or centrality, upon the man seduced. I think rather that she was appropriating the role of the femme fatale in order to gain control of her body and of the text in which the body was being (re)written.

It is important to note that Freud labelled incest a taboo, and as Herman aptly summarizes his ideas, he propogated the theory that its prohibition was a way of ensuring the peaceful evolution of the family.[39] The families he envisioned and wanted to protect were patriarchal ones. Nin arguably disrupted the authority of her father when she consented to incest, in that she threatened the continuation of his line. She thus radically rewrote DuPlessis's romance ending.

Her ability to rewrite her past is further borne out when we note Broe's suggestion: "One way of looking at dreams is to consider them active reenactments of things passively endured in childhood."[40] Artaud's insistence that his Theatre must provide "the audience with truthful distillations of dreams" was realized by Nin, who marvelled about her intimacy with her father, "We looked at each other as in a dream " (I, 208); "I was living a dream" (I, 215). This description recalls the surreal directive of Breton. Artaud's assertion that the theatre "restores all our dormant conflicts"[41] is proven by Nin's recognition of her father as the man who had abused her in the past. Staring at this face, she "realized how this mask had terrorized me [...] How as a child I had the obscure terror that this man could never be satisfied" (I, 205). Nin rewrote the past by casting herself as the one who would "never be satisfied" by her father as lover.

In writing about Ford's Annabella, Artaud had praised her "rebellious and heroic passion," and in a sense it seems that Nin was approaching the incest as a kind of self-imposed dare, stimulated by her analysis and by her reading, to prove that she was capable of transcending the rational world, of breaking the "barriers" in the dramatic spirit of Ford's protagonists. In this way she would emerge from being a victim in childhood to become a survivor in adulthood, one who controlled how the incest was (re-)experienced and narrated.

THE TORTURE DIARY

In order to understand this control, we must consider other influences on Nin. One of these was Octave Mirbeau, whose *Torture Garden* (1899) elicited this response from her: "I remember being struck with the limitations of physical cruelty and pain. I also remember that I felt obsessions and anxieties were just as cruel and painful, only no one had described them vividly [...] I wanted to do, in *House of Incest*, the counterpart to physical torture in the psychic world, in the psychological realm" (D, 1:265). In February 1934 she repeated the observation that "the description of physical torture was, for me, so much less potent than mental tortures [...] Mental tortures we are only now beginning to delve into" (D, 1:311). Mirbeau's work, described as "the most sickening work of art of the nineteenth century,"[42] confronts, like Artaud's theatre, the boundaries between respectable social behaviour and instinctual sexual and spiritual depravity.

Clara, a sado-masochistic woman who leads the unnamed male narrator through the *Torture Garden*, mocks: "It is that permanent contradiction between your ideas and desires and all the dead formalities and vain pretenses of your civilization which makes you sad, troubled and unbalanced. In that intolerable conflict you lose all joy of life and all feeling of personality, because at every moment they suppress and restrain and check the free play of your powers."[43] In this tension, Nin had said of herself and her father: "We are barbaric and subliminal. We have lived like civilized barbarians. The most barbaric and the most sublimated" (*I*, 204). Perhaps Nin, eager to test "the free play" of her powers, conceived the incest as a challenge to "dead formalities and vain pretenses," and determined to rewrite the incest narrative from a woman's perspective. It is likely that in doing so, she imagined herself as Clara, for Clara is a woman who thrives on watching the tortures in the garden, and she believes that love is equivalent to torture[44] – just as Nin announced that she was a femme fatale who was "wreaking a kind of revenge upon men" (*I*, 196).

In addition to Mirbeau, the diary also reflects the hellish world of Arthur Rimbaud, the nineteenth-century French symbolist poet. Nin was particularly affected by his "A Season in Hell" (1873), in which he made the provocative statement "It is necessary to be absolutely modern."[45] I believe that Nin took him at his word. She called her novella *House of Incest*, which she was working on at this time, "my season in hell" (*D*, 1:289). Rimbaud's work depicts a journey into the unconscious through his tortured psyche. He introduces his poem to "dear Satan": "I detach for your benefit these few hideous pages from my damned man's diary."[46] Likewise, Nin "detaches" the "few hideous pages" of her description of incest from *her* diary for the benefit of her readers.

It was two years before "A Season," in 1871, that Rimbaud had outlined his poetic theory. In his "Lettres du voyant," he advised, "The first study for a man who wants to be a poet is the knowledge of himself, entire." This knowledge comes from going on a particular kind of journey: "The poet makes himself a *visionary* through a long, a prodigious and rational disordering of all the senses. Every form of love, of suffering, of madness; he searches himself, he consumes all the poisons in him, keeping only their quintessences. Ineffable torture in which he will need all his faith." The rewards of this journey are that the poet "arrives at the unknown," and even though he may be destroyed "by those unnamable, unutterable and innumerable things," he will have had his vision.[47]

Nancy Scholar believes that "*House of Incest* is Nin's response to Rimbaud's advice."[48] While this interpretation is certainly true, I suggest that Nin's more dramatic response was the actual act of incest and/or the textual reconstruction of such as act, either or both of which were translated first of all into the diary. Nin made it clear that her journey into her unconscious was launched there, for it is within the diary's pages that she confessed: "There are experiences I shy away from. But my curiosity, creativeness, urge me beyond these boundaries, to transcend my character. My imagination pushes me into unknown, unexplored, dangerous realms" (D, 1:29).

If Nin wanted to prove that she was the genuine "visionary" artist as defined by Rimbaud, she might have found it necessary, in fulfilling her task, to take him at his word and plunge into experiencing the "poison" of incest. Just as he described the poet's visions as "unnamable," so Nin, as we have seen, referred to the "joy of something unnameable" when she kissed her father. Elsewhere, she states: "Hell is a different place for each man, or each man has his own particular hell. My descent into the inferno is a descent into the irrational level of existence, where the instincts and blind emotions are loose, where one lives by pure impulse, pure fantasy, and therefore pure madness" (D, 1:36). These are precisely the conditions for and the consequences of her incestuous relationship.

Having considered these influences, then, we can now make further connections between Artaud's Theatre of Cruelty, Rimbaud's "A Season in Hell," Mirbeauesque psychic tortures, and Nin's textual incest with her father. Just as the Theatre of Cruelty advocates the release of pain, cruelty, and violence and a confrontation with instinctual obsessions, so Rimbaud urges a dangerous voyage into the psyche, where these obsessions are hiding. Moreover, the dangers of which he warns are the psychic tortures associated with Mirbeau and Artaud; as Nin said, "I also remember that I felt obsessions and anxieties were just as cruel and painful." Her incestuous encounter with her father was specifically her "season in hell." She titled the fiction – her "season in hell" – *House of Incest*, and the diary volume *Incest*.

The relationship can be considered a journey into Nin's deepest, most instinctual and primitive fears – her paradoxical taboo desire for the father coupled with the horror of childhood abuse – and she necessarily experienced psychic tortures, the stuff of which Artaud's theatre is made. As she described her father's kiss: "I was *tortured* by a complexity of feelings" (my emphasis). It is further interesting to consider this kiss, the father's poisonous sperm, and the poisonous kiss of Artaud together with Rimbaud's protagonist. For it is through poison that this character enters his "Night in Hell": "I have swallowed a famous throatful of poison";[49] he later refers to "this poison, this kiss a thousand times accursed!"[50] And it was through her father's kiss that

Nin entered her "season in hell." In addition, poison spreads through Mirbeau's Garden. The narrator notes that the heat "was deadly as poison,"[51] and he recognizes his inability "to cure myself of the frightful poison that woman [Clara] had injected into my flesh."[52]

Ultimately, it was by journeying into her "inferno," or participating in the Theatre of Cruelty, that Nin was able to confront her father to the point of extracting him from herself, purging herself, as it were, from that which had previously been unacknowledged, repressed. She was then able to utilize her experiences and discoveries for artistic purposes, as both Artaud and Rimbaud directed. She confessed, "I do not understand abstract art. Only art born of love, passion, pain" (D, 1:223). The art that she delivered includes her "performance" in the Theatre of Cruelty, her first novella *House of Incest*, and the passages within her diary.

To appreciate how the diary both is affected by and affects Nin's purgation, we must follow her from her father's bed to a bed in Avignon with Miller. Writing there, she discussed the impact of her father on the diary: "I had wanted at least my incestuous love to remain unwritten. I had promised Father utter secrecy." That is, she had promised to remain loyal to him as against the diary. However, "one night here in the hotel, when I realized there was no one I could tell about my Father, I felt suffocated. I began to write again." Admitting the psychic torture of the incest, she noted that her journal helped to preserve her sanity: "I need this order. I am more ill than ever, more neurotic, and I must keep my balance" (I, 216–7). We can recall Djuna Barnes's advice: "Keep writing. It's a woman's only hope."

Nin tells us that she and her father continued to meet as lovers. And yet she could not wholly forget that this was still the same man who had caused and continued to cause her so much pain. In August she repeated how significant her diary was to her: "It is a kind of supreme treachery. Because Father has begged me not to write. Faithfulness to the journal seems to force me each time to write in spite of [. . .] my promise to Father" (I, 244). Whereas she had previously used her diary to seduce, she was here using it to assert autonomy. Her diary inscribes both "the survival story and the incest story" described by Broe, and thus it is the ideal space in and of which Nin took control.

Even more, the fact that she was being "treacherous" is evidenced in a comment made in the journal the day before her first act of incest. Speaking of the diary, she threatened: "With the power I have, what evil I could do [. . .] and this evil I do in my journal. My evil will be posthumous – the ruthless truths!" (I, 203). In 1937 she admitted of this diary volume: "To me it is intensely humorous, my giving the *Incest* title, knowing it will give my Father chills of fear [...] I love to throw bombs" (*F*, 406). Nin's sentiments reflect Rimbaud's protagonist at the end of his journey, after he has confronted and conquered his demons: "For I can say that victory is mine."[53] Nin's "bomb" may be contextualized within Herman's study, in which Herman found that many incest survivors who felt extreme power over men were in fact recognizing that they "had the potential to destroy their families."[54] That is, they "could bring disaster upon their families by revealing what they knew." Though Nin waited until both she and her father were dead, she nonetheless made her diary the whistle she blew against him. She has had the last word, and it is one of "ruthless truths" indeed, her final and unequivocal "revenge upon men."

Nin had been lured by her father, succumbing to his power over her because she had always longed for his paternal love. But there was clearly a part of her which was able to stand back, record her repulsion, and recognize the abuse that had gone on. On 10 June 1934, when her father came to visit, she was relieved that her response to him had died: "And I smile to see I have no emotion – no feeling for this stiff inhuman schoolteacher." She rejoiced, "Oh, I'm free! I'M FREE" (*I*, 339–40). Nin echoes Rimbaud's protagonist as he emerges from hell: "Yet I believe that to-day I have finished the tale of my hell."[55]

By participating in the Theatre of Cruelty and travelling through her "inferno," Nin experienced a necessary purgation. In August she confronted her father: "I begin a letter to my Father and I am stopped by sobbing. Frustration and despair." And she concluded, "He is no *Father*" (*I*, 367). Nin's diary not only depicts in detail the sexual relations but judges them as wrong, herself the victim she was. It is likely that she had her own experiences in mind when she alluded to Mirbeau in February 1934, after the incest – "Mental tortures we are only now beginning to delve into."

Artaud predicted that both the plague and the Theatre of Cruelty would bring about a crisis, "after which there is nothing left except death or drastic purification." Nin's assertion that she was "FREE" heralds her purification. Her energy had been intensified by the delirium of the crisis, manifested in her ability to channel her energy into writing. The June entry ends with a significant question: "Why has the diary come to life again?" (*I*, 340). Having said that she was "FREE" of her father, she was now able to return to herself and to the diary, which proved both a less-threatening lover – that "rival" against whom the father fought – and the receptacle for her creative energy.

Writing in her diary on 6 August 1932, Nin offered a prophetic passage about the diary itself, possibly recognizing the role that it would play in absorbing and enacting the texts of Artaud, Mirbeau, and Rimbaud: "I have a poisonous passion for remembering. I love what I remember better than what has not yet been recorded, because what is remembered is charged with intolerable regrets, with the anguish of unfinished gestures, of irretrievable wrongs and blunders ... There is remembrance the most intricate form of torture [*sic*] – Pour souffrire il suffis de se rappeler" (book 35). Words such as "poisonous," "gestures," and "torture" anticipate both the actual experience and the literary depiction of Nin's adult incest. Her diary stands as the greatest testimony that, indeed, "in order to suffer all one has to do is remember." In her study of incest texts, Broe asserts that "the various enclosures are transformed into embodied forms for dis-closure, for remembering and releasing the woman's body." The diary is the enclosure within which Nin's memory and body are released.

THE WRITING WOMAN

If Anaïs Nin was abused by her father, she was, according to her diary, often sexually violated by her husband as well. From the moment that she married Guiler, she determined to play the perfect wife; although in reality she was far from being so, she continued to act this part. She had no physical desire for her husband, but slept with him in order to keep up appearances, to write a sham "romance plot," even as she was busily making love beyond its ending. This dichotomy is registered throughout the diary in tones of traumatic endurance. It is Nin's inflated passion for Miller and others that is set against her growing repulsion towards her husband. She offers a horrific description of Guiler which invokes the rape of Leda by the swan: "I submit to his caresses. My body is so indifferent. But before his desire, then, I am in revolt. I hate his mouth on mine. And the pain, the big, clumsy ravages, always like a violation. My face is twisted with pain [...] Fortunately, he is swift, like a heavy-clawed bird" (I, 165).

Nin's "violation" is problematized by the fact that the main reason she stayed with Guiler was financial. Although she would have many opportunities to leave him for Miller and other men less well off, she stayed with him almost until she died, preferring to take other lovers and even one common-law husband on the side while preserving ties to Guiler.[56] She conceded that she was "a prisoner of material necessity" (I, 332). Guiler must have been aware of her infidelities – Nin implied as much on several occasions[57] – and it is possible that he was also aware of her need of the luxuries that he could offer her, and that he used money to keep her, control her. Nin drew attention to this with statements such as "Hugh punishes me by depriving me of money" (I, 395). Guiler put a price tag on the freedom that he permitted his wife, forcing her to have sex with him: "You have to pay me or I won't let you go out" (*F*, 113). Nin believed that as much as she used Guiler, he used her: "I am an acquisition. I am an instrument to his *rise*. He has selected an artist, and a woman who can charm. He uses me" (*I*, 74).

The connection between power, money, and sex is intensified by Nin's obsession with prostitution, a common trade for adult survivors of childhood incest.[58] The unexpurgated volumes are filled with references to her fascination with and conception of herself as "the Whore" (*F*, 235). At one point, "Hugo almost threw himself on me, and I opened my legs passively, like a prostitute" (*HJ*, 245). With Miller, she leaped "up like a gay little whore" (*I*, 102). It should be noted that perhaps the only time Nin seems capable of sarcasm or irony is when she confronts herself as a woman obsessed with sex. For example, she commented in 1936, "Coming back to the hotel I said to myself, My only exercise in New York consists of fucking" (*F*, 214). And she mocked herself as someone "Spending three-quarters of my life in bed." She went on: "I know only one recipe for happiness: Take the sperm of three different men (as different as possible!), let it mix in your womb. If the transfusion can take place the same day the alchemy will produce perfection" (*F*, 335).

Ever dichotomized, Nin would "always be the virgin-prostitute, the perverse angel, the two-faced sinister and saintly woman" (*HJ*, 2). As Nussbaum has argued, "The self presented in diary lacks an obvious center," and it is this decentring which allowed Nin to strategically claim that she felt "innocent" while writing of her affairs in her diary beside Guiler (*HJ*, 211), while after months of sex with Miller, "I have come to Henry like a virgin" (*HJ*, 217).

The virgin-prostitute persona was connected to Nin's sense of self as mother. On the one hand, she was the Virgin Mary, the divine mother of all (*I*, 86). In her innocence she gave birth to the artist-god, announcing, "if I am not a great artist, I don't care. I will have been good to the artist, the mother and muse and servant and inspiration" (*D*, 1:223). However, the artists whom Nin "inspired," her children, were often the same men she slept with, and thus she was that other Mary, Magdalene. Herman observes how incest survivors "perceived their assignment as substitute mothers as due to their sex and viewed boys as freer to be children."[60] Nin's sense of self as "mother" to her artist-children may have had its origins in her own experience of abuse.

Nin, however, refused the most tangible maternal role, that of mother to a baby. When she discovered that she was pregnant, she immediately contextualized the unborn child within the dichotomies of being a mother versus being an artist, and between serving oneself and serving a man. She was certain that it was Miller's baby and concluded, "I must destroy it." She examined her feelings: "I have experienced the most terrible mixture of emotions – pride to be a mother, a woman, a complete woman, the love of a human creation, the infinite possibilities of motherhood." Recapping the various roles that she had played, she tried to enter into one and thereby stabilize her identity. She was "awed, and all devilry and passion are stilled. No longer the virgin, the sterile artist woman, the mistress, the diabolical half-human woman – the full bloom of woman." But in the final analysis, she wrote of motherhood: "I still regard it as an abdication, as an abnegation, as the supreme immolation of the ego. I am offered this at the time when I am most awake to myself as an artist, as a solitary, unmated woman" (I, 329).

Nin was honest in her admission that she simply did not want to have a child for "selfish" reasons, positioning herself as the woman who wanted a lover and a career only. In this, as with other women of the period, she boldly anticipated the Pro-Choice Movement of the sixties on. Though Nin continued to serve men, she resolved the dichotomy between being a mother and being an artist: "I refuse to continue to be the mother [...] I want to live only for the love of man, and as an artist – as a mistress, as a creator. Not motherhood, immolation, selflessness. Motherhood, that is solitude again, giving, protecting, serving, surrendering. No. No. No" (I, 330).

Nin's emphatic refusal may be understood in terms of the sociological studies by Chodorow and the analysis presented by Friedman. Throughout her life, Nin had positioned herself in relational terms, always ready to serve and nurture others, as when she stated that "woman's universe" was "always revolving around *persons*" (I, 79–80); and that "People mingle within me. There is a flow between them all, an absence of separateness" (D, 1:188). In this way her self contains Chodorow's "flexible or permeable ego boundaries." As Friedman argues, this fluidity proved dangerous because Nin so wholly gave herself over to the flow and consistently risked psychic breakdown.[61] Her triple "No" in the passage cited above is an instance of her trying to dam up the relational flow, establish some boundaries with a degree of autonomy.

Other comments testify to her attempts to assert herself as subject and centre of her art and life; for example, "it is the cursed woman in me who causes the madness, the woman with her lover, her devotion, her shackles. Oh, to be free, to be masculine and purely artist. To care only about the art" (I, 308). There were times when Nin indeed cared "only about the art." She could assert that "my temperament belongs to the writer, not to the woman" (HJ, 12); and in this state she could accept her "horribly monstrous ego," which drove her "to create" (F, 224). Nin's divided selves – the "masculine and purely artist" and the feminine and purely woman – were reconciled when she came to recognize that within her, the two might be fused, rendering her a uniquely female artist. It was here that woman's potential for giving birth was most profoundly tied to artistic creation.

Earlier, when contemplating how to craft a story about June Miller, Nin had realized that she must "write as a woman, and as a woman only" (D, 1:128). It was during conversations with Henry Miller and his friend Lawrence Durrell in 1937 that Nin was able to articulate what such writing entailed. Although I am jumping ahead a few years, her more mature perspective bears mentioning here. Nin copied into her diary a letter from Durrell in March 1937, in which he praised her "Birth" story. Nin responded, "Writing as a woman. I am becoming more and more aware of this" (D, 2:183–4). Significantly, the story was taken directly from the diary, proving that it was within this text that she first wrote "as a woman." By August, Durrell and his wife, Nancy, were visiting Paris, and with Miller they enjoyed long literary talks. When Durrell and Miller complained that Nin must become more objective, "make the leap outside of the womb," she refused, realizing it was "at this moment that we each go different ways," and that her way was "the woman's way" (D, 2:232–3). She positioned herself as a Woolfian "outsider."

In explaining what this "woman's way" was, Nin prefigured Chodorow and her notion of permeable ego boundaries, and she dismantled the aesthetic upon which Eliot had built his great Tradition: "woman's creation far from being like man's must be exactly like her creation of children, that is it must come out of her own blood, englobed by her womb, nourished with her own milk" (D, 2:233). (Here we can also see how Nin was once again anticipating l'écriture féminine.) She went further: "The woman was born mother, mistress, wife, sister, she was born to represent union, communion, communication, she was born to give birth to life, and not to insanity. It is man's separateness, his so-called objectivity, which has made him lose contact, and then his reason. Woman was born to be the connecting link between man and his human self. Between abstract ideas and the personal pattern which creates them." Nin thus criticized the male artist who works alone: "I do not delude myself as man does, that I create in proud isolation. I say we are bound, interdependent. Woman is not deluded. She must create without these proud delusions of man" (D, 2:234).

I raised the point earlier that Nin's sense of interdependence was often debilitating. Friedman believes that "Nin's conflation of creativity and the relational feminine self leads her into troubling cycles of giving, breakdown, and recovery, each stage of which feeds into her writing."[62] While I agree with this evaluation, I would also argue that Nin was transforming the traditional and genuine reality of women's lives – interdependence – into an enabling aesthetic agenda. And nowhere is this agenda more clearly realized than in and through the diary. She recorded Durrell as saying: "I have only smelled the diary writing, just read a page here and there. You have done it, the real female writing" (D, 2:254); "The diary cannot stop until the quest is over [...] We are all writing about the Womb, but you *are* the Womb"(D, 2:256). Nin made this connection to the diary explicit when, missing her diary, she yearned, "I wanted nothing else but the diary, to rest upon, as in a womb" (I, 306).

The fact that her diary was gendered female, complete with its own metaphorical womb, goes a long way in explaining why she wrote in it. This concept can further be understood by considering a comment made by Theodore Dreiser to Nin during their meeting in January 1935: "He asked me how I managed to have an individuality and yet retain my femininity and be unobtrusive" (D, 2:12). The question underscores the basic tenet, put forward in various ways by theorists such as Smith, DuPlessis, and Benstock, that women (must) learn to negotiate traditional gender roles with more self-directed and autonomous desires.

Although Nin did not provide an answer as to how she did so, it is possible to offer one here. The diary stands as the site of her artistic self – her "individuality." She was a writer who could still "retain" her "femininity" because, for one thing, the diary itself is "feminine," being the site and product of "interdependence," and secondly, it is, just as a woman should be, "unobtrusive." But Nin was all along planning to publish the diary, and thus both her "silence" and her "cunning" are manifest here.

Moreover, her negotiations can be contextualized within postmodern autobiography, as theorized by Neuman and others, while Dreiser's question helps us to answer the rhetorical query posed by Benstock – "we have yet to discover whether the 'Modernist Mime' constituted an enforcement of the patriarchal poetic law or a skillful subversion of it."[63] Nin was doing both, for she embraced what was expected of her as a woman within a patriarchy, and she used her position on the margins to slide "unobtrusively" into the centre of a very modernist life, and life work.

THE NOVEL OF THE FUTURE

Having thus far considered the diary as a site of Nin's modernism and as a place where she constructed identity, I would now like to reveal, with a broader sweep, how this work was publicly realized as such, and how this process affected and was affected by Nin's later sense of self.

On 24 October 1931 she announced: "I have begun to copy my Journal from the very beginning, that is, from 11 years old on." Two days later she acknowledged: "A strange life I'm leading, because copying out the first part of my Journal I seem to be spinning the whole web out from the beginning while at the same time working on the end" (book 32). By April 1932 she had hired "Marguerite S.," who was "helping me to copy the diary" (D, 1:74). The diary started to assume an especially valuable status, for Nin began to store the originals in a bank vault.

From this point on, there are countless references to her making transcripts, a practice she would continue for the rest of her life, so that new, "present" diaries were always being written while older ones were being transcribed. This pattern underscores how the diary was conceived in terms of a manuscript, one that Nin had many opportunities to revise and edit. This practice enabled her to carefully shape and control the versions of herself that she put forward. In *The Novel of the Future*, her treatise on the process of creation, she noted that her "fictionalizing" of the people whom she wrote about in her diary had "two motives: one, protection of the personalities; the other symbolization, the creation of the myth."[64] She ended this book with a quotation from Daniel Stern's 1968 review of the published *Diary*: "We learn too ... that an obsession with recording reality need not be at odds with the creation of other worlds. That we need give up neither reality nor fantasy in our lives nor in our art."[65] Nin took these words as her modus operandi, once again claiming kinship with postmodern autobiographers whose strategy is the negotiating of history and art. Within the diary she grounded her life in real social, political, and cultural terms while she built an edifice of art on which she transformed and transcended these realities.

Through Miller, Nin had met William Bradley, a literary agent. In April 1933 she showed him her childhood journal, and he said, "it is remarkable" (I, 138). This comment marks the first professional interest in the diary, in that Bradley was in a position to make contacts for her. He did so by giving the diary to Alfred Knopf. Knopf would not publish it, though, and over time Bradley was replaced by an agent who showed more determination to market the diary. In August 1936 Nin met Denise Clairouin, who wanted "all the diaries to be published" (D, 2:107). But within a year, Clairouin's opinion took a dramatic turn, and Nin was forced to write: "Denise Clairouin said: 'The diary will never be published. People can't bear such nakedness. You are so much in life. Never write for intellectuals. The childbirth story will immediately be censored'" (D, 2:167).

In 1935 Nin had realized, "Diary my chief work" (F, 49); "I am gifted for the diary and nothing else" (F, 99). In January 1937 she reiterated, "The diary is my form" (F, 374). That fall Miller published an essay on Nin's diaries, entitled "Un Être Étoilique," which not only celebrated the diary as a major artistic achievement but drew attention to it, bringing it to public awareness for the first time. Miller continued his crusade, "collecting subscriptions to publish the first volume of the diary" (D, 1:270). Meanwhile, Clairouin returned with optimism, informing Nin: "I gave the diaries to Maxwell Perkins, of Scribner [...] He was thunderstruck [...] He wants you to make an abridged copy" (D, 2:268). Despite these efforts, Scribner rejected Nin's edited version, and the Miller subscription scheme failed.[66]

These events were documented in volume 2 of the *Diary*, and it is within this volume that Nin discussed how the journal had changed: "The diary was once a disease. I do not take it up for the same reason now. Before it was because I was lonely, or because I did not know how to communicate with others [...] Now it is to write not for solace but for the pleasure of describing others, out of abundance" (D, 2:205). Although she had all along conceived the diary as a book to be published, it was at the point when the diary became about others that she actively began to market it for them. Nin could manipulate her concept of an interdependent feminist aesthetic into one which would justify the publishing of the diary.

In September 1939, forced out of France by war, she and her husband returned to New York, where she resumed her quest to find a publisher. Having met Dorothy Norman, the publisher of the magazine *Twice a Year*, Nin was able to report in April 1941 that "Dorothy Norman will publish sections of the childhood diary" (D, 3:118). These appeared in the October 1941 issue, "seven pages out of the manuscript of the first diary volume, translated by me [Nin] from the French." The only response that she recorded in her diary was a negative one: "Veronica Jennings, of the *Saturday Review of Literature*, says my diary has 'no universal quality'" (D, 3:156), a judgment which reinforces how the personal was devalued in the marketplace.

It needs to be stressed that although Nin seems preoccupied with publishing the diaries, she was equally, if not more, eager to see her fiction in print. Because it was so frequently rejected by commercial publishers, she decided to take matters into her own hand. Demonstrating courage and confidence, during the years between 1935 and 1941 Nin bought a total of three printing presses in order to bring out her work herself.

The novellas she printed on her first two presses in Paris were unsuccessful; once back in New York, she bought her third press. But it was not until January 1944, when she printed her collection of stories *Under a Glass Bell*, that she received the critical praise she was convinced she had deserved all along. It was Edmund Wilson's favourable review for the *New Yorker* that brought Nin her first mainstream recognition, allowing her to feel, for the first time, "visible and tangible" (*D*, 3:312). She and her introspective prose were shifting from the margins to the centre. Then in September 1945 she printed her new novel, *This Hunger*. Once again receiving critical acclaim from Wilson, Nin finally received full attention from the commercial publishing world, and in December she signed a contract with E.P. Dutton for all her novels.

These events are important in terms not only of her development as a writer, but also of the diary's development as a public text. The fact that Nin, with the means to publish anything she wanted, chose to print her fiction rather than portions of the diary needs to be considered. In a letter of May 1944, written from Big Sur, Miller reveals why she may not have printed the diary: "[Bern] Porter writes me that you have abandoned all thought of bringing out the Diary here in America. Because your lawyer advises that it will get you into trouble. But – if you began at the beginning, as I always hoped you would, if you bring out the first volumes (in French), nothing could happen to you." He promised to send her "each month one hundred dollars, for the printing of the first few volumes of the Diary in French."[67] Nin had been convinced by Miller's enthusiasm, for she prepared to publish the diary. It must be stressed that this was after she had achieved recognition from Wilson for her short stories. Typically, though, Miller's generosity turned in on itself when he needed his money back, and Nin was forced to put her project on hold.

Though publication had been delayed, the diary continued to gain a public reputation. From late 1946 to early 1947 Nin travelled around the United States on a lecture tour, often reading selections from her diary in addition to her stories. Through speeches delivered at each reading, she promoted the diary, as evidenced by her notes for the tour which she copied into her diary. For instance, she told her listeners: "The theme of the diary is always the personal, but it does not mean only a personal story: it means a personal relation to all things and people. The personal, if it is deep enough, becomes universal, mythical, symbolic" (*D*, 4:153). With this statement, she was preparing her audience to be the future readers of the diary. It was to become her "novel of the future," a text in which life and art are perhaps unprecedentedly fused. Nin promised that it had, contrary to Veronica Jennings's earlier assessment, "universal quality" – but a quality which speaks to and validates female experience, for like women, the diary has "relation to all things and people." This quality increases the degree to which the diary has become for and about "others."

Nin's rising anger and frustration at being ignored by the American writing scene contributed to the diary's being directed towards others, for in a desperate desire to be noticed, she turned more and more to her diary as her life work. In the winter of 1952–53 she copied a letter into the diary from friend and critic Maxwell Geismar. She had given him some of her journals to read, and he was full of praise: "Yesterday and last night I read the last two sections with increasing admiration [...] This is literature of the first order" (D, 5:101). Following this quotation, she copied a letter from Miller, who in his postscript added, "If only you could bring yourself to publish the diary! Or unmutilated big fragments of it" (D, 5:102). By the fall of 1953 Geismar and his wife, Anne, had been encouraging her to do so: "Talk with Geismars about problems of publishing the diary. Aside from the human problem of those who have to be protected, there is also the problem that the diary is not finished. The condition of its continuation is secrecy [...] The public eye and spotlight will kill it" (D, 5:135).

Given that Nin had spent her lifetime turning over portions of her diary to other people to read, reading it herself in lecture halls, and trying to publish it, this last comment is ironic. And yet she had many opportunities during which she could have published the diary instead of her fiction. In addition to her legal concerns, she was unwilling to compromise, to take criticism constructively, to heed the advice of others. In short, for better or worse, she remained loyal to *her* vision of the diary, as she made clear: "Once in Paris in the late thirties, encouraged by Maxwell Perkins' interest, I prepared according to his suggestion six hundred pages of excerpts from the diary [...] Today I burnt these pages in the fireplace. If the novels are symbolic and composites, the diary at least must be intact" (D, 5:208). With respect to Gertrude Stein's work, Benstock has suggested that "our feminist rereadings of Modernism cannot remain comfortably within the limits of the old logic, within the boundaries of the old definitions, within the conventions of old strategies."[68] Having rejected the patriarchal "logic" of grammar when she dropped out of high school, Nin continued to privilege her own system of editing, and for this reason she too forces us to re-evaluate how we read and rank literature.

She sent a letter to Geismar, reiterating not only that she considered the diary her major work but that she would publish it only when she felt that she and it were ready. Writing out of her experience as a failed commercial writer, she sent her spirit into exile: "America, for me personally, has been oppressive and destructive. But today I am completely free of it [...] I don't need to be published. I only need to continue my personal life [...] and to do my major work, which is the diary. I merely forgot for a few years what I had set out to do." She went on:

"I have settled down to fill out, round out the diary. I am at work now on what I call the volume of superimpositions, which means that while I copy out volume 60, I write about the developments and conclusions which took place twenty years later [...] It can wait for publication" (D, 5:216–7). Exiled to her imagination, then, Nin found refuge in her diary, itself in exile of genre.

The diary would of course be published, as she affirmed in the spring of 1955: "I think what I should do is devote the rest of my time to preparing diaries for publication" (D, 5:237). In the spring of 1961 she offered Alan Swallow, an independent publisher in Denver, the chance to publish all of her novels, including the new manuscript, *Seduction of the Minotaur*. She sweetened the offer thus: "There is one added factor, that I have always said whatever publisher puts out my novels I will give an option on the diaries (for the future)" (D, 6:253–4). Swallow responded positively, and a contract was signed. Having announced in the summer of 1937 that the diary was "for the pleasure of describing others," by the winter of 1962–63, Nin was now making it explicitly for them. In a gesture of giving, she "decided to retire as the major character of this diary. From now on the diary will be called *Journal des Autres* (Diary of Others)" (D, 6:319); it had become, in name and in spirit, the quintessential text of female interdependence.

This gesture had everything to do with Nin's desire to communicate, to bridge the gap which she felt existed between herself and the world. In 1941 she had discussed her motivation for beginning the diary: "The bridge. It was my first bridge. To reach my father. To reach Europe" (D, 3:115). She later updated this explanation: "My connection with the world broke twice: the first time when my father left me. The second time when America slammed the door on my writing. What I have been busy reconstructing is my bridge to the world" (D, 6:121). Through the publication of the diary, she would build a bridge from the banks of her private exile to the shores of her public success.

This bridge required careful labour. In a letter to her correspondent Roger Bloom, she explained: "I have been working at copying and editing the diaries [...] But for human reasons (hurting others) I cannot publish it yet. This is a secret which is becoming harder and harder to keep as it is my major work" (D, 6:224). But by the spring of 1962 she had figured out a way of editing so as to "avoid hurting or damaging people"; she confessed: "It was a complex problem of ethics and humanism" (D, 6:298). Now satisfied with her methods, she collected her building materials and began to show the diary to Swallow and to Gunther Stuhlmann, her agent since the mid-fifties. Though they both responded with encouragement, Swallow unfortunately realized that the job was too big for him. Once again Nin was left without a publisher (D, 6:363-4).

She had a hard time marketing the diaries. It was rejected by Random House, Putnam, and William Morrow. Swallow finally convinced Hiram Haydn of Harcourt Brace to take on the task, and after much preparation, Nin was able to exclaim in her diary in the summer of 1966, "Volume 1 of the Diary is published!" (D, 6:396). She received extremely good reviews, but the one that impressed her the most was the article by Robert Kirsch in the *Los Angeles Times*. He called the diary "one of the most remarkable in the history of letters," and he considered it "a literary accomplishment" (D, 6:397–8). Nin basked in his apparent understanding, claiming, "I will no longer be vulnerable to the old cliché that I am only interested in the personal" (D, 6:399). Her dream of being recognized as a literary diarist had finally come true.

Fame affected both Nin and the diary. These changes are registered in volume 7 of the *Diary*, which not only records the successful results of the publication of volume 1 in 1966, but traces Nin's preparation and publication of all subsequent volumes through to volume 6. In the fall of 1966 she documented her metamorphosis: "I am like a new woman, born with the publication of the Diary" (D, 7:35). This "new woman" was the antithesis of her earlier self, as Nin would comment in 1973: "Ever since this communion with the world has happened I no longer suffer from loneliness" (D, 7:284). The desire to bridge the gap between herself and the world was fully realized. She noted of her readers, "I had to accept that my Diary was theirs" (D, 7:214), and of her diary, "I gave it away to the world. It was open and shared" (D, 7:219).

Specifically, the diary is shared through dialogue. In 1972 she told how "Bebe Herring gave me the word *furrawn*, which she had discovered in Joyce [...] The Welsh word meant 'talk that leads to intimacy.' It had inspired all my lectures this year" (D, 7:213). Nin had told Herring in 1970 that "Furrawn" "is the overall title of the Diaries" (D, 7:154). She confirmed, "The Diary has become a correspondence with the world" (D, 7:228). Its form necessarily changed: the diary moved from being a book about Nin and then a book about others to a book actually composed by others. That is, it collapsed into a scrapbook, a fact that Nin recognized: "Whenever I was asked if I still wrote in the Diary, I answered automatically, 'Of course.' But one day I realized this was not true. I was binding 1970 together and found many letters, photographs, testimonies, programs, clippings, but no Diary" (D, 7:168).

This new diary continued to encode a modernist agenda. Its plurality of voices represents the breakdown in the subject's authority, seen in such masterpieces as *Ulysses*, *The Waves*, and *As I Lay Dying*. In a different sense, if we think of Roland Barthes, the diary may be an example of the writerly, postmodern text. In *S/Z* Barthes distinguishes between the "readerly" text, which is a product, and the "writerly" text, which is a production. The writerly text transforms the reader from a passive consumer of a text to a producer of one. He states, "The writerly text is a perpetual present ... [it] is *ourselves* writing."[69] In its status as a scrapbook-dialogue, Nin's diary literally invites the reader to participate in its production. Further, the diary, like the writerly text, is never ultimately completed; it is naturally open-ended. As Nin asserted, "The Diary is true to becoming and to continuum" (D, 7:109); "the Diary will never be finished" (D, 7:145). She has pre-served a kind of "perpetual present" associated with Barthes, for as they stand, the *Diary* volumes are incomplete. It will be for future read-ers, and generations, to continue the "writing" as further portions of unexpurgated materials are released – just as further versions of Nin's textual selfhood will be released, decentred by the multiplicity of vol-umes, always in a state of "becoming." But her self is not only con-signed to a postmodern fragmentation, for Nin enforced closure by summing up individual entries and volumes, and by publishing the diary in bound, "finished" volumes, a process that allows us to see the self as even momentarily fixed and unified.

Nin asked herself in 1972, "Anaïs, what have you become? Where are you?" In answer to "where?" she is within history and within her diary. In answer to "what?" she was a real woman and she remains a textual construction. She cunningly told her diary: "There was once a woman who had one hundred faces. She showed one face to each per-son, and so it took one hundred men to write her biography" (ED, 4:419). Nin left a hoard of fragments to shore against her ruins, but she was determined that her biographers would not easily be able to set her self in order.

Conclusion

One of the most rewarding aspects of this study for me, personally, was the opportunity to travel to different locations in order to examine the original diary manuscripts of Virginia Woolf, Antonia White, Elizabeth Smart, and Anaïs Nin. It was a particular pleasure to meet Rupert Pole, Nin's common-law husband for the last thirty years of her life. As well, I appreciated the fact that White's daughter and son-in-law, Susan and Thomas Chitty, invited me to their Sussex cottage so that I could examine the original diaries. The effect of these two experiences and the excitement of seeing Smart's and Woolf's manuscripts have been that the four writers are more real to me; they are no longer only textual constructs. My fascination with them as people was increased by research which brought to light the fact that not only did they share many friends, lovers, and acquaintances, but they admired and knew of each other. Thus, before making any final comments about the diaries themselves, I would like to consider briefly these biographical connections, for they reveal the possibility that Woolf, White, Smart, and Nin may have influenced, albeit indirectly, each other's diaristic work. Significantly, these connections are often registered within their diaries.

Though Woolf never met Smart or Nin, Smart was certainly inspired by Woolf. In 1933 she read *The Waves* and *To the Lighthouse* and was so impressed that she wished she had written them. In London in 1936 she yearned to be part of an artistic circle, one that included Woolf: "O that I knew as my comfortable friends Yeats, MacNeice, Roger Fry, Virginia Woolf, A. Huxley, Spender, Auden, McLeish, G.B. Shaw, etc!"

(NS, 165). Woolf had a particular impact on Smart's diary, since Smart rationalized that in "copying Virginia Woolf," she was benefiting from her instruction: "isn't it permissible to be stimulated by people honourably, to be made more alert and alive and noting things by others?" (NS, 38).

Woolf met White at least once, as she documented in her diary on 3 November 1936: "after tea, we went to the Sunday Times book show ... And Miss White came up, a hard little woman, with a cheery wooden face, & talked about her book & reviews" (D, 5:29). White's diary at this time was sporadic, and there is no corresponding entry or later reference to such a meeting. We do know, however, that she greatly admired Woolf's work. White documented reading Woolf's *Jacob's Room*, and *To the Lighthouse* – "her one real masterpiece" (D, 2:216). Of *The Years*, she noted: "*How* marvellously she writes – or rather *paints*" (D, 2:197). In 1967 she "Read several of Virginia Woolf's essays [...] how brilliant, how witty, how acute V.W. is – and what sharp claws she has too" (D, 2:169). Three years later she referred to Woolf as "The great heroine-writer of my youth." White also connected her depression with Woolf's: "She will always interest me extremely [...] And of course she was mad too – more officially mad, in a way, than I am. I understand very well her intense sense of the thousand things pressing on one's mind simultaneously" (D, 2:216). And in 1978 she read Woolf's diary, in Leonard Woolf's abridged version: "I have been reading – in snatches – V. Woolf's extracts from her diary – It produces a feeling of extreme depression. Enough to discourage me from ever *attempting* to write again" (D, 2:295).

Earlier, in 1961, White had recorded: "I had a curious dream last night. I was being married to Virginia Woolf! I often have this dream of being married to a woman but this was peculiarly realistic. It appeared to be 'love' on her side." She examined the impact of this dream: "I was sad at leaving my little flat, though it was to live in far more elegant surroundings in the beautiful house in Gordon Square, inhabited by other 'Bloomsburies.' I was rather nervous of *them*. They were obviously looking one over critically. However I managed to say spontaneously something they thought 'amusing'" (D, 2:52). White's dream helps to explain why, though contemporaries, she and Woolf were not friends: Woolf was part of the Bloomsbury group, and membership was exclusive. Though White lived close to Woolf, the artists who inhabited her Chelsea neighbourhood did not mix well with the "critical" "Bloomsburies." Woolf acknowledged in a letter to Logan Pearsall Smith what Hermione Lee refers to as "Bloomsbury-Chelsea hostilities": "Why should not Chelsea and Bloomsbury meet and laugh at each other to their faces and quite genuinely enjoy themselves?"[1]

If Woolf remained a spiritual presence for Smart and White, during the 1930s and 1940s Smart, White, and Nin came into physical contact with many of the same people, most notably George Barker, Lawrence Durrell, Henry Miller, and the British surrealist poet David Gascoyne. In 1936 White was introduced to Barker by her friend, the American writer Emily Coleman. Barker, in addition to becoming White's lover, gave her artistic inspiration. Recall her gratitude to him in her diary: "As regards work he gives me more hope and stimulus than anyone I know" (book 5).

Through Barker, White became intimate with Gascoyne. He was a friend of Durrell's, and in October 1937, after reading *The Black Book* (which had so inspired Smart), he had sent his own diary to Durrell so that Durrell could see how closely the fictional diary resembled his own. In this same month, Gascoyne went to see Nin in Paris, and the two exchanged diaries.[2] Shortly after, in January 1938, White visited Gascoyne for a week in Paris. During this trip she was introduced to, among Gascoyne's friends, Durrell, Miller, and Alfred Perlès, the editorial team of *The Booster*.[3] Nin made up the fourth member of this group.

Gascoyne's literary introductions proved professionally important to White, since they facilitated the acceptance of some of her work by *The Booster*, which was renamed *Delta* in April 1938. White would have three poems in this first issue of *Delta*, and her short story "House of Clouds" was published in the second. Further, her contact with Gascoyne would likely have given her an awareness of his diaristic fragment published in the November 1937 issue of *Booster* and of Nin's diary excerpt, which would appear in the 1938 summer issue of *Seven*.

With the outbreak of the World War II, Barker decided to go to Japan. Chitty recalls that in late 1939 he sent White a letter in which he informed her of his plans: "Barker, fearing that 'military conscription' might interrupt his 'communication with Parnassus,' had accepted the chair of English at Sendal University [*sic*], Japan. He closed the letter with a request for a small loan."[4] Barker's "request for a small loan" from White to help him get into Japan was topped by his request to another woman for a large donation to help him get out of Japan less than a year later. The woman to whom he made this financial appeal was the young and aspiring Canadian writer Elizabeth Smart.

Just as Durrell had helped to publish White in *Delta*, so he assisted Smart. In 1938 he published her poem "Comforter, Where, Where is Your Comforting?" in the last issue of *Delta*, and after the magazine folded, the two maintained an intermittent correspondence. In a letter of 15 January 1939 Smart confided to Durrell: "About my favourite younger poet is George Barker. He excites me most, even when immature." She went on to announce: "I liked a woman I discovered in the only copy of Delta I've seen, called Antonia White."[5] The impressionable Smart was finding stimulation in Barker and White at a time when Barker had already been encouraging White. Smart was also likely inspired by Durrell, for at some point at the end of 1939 he sent her some of his work: typed sheets containing six of his poems. One of these poems, "Journal (to David Gascoyne),"[6] has particular relevance given that, while Smart did not yet know Gascoyne, she did keep a diary, and Durrell's poem about Gascoyne's journal would reinforce her sense of the diary's connection to literature.

To a writer in Smart's position – young, inexperienced, full of overblown romantic sensibilities, and yet fully serious about becoming a poet – Durrell must have seemed a key man to know. For in addition to putting her in touch with Barker, he provided her with updates about many of his literary friends, thus making her feel somehow part of a group. For instance, referring to the start of the war, he wrote to tell her, "David Gascoyne is having mystical adventures on the Siegfried line of the soul, Anaïs Nin is miserably blacked out in Paris poor darling, writing and moaning. Me I'm sticking to Greece as long as I possibly can. Miller too he says."[7]

Aware of Durrell's friendship with Nin, Smart must have mentioned her in her letters to Durrell. That she did so is confirmed in one of his responses: "And Anaïs, you know, is the first woman, really the *first*. That is why she is such a lovely monster, and my most adored of friends." And just as he encouraged Smart to contact Barker, so Durrell urged her to look up Nin: "Do find her in NY if you go. Tell you like her books [*sic*], write to her. She will be so happy, because she had had a long neglect."[8] Despite this suggestion, there is no record of a meeting between Smart and Nin. That they had met could be inferred from Smart's review of Nin's first volume of diaries for *Queen* magazine in July 1966. She began the article: "The monumental volumes were carefully locked in safes, but sometimes, if you went to tea with her, she would show you what she had written about you the last time you went to tea with her. This was a shocking, embarrassing, exciting experience."[9] For Smart's claim to have been personal, Nin must have met her at least twice in order to have shown her what she wrote about her on the first occasion. In all of Nin's diaries, however, there is not one word about Smart. Neither does Smart herself mention such a meeting in her diaries.

While there is no proof that Smart actually met Durrell, she did meet Miller, Nin's great love. She had been thinking of him during her stay in Mexico: "I dreamt a long dream of Henry Miller and his friends and of escaping and indoor swimming pools" (NS, 212). In her waking hours Smart wrote to Miller; there is one extant letter from him to her dated 9 February 1940. Here he warms to her: "Hope we can meet. Betty [Ryan] speaks glowingly of you. And Durrell too wanted me to meet you. I think he liked your letters." Having been asked to send her some of his books, he was forced to reply: "None here. Only hope is to write publisher direct, enclosing check ... Sorry I can't help you out. I haven't even a copy of my books for my self."[10] The two did meet eventually, as evidenced by Miller's comment about her in a letter he sent to Durrell in December 1941: "Betty Smart sends her warm greetings – saw her the other day. A blonde Viking type – Canadian."[11]

Just as Smart made contact with Nin's lover Miller, so Nin would later become close to Smart's first lover, Varda. She described in her diary how "One morning what appeared in place of a letter was a big square package, one yard around. I opened it and it was a collage by Jean Varda. He calls it 'Women Reconstructing the World.' Against a background of sand the color of champagne, with its tiny grains of sparkling glass, five women in airy cutouts" (D, 3:312). I stood in front of this collage when I visited Nin's and Rupert Pole's home, marvelling not only at the beauty of the work but at the connection between Varda, Smart, and Nin.

Moreover, Smart's lover Barker also linked up with Nin. By the end of 1940 Smart was pregnant with Barker's child. As we have seen, she went to live in an isolated cabin in British Columbia, hoping that he would join her – he was living in New York. Though he came to visit in May 1941, he stayed only a month before returning to the United States. In September he did try to get back to her, but he was denied entry into Canada.[12] By this time he had become involved with Nin, who had moved to New York after being driven out of Paris because of the war.

Just as Smart had earlier admired the work of White, so we should recall that she was inspired by Nin's writing. She had told her diary: "*Winter of Artifice* by Anaïs Nin [...] ALL ALL ALL. And a WOMAN, a real woman, only by or from a woman, ALL. It fertilizes. It empowers" (NS, 205). She added: "Anaïs Nin exposes me. She sees so clearly, and she dares to speak, she rouses herself to examine, not flops into the moment. She knows, she puts it all gathered and whole and true" (NS, 211).

Smart would have been pleased to receive Barker's personal accounts of Nin in his letters from New York. In November 1941, for instance, he wrote, "I've seen Anaïs Nin but I spent two hours telling her that her prose was largely blank verse when it was good and just bad when it was bad."[13] In another letter written around this time, he humorously updated Smart on his encounters: "Anaïs Nin left her card here but I was out and as I dont approve of her have ignored it. Any woman who can write fifty volumes of journals is too dangerous."[14]

Barker approved of Nin enough to work for her, though. Needing to make money in the wake of having her novels rejected by U.S. publishers, she began writing erotica for a wealthy "collector." When the demand for stories became too great for her alone, she drew some of her friends into her "firm," including Barker. While he was thus engaged, Smart had gone to Washington to work for the British embassy. By March 1943 she had moved to England, and Barker followed her there shortly after. It was through him that she was introduced to the London literary scene of Soho, where she met Gascoyne and White. According to Chitty, some time in the early forties Smart had gone to the BBC, where White was working, to complain to her about the fact that she was a woman alone with four (of Barker's) children.[15] Though the details of the relationship are vague, there is no disputing that the two women established an acquaintanceship. White told her diary in 1964, "Just as I was packing the last parcel, Elizabeth Smart rang out of the blue asking if I'd interview the Archbishop of York for *The Queen* [magazine] on Thursday" (*D*, 2:103).

Though this is the only reference to Smart in White's diary, there are three extant letters from White to her. The first one, dated 28 November 1965, refers to Smart's efforts, described above, to solicit work for White. White wrote: "At the moment I'm in the midst of a rush translation ... of what do you think? ... a Violette Leduc article for American Vogue! I've done 5 or 6 of these this year and they've kept me solvent. All due to *you* ... for it all started with Vogue Feature Editor reading the piece I did for you in *The Queen* about a year ago."[16]

At the beginning of this letter we find further evidence of Smart's trying to assist White. She had offered her positive response to White's writing, and White replied, "I was so touched by your letter and so delighted that you like *The Hound and the Falcon*." Smart had tried to help her with a paperback deal for the book, as White noted: "It is awfully nice of you to have recommended it to Panther Books." She then moved on to more social matters and signed the letter affectionately, "Thank you again and love, Antonia."

On 25 June 1967 White in turn wrote to Smart to congratulate her on the paperback edition of *By Grand Central Station*, which had been published in July the previous year. She established a degree of intimacy with "My dear Elizabeth" and began by thanking her: "How very nice of you to send me the books as you said. I am delighted to have them, especially your own, as I have wanted to read it ever since I first heard of it."

White continued: "I can see, even from the first few pages, that it's the kind of book one will want to read many times, as one does a poem so it is wonderful to *possess* it. I do hope that it is going to have the recognition it deserves now that it's available in paper-back." More socially, White apologized, "Alas, I won't be able to come to your party on July 14th." But she stressed, "I *did* so enjoy seeing you at Longmans' party."[17]

On 12 July she wrote again because she feared that Smart had not received the letter of 25 June. She added some comments about *By Grand Central Station*: "I had only just begun yours then. Now I have read it and found it almost unbearably moving. In fact I haven't quite recovered from the vicarious experience of such passion and such suffering and am still 'living in' your amazing book."[18]

These biographical connections show that Smart, White, and Nin were aware of each other and of Woolf, not only as novelists but as diarists as well. Personally, they shared certain friends and lovers. Professionally, they were writing for the same innovative magazines, developing literary strategies based on similar desires to create new forms in fiction, and most significantly here, applying these forms to their journals. In concluding this work, then, I would like to return to the theses outlined in the first three chapters in order to show how they have been realized in the diaries of Woolf, White, Smart, and Nin.

Robert Fothergill remains one of the most insightful scholars in recognizing the literary potential of the diary. The aim of my analysis has been to illuminate the extent to which the diaries of the four women were clearly written, as he puts it, "out of a conscious respect for the diary as a literary form," and to prove that they are indeed "major achievements," not only in terms of diary writing but in terms of their status as modernist works.[19]

Complementing Fothergill's work is Lawrence Rosenwald's "Prolegomena" in his *Emerson and the Art of the Diary*. Here, as we have seen, he offers a concise and challenging analysis of the diary in general, successfully undermining preconceived ideas about the genre. In particular, he stresses that "the notion that diaries are necessarily private is simply false."[20] If the diarist is conscious of an audience, then she or he will necessarily be concerned with the aesthetic potential of the diary. Denying the assumption that diaries must be "artless," Rosenwald forces us to consider more startling, yet valid possibilities: diarists very often write for some form of audience; they frequently revise entries; and given that they are likely to reread past entries, they are able to shape future ones in a thematic manner. It is with these possibilities in mind that he conceives a continuum of artful construction and offers criteria to help us locate where on the continuum an individual diarist may be found.[21]

It was these criteria that I applied to my examination of the original diary manuscripts. Although my analysis is detailed, I can offer a few general observations here. The diarists exhibit many of the same writing habits and techniques. For example, they all reread their diaries at various intervals, as evidenced by their additions to the margins, footnotes, or scratchings-out in different pens and by the fact that they wrote about rereading portions of a certain volume, or year, within the diary itself. They all considered the diary as a text in itself, for they gave each volume a formal beginning and ending, in terms of acknowledging a new book and signing off or summing up a completed one. And both Smart and Nin, and to a lesser extent Woolf, took great care to produce often elaborate and creative title pages, prefaces, and indexes.

As well, the four women shared a vast knowledge of a tradition of literary diaries. Throughout their lives, and especially at a young age, they were reading the published journals of writers such as Dorothy Wordsworth, Marie Bashkirtseff, Barbellion, Katherine Mansfield, James Agate, and Henri Amiel, to name a few. This awareness of the market potential of diaries would surely have impacted on their impressionable and aspiring literary sensibilities. Further, they had a penchant for showing their diaries to other people, notably family members, friends, and lovers, thus indicating that for them the diary was never a solely private document.

In addition to being well-read in a diaristic sense, these women shared a background in modernist literature. It is important to emphasize that none of them had a full or formal post-secondary education. Smart, White, and Nin went to high school, but Smart was the only one to complete her program – both White and Nin dropped out, White to work as a governess and then copywriter, and Nin to work for her mother at home. Despite this record, all four were determined to educate themselves in their independent ways. Nin engaged a teacher in Paris. Woolf took lessons from private tutors, and she, like Smart, enrolled in extension courses at King's College in the University of London. No matter what level of education they received, they all set up personally designed, extensive reading programs which they conscientiously followed. They studied writers such as Proust, Lawrence, Mansfield, Eliot, Joyce, Gide, Freud, Jung, Breton, and Rimbaud.

Learning as they did from these and other writers, the four women employed and developed modernist strategies not only in the fiction they were writing but in their diaries as well, for they were writing diaries concomitant with their novels. Specifically, they constructed their diaries as modernist texts. Woolf's diary inscribes the aesthetic theories that directed her experimental fiction and essays. White drew on her anxieties, dreams, and neuroses to investigate her psyche in a text modelled on Freud's psychoanalytic genre. Smart's particular achievement is her use of allusion and quotation in the style of, for instance, *The Waste Land*, coupled with her unabashed celebration of erotic passion. Nin, too, expressed love in a highly Lawrentian, self-conscious manner, and she incorporated her interest in psychoanalysis to create a surreal and symbolic text in the spirit of Artaud and Rimbaud.

Perhaps the most explicit proof that these diaries were considered and constructed as works in themselves comes from the revelation that Smart, White, and Nin all sought ways of publishing portions of their diaries at a fairly early stage in their literary lives. Smart began to craft her travel diary into a book modelled on the example of James Agate's published diary series, *Ego*, when she was only twenty-three, with no other literary publications to speak of. White sent a portion of her 1935 diary to publishers in 1937, shortly after her first novel had appeared. Nin began submitting her diary to literary agents in 1933, with only a critical study of D.H. Lawrence to her name, and she had a fragment of her diary published in the summer 1938 issue of *Seven*. These women considered their diaries to be significant works by which they could earn a literary reputation. Their diaries were central, not marginal, to their sense of self as public writers.

While all three tried to publish their diaries early on, the reality is that the diaries did not actually appear until much later. White's diaries were published posthumously, but she had discussed the prospect with her daughter Susan. Smart had sought Alice Van Wart as editor for her diary and approved the proofs, but she died while the work was in production. Nin was sixty-three when her first volume appeared. Because Woolf's life ended as early as it did, it is impossible to know what she would finally have done with her diaries. However, just as the others entrusted their diaries to editors, so Woolf effectively left hers to Leonard to publish. In 1926 she wondered of her journals, "If I died, what would Leo make of them? [...] Well, he should make up a book from them" (*D*, 3:67). And in 1927 "L. taking up a volume the other day said Lord save him if I died first & he had to read through these" (*D*, 3:125). Virginia did die first, and Leonard did "read through" the diaries, producing the single volume *A Writer's Diary* in 1954.

Though the reasons why White, Smart, and Nin would hold off for so long publishing a work that they were eager to see printed in their youth must be complex, it is possible to speculate on what they were. The reasons have to do with the diary's status as a female text, and so this issue must first be addressed before we move on.

My investigation of the diaries has been informed by a plethora of feminist revisionists who explore how and why the diary is a particularly characteristic and necessary female space. Blodgett, Simons, and Gannett each trace a comprehensive history of a women's diaristic tradition, while others such as Nussbaum, Hogan, and Lensink, to name only a few, offer a poetics of the diary as a specifically female and feminine genre. Smith, Spender, Spencer, and DuPlessis examine women's positions throughout history in a patriarchal culture and their attempts at both conforming to and rejecting prescriptive roles. And theorists such as Neuman, Brodzki, and Schenck have been helpful in my discussion of how diarists negotiate concepts of a unified, central selfhood with the post-structuralist breakdown of such a selfhood.

That women struggle with their identity is dramatically supported by the degree to which Woolf, White, Smart, and Nin were always trying to reconcile their various selves. This endeavour is most evident in terms of how they fashioned identities through names. Woolf went by the name of "Mrs Woolf," but she admitted that as an adult she still played the social games expected of "Virginia Stephen." White was "Eirene Botting" and "Antonia White," the father's daughter versus the self-determined novelist. Smart, too, divided herself into "Mrs Barker," the unwed wife, and "Elizabeth Smart," the author. Nin was "Miss Nin," the obedient daughter, "Mlle Linotte," the selfish scribbler, "Mrs Guiler," the legal wife, "Mrs Miller," the adulterous wife, and "Anaïs Nin," the writer.

These women shared many sensibilities and performed similar roles, which indicate how they "grappled" with being rebel-conformists. All four were raised in conservative homes. Woolf and White grew up in Kensington in families governed by overbearing fathers. Smart's Ottawa neighbourhood of Sandy Hill was perhaps a Canadian equivalent of Kensington, and while her father was a benign figure, his world was a "socially respectable" one. Unlike the others, Nin lived a lower-middle-class life until she married Guiler. Though her father was absent, he exerted an epistolary control over her. But as soon as they were able, these women left their childhood homes and set up residences which could accommodate, and which reflected, their independent and artistic desires. Woolf moved to Bloomsbury, White to Chelsea, Smart to London, and Nin to Paris.

One shared element of their upbringing is that they were taught to construct themselves as "feminine." Smart's adage serves for all when she noted that her function was to "pass ashtrays gracefully, be a Blonde" (A, 140). As a result, it is not surprising that White, Smart, and Nin recognized that the fastest, or perhaps only likely, way to enter the literary world was through a man – that is, by being the lover of a writer. These women, however, like Woolf, had literary talents and ambitions of their own. The dichotomy which was then set up and which plagued them for most of their lives was the importance of love over work, self-sacrifice over self-expression, passivity over activity. This dichotomy is manifested in the women's remarkably similar conceptions of the diary as being at once a site of pleasure and selfishness, duty and discipline, and a life-sustaining comfort.

Struggling with polar roles and divided selves, these women turned to the diary as a place in which they could cast themselves as protagonists in a narrative of their own making, one which could both reflect and challenge their culturally prescribed life stories. On the one hand, they charted their lives through traditional narratives of daughterhood, marriage, and motherhood, with accompanying qualities such as obedience, passivity, and femininity. On the other, they subverted these narrative expectations and, in the spirit of DuPlessis, "rewrote the ending" by offering subject matter which had generally been considered radical or taboo.

It is necessary to comment further on the fact that all four diarists had lesbian experiences, and three of the four were probably victims of childhood sexual abuse. Woolf's, White's, Smart's, and Nin's documentation of their sexuality may be considered in light of the fact that, given that they happened to have lesbian tendencies, they were courageous enough to register their challenges to heterosexual imperatives. Similarly, within the scope of this study, it would be irresponsible to consider the issue of incest in any light beyond its representation within the diaries. Woolf likely used her journal to encode abuse, while at the other end of the spectrum is Nin, who used hers to exploit it, graphically depicting with passion and repulsion her seemingly consensual experiences of incest. White is somewhere in the middle. She turned to her diary to confront the possibility of incest, registering the impact and implications of such a reality. But whatever the differences in representation, the diaries were coping spaces – places in which they could at least attempt to come to terms with their past: Woolf to repress it, Nin to seek revenge, and White to probe uncertainties.

To return, then, to the question of why White, Smart, and Nin gave up trying to publish their diaries early on and why Woolf never tried, the answer could be that they felt the marketplace was not ready to receive their material. What Denise Clairouin said of Nin's rejected diary in 1937 may apply to the others' as well: "The diary will never be published. People can't bear such nakedness. You are so much in life [...] The childbirth story will immediately be censored" (D, 2:167). Appealing to a marketplace at the height of the New Criticism, which advocated impersonality on the part of the author, these diarists were almost bound to be spurned. By the nineteen sixties, though, the stronghold of New Criticism had weakened, and its decline, coupled with the rise of new feminist movements, paved the way for a greater receptivity to (female) autobiographical writing. These developments would have increased the market potential of the diaries later on in the writers' careers.

Beyond the market, Woolf draws attention to the fact that a diarist might not want her "real" or raw stories exposed during her lifetime. She began her review of Evelyn's diary on this note: "There can be no doubt that the good diarists are those who write either for themselves or for a posterity so distant that it can safely hear every secret and justly weigh every motive. For such an audience there is no need either of affectation or of restraint. But a diary written to be published in the author's lifetime is no better than a private version of the newspaper, and often worse. The good opinion of our contemporaries means so much to us that it is well worthwhile to tell them lies."[22]

In a different sense, the four writers may have felt the need to keep up a pretence that their diaries were private, not public documents. That they did keep it up is supported by Nin, who recognized in 1925: "In short, I am afraid. I have no faith in myself. Which does not mean that I will stop writing, but which means that I can never look at writing as a profession, as a 'public' work. I think I am doomed to loving and practicing it in secret" (D, 3:159). This was precisely White's sentiment, expressed in 1965: "I can only write if I think it is not going to be published" (D, 2:131). Her controlling fear, one reinforced by the marketplace, was that her "real" writing would be seen and judged, and she herself, the subject of the text, condemned. Smart, too, was afraid "to speak out, to dare to be myself" (NS, 185).

It may also be that these women deliberately delayed publishing their diaries because they were already sabotaging distinctions between their diaries and their lives. That is, they were living their diaries as much as writing them, and what they wrote informed who they were and how they behaved. For instance, it was seen how Smart constructed herself as Dido in words and then, carried away by this literary persona, actually became Dido abandoned in Pender Harbour. Distinctions between the diary and the novel were also blurred to some extent in that Woolf, White, Smart, and Nin all wrote fiction that not only was autobiographical but had come, in the case of Smart and Nin, directly from their journals.

As the women grew older, their diaries became more concerned with looking back on the past, reflecting on the lives lived and on death. It was at this stage that the desire to communicate what had not been said in their fiction, and what had not been admitted in their lives, became paramount for all of them. Woolf began her memoirs, and White and Smart started autobiographies in old age. White and Smart suffered from severe writer's block, and both left their autobiographies unfinished, as did Woolf. But all along they had been documenting their struggles to live, write, and come to terms with themselves within their diaries.

Eventually, the four authors recognized how their diaries were the public texts they had been trying to deliver. Nin, for her part, came to this awareness earlier and perhaps more consciously, conceding that her diary was no longer hers alone. As she said of the readers of her first volume, "I had to accept that my Diary was theirs" (D, 7:214), and of her diary, "I gave it away to the world. It was open and shared" (7:219). The diary was given away because it was a means of communication and self-affirmation. Three months before her death, Woolf walked "over the marsh saying, I am I" (D, 5:347). Smart echoed her in her own diary: "Somebody's got to say I am I" (A, 171). And White stressed, "you want to tell someone something" (D, 1:168).

The diary proved an ideal space not only for telling things, but for shoring up selves. Woolf turned to her journal to "achieve a symmetry by means of infinite discords" and to "achieve in the end, some kind of whole made of shivering fragments." White similarly achieved, as Drabble phrased it, a "final effect" which is, "oddly, not of fragmentation, but of a powerful urge towards synthesis." Smart refused to remain "simpering on the sidelines, bashfully self-effacive," and like Nin, who at times suffered "from a lack of wholeness," Smart used her journal to ensure that she would assume centre position, the fragments of selfhood collected into the unified pattern of her text.

The diary was also a place in which to experiment with ways of telling and shoring. Here it is helpful to recall Marlene Kadar's assertion "Like water, the shape of genres does not really exist, and their essence can never really be captured." While I have celebrated Woolf, White, Smart, and Nin as extraordinary diarists, I have also shown how they spent their creative lives blurring the boundaries of genre, writing their fiction as autobiography, their diary as autobiography, and their diary as fiction. According to Kadar, the result of such "disregard for genre and its rules" is the creating of new genres.[23]

Woolf once noted, "I have an idea that I will invent a new name for my books to supplant 'novel.' A new ——— by Virginia Woolf. But what?" (D, 3:34). White similarly remarked, "There can never be 'THE NOVEL' because there is no such thing as a novel" (book 10). In a letter to her publisher, Jay Landesman, Smart emphasized that her books "are not novels or novellas. They are short but that is their right length, the length they have to be, and I don't see why they *have* to be put into the old categories."[24] She further registered her frustration with the traditional categories of form: "But what form? Infinite pains for a poem. But I need a new form even for a poem. I have used up my ones" (NS, 202). This sentiment is reiterated by Nin: "I have a feverish desire to invent a form for myself" (ED, 3:143).

Smart's question – "But what form?" – posed by the four diarists here, is answered by Woolf. In April 1933 she described in detail her intentions for "Here and Now," the work-in-progress that would become *The Years*: "It should include satire, comedy, poetry, narrative, & what form is to hold them all together? Should I bring in a play, letters, poems? I think I begin to grasp the whole. And its [*sic*] to end with the press of daily normal life continuing. And there are to be millions of ideas but no preaching – history, politics, feminism, art, literature – in short a summing up of all I know, feel, laugh at, despise, like, admire hate & so on" (D, 4:152). She later remarked, "The lesson of Here & Now is that one can use all kinds of 'forms' in one book" (D, 4:238).

In these passages, Woolf could just as easily have been describing the diary, a text that is made up of "all kinds of 'forms.'" Each entry necessarily ends and begins again "with the press of daily normal life continuing," while the text as a whole offers "a summing up of all" that a diarist "knew, felt, laughed at, despised, liked, admired, hated and so on." Woolf, White, Smart, and Nin have produced through their living, and through their persistent documentation of this living, texts which at once are recognizable as diaries and yet refuse to be pinned down as such, texts whose innovative forms frustrate the distinction between genres and between art and life.

Notes

INTRODUCTION

1 Nussbaum, "Toward Conceptualizing Diary," 128.
2 Lensink, "Expanding the Boundaries of Criticism," 40.
3 Ponsonby, *English Diaries*, 1.
4 Rosenwald, *Emerson*, 22.
5 Fothergill, *Private Chronicles*, 40.
6 Ibid., 38–40.
7 Bloom, "I Write," 24–5.
8 Neuman, "Autobiography: From Different Poetics," 214.
9 Blodgett, *Centuries of Female Days*, 5.
10 Ibid., 2.
11 Benstock, *Women of the Left Bank*, 245.
12 Scott, *Refiguring Modernism*, 1: 250.
13 Ibid., 256.
14 Bunkers, "What Do Women *Really* Mean?" 217.
15 Scott, *Refiguring Modernism*, 1: 257.
16 Lensink, "Expanding the Boundaries of Criticism," 52.
17 Kadar, "Coming to Terms," 10.
18 Kadar, "Whose Life Is It Anyway?" 152.
19 Ibid., 153.
20 Hanscombe and Smyers, *Writing for Their Lives*, 11.
21 Scott, *Gender of Modernism*, 4.
22 Bair, *Anaïs Nin*, xviii.
23 Mudge, "Exiled as Exiler," 215–16.

24 Schenck, "All of a Piece," 282.
25 Mudge, "Exiled as Exiler," 216–17.
26 Quoted in Schenck, "All of a Piece," 285.
27 There are a few entries missing from volume 1 of Anne Olivier Bell's series which were subsequently published in *The Charleston Magazine* 9 (1994): 27–35.
28 Bair, *Anaïs Nin*, xvii.
29 Ibid., xvi.
30 Ibid., 518.

CHAPTER ONE

1 Hart, "Notes for an Anatomy," 485.
2 Ponsonby, *English Diaries*, 5.
3 Mallon, *A Book of One's Own*, 1.
4 Nussbaum, "Toward Conceptualizing Diary," 130.
5 Simons, *Diaries and Journals*, 7.
6 "Journal," in *Oxford English Dictionary*, 1989 ed.
7 "Diary," ibid.
8 Smith, *A Poetics of Women's Autobiography*, 20–6.
9 Gannett, *Gender and the Journal*, 105.
10 Smith, *A Poetics of Women's Autobiography*, 26.
11 Both Blodgett and Gannett acknowledge their debt to Fothergill, such that their overviews of the diaristic tradition are based on his work.
12 Fothergill, *Private Chronicles*, 14.
13 Dobbs, *Dear Diary*, 18.
14 "Biography," in *Oxford English Dictionary*, 1989 ed.
15 "Autobiography," ibid.
16 Defoe, *Robinson Crusoe*, 1.
17 Defoe, *Moll Flanders*.
18 Quoted in Gannett, *Gender and the Journal*, 113.
19 Gannett, *Gender and the Journal*, 113.
20 Simons, *Diaries and Journals*, 10.
21 Fothergill, *Private Chronicles*, 15.
22 Bacon, "Of Travel," 113.
23 Blodgett, *Centuries of Female Days*, 34.
24 Fothergill, *Private Chronicles*, 15.
25 Ibid., 16.
26 Ibid., 17-18.
27 Ibid., 15-17.
28 Rosenwald, *Emerson*, 10.
29 Spalding, *Self-Harvest*, 36.
30 Fothergill, *Private Chronicles*, 19.

31 Blodgett, *Centuries of Female Days*, 22–23.

32 Blodgett, Ibid., 23–26.

33 Fothergill, *Private Chronicles*, 22.

34 Quoted in Gannett, *Gender and the Journal*, 112.

35 Pepys's diary was not initially published in full. The first published text to which I refer here, the 1825 edition, was only a selection. An expanded version came out in 1875–9, followed by the more complete ten-volume edition of 1893–99. R. Latham and W. Matthews's unbowdlerized transcription appeared in 1970–83.

36 Dobbs, *Dear Diary*, 224. This personal diary was a pocket diary, and in its earliest manifestation, in addition to including Christian holidays, it was a small book that had spaces for day-to-day recording of transactions, activities, and the like. It has retained this quality in its modern form, but has been developed to include metrification information, world populations, and time variations from Greenwich Mean Time (ibid., 222–223).

37 Bowle, *The Diary of John Evelyn*, vii.

38 "Memoir," in *Oxford English Dictionary*, 1989 ed.

39 "Evelyn, John," in *The Oxford Companion to English Literature*, 1985 ed.

40 Bowle, *The Diary of John Evelyn*, vii–viii.

41 Mallon, *A Book of One's Own*, 1–2.

42 Matthews, "Introduction,", cii–ciii.

43 Ponsonby, *English Diaries*, 82.

44 O'Brien, *English Diaries and Journals*, 16.

45 Aitken, *English Diaries*, vii.

46 Spalding, *Self-Harvest*, 33.

47 Dobbs, *Dear Diary*, 6.

48 Marchand, "In My Hot Youth," 25.

49 Simons, *Diaries and Journals*, 19–32.

50 Rosenwald, *Emerson*, 22.

51 Fothergill, *Private Chronicles*, 32.

52 Rosenwald, *Emerson*, 11.

53 Blodgett, *Centuries of Female Days*, 34.

54 Blind, "Introduction," vii.

55 Bashkirtseva, *Journal*, xxix.

56 Rosenwald, *Emerson*, 7, 11.

57 Fothergill, *Private Chronicles*, 35.

58 Spalding, *Self-Harvest*, 69, 21.

59 Franklin, "The Diaries of Forgotten Women," 473.

60 Kagle and Gramegna, "Rewriting Her Life," 38.

61 Blodgett, *Centuries of Female Days*, 24, 38.

62 Huff, *British Women's Diaries*, xviii.

63 Gannett, *Gender and the Journal*, 133.
64 Bunkers, "Diaries and Dysfunctional Families," 221.
65 Rosenwald, *Emerson*, 10.
66 Rosenwald, Ibid., 10–12.
67 Mallon, *A Book of One's Own*, xvi–xvii.
68 Godwin, "A Diarist on Diarists," 14.
69 Gristwood, *Recording Angels*, 5–7.
70 Lifshin, *Ariadne's Thread*, 15–16.
71 Wilde, *The Portable Oscar Wilde*, 473.
72 Smith, *A Poetics of Women's Autobiography*, 19.
73 Spacks, "Selves in Hiding," 112.
74 Jelinek, *The Tradition of Women's Autobiography*, xii.
75 Rosenwald, *Emerson* 5–6.
76 Gusdorf, "Conditions and Limits," 35.
77 Pascal, *Design and Truth*, 2-9.
78 Lejeune,"The Autobiographical Contract," 193–202.
79 Ibid.
80 Ibid., 202.
81 Ibid.
82 Ibid., 219.
83 Bruss, *Autobiographical Acts*, 10.
84 Bloom and Holder, "Anaïs Nin's Diary in Context," 192.
85 Hart, "Notes for an Anatomy," 511.
86 Ibid., 497.
87 Ibid., 501.
88 Eakin, *Fictions in Autobiography*, 3.
89 Ibid., 11.
90 Helen Buss, in *Mapping Our Selves*, explores the serial autobiographies of Canadian women such as Fredelle Bruser Maynard and Emily Carr.
91 Blodgett, *"Capacious Hold-All"*, 10.
92 Mandel, "Full of Life Now," 65- 7.
93 Gusdorf, "Conditions and Limits," 42.
94 Mandel, "Full of Life Now," 63.
95 Olney, "Some Versions of Memory," 237–8.
96 Mazlish, "Autobiography & Psycho-analysis," 32.
97 Olney, *Metaphors of Self*, 35.
98 Olney, "Some Versions of Memory," 240.
99 Fothergill, *Private Chronicles*, 44.
100 Bell, *Editing Virginia Woolf's Diary*, 7.
101 Gusdorf, "Conditions and Limits," 47.
102 Barthes, *Roland Barthes*, 188.
103 Stanton, *The Female Autograph*, 10.
104 Rosenwald, *Emerson*, 12.

105 Ibid., 24–5.
106 Fothergill, *Private Chronicles*, 41.
107 Hampsten, *Read This Only to Yourself*, 95.
108 Buss, *Mapping Our Selves*, 39.
109 Huff, *British Women's Diaries*, xviii–xix.
110 Bunkers, "What Do Women *Really* Mean?" 214.
111 Lensink, "Expanding the Boundaries," 46–50.
112 Spacks, *Imagining a Self*, 300–12.
113 Eakin, *Fictions in Autobiography*, 3–7.
114 Hart, "Notes for an Anatomy," 486.
115 Benstock, "Authorizing the Autobiographical," 11.
116 Gusdorf, "Conditions and Limits," 43–5.
117 Adams, *Telling Lies*, 12.
118 Jelinek, *The Tradition of Women's Autobiography*, xiii.
119 Bloom and Holder, "Anaïs Nin's Diary in Context," 194, 197.
120 Stanton, *The Female Autograph*, 13.
121 Jay, *Being in the Text*, 27.
122 Nietzsche, *Will to Power*, 267; quoted ibid., 28.
123 De Man, "Autobiography as De-facement," 920.
124 Eakin, "Narrative," 34, 37.
125 Ibid., 35.
126 Ibid., 37–8.
127 Eakin, *Fictions in Autobiography*, 192.
128 Rosenwald, *Emerson*, 16–20.
129 Fothergill, *Private Chronicles*, 55–6.

CHAPTER TWO

1 Rich, On Lies, 217, 215.
2 Blodgett, *Centuries of female Days*, 26–7.
3 Ibid., 30.
4 Fothergill, *Private Chronicles*, 19.
5 Pomerleau, "The Emergence of Women's Autobiography in England," 28.
6 Nussbaum, "Toward Conceptualizing Diary," 134.
7 Stanton, *The Female Autograph*, 6.
8 Gannett, *Gender and the Journal*, 116, 100–1.
9 Mallon, *A Book of One's Own*, 19.
10 Gannett, *Gender and the Journal*, 123–4.
11 Franklin, *Private Pages*, xiv.
12 Hampsten, *Read This Only to Yourself*, xi.
13 Woolf, *A Room*, 46–7.
14 Pepys, *The Illustrated Pepys*, 47.

15 Simons, "Invented Lives," 253.
16 Gannett, *Gender and the Journal*, 123.
17 Mallon, *A Book of One's Own*, 279.
18 Simons, "Invented Lives," 253.
19 Gannett, *Gender and the Journal*, 122.
20 Bell, *Editing Virginia Woolf's Diary*, 7.
21 Simons, *Diaries and Journals*, 150.
22 Ponsonby, *English Diaries*, 29–30.
23 Ponsonby, *More English Diaries*, 26–7.
24 Spalding, *Self-Harvest*, 69-70.
25 Dobbs, *Dear Diary*, 178.
26 See, for instance, Frank Kermode's history of the canon in "Institutional Control of Interpretation."
27 Culley, *A Day at a Time*, 3–4. The term "female" should be understood to mean biologically determined, and the term "feminine" to refer to social, historical, and cultural conditioning.
28 Blodgett, *Centuries of Female Days*, 24, 35, 37–8.
29 Culley, *A Day at a Time*, 3.
30 Ibid., 4.
31 White, *The Sugar House*, 256.
32 Smith, *A Poetics of Women's Autobiography*, 41-3.
33 Gannett, *Gender and the Journal*, 136.
34 Blodgett, *Centuries of Female Days*, 5.
35 Spender, *Mothers of the Novel*, 115–37, 162.
36 Spencer, *The Rise of the Woman Novelist*, viii.
37 Spender, *Mothers of the Novel*, 4.
38 Schenck, "All of a Piece," 285.
39 Woolf, *A Room*, 74.
40 Woolf, "Professions for Women," 284.
41 Ibid., 285.
42 Woolf, *A Room*, 74.
43 Schenck, "All of a Piece," 294; Rich, *On Lies*, 44.
44 Spencer, *The Rise of the Woman Novelist*, 13–20.
45 Spender, *Mothers of the Novel*, 161-2.
46 Gannett, *Gender and the Journal*, 107, 149.
47 Russ, *How to Suppress Women's Writing*, 76.
48 Blodgett, *Centuries of Female Days*, 120–47, 195–6.
49 Smith, *A Poetics of Women's Autobiography*, 52-4.
50 Smith, "The Impact of Critical Theory," 5.
51 DuPlessis, Writing beyond the Ending, x.
52 Ibid., x.
53 Ibid., 4–6.
54 Smith, *A Poetics of Women's Autobiography*, 56.

55 Bonnie Kime Scott defines gender as "a category constructed through cultural and social systems. Unlike sex, it is not a biological fact determined at conception ... Gender is more fluid, flexible, and multiple in its options that the (so far) unchanging biological binary of male and female" (*The Gender of Modernism*, 2).
56 Woolf, *Orlando*, 150.
57 Kadar, "Whose Life Is It Anyway?" 160.
58 Stanton, *The Female Autograph*, 7.
59 Schenck, "All of a Piece," 286.
60 Smith, *A Poetics of Women's Autobiography*, 31.
61 Woolf, *A Room*, 35.
62 Ibid., 95, 97.
63 Chodorow, *The Reproduction of Mothering*, 169; and quoted in Friedman, "Women's Autobiographical Selves," 41.
64 Friedman, "Women's Autobiographical Selves," 38–56.
65 Stanton, *The Female Autograph*, 15–16.
66 Smith, *A Poetics of Women's Autobiography*, 8.
67 Neuman, "Autobiography," 217.
68 Ibid., 217, 226.
69 Brodzki and Schenck, *Life/Lines*, 14.
70 Schenck, "All of a Piece," 286, 305.
71 Smith, *A Poetics of Women's Autobiography*, 176, 58–9.
72 Ibid., 58.
73 Blodgett, *Centuries of Female Days*, 71.
74 Simons, *Diaries and Journals*, 7.
75 Woolf, *Orlando*, 150, 290–96.
76 Franklin, *Private Pages*, xix.
77 Moffat and Painter, *Revelations*, 5.
78 Buss, *Mapping Our Selves*, 164, 170.
79 DuPlessis, "For the Etruscans," 140–41.
80 Freedman, "Border Crossings," 13.
81 Buss, *Mapping Our Selves*, 23.
82 Ibid., 17.
83 Hogan, "Engendered Autobiographies," 95; Schor, *Reading in Detail*, 4.
84 Hogan, "Engendered Autobiographies," 95–6; Hampsten, *Read This Only to Yourself*, 80–81.
85 Hogan, "Endendered Autobiographies," 95; Juhasz, "Towards a Theory," 224.
86 Hogan, "Engendered Autobiographies," 99–100.
87 Ibid., 100.
88 Hogan, "Engendered Autobiographies," 100; Chodorow, *The Reproduction of Mothering*, 93.

89 Hogan, "Engendered Autobiographies," 103; DuPlessis, "For the Etruscans," 131.

90 Hogan, "Engendered Autobiographies," 105.

CHAPTER THREE

1 Spengemann, *Forms of Autobiography*, xiii.
2 See, for example, Shari Benstock, "Authorizing the Autobiographical," 21; Scott, *The Gender of Modernism*, 1–4.
3 Ibid., 2, 4.
4 Benstock, "Expatriate Modernism," 20.
5 Friedman, "Exile in the American Grain," 88.
6 Ibid., 88.
7 Joyce, *A Portrait*, 268–9.
8 I have in mind especially the work of Gillian Hanscombe, Virginia Smyers, Shari Benstock, Bonnie Kime Scott, and Susan Stanford Friedman.
9 Hanscombe and Smyers, *Writing for their Lives*, xvii.
10 Ibid., 10.
11 Friedman, "Exile in the American Grain," 96, 94–5.
12 Benstock, "Expatriate Modernism," 20.
13 Smart, "Fact and Emotional Truth," 193.
14 Friedman, "Exile in the American Grain," 92.
15 Scott, *Refiguring Modernism*, 1:79.
16 See, for instance, Scott's *Refiguring Modernism*, Nicholl's *Modernisms*, and Hugh Kenner's *The Pound Era*.
17 Benstock, "Expatriate Modernism," 29.
18 Eliot, "Tradition," 1226.
19 Quoted in Lee, *Virginia Woolf*, 439.
20 Scott, *Refiguring Modernism*, 1:79.
21 From the unpublished diary of Emily Coleman, 11 November 1929, Emily Holmes Coleman Papers, University of Delaware, box 77, file 625.
22 Scott, *Gender of Modernism*, 10.
23 Richardson, "Oberland," 93.
24 Richardson, "Deadlock," 218.
25 Eliot, "*Ulysses*," 177.
26 Showalter, *Sexual Anarchy*, 76–7.
27 Huyssen, *After The Great Divide*, vii.
28 Ibid., 52.
29 Richardson, "Women and the Future," 413.
30 Richardson, "Deadlock," 219.
31 Scott suggests that Eliot entered the high Anglican church to impose "order" on his life in order to offset the "chaos" of the behaviour of his wife, Vivien. (*Refiguring Modernism*, 1:126).

32 Huyssen, *After the Great Divide*, 47, 53. The notion that a female threat resulted in the devaluing of mass culture as feminine recalls the arguments put forward by Spender and Spencer to account for the devaluing of women's novels as "romance."

33 Ibid., 59.

34 See, for instance, Kershner, *Joyce and Popular Culture*.

35 Woolf, "Modern Fiction," 189, 194–5.

36 Hogan, "Engendered Autobiographies," 95–6.

37 Nicholls, *Modernisms*, 76.

38 Lejeune, "The 'Journal de Jeune Fille,'" 118–19.

39 Joyce, *A Portrait*, 233.

40 Eliot, "Tradition," 1228, 1231.

41 Ibid., 1231.

42 Nicholls, *Modernisms*, 194, 167.

43 Ibid., 19.

44 Eliot, "Love Song," 2259, 2260.

45 Waugh, *Feminine Fictions*, 18–19; Woolf, "Women and Fiction," 147.

46 Woolf, *To the Lighthouse*, 53.

47 Woolf, *A Room*, 41.

48 Eliot, "Tradition," 1230.

49 Lawrence, *Women in Love*, 525–6.

50 Joyce, *Ulysses*, 269.

51 See Olney's *Metaphors of Self* and Jay's *Being in the Text* for autobiographical treatments of Eliot's *Four Quartets*.

52 Miller, *T.S. Eliot's Personal Waste Land*, 2–3.

53 Eliot, "In Memoriam," 239–43; Miller, *T.S. Eliot's Personal Waste Land*, 4.

54 Miller, *T.S. Eliot's Personal Waste Land*, 9–10.

55 Hall, *A Primer of Freudian Psychology*, 17.

56 Scott, *Refiguring Modernism*, 1:59.

57 Culley, *A Day at a Time*, 3–4.

58 Freud, "Femininity," 146.

59 Jones, *The Life and Work of Sigmund Freud*, 474.

60 Freud, "Femininity," 169.

61 In a chapter entitled "The Stream of Consciousness," James writes: "Consciousness, then, does not appear to itself chopped up in bits ... It is nothing jointed; it flows ... *In talking of it hereafter, let us call it the stream of thought, of consciousness, or of subjective life*" (James, *Psychology*, 26.

62 Sinclair, "The Novels of Dorothy Richardson," 444.

63 Freud, "The Psychogenesis of a Case of Homosexuality," 386.

64 DuPlessis, "For the Etruscans," 136.

65 Quoted in Mallon, *A Book of One's Own*, 146.

66 Nussbaum, "Toward Conceptualizing Diary," 132.
67 Quoted in Kaufmann, "T.S. Eliot's," 77.
68 Ibid., 76.
69 Ibid., 75.
70 Quoted ibid., 77.
71 Benstock, "Expatriate Modernism," 28.
72 Herman, *Father-Daughter Incest*, 3.
73 See, for instance, Freud's *Studies on Hysteria* and *The Interpretation of Dreams*.
74 Broe, "My Art," 66; Chitty, *Now to My Mother*, 94.
75 Schenck, "Exiled by Genre," 229–31.
76 Ingram, "Introduction," 5–6, 9.
77 Schenck, "Exiled by Genre," 231.
78 Friedman, "Exile in the American Grain," 87.

CHAPTER FOUR

1 Woolf, "Modern Fiction," 194.
2 Virginia Stephen did not take the name of Woolf until her marriage to Leonard Woolf in 1912. However, because she is known as a writer by this surname, I will refer to her as Woolf throughout.
3 Abbott, "Old Virginia," 236.
4 Quentin Bell, in Woolf, *Diary*, 1: xiii.
5 Lee, *Virginia Woolf*, 769.
6 Rosenwald, *Emerson*, 19. All references to his physical criteria are from this page.
7 Book II of the manuscript series. Both Leaska (*PA*, 405–6) and Olivier Bell (*D*, 1: 321–4) provide catalogue descriptions of the diaries in appendices. For the sake of coherence, when referring to the holograph volumes, I will use the same numbering systems and the term "book". These references will be included in the body of the text.
8 "palimpsest," in *Oxford English Dictionary*, 1989 ed.
9 Gilbert and Gubar, *A Madwoman in the Attic*, 73.
10 Anne Olivier Bell, in Woolf, *Diary*, 1: 321.
11 Gilbert and Gubar, *A Madwoman in the Attic*, 73.
12 Simons, *Diaries and Journals*, 182.
13 Rosenwald, *Emerson*, 11.
14 Woolf, "Papers on Pepys," 234.
15 Woolf, "Rambling round Evelyn," 111.
16 Ibid., 118–19.
17 Woolf, "The Journal of Elizabeth Lady Holland," 231–2.
18 Woolf, "The Diary of a Lady in Waiting," 195.
19 Woolf, "Emerson's *Journals*," 338.

20 Woolf, "Letters and Journals of Anne Chalmers," 398–9.
21 Woolf, "Genius," 154.
22 Woolf, "Dorothy Wordsworth," 167.
23 Hassam, "Reading Other People's Diaries," 440.
24 Rosenwald, *Emerson*, 11.
25 Woolf, "Old Bloomsbury," 185; 193.
26 Charleston was the farmhouse in Sussex to which Vanessa Bell and her family moved in 1916, along with Duncan Grant, her lover. David Garnett ("Bunny") was also a lover of Grant's.
27 Woolf, "The Legacy," 281.
28 Blodgett, *Centuries of Female Days*, 71–2.
29 Woolf, "A Sketch of the Past," 64.
30 Abbott, "Old Virginia," 241.
31 Ibid., 241.
32 As Leaska informs us, "Collins and Renshaw were and are printers and publishers of diaries" (*PA*, 10n40).
33 This diary is not extant.
34 Woolf, "A Sketch of the Past," 111, 115, 124.
35 Woolf, "Modern Fiction," 189.
36 Woolf, "Papers on Pepys," 235.
37 Hinz, "Mimesis," 195.
38 Ibid., 196.
39 Ibid., 205.
40 Woolf, "James Woodforde," 93.
41 Woolf, "Modern Fiction," 189. Note that this essay of 1925 is a revised version of her 1919 essay "Modern Novels," which does not have the reference to "Monday or Tuesday." Woolf thus added the reference only after she had written the story "Monday or Tuesday" in 1921.
42 James, "Art of Fiction," 486.
43 Conrad, *Nigger*, xlix.
44 Ford, *Critical Writings*, 41.
45 Ibid., 73.
46 Quoted in Van Gunsteren, *Katherine Mansfield*, 69.
47 Pater, "From *The Renaissance*," 60.
48 Joyce, *Stephen Hero*, 216.
49 Joyce, *Portrait*, 186.
50 Mansfield, *Journal*, 148; quoted in Van Gunsteren, *Katherine Mansfield*, 80.
51 Woolf, "A Terribly Sensitive Mind," 356.
52 Woolf, "The Moment," 9.
53 Woolf, *To the Lighthouse*, 142, 218.
54 Ibid., 150, 281.
55 Woolf, "The Journal of Mistress Joan Martyn," 254.

56 Woolf, *Mrs Dalloway*, 28–9, 135.
57 Woolf, "A Sketch of the Past," 71–2.
58 Sinclair, "The Novels of Dorothy Richardson," 444.
59 Lee, *Virginia Woolf*, 391.
60 Woolf, "Modern Fiction," 190.
61 Virginia and Leonard Woolf published *The Waste Land* at their Hogarth Press in 1923.
62 Woolf, "Modern Fiction," 190.
63 Ibid., 188–9, 194–5.
64 Woolf, "Papers on Pepys," 234–5.
65 Woolf, "Mr. Bennett and Mrs. Brown," 102, 118–9.
66 Woolf, "A Sketch of the Past," 158.
67 Lee, *Virginia Woolf*, 7–8.
68 Woolf, "Life and the Novelist," 135, 131.
69 Woolf, *A Room*, 76, 99.
70 Ibid., 6, 95–8.
71 Woolf, "Romance and the Heart," 367.
72 Woolf, *A Room*, 99.
73 Woolf, "Women and Fiction," 147.
74 Lee, *Virginia Woolf*, 72.
75 Woolf, "Professions for Women," 285, 288.
76 Woolf, "Personalities," 273–4, 276, 277.
77 Woolf, "Montaigne," 84, 95.
78 Woolf, "Modern Fiction," 185, 188.
79 Woolf, "Montaigne," 92, 88, 96, 95.
80 Woolf, "Modern Fiction," 189.
81 Woolf, "Montaigne," 96.
82 Woolf, *A Room*, 41.
83 "East Coker" is the second section of Eliot's *Four Quartets*.
84 DeSalvo, "As 'Miss Jan Says,'" 112.
85 DeSalvo, *Virginia Woolf*, 239.
86 Lee, *Virginia Woolf*, 102.
87 DeSalvo, *Virginia Woolf*, 258.
88 A group of "Bloomsbury" members who met between 1920 and 1936 for the purpose of reading memoirs.
89 Woolf, "22 Hyde Park Gate," 177.
90 Broe, "My Art," 50.
91 Ibid., 51.
92 Woolf, "A Sketch of the Past," 157.
93 Ibid., 148–9.
94 Ibid., 150.
95 Ibid., 148–151.
96 Friedman, "Exile in the American Grain," 88.

97 Woolf, "Old Bloomsbury," 184.

98 Ibid., 184-5.

99 Ibid., 190.

100 Ibid., 186.

101 DeSalvo, *Virginia Woolf*, 260.

102 Conrad, *Heart of Darkness*, 10, 41.

103 Bell, *Virginia Woolf*, 2: 19.

104 Woolf, "Mr. Bennett and Mrs. Brown," 96.

105 Woolf, *The Waves*, 51, 176.

106 Ibid., 85.

107 Woolf, *To the Lighthouse*, 266.

108 Woolf, "A Sketch of the Past," 159.

109 Lee, *Virginia Woolf*, 191–2.

110 As Lee points out, Woolf never underwent analysis not only because she would have resisted it but because it would not have been recommended for a suicidal patient (*Virginia Woolf*, 197).

111 Woolf, "A Sketch of the Past," 149.

112 Woolf, *Letters*, 1: 496.

113 Blodgett, "A Woman Writer's Diary," 67.

114 Woolf, "Reminiscences," 39.

115 Woolf, *The Flight of the Mind*, 496.

116 Ethel Sands (1873–1962) was an American painter who lived in Europe.

117 Woolf, "Old Bloomsbury," 195.

118 Scott, Refiguring Modernism, 1:169.

119 Woolf, *To the Lighthouse*, 67, 265.

120 Friedman, "Exile in the American Grain," 93.

121 Woolf, *Three Guineas*, 234.

122 DeSalvo, "As 'Miss Jan Says,'" 103.

123 Woolf, "James Woodforde," 100.

124 Woolf, "John Evelyn," 266.

CHAPTER FIVE

1 White, *Antonia White Diaries*, 1: 168.

2 Chitty, introduction, *Antonia White Diaries*, 1: 7–8.

3 Drabble, Rev. of *Antonia White Diaries*.

4 Ibid., 103.

5 Freud, "Dreams," 90–1.

6 White underwent only a partial analysis with the psychologist James Robb in 1934; in February 1935 she would begin a more extenisve analysis with Dr Dennis Carroll.

7 Drabble, "Women Novelists," 89.

8 Drabble, Rev. of *Antonia White Diaries*, 103.

9 White was born Eirene Botting. However, she grew up disliking this name, and eventually adopted the pseudonym Antonia White in 1928, a fact that will be explored in detail later. Because White was not only her preferred but her professional name, I will use it to refer to her.

10 Drabble, Rev. of *Antonia White Diaries*, 102.

11 The notebooks have been numbered by the Chittys 1 through 39. All further references to these books will be included in the text, identified by book number.

12 Rosenwald, *Emerson*, 25.

13 Ibid., 19.

14 Ibid.

15 Ibid., 11.

16 Chitty, *Now to My Mother*, xiv.

17 Gascoyne, *Collected Journals*, 16.

18 Chitty, *Now to My Mother*, xiii-xiv.

19 Interview with Susan Chitty, 2 August 1994.

20 In her foreword to *The Hound and the Falcon*, White states that "Peter" was not Thorp's "real name but one he liked to be called by" (*HF*, xvii).

21 Maritain was a Jewish emigré from Rostov on the Don who converted to Catholicism with her husband, Jacques. He had asked White to translate Raïssa's journal.

22 White, *As Once in May*, 57-9.

23 White, *Frost in May*, 158.

24 Ibid., 201.

25 Ibid., 209.

26 Ibid., 217.

27 Broe, "My Art," 73.

28 About the change in name, White explains: "Of course Clara is a continuation of Nanda. Nanda became Clara because my father had a great passion for Meredith and a particular passion for Clara Middleton (heroine of *The Egoist*)" quoted in Carmen Callil's introduction to *The Lost Traveller*.

29 White, *The Sugar House*, 154.

30 The real incident of writing the convent novel took place when White was fifteen.

31 White, *The Sugar House*, 162-3.

32 In "Psychic Bisexuality," Charlotte Painter draws attention to the pseudonymous Joanna Field, an English psychologist who used her diary to conduct a self-analysis. The diary was published in 1934 as *A Life of One's Own* (Moffat and Painter, *Revelations: Diaries of Women*, 393). Though there is no proof that White read this text, in 1938 she did mention reading another of Field's books, *Experiment in Leisure* (D, 1:131), and thus

it is possible to speculate that she was aware of, or had even read, the diary study.

33 Berman, *Essential Papers*, 14.
34 Rieff, introduction, in Freud, *Dora*, 8–9.
35 Berman, *Essential Papers*, 21.
36 Marcus, "Freud and Dora," 48.
37 Quoted ibid., 77.
38 Ibid., 36, 39.
39 Ibid., 47.
40 Woolf, *A Room*, 41.
41 Marcus, "Freud and Dora," 47.
42 Kartiganer, "Freud's Reading Process," 3–4.
43 Ibid., 8.
44 Ibid., 17.
45 Freud, *Dora*, 22. A portion of this quotation appears in Marcus, "Freud and Dora," 52.
46 Freud, *Dora*, 23.
47 Marcus, "Freud and Dora," 52.
48 Freud, *Dora*, 22–3.
49 Marcus, "Freud and Dora," 49.
50 Freud, *Dora*, 27.
51 Ibid., 45; Marcus, "Freud and Dora," 62.
52 Freud, *Dora*, 24.
53 Freud, "The Psychogenesis of a Case of Homosexuality," 160.
54 Freud, *Dora*, 26–7.
55 Marcus, "Freud and Dora," 59.
56 Freud, *Dora*, 89; Marcus, "Freud and Dora," 59.
57 Marcus, "Freud and Dora," 46–7.
58 Ibid., 76.
59 Ibid., 64.
60 Ibid., 55–7.
61 Friedman, "Hysteria," 62.
62 Ibid., 42–4.
63 Ibid., 59-60.
64 Ibid., 62–3.
65 Ibid., 64.
66 Chitty, *Now to My Mother*, 155.
67 Broe, "My Art," 49.
68 Chitty, introduction, in White, *Diaries* 1: 8.
69 Hopkinson, *Nothing to Forgive*, 427.
70 White, *Lost Traveller*, 277–8.
71 Chitty, *Now to My Mother*, 3.
72 Broe, "My Art," 75.

73 Herman, *Father-Daughter Incest*, 30.
74 Ibid., 99.
75 Ibid., 29.
76 Ibid., 103.
77 Ibid., 30.
78 Chitty, *Now to My Mother*, 30.
79 Ibid., 95.
80 Herman, *Father-Daughter Incest*, 100.
81 Ibid., 100.
82 White, *Lost Traveller*, 164.
83 Chitty, introduction, White, *Diaries*, 1: 8.
84 Freud, "Feminity,", 158–9.
85 Freud, "Some Psychological Consequences," 192.
86 See also, for example, D, 2: 29, 59, 109, 112, 164, 195.
87 See, for example, Woolf, D, 1: 259; 3: 167; 4: 123; 5: 48, 53, 72, 79, 142, 178, 191, 270.
88 Gilbert and Gubar, *The Madwoman in the Attic*, 3–4.
89 Smith, *A Poetics of Women's Autobiography*, 43.
90 During their marriage, White and Hopkinson lived, with the two children, in a mansion flat in Fulham. After they separated, White stayed in the home with the children. She received some financial support from Hopkinson by way of alimony payments.
91 Chodorow, *The Reproduction of Mothering*, 5.
92 White, *As Once*, 82–4.
93 Rose, "Antonia White," 240–41.
94 Hall, *Primer*, 107–109.
95 White, *As Once in May*, 82.
96 Ibid., 258.
97 White, *Frost in May*, 158.
98 Stanislaus Joyce, *My Brother's Keeper*, 238.
99 Joyce, *Ulysses*, 11.
100 Joyce, *Portrait*, 15.
101 White, *Frost in May*, 32–3.
102 Joyce, *Portrait*, 22.
103 Ibid., 184.
104 Ibid., 186.
105 Ibid., 276.
106 Rose, "Antonia White," 239.
107 White, "Antonia White," 73.
108 Ibid., 76–7.
109 Stanislaus Joyce, *My Brother's Keeper*, 107.
110 Joyce, *Portrait*, 220.
111 Ibid., 268–9.

112 Stanislaus Joyce, *My Brother's Keeper*, 104–5.

113 White, "Antonia White," 81.

114 Ibid., 81–2.

115 Ibid., 81.

116 Ellman, *James Joyce*, 97.

117 Joyce, *Letters*, 2: 221.

118 Ellmann, *James Joyce*, 337.

119 Joyce, *Letters*, 2: 386.

120 Ibid., 89.

121 White, *Frost in May*, 122.

122 Ellmann, *James Joyce*, 50, 65.

123 James Joyce, *Stephen Hero*, 211.

124 Joyce, *A Portrait*, 233.

125 Bowen, introduction, White, *Frost in May*, 9. "Lippington" is a fictionalized name for the village of Roehampton.

126 Hynes, "Antonia White," 733.

127 Jane Marcus, "Antonia White," in Scott, *The Gender of Modernism*, 599.

128 In 1964 White referred to this incident and acknowledged that de Bezer "persuaded me (wrongly, I think) to burn the first 2" (*D*, 2:97).

129 Chitty, *Now to My Mother*, 151.

130 Hopkinson, *Nothing to Forgive*, 286.

131 Joyce, *Letters*, 2: 108.

132 Ellmann, *James Joyce*, 637.

133 Ibid., 638.

134 White, *As Once in May*, 2.

135 Hopkinson, *Nothing to Forgive*, 428.

136 Freud, *Dora*, 26.

137 Marcus, "Freud and Dora," 49.

CHAPTER SIX

1 From an unpublished title page to Smart's diary for 18 December 1933 to 19 April 1934, box 2, f. 5.

2 Sullivan, *By Heart*, 378.

3 Smart, "Fact and Emotional Truth," 187.

4 Van Wart, "Preface," 8.

5 Sullivan, *By Heart*, 32.

6 Van Wart, "Life Out of Art," 27.

7 Sullivan, *By Heart*, 331.

8 Drabble, "Women Novelists," 88–9.

9 Hassam, "Reading," 441.

10 Ibid., 438.

11 Sullivan, *By Heart*, 229–30.

12 Rosenwald, *Emerson*, 19.

13 Defoe, *Robinson Crusoe*, preface.

14 Graham Spry was a co-founder of the Canadian Radio League in the 1930s. A friend of the Smart family, he had met Elizabeth when she was a young girl. He took an interest in her work, encouraging her to read and write.

15 Sullivan, *By Heart*, 97.

16 Nicholls, *Modernisms*, 19.

17 Sullivan, *By Heart*, 102–3.

18 Durrell, *The Black Book*, 81.

19 "Agate, James Evershed," in *Dictionary of National Biography, 1941–1950*.

20 Agate, *The Selective Ego*, 1.

21 Sullivan, *By Heart*, 58, 79.

22 Not only would Smart transcribe whole portions of her diary into her novel *By Grand Central Station*, but in imitation of Eliot, she would offer her publisher a list of sources.

23 McGee was the grandson of Thomas D'Arcy McGee, the Canadian poet and politician who was involved in Confederation.

24 Van Wart has footnoted most of Smart's innumerable allusions.

25 Donne, "The Sun Rising."

26 Shakespeare, *Macbeth*, 132.

27 Ibid., 77.

28 Eliot, "The Love Song of J. Alfred Prufrock," 2262.

29 Van Wart, "Life Out of Art," 21.

30 Waugh, *Feminine Fictions*, 18.

31 Smart to Lawrence Durrell, 15 January 1939, Lawrence Durrell Collection, Special Collections, Southern Illinois University at Carbondale.

32 Gardiner, "Exhiliration," 134. Rhys grew up in the West Indies, Stead in Australia, and Lessing in Rhodesia.

33 Ibid., 134–5.

34 Smart, "Fact and Emotional Truth," 193.

35 Smart, *By Grand Central Station*, 67.

36 Smart, "Fact and Emotional Truth," 188, 191.

37 Sullivan, *By Heart*, 62.

38 Smart, *Juvenilia*, 97–8.

39 Sullivan, *By Heart*, 80.

40 Benstock, "Expatriate Modernism," 28.

41 The works in question are Nin's fictional pieces. The first volume of her diary was not published until 1966. However, a fragment from one of her diaries was published in the summer 1938 issue of the magazine *Seven*. Given that Smart would have three poems published in the spring 1940

issue of *Seven*, it is likely that she would have read Nin's diary from the earlier number.

42 Breton, "Manifesto," 14.

43 "Moon," in *A Dictionary of Symbols*, ed. J.E. Cirlot, 215.

44 Emily Coleman Papers, Special Collections, University of Delaware. F635, 12 March 1936.

45 Ibid., 22 March 1936.

46 In a different diary, covering the same period of August 1937, Smart records reading *Janus* on 30 August (ESF, box 3, f.2).

47 Sullivan, *By Heart*, 120.

48 Smart to Lawrence Durrell, 15 January 1939, Lawrence Durrell Collection, Special Collections, Southern Illinois University at Carbondale.

49 Sullivan, *By Heart*, 120.

50 Eliot had arranged for Barker to be a professor of English literature at Sendai Imperial University in Japan, but Barker was soon unhappy in his position there and wanted to come home (Sullivan, *By Heart*, 142–3).

51 Smart had two sisters; Helen was the eldest and Jane the youngest of the three.

52 Van Wart identifies Gene as "Gene Derwood, poet and painter, married to Oscar Williams, compiler of several poetry anthologies. Barker's friends, with whom Smart and Barker stay in New York" (NS, 284).

53 Scott, Refiguring Modernism, 1: 79.

54 Sullivan, *By Heart*, 112.

55 Chodorow, *The Reproduction of Mothering*, 3.

56 Ibid., 7.

57 Sullivan, *By Heart*, 153.

58 Smart, "Fact and Emotional Truth," 192–3.

59 Smart had been listening to Henry Purcell's opera *Dido and Aeneas*.

60 Ovid, *Heroides*, 58.

61 Katharine Goodson was Smart's piano teacher in London.

62 Sullivan, *By Heart*, 274.

63 Telephone conversation with Van Wart, Toronto, 27 January 1994.

64 In 1985 Smart titled a small notebook "Instructions on *Necessary Secrets*." She made several small, insignificant corrections and editorial remarks in it (ESF, box 12, f.9).

65 Ledger, Rev. of *Necessary Secrets*.

66 Henderson, Rev. of *Necessary Secrets*.

67 Thomas, Rev. of *Necessary Secrets*.

68 Although this is the more recent publication, the material I have selected for use was published earlier, in *In the Meantime*. There is some discrepancy in the dating between these two works. In *On the Side of the Angels*, the diary entries from 15 March to 17 July appear under the year of "The Eighties" (114–24). In contrast, the same entries from 15 March to 6

April are dated 1979 in *In the Meantime* (132–59). My own research at the National Library of Canada has confirmed that the entries are dated correctly in *In the Meantime*.

CHAPTER SEVEN

1 Nin, *Early Diary*, 1: 175.
2 Fothergill, *Private Chronicles*, 38–9.
3 Bair, *Anaïs Nin*, xviii.
4 Fitch, *Anaïs*, 4.
5 See, for instance, Bair, *Anaïs Nin*, 212, 242–3, 279–80, 324–5.
6 Ibid., 518.
7 Fitch, *Anaïs*, 18–19.
8 Nin describes this event often. See, for example, ED, 2:34–6, 365; and 2:88.
9 Rosenwald, *Emerson*, 19. All references in this chapter are from this page.
10 This diary is listed as book 1 in box 2 of the Anaïs Nin Collection at the University of California, Los Angeles. Nin's diaries from this date, 25 July 1914, through to November 1934 are available to the public. The contents are listed thus: box 2, books 1–8; box 9, books 9–17; box 10, books 18-24; box 15, books 25–31; box 16, books 32–42; box 17, books 43–46. All further references to the collection will be included in the text, identified only by book number.
11 Fitch, *Anaïs*, 6.
12 Friedman, "Exile in the American Grain," 89.
13 Eugene Graves was a friend of Guiler's.
14 Herman, *Father-Daughter Incest*, 29.
15 Woolf, "Professions for Women," 284.
16 Scholar, *Anaïs Nin*, 4.
17 Bair, *Anaïs Nin*, 36–37.
18 Benstock, "Expatriate Modernism," 33–34.
19 Brodzki and Schenck, *Life/Lines*, 14.
20 Nin, *D.H. Lawrence*, 32–3.
21 Bair, *Anaïs Nin*, 493.
22 Nin, *D.H. Lawrence*, 33.
23 The editors, "Introduction," *transition* 1 (April 1927): 137.
24 Benstock, "Expatriate Modernism," 28.
25 White, *As Once in May*, 59.
26 Bair, *Anaïs Nin*, 17–8.
27 Fitch, *Anaïs*, 127–8.
28 Herman, *Father-Daughter Incest*, 97.
29 Bair, *Anaïs Nin*, 174. Note that Bair also documents Nin's diaristic testi-

mony that she engaged in incest with her brother Thorvald three times (221–2).

30 Meiselman, *Resolving the Trauma of Incest*, 137.
31 Broe, "My Art," 67.
32 Bair, *Anaïs Nin*, 139.
33 Nicholls, *Modernisms*, 281–2.
34 Artaud, "Theatre of Cruelty," 70–6.
35 Artaud, "Theatre and the Plague," 17–20.
36 Broe, "My Art," 67.
37 Artaud, "Antonin Artaud: Letters – 1933," 57.
38 Herman, *Father-Daughter Incest*, 36–7.
39 Ibid., 53.
40 Broe, "My Art," 69; Broe is paraphrasing Alice Miller's *Thou Shalt Not Be Aware*.
41 Artaud, "Theatre and the Plague," 17.
42 Juno and Vale, Introduction, 7.
43 Mirbeau, *The Torture Garden*, 50.
44 Ibid., 73.
45 Rimbaud, "A Season," 304.
46 Ibid., 274.
47 Rimbaud, "By Way of a Preface," xxx–xxxi.
48 Scholar, *Anaïs Nin*, 74.
49 Rimbaud, "A Season," 281.
50 Ibid., 284.
51 Mirbeau, *The Torture Garden*, 56.
52 Ibid., 58.
53 Rimbaud, "A Season," 303.
54 Herman, *Father-Daughter Incest*, 98.
55 Rimbaud, "A Season," 302.
56 Nin met Rupert Pole in 1947, and though they were never legally married, they lived together for the next thirty years, until Nin's death.
57 For example, in May 1933 she wrote: "But Hugo had seen Henry's coat and hat in the hall. A profoundly suspicious and angry look came over his face. I have never seen such a look on Hugo's face, of *absolute knowingness*" (I, 162).
58 Herman, *Father-Daughter Incest*, 29–30.
59 Nussbaum, "Conceptualizing," 132.
60 Herman, *Father-Daughter Incest*, 31.
61 Friedman, "Women's Autobiographical Selves," 45.
62 Ibid., 46.
63 Benstock, "Expatriate Modernism," 29.
64 Nin, *Novel of the Future*, 158.
65 Ibid., 200.

66 Fitch, *Anaïs*, 212–13.
67 Nin and Miller, *A Literate Passion*, 360–2.
68 Benstock, "Expatriate Modernism," 34.
69 Barthes, *S/Z*, 4–5.

CONCLUSION

1 Quoted in Lee, *Virginia Woolf*, 633.
2 Gascoyne, *Collected Journals*, 139–42.
3 Ibid., 362.
4 Chitty, *Now to My Mother*, 116.
5 Elizabeth Smart to Lawrence Durrell, 15 January 1939, Lawrence Durrell Collection, Special Collections, Southern Illinois University at Carbondale.
6 ESF, box 71, f. 12.
7 Lawrence Durrell, Athens, to Elizabeth Smart, New York, (undated), ESF, box 33.
8 Lawrence Durrell to Elizabeth Smart, Mexico, ESF, box 33.
9 Smart, Rev. of *The Journals of Anaïs Nin*, 17.
10 Henry Miller to Elizabeth Smart, 9 February 1940, ESF, box 35.
11 Durrell and Miller, *The Durrell-Miller Letters*, 153.
12 Sullivan, *By Heart*, 182–4.
13 George Barker to Elizabeth Smart, (undated), ESF, box 18, f. 4.
14 George Barker to Elizabeth Smart, 30 November 1941, ESF, box 18, f. 4.
15 Interview with Susan Chitty, Sussex, 2 August 1994.
16 Antonia White to Elizabeth Smart, 28 November 1965, ESF, box 37.
17 Antonia White to Elizabeth Smart, 25 June 1967, ESF, box 37.
18 Antonia White to Elizabeth Smart, 12 July 1967, ESF, box 37.
19 Fothergill, *Private Chronicles*, 38–40.
20 Rosenwald, *Emerson*,10.
21 Ibid., 21–4.
22 Woolf, "John Evelyn," 259.
23 Kadar, "Whose Life Is It Anyway," 152–3.
24 Sullivan, *By Heart*, 331.

Bibliography

ARCHIVAL SOURCES

BRITISH LIBRARY, London, England
The Virginia Woolf Manuscripts

SUSAN AND THOMAS CHITTY PERSONAL ARCHIVE
Antonia White Papers

NATIONAL LIBRARY OF CANADA, Ottawa
Elizabeth Smart Fonds
Alice Van Wart Collection of Elizabeth Smart Papers

NEW YORK PUBLIC LIBRARY, New York
Astor, Lenox and Tilden Foundations
The Henry W. and Albert A. Berg Collection of English and American Literature
The Virginia Woolf Manuscripts

SOUTHERN ILLINOIS UNIVERSITY AT CARBONDALE
The Lawrence Durrell Collection

UNIVERSITY OF CALIFORNIA AT LOS ANGELES RESEARCH LIBRARY
The Anaïs Nin Collection

UNIVERSITY OF DELAWARE, Newark
The Emily Holmes Coleman Papers

PUBLISHED SOURCES

Abbott, H. Porter. "Old Virginia and the Night Writer: The Origins of Woolf's Narrative Meander." In *Inscribing the Daily*, ed. Suzanne L. Bunkers and Cynthia Huff, 236–51. Amherst: University of Massachusetts Press 1996.

Ackroyd, Peter. *T.S. Eliot: A Life*. New York: Simon and Schuster 1984.

Adams, Timothy Dow. *Telling Lies in Modern American Autobiography*. Chapel Hill: University of North Carolina Press 1990.

Agate, James. *The Selective Ego: The Diaries of James Agate*. Ed. Tim Beaumont. London: Harrap 1976.

Aitken, James, ed. *English Diaries of the XVI, XVII and XVIII Centuries*. Harmondsworth: Allen Lane–Penguin Books 1941.

Artaud, Antonin. "Letters – 1933." *Anaïs: An International Journal*, 1 (1983): 52–9.

– "Theatre and the Plague." In *Antonin Artaud: Collected Works*, trans. Victor Corti, 4: 7–21 . London: Calder & Boyars 1974.

– "The Theatre Of Cruelty, First Manifesto." In *Antonin Artaud: Collected Works*, trans. Victor Corti, 4: 68–76. London: Calder & Boyars 1974.

Bacon, Francis. "Of Travel." In *The Essays*, ed. with introduction by John Pitcher, 113–114. Harmondsworth: Penguin 1985.

Bair, Deirdre. *Anaïs Nin: A Biography*. New York: G.P. Putman's Sons 1995.

Barthes, Roland. *Roland Barthes*. Trans. Richard Howard. New York: Hill and Wang 1977.

– *S/Z*. Trans. Richard Miller. New York: Hill and Wang 1974.

Bashkirtseva, Mariia. *The Journal of Marie Bashkirtseff*. Trans. Mathilde Blind. London: Cassell & Company 1891.

Bell, Anne Olivier. *Editing Virginia Woolf's Diary*. London: The Bloomsbury Workshop 1990.

Bell, Quentin. *Virginia Woolf: A Biography*. 2 vols. London: Hogarth Press 1972.

Benstock, Shari. "Authorizing the Autobiographical." In *The Private Self*, ed. Shari Benstock, 10–33. Chapel Hill: University of North Carolina Press 1988.

– "Expatriate Modernism: Writing on the Cultural Rim." In *Women's Writing in Exile*, ed. Mary Lynn Broe and Angela Ingram, 19–40. Chapel Hill: University of North Carolina Press 1989.

– *Women of the Left Bank*. Austin: University of Texas Press 1986.

Berman, Emanuel, ed. *Essential Papers on Literature and Psychoanalysis*. New York: New York University Press 1993.

Blind, Mathilde. Introduction. In *The Journal of Marie Bashkirtseff*, vii–xxviii. London: Cassell & Company 1891.

Blodgett, Harriet. ed. *"Capacious Hold-All": An Anthology of English-*

women's Diary Writings. Charlottesville: University Press of Virginia 1991.

– *Centuries of Female Days: Englishwomen's Private Diaries*. New Brunswick: Rutgers University Press 1988.

– "A Woman Writer's Diary: Virginia Woolf Revisited." *Prose Studies* 12 (May 1989): 57–71.

Bloom, Lynn Z. "'I Write for Myself and Strangers': Private Diaries as Public Documents." In *Inscribing the Daily*, ed. Suzanne L. Bunkers and Cynthia A. Huff, 23–37. Amherst: University of Massachusetts Press 1996.

– and Orlee Holder. "Anaïs Nin's Diary in Context." *Mosaic* 2 (1977–8): 191–202.

Bobbitt, Joan. "Truth and Artistry in the *Diary of Anaïs Nin*." *Journal of Modern Literature* 9 (1981–82): 267–76.

Bowle, John. Introduction. In *The Diary of John Evelyn*, ed. John Bowle. Oxford: Oxford University Press 1983.

Breton, André. "Manifesto of Surrealism." In *Manifestoes of Surrealism*, trans. Richard Seaver and Helen R. Lane, 3–47. Ann Arbor: The University of Michigan Press 1972.

Breuer, Josef, and Sigmund Freud. *Studies on Hysteria*. Trans. and ed. James and Alix Strachey. London: Penguin Books 1991.

Brodzki, Bella, and Celeste Schenck, eds. *Life/Lines: Theorizing Women's Autobiography*. Ithaca: Cornell University Press 1988.

Broe, Mary Lynn. "My Art Belongs to Daddy: Incest as Exile, The Textual Economics of Hayford Hall." In *Women's Writing in Exile*, ed. Mary Lynn Broe and Angela Ingram, 41–86. Chapel Hill: University of North Carolina Press 1989.

Bruss, Elizabeth W. *Autobiographical Acts: The Changing Situation of a Literary Genre*. Baltimore: Johns Hopkins University Press 1976.

Bunkers, Suzanne. "Diaries and Dysfunctional Families: The Case of Emily Hawley Gillespie and Sarah Gillespie Huftalen." In *Inscribing the Daily*, ed. Suzanne L. Bunkers and Cynthia A. Huff, 220–35. Amherst: University of Massachusetts Press 1996.

– "What Do Women *Really* Mean? Thoughts on Women's Diaries and Lives." In *The Intimate Critique: Autobiographical Literary Criticism*, ed. Diane P. Freedman, Olivia Frey, and Frances Murphy Zauhar, 207–21. Durham: Duke University Press 1993.

– and Cynthia A. Huff, eds. *Inscribing the Daily*. Amherst: University of Massachusetts Press 1996.

Buss, Helen M. *Mapping Our Selves: Canadian Women's Autobiography in English*. Montreal and Kingston: McGill-Queen's University Press 1993.

Chitty, Susan. *Now to My Mother: A Very Personal Memoir of Antonia White*. London: Weidenfeld and Nicolson 1985.

Chodorow, Nancy. *The Reproduction of Mothering: Psychoanalysis and the Sociology of Gender.* Berkeley: University of California Press 1978.

Conrad, Joseph. *Heart of Darkness.* Harmondsworth: Penguin Books 1973.

- "Preface." In *The Nigger of the "Narcissus,"* ed. Cedric Watts, xlvii–li. Harmondsworth: Penguin Books 1988.

Culley, Margo, ed. *A Day at a Time: The Diary Literature of American Women from 1764 to the Present.* New York: The Feminist Press at the City University of New York 1985.

Defoe, Daniel. *Moll Flanders.* New York: Random House n.d.

- *Robinson Crusoe.* New York: Walter J. Black 1941.

De Man, Paul. "Autobiography as De-facement." *Modern Language Notes* 94 (1979): 919–30.

DeSalvo, Louise A. "As 'Miss Jan Says': Virginia Woolf's Early Journals." In *Virginia Woolf and Bloomsbury,* ed. Jane Marcus, 96–124. Basingstoke: Macmillan Press 1987.

- *Virginia Woolf: The Impact of Childhood Sexual Abuse on Her Life and Work.* Boston: Beacon Press 1989.

Dobbs, Brian. *Dear Diary ...: Some Studies in Self-Interest.* London: Hamish Hamilton 1974.

Donne, John. "The Sun Rising." In *The Norton Anthology of English Literature,* ed. M.H. Abrams et al., 4th ed., 1: 1073. New York: W.W. Norton & Co. 1979.

Drabble, Margaret. Rev. of *Antonia White Diaries, 1926–57. Vogue* (British), September 1991, 102–3.

- "Women Novelists." *National Book League Periodical,* 1968, 87–90.

Dunn, Jane. *Antonia White: A Life.* London: Jonathan Cape 1998.

DuPlessis, Rachel Blau. "For the Etruscans: Sexual Difference and Artistic Production – The Debate over a Female Aesthetic." In *The Future of Difference,* ed. Hester Eisenstein and Alice Jardine, 128–56. Boston: G.K. Hall & Co. 1980.

- *Writing beyond the Ending: Narrative Strategies of Twentieth-Century Women Writers.* Bloomington: Indiana University Press 1985.

Durrell, Lawrence. *The Black Book.* New York: Carroll & Graf Publishers 1990.

- and Henry Miller. *The Durrell-Miller Letters, 1935–80.* Ed. Ian S. MacNiven. London: Faber and Faber 1988.

Eakin, Paul John. *Fictions in Autobiography: Studies in the Art of Self-Invention.* Princeton: Princeton University Press 1985.

- "Narrative and Chronology as Structures of Reference and the New Model Autobiographer." In *Studies in Autobiography,* ed. James Olney, 32–41. New York: Oxford University Press 1988.

Eliot, T.S. "In Memoriam." In *Selected Prose of T.S. Eliot,* ed. Frank Kermode, 239–47. New York: Harcourt Brace Jovanovich 1975.

– "The Love Song of J. Alfred Prufrock." In *The Norton Anthology of English Literature*, ed. M.H. Abrams et al., 4th ed., 2: 2259–62. New York: W.W. Norton & Company 1979.

– "Tradition and the Individual Talent." In *The Norton Anthology of American Literature*, ed. Ronald Gottesman et al., 2: 1225–32. New York: W.W. Norton & Company 1979.

– "*Ulysses*, Order and Myth." In *Selected Prose of T.S. Eliot*, ed. Frank Kermode, 175–8. New York: Harcourt Brace Jovanovich 1975.

Ellmann, Richard. *James Joyce.* New York: Oxford University Press 1965.

Evelyn, John. *The Diary of John Evelyn.* Ed. John Bowle. Oxford: Oxford University Press 1983.

– *Memoirs, Illustrative of the Life and Writings of John Evelyn, Esq. F.R.S.* Ed. William Bray. London: Henry Colburn 1819.

Fitch, Noël Riley. *Anaïs: The Erotic Life of Anaïs Nin.* Boston: Little, Brown and Co. 1993.

– ed. *In transition: A Paris Anthology.* London: Secker & Warburg 1990.

Fleishman, Avrom. *Figures of Autobiography: The Language of Self-Writing in Victorian and Modern England.* Berkeley: University of California Press 1983.

Ford, Ford Madox. *Critical Writings of Ford Madox Ford.* Ed. Frank MacShane. Lincoln: University of Nebraska Press 1964.

Fothergill, Robert A. *Private Chronicles: A Study of English Diaries.* London: Oxford University Press 1974.

Franklin, Penelope. "The Diaries of Forgotten Women." *Book Forum* 4 (1979): 467–74, 557–8.

– ed. *Private Pages: Diaries of American Women, 1830s–1970s.* New York: Ballantine Books 1986.

Freedman, Diane P. "Border Crossings as Method and Motif in Contemporary American Writing, or, How Freud Helped Me Case the Joint." In *The Intimate Critique: Autobiographical Literary Criticism*, ed. Diane P. Freedman, Olivia Frey, and Frances Murphy Zauhar, 13–22. Durham: Duke University Press 1993.

Freud, Sigmund. *Dora: An Analysis of a Case of Hysteria.* Ed. Philip Rieff. New York: Macmillan 1963.

– "Dreams." In *The Complete Introductory Lectures on Psychoanalysis*, trans. and ed. James Strachey, 81–239. New York: W.W. Norton 1966.

– "Femininity." In *Sigmund Freud: New Introductory Lectures on Psycho-analysis*, ed. and trans. James Strachey, 2: 145–69. London: Penguin 1991.

– *The Interpretation of Dreams.* Trans. James Strachey, ed. Angela Richards. London: Penguin 1991.

– "The Psychogenesis of a Case of Homosexuality in a Woman." In *The Standard Edition of the Complete Psychological Works of Sigmund Freud*, trans.

and ed. James Strachey, in collaboration with Anna Freud, assisted by Alix Strachey and Alan Tyson, 18: 147–72. London: Hogarth Press 1955.

– "Some Psychological Consequences of the Anatomical Distinction Between the Sexes." In *Sigmund Freud: Collected Papers*, ed. James Strachey, 5: 186–97. London: Hogarth Press 1950.

Friedman, Susan Stanford. "Exile in the American Grain: H.D.'s Diaspora." In *Women's Writing in Exile*, ed. Mary Lynn Broe and Angela Ingram, 87–112. Chapel Hill: University of North Carolina Press 1989.

– "Hysteria, Dreams, and Modernity: A Reading of the Origins of Psychoanalysis in Freud's Early Corpus." In *Rereading the New: A Backward Glance at Modernism*, ed. Kevin J.H. Dettmar, 41–71. Ann Arbor: The University of Michigan Press 1992.

– "Women's Autobiographical Selves: Theory and Practice." In *The Private Self*, ed. Shari Benstock, 34–62. Chapel Hill: University of North Carolina Press 1988.

Gannett, Cinthia. *Gender and the Journal: Diaries and Academic Discourse.* Albany: State University of New York Press 1992.

Gardiner, Judith Kegan. "The Exhilaration of Exile: Rhys, Stead, and Lessing." In *Women's Writing in Exile*, ed. Mary Lynn Broe and Angela Ingram, 133–50. Chapel Hill: University of North Carolina Press 1989.

Gascoyne, David. *Collected Journals, 1936–42.* London: Skoob Books Publishing 1991.

Gilbert, Sandra M., and Susan Gubar. *The Madwoman in the Attic.* New Haven: Yale University Press 1979.

Godwin, Gail. "A Diarist on Diarists." *Antaeus* 61 (1988): 9–15.

Gristwood, Sarah. *Recording Angels.* London: Harrap 1988.

Gusdorf, Georges. "Conditions and Limits of Autobiography." In *Autobiography: Essays Theoretical and Critical*, ed. James Olney, 28–48. Princeton: Princeton University Press 1980.

Hall, Calvin S. *A Primer of Freudian Psychology.* New York: New American Library 1979.

Hampsten, Elizabeth. *Read This Only to Yourself: The Private Writings Of Midwestern Women, 1880–1910.* Bloomington: Indiana University Press 1982.

Hanscombe, Gillian, and Virginia L. Smyers. *Writing for Their Lives: The Modernist Women, 1910–1940.* London: The Women's Press 1987.

Hart, Francis R. "Notes for an Anatomy of Modern Autobiography." *New Literary History* 1 (1970): 485–511.

Hassam, Andrew. "Reading Other People's Diaries." *University of Toronto Quarterly* 56 (1987): 435–42.

Heilbrun, Carolyn G. *Writing a Woman's Life.* New York: Ballantine Books 1988.

Henderson, Heather. Rev. of *Necessary Secrets*, by Elizabeth Smart. *Maclean's*, 17 November 1986, 76a.

Herman, Judith Lewis. *Father-Daughter Incest*. Cambridge: Harvard University Press 1981.

Hinz, Evelyn J. "Mimesis: The Dramatic Lineage of Auto/Biography." In *Essays on Life Writing: From Genre to Critical Practice*, ed. Marlene Kadar, 195–212. Toronto: University of Toronto Press 1992.

Hogan, Rebecca. "Engendered Autobiographies: The Diary as a Feminine Form." In *Autobiography and Questions of Gender*, ed. Shirley Neuman, 95–107. London: Frank Cass 1991.

Hopkinson, Lyndall P. *Nothing to Forgive: A Daughter's Life of Antonia White*. Great Britain: Sceptre–Hodder and Stoughton Ltd. 1990.

Howarth, William L. "Some Principles of Autobiography." In *Autobiography: Essays Theoretical and Critical*, ed. James Olney, 84–114. Princeton: Princeton University Press 1980.

Huff, Cynthia. *British Women's Diaries: A Descriptive Bibliography of Selected Nineteenth-Century Women's Manuscript Diaries*. New York: AMS Press 1985.

Huyssen, Andreas. *After the Great Divide: Modernism, Mass Culture, Postmodernism*. Bloomington: Indiana University Press 1986.

Hynes, Samuel. "Antonia White." *Times Literary Supplement*, 7 March 1969, 733.

Ingram, Angela. "Introduction: On the Contrary, Outside of It." In *Women's Writing in Exile*, ed. Mary Lynn Broe and Angela Ingram, 1–15. Chapel Hill: University of North Carolina Press 1989.

James, Henry. "The Art of Fiction." In *The Norton Anthology of American Literature*, ed. Ronald Gottesman et al., 2: 482–99. New York: W.W. Norton & Co. 1979.

James, William. *Psychology: The Briefer Course*. Ed. Gordon Allport. Notre Dame: University of Notre Dame Press 1985.

Jay, Paul. *Being in the Text: Self-Representation from Wordsworth to Roland Barthes*. Ithaca: Cornell University Press 1984.

Jelinek, Estelle C., ed. *The Tradition of Women's Autobiography: From Antiquity to the Present*. Boston: Twayne Publishers 1986.

– ed. *Women's Autobiography: Essays in Criticism*. Bloomington: Indiana University Press 1980.

Jones, Ernest. *The Life and Work of Sigmund Freud*. Ed. and abr. Lionel Trilling and Steven Marcus. Harmondsworth: Penguin Books with Hogarth Press 1961.

Joyce, James. *Letters of James Joyce*. Vol. 2. Ed. Richard Ellmann. London: Faber and Faber 1966.

– *A Portrait of the Artist as a Young Man*. Ed. Seamus Deane. London: Penguin Books 1992.

– *Stephen Hero*. Ed. Theodore Spencer, John J. Slocum, and Herbert Cahoon. London: Jonathan Cape 1956.

– *Ulysses*. London: Penguin 1992.

Joyce, Stanislaus. *My Brother's Keeper: James Joyce's Early Years*. Ed. Richard Ellmann. New York: The Viking Press 1958.

Juhasz, Suzanne. "Towards a Theory of Form in Feminist Autobiography: Kate Millet's *Flying* and *Sita*; Maxine Hong Kingston's *The Woman Warrior*." In *Women's Autobiography: Essays in Criticism*, ed. Estelle C. Jelinek, 221–37. Bloomington: Indiana University Press 1980.

Juno, Andrea, and V. Vale. Introduction. In *The Torture Garden*, by Octave Mirbeau, ed. Andrea Juno and V. Vale, trans. Alvah C. Bessie, 6–7. San Francisco: Re/Search Publications 1989.

Kadar, Marlene. "Coming to Terms: Life Writing – from Genre to Critical Practice." In *Essays on Life Writing: From Genre to Critical Practice*, ed. Marlene Kadar, 3–16. Toronto: University of Toronto Press 1992.

– "Whose Life Is It Anyway? Out of the Bathtub and into the Narrative." In *Essays on Life Writing: From Genre to Critical Practice*, ed. Marlene Kadar, 152–61. Toronto: University of Toronto Press 1992.

Kagle, Steven E., and Lorenza Gramegna. "Rewriting Her Life: Fictionalization and the Use of Fictional Models in Early American Women's Diaries." In *Inscribing the Daily*, ed. Suzanne L. Bunkers and Cynthia A. Huff, 38–55. Amherst: University of Massachusetts Press 1996.

Kartiganer, Donald M. "Freud's Reading Process: The Divided Protagonist Narrative and the Case of the Wolf-Man." In *The Psychoanalytic Study of Literature*, ed. Joseph Reppen and Maurice Charney, 3–36. New Jersey: The Analytic Press 1985.

Kaufmann, Michael Edward. "T.S. Eliot's New Critical Footnotes to Modernism." In *A Backward Glance at Modernism*, ed. Kevin J.H. Dettmar, 73–85. Ann Arbor: University of Michigan Press 1992.

Kazin, Alfred. "Autobiography as Narrative." *Michigan Quarterly Review* 3 (1964): 210–16.

Kenner, Hugh. *The Pound Era*. Berkeley: University of California Press 1971.

Kermode, Frank. "Institutional Control of Interpretation." *Salmagundi* 43 (winter 1979): 72–86.

Kershner, R.B., ed. *Joyce and Popular Culture*. Gainesville: University Press of Florida 1996.

Lawrence, D.H. *Women in Love*. Ed. Charles L. Ross. London: Penguin 1982.

Ledger, Brent. Rev. of *Necessary Secrets*, by Elizabeth Smart. *Quill and Quire*, February 1987, 16.

Lee, Hermione. *Virginia Woolf*. London: Chatto & Windus, 1996.

Lejeune, Philippe. "The Autobiographical Contract." In *French Literary Theory Today: A Reader*, ed. Tzvetan Todorov, trans. R. Carter, 192–222. Cambridge: Cambridge University Press 1982.

- "The 'Journal de Jeune Fille' in Nineteenth-Century France." Trans. Martine Breillac. In *Inscribing the Daily*, ed. Suzanne L. Bunkers and Cynthia A. Huff, 107–22. Amherst: University of Massachusetts Press 1996.

Lensink, Judy Nolte. "Expanding the Boundaries of Criticism: The Diary as Female Autobiography." *Women's Studies* 14 (1987): 39–53.

Lifshin, Lyn, ed. *Ariadne's Thread: A Collection of Contemporary Women's Journals*. New York: Harper and Row 1982.

Mallon, Thomas. *A Book of One's Own: People and Their Diaries*. London: Penguin Books Ltd. 1986.

Mandel, Barrett J. "Full of Life Now." In *Autobiography: Essays Theoretical and Critical*, ed. James Olney, 49–72. Princeton: Princeton University Press 1980.

Marchand, Leslie A., ed. *"In My Hot Youth": Byron's Letters and Journals*. Vol 1. 1. London: John Murray 1973.

Marcus, Jane. "Alibis and Legends: The Ethics of Elsewhereness, Gender and Estrangement." In *Women's Writing in Exile*, ed. Mary Lynn Broe and Angela Ingram, 269–94. Chapel Hill: University of North Carolina Press 1989.

Marcus, Steven. "Freud and Dora: Story, History, Case History." In *Essential Papers on Literature and Psychoanalysis*, ed. Emanuel Berman, 36–80. New York: New York University Press 1993.

Matthews, William. *British Diaries: An Annotated Bibliography of British Diaries Written between 1442 and 1942*. Berkeley: University of California Press 1950.

- "The Diary as Literature." In *The Diary of Samuel Pepys*, ed. Robert Latham and William Matthews, 1: xcvii–cxiii. Berkeley: University of California Press 1970.

Mazlish, Bruce. "Autobiography & Psycho-analysis: Between Truth and Self-Deception." *Encounter* 35 (1970): 28–37.

Meiselman, Karin C. *Resolving the Trauma of Incest: Reintegration Therapy with Survivors*. San Francisco: Jossey-Bass 1990.

Miller, James E., Jr. *T.S. Eliot's Personal Waste Land: Exorcism of the Demons*. University Park: The Pennsylvania State University Press 1977.

Mirbeau, Octave. *The Torture Garden*. Ed. Andrea Juno and V. Vale. Trans. Alvah C. Bessie. San Francisco: Re/Search Publications 1989.

Moffat, Mary Jane, and Charlotte Painter, eds. *Revelations: Diaries of Women*. New York: Vintage Books 1975.

Mudge, Bradford K. "Exiled as Exiler: Sara Coleridge, Virginia Woolf, and the Politics of Literary Revisionism." In *Women's Writing in Exile*, ed. Mary Lynn Broe and Angela Ingram, 199–223. Chapel Hill: University of North Carolina Press 1989.

Neuman, Shirley, ed. *Autobiography and Questions of Gender*. London: Frank Cass 1991.

– "Autobiography: From Different Poetics to a Poetics of Differences." In *Essays on Life Writing: From Genre to Critical Practice*, ed. Marlene Kadar, 213–30. Toronto: University of Toronto Press 1992.

Nicholls, Peter. *Modernisms: A Literary Guide.* Berkeley: University of California Press 1995.

Nin, Anaïs. *D.H. Lawrence: An Unprofessional Study.* Chicago: The Swallow Press Inc. 1964.

– *The Diary of Anaïs Nin.* Ed. Gunther Stuhlmann. 7 vols. San Diego: The Swallow Press and Harcourt Brace Jovanovich 1966–80.

– *The Early Diary of Anaïs Nin.* 4 vols. 1978–85. Vol. 1, 1914–1920: *Linotte*, trans. Jean Sherman, ed. John Ferrone (New York: Harcourt Brace Jovanovich 1978); vol. 2, 1920–1923, ed. Rupert Pole (New York: Harcourt Brace Jovanovich 1982); vol. 3, 1923–27: *Journal of a Wife*, ed. Rupert Pole (London: Peter Owen Publishers 1983); vol. 4, 1927–1931, ed. Rupert Pole (San Diego: Harcourt Brace Jovanovich 1985).

– *Fire: From a Journal of Love: The Unexpurgated Diary of Anaïs Nin, 1934–1937.* Ed. Rupert Pole and Gunther Stuhlmann. New York: Harcourt Brace & Co. 1995.

– *Henry and June: From the Unexpurgated Diary of Anaïs Nin.* ed. Rupert Pole and Gunther Stuhlmann. San Diego: Harcourt Brace Jovanovich 1986.

– *Incest: From a Journal of Love: The Unexpurgated Diary of Anaïs Nin, 1932–1934.* Ed. Gunther Stuhlmann. New York: Harcourt Brace Jovanovich 1992.

– *The Novel of the Future.* Athens: Swallow Press/Ohio University Press 1968.

– and Henry Miller. *A Literate Passion: Letters of Anaïs Nin and Henry Miller, 1932–1953.* Ed. Gunther Stuhlmann. San Diego: Harcourt Brace Jovanovich 1987.

Nussbaum, Felicity A. "Toward Conceptualizing Diary." In *Studies in Autobiography*, ed. James Olney, 128–40. New York: Oxford University Press 1988.

O'Brien, Kate. *English Diaries and Journals.* London: William Collins 1943.

Olney, James. "Autobiography and the Cultural Moment: A Thematic, Historical, and Bibliographical Introduction." In *Autobiography: Essays Theoretical and Critical*, ed. James Olney, 3–27. Princeton: Princeton University Press 1980.

– *Metaphors of Self: The Meaning of Autobiography.* Princeton: Princeton University Press 1972.

– "Some Versions of Memory / Some Versions of Bios: The Ontology of Autobiography." In *Autobiography: Essays Theoretical and Critical*, ed. James Olney, 236–67. Princeton: Princeton University Press 1980.

Ovid. *Heroides.* Trans. Harold Isbell. London: Penguin Books 1990.

Pascal, Roy. *Design and Truth in Autobiography.* London: Routledge & Kegan Paul 1960.

Pater, Walter. "From *The Renaissance: Studies in Art and Poetry.*" In *Selected Writings of Walter Pater*, ed. Harold Bloom, 17–63. New York: Columbia University Press 1974.

Pepys, Samuel. *The Diary of Samuel Pepys.* Ed. Robert Latham and William Matthews. 11 vols. Berkeley: University of California Press 1970.

– *The Illustrated Pepys: Extracts from the Diary.* Selected and ed. Robert Latham. London: Bell & Hyman Ltd. 1978.

Pomerleau, Cynthia S. "The Emergence of Women's Autobiography in England." In *Women's Autobiography: Essays in Criticism*, ed. Estelle C. Jelinek, 21–38. Bloomington: Indiana University Press 1980.

Ponsonby, Arthur. *English Diaries.* London: Methuen & Co. 1923.

– *More English Diaries.* London: Methuen & Co. 1927.

Rich, Adrienne. *On Lies, Secrets, and Silence: Selected Prose, 1966–1978.* New York: W.W. Norton & Co. 1979.

Richardson, Dorothy M. "Deadlock." In *Pilgrimage 3*, 9–229. London: Virago 1979.

– "Oberland." In *Pilgrimage 4*, 9–127. London: Virago 1979.

– "Women and the Future." In *The Gender of Modernism*, ed. Bonnie Kime Scott, 411–14. Bloomington: Indiana University Press 1990.

Ricoeur, Paul. "Life: A Story in Search of a Narrator." In *A Ricoeur Reader: Reflection and Imagination*, ed. Mario J. Valdes, 425–37. Toronto: University of Toronto Press 1991.

Rieff, Philip. Introduction. In *Dora: An Analysis of a Case of Hysteria*, by Sigmund Freud, 7–20. New York: Collier Books–Macmillan Publishing Co. 1963.

Rimbaud, Arthur. "By Way of a Preface (*Les Lettres du Voyant*)." *Rimbaud: Illuminations and Other Prose Poems*, trans. Louise Varèse, xxv–xxxv. New York: New Directions Publishing 1946.

– "A Season in Hell." Trans. J.S. Watson, Jr. In *A Season In Hell: The Life of Arthur Rimbaud*, by Jean-Marie Carre, trans. Hannah and Matthew Josephson, 273–304. New York: The Macaulay Company 1979.

Rose, Ellen Cronan. "Antonia White: Portrait of the Artist as a Dutiful Daughter." LIT 2 (1991): 239–48.

Rosenwald, Lawrence. *Emerson and the Art of the Diary.* New York: Oxford University Press 1988.

Russ, Joanna. *How to Suppress Women's Writing.* Austin: University of Texas Press 1983.

Schenck, Celeste M. "All of a Piece: Women's Poetry and Autobiography." In *Life/Lines: Theorizing Women's Autobiography*, ed. Bella Brodzki and Celeste Schenck, 281–305. Ithaca: Cornell University Press 1988.

– "Exiled by Genre: Modernism, Canonicity, and the Politics of Exclusion." In *Women's Writing in Exile*, ed. Mary Lynn Broe and Angela Ingram, 225–50. Chapel Hill: University of North Carolina Press 1989.

Scholar, Nancy. *Anaïs Nin.* Boston: Twayne Publishers 1984.

Schor, Naomi. *Reading in Detail: Aesthetics and the Feminine.* New York: Methuen 1987.

Scott, Bonnie Kime, ed. *The Gender of Modernism: A Critical Anthology.* Bloomington: Indiana University Press 1990.

– *Refiguring Modernism.* Vol. 1. Bloomington: Indiana University Press 1995.

Shakespeare, William. *Macbeth.* Ed. G.K. Hunter. London: Penguin Books 1967.

Showalter, Elaine. *Sexual Anarchy: Gender and Culture at the Fin de Siècle.* New York: Penguin Books 1990.

Simons, Judy. *Diaries and Journals of Literary Women from Fanny Burney to Virginia Woolf.* Iowa City: University of Iowa Press 1990.

– "Invented Lives: Textuality and Power in Early Women's Diaries." In *Inscribing the Daily*, ed. Suzanne L. Bunkers and Cynthia A. Huff, 252–63. Amherst: University of Massachusetts Press 1996.

Sinclair, May. "The Novels of Dorothy Richardson." In *The Gender of Modernism*, ed. Bonnie Kime Scott, 442–8. Bloomington: Indiana University Press 1990.

Smart, Elizabeth. *The Assumption of the Rogues & Rascals.* Hammersmith: Paladin–Harper Collins 1991.

– *Autobiographies.* Ed. Christina Burridge. Vancouver: William Hoffer/Tanks 1987.

– *By Grand Central Station I Sat Down and Wept.* Ottawa: Deneau Publishers 1981.

– "Fact and Emotional Truth." In *In Their Words: Interviews with Fourteen Canadian Writers*, by Bruce Meyer and Brian O'Riordan, 185–96. Toronto: Anansi 1984.

– *In the Meantime.* Ed. Alice Van Wart. Ottawa: Deneau Publishers 1984.

– *Juvenilia: Early Writings of Elizabeth Smart.* Ed. Alice Van Wart. Toronto: The Coach House Press 1987.

– *Necessary Secrets: The Journals of Elizabeth Smart.* Ed. Alice Van Wart. Toronto: Deneau Publishers 1986.

– *On the Side of the Angels: The Second Volume of the Journals of Elizabeth Smart.* Ed. Alice Van Wart. Hammersmith: HarperCollins 1994.

– Review of *The Journals of Anaïs Nin, 1931–1934. Queen*, 6 July 1966, 17.

Smith, Sidonie. "The Impact of Critical Theory on the Study of Autobiography: Marginality, Gender, and Autobiographical Practice." *A/B: Auto/Biography Studies* 3 (1987): 1–12.

– *A Poetics of Women's Autobiography: Marginality and the Fictions of Self-Representation.* Bloomington: Indiana University Press 1987.

Spacks, Patricia Meyer. *Imagining a Self: Autobiography and Novel in Eighteenth-Century England.* Cambridge: Harvard University Press 1976.

- "Reflecting Women." *Yale Review* 63 (1973): 26–42.
- "Selves in Hiding." In *Women's Autobiography: Essays in Criticism*, ed. Estelle C. Jelinek, 112–32. Bloomington: Indiana University Press 1980.

Spalding, P.A. *Self-Harvest: A Study of Diaries and the Diarist*. London: Independent Press Ltd. 1949.

Spencer, Jane. *The Rise of the Woman Novelist: From Aphra Behn to Jane Austen*. Oxford: Basil Blackwell 1986.

Spender, Dale. *Mothers of the Novel*. London: Pandora Press 1986.

Spengemann, William. *The Forms of Autobiography: Episodes in the History of the Literary Genre*. New Haven: Yale University Press 1980.

Stanton, Domna C., ed. *The Female Autograph*. New York: New York Literary Forum 1984.

Starobinski, Jeane. "The Style of Autobiography." In *Autobiography: Essays Theoretical and Critical*, ed. James Olney, 73–83. Princeton: Princeton University Press 1980.

Sullivan, Rosemary. *By Heart: Elizabeth Smart: A Life*. Toronto: Viking–Penguin Books Canada Ltd. 1991.

Thomas, Audrey. Rev. of *Necessary Secrets*, by Elizabeth Smart. *Books in Canada*, April 1987, 17.

Van Gunsteren, Julia. *Katherine Mansfield and Literary Impressionism*. Amsterdam: Rodopi 1990.

Van Wart, Alice. "'Life Out of Art': Elizabeth Smart's Early Journals." In *Essays on Life Writing*, ed. Marlene Kadar, 21–7. Toronto: University of Toronto Press 1992.
- "Preface." In *Juvenilia: Early Writings of Elizabeth Smart*, ed. Alice Van Wart, 7–8. Toronto: The Coach House Press 1987.

Waugh, Patricia. *Feminine Fictions: Revisiting the Postmodern*. London: Routledge 1989.

White, Antonia. "Antonia White." In *Born Catholics*, ed. F.J. Sheed, 72–89. New York: Sheed and Ward 1954.
- *Antonia White Diaries*. Ed. Susan Chitty. 2 vols. London: Constable and Company 1991–92.
- *As Once in May: The Early Autobiography*. Ed. Susan Chitty. London: Virago Press 1991.
- *Beyond the Glass*. London: Virago Press 1979.
- *Frost in May*. Toronto: Lester & Orpen Dennys 1981.
- *The Hound and the Falcon: The Story of a Reconversion to the Catholic Faith*. London: Virago Press 1980.
- *The Lost Traveller*. London: Virago Press 1979.
- *The Sugar House*. London: Virago Press 1979.

Wilde, Oscar. *The Portable Oscar Wilde*. Ed. Richard Aldington and Stanley Weintraub. New York: Penguin 1981.

Woolf, Virginia. "The Diary of a Lady in Waiting." In *The Essays of Virginia Woolf*, ed. Andrew McNeillie, 1: 195–200. London: Hogarth Press 1986.

– *The Diary of Virginia Woolf*. Edited by Anne Olivier Bell. 5 vols. Harmondsworth: Penguin, 1977–84. Vols. 2, 4, and 5 edited with the assistance of Andrew McNeillie.

– "Dorothy Wordsworth." In *The Common Reader*, 2: 164–72. London: Hogarth Press 1932.

– "Emerson's *Journals*." In *The Essays of Virginia Woolf*, ed. Andrew McNeillie, 1: 335–340. London: Hogarth Press 1986.

– *The Flight of the Mind: The Letters of Virginia Woolf*. Vol. 1, 1888–1912. Ed. Nigel Nicolson. London: Hogarth Press 1975.

– "Genius: R.B. Haydon." In *The Moment and Other Essays*, 150–5. London: Hogarth Press 1947.

– "James Woodforde." In *The Common Reader*, 2:93–100. London: Hogarth Press 1932.

– "John Evelyn." In *The Essays of Virginia Woolf*, ed. Andrew McNeillie, 3: 259–68. London: Hogarth Press 1988.

– "The Journal of Elizabeth Lady Holland." In *The Essays of Virginia Woolf*, ed. Andrew McNeillie, 1:230–9. London: Hogarth Press 1986.

– "The Journal of Mistress Joan Martyn." *Twentieth Century Literature* 25 (1979): 240–69.

– "The Leaning Tower." In *The Moment and Other Essays*, 105–25. London: Hogarth Press 1947.

– "The Legacy." In *The Complete Shorter Fiction of Virginia Woolf*, ed. Susan Dick, 281–7. London: Hogarth Press 1985.

– "Leslie Stephen." In *The Captain's Death Bed and Other Essays*, 69–75. New York: Harcourt Brace Jovanovich 1950.

– "Letters and Journals of Anne Chalmers." In *The Essays of Virginia Woolf*, ed. Andrew McNeillie, 3: 398–9. London: Hogarth Press 1988.

– "Life and the Novelist." In *Collected Essays by Virginia Woolf*, 2: 131–6. London: Hogarth Press 1966.

– "Mr. Bennett and Mrs. Brown." In *The Captain's Death Bed and Other Essays*, 94–119. New York: Harcourt Brace Jovanovich 1950.

– *Mrs Dalloway*. London: Grafton Books 1976.

– "Modern Fiction." In *The Common Reader*, 1: 184–95. London: Hogarth Press 1948.

– "The Moment: Summer's Night." In *The Moment and Other Essays*, 9–13. London: Hogarth Press 1947.

– *Moments of Being*. Ed. Jeanne Schulkind. San Diego: Harcourt Brace & Co 1985.

– "Montaigne." In *The Common Reader*, 1: 84–97. London: Hogarth Press 1948.

– "The New Biography." In *The Essays of Virginia Woolf*, ed. Andrew McNeillie, 4: 473–9. London: Hogarth Press 1994.
– "Old Bloomsbury." In *Moments of Being*, ed. Jeanne Schulkind, 179–201. San Diego: Harcourt Brace 1985.
– *Orlando*. Ed. Rachel Bowlby. Oxford: Oxford University Press 1992.
– "Papers on Pepys." In *The Essays of Virginia Woolf*, ed. Andrew McNeillie, 2: 233–8. London: Hogarth Press 1987.
– *A Passionate Apprentice: The Early Journals of Virginia Woolf, 1897–1909*. Ed. Mitchell A. Leaska. Toronto: Lester & Orpen Dennys 1990.
– "Personalities." In *Collected Essays by Virginia Woolf*, 2: 273–7. London: Hogarth Press 1966.
– "Professions for Women." In *Collected Essays by Virginia Woolf*, 2: 284–9. London: Hogarth Press 1966.
– *The Question of Things Happening: The Letters of Virginia Woolf*, Vol. 2, 1912–22. Ed. Nigel Nicolson. London: Hogarth Press 1976.
– "Rambling Round Evelyn." In *The Common Reader*, 1: 110–20. London: Hogarth Press 1948.
– "Reminiscences." In *Moments of Being*, ed. Jeanne Schulkind, 25–59. San Diego: Harcourt Brace 1985.
– "Romance and the Heart." In *The Essays of Virginia Woolf*, ed. Andrew McNeillie, 3: 365–8. London: Hogarth Press 1988.
– *A Room of One's Own*. London: Granada Publishing Ltd. 1977.
– "A Sketch of the Past." In *Moments of Being*, ed. Jeanne Schulkind, 61–159. San Diego: Harcourt Brace 1985.
– "A Terribly Sensitive Mind." Collected Essays by Virginia Woolf, Vol. 1, 356–8. London: Hogarth Press 1966.
– *Three Guineas*. In *A Room of One's Own and Three Guineas*, ed. Michèle Barrett, 115–334. London: Chatto & Windus 1984.
– *To the Lighthouse*. Ed. Margaret Drabble. Oxford: Oxford University Press 1992.
– "22 Hyde Park Gate." In *Moments of Being*, ed. Jeanne Schulkind, 162–77. San Diego: Harcourt Brace & Co 1985.
– *The Waves*. London: Grafton Books 1977.
– "Women and Fiction." In *Collected Essays by Virginia Woolf*, 2: 141–8. London: Hogarth Press 1966.

Index

Abbott, H. Porter, 97, 113–14
Adams, Timothy Dow, 39, 286
Agate, James, 240, 352, 353
Aitken, James, 23
Allendy, René, 317, 321
allusion, 9. *See also* Smart
Amiel, Henri Frédéric, 305, 352
"angel in the house," 55, 74, 84, 199, 222. *See also* Woolf
Artaud, Antonin, 322–8; "Theatre and the Plague," 323–4; "The Theatre of Cruelty, First Manifesto," 322–3, 330, 331, 332
Auden, W.H., 243
Augustine, St, 40
Austen, Jane, 54, 57
autobiography: critical evaluation of, 29–36, 62–4, 71; development of, 15–16, 17, 53; and fiction, 7, 13, 31, 38–9, 41, 86–8; and gender, 40, 47, 53, 58–9, 62;

and modernism, 71, 76; "proper," 4, 15, 28–30; and truth, 39; women's, 40, 46–7, 53, 58–9, 61–4, 69. *See also* diary
"autogynography," 63

Bacon, Francis, 18; "Of Travel," 18, 236
Bailey, Louise, 37
Bair, Deirdre, 9, 11, 12, 84, 283, 305, 319–20, 321
Barbellion (Bruce Frederick Cummings), 25, 174, 175, 352
Barker, George, 262–3, 347, 349–50. *See also* Smart
Barker, Jessica, 264, 266, 271
Barnacle, Nora, 213, 218
Barnes, Djuna, 6, 7, 94, 146, 190; *Ladies Almanack*, 6; *Nightwood*, 83, 88
Barthes, Roland, 35–6, 38, 41–2, 343–4
Bashkirtseva, Mariia, 24–5; *The Journal of*

Marie Bashkirtseff, 24–5, 81, 305, 306, 352
Bell, Anne Olivier, 35, 49, 97
Bell, Clive, 102
Bell, Deborah, 46
Bell, Quentin, 97
Bell, Vanessa Stephen, 102, 110, 113
Bennett, Arnold, 132, 137, 240
Benstock, Shari: and autobiography, 39; and exile, 72, 75, 159; and modernist principles, 76, 96, 152; and sexualized writing, 93, 259, 313, 317; and Gertrude Stein, 6, 306, 341; and *Women of the Left Bank*, 74
Berman, Emanuel, 180
biography, 16, 17, 36
Birrells, the, 121
Blake, Kathleen, 10
Blake, William, 237, 242
Blind, Mathilde, 24–5
Blodgett, Harriet: and diary aesthetics, 37; and diary as female form, 5,

46, 53, 147–8, 354; and
diary "proper," 20; and
diary vs. autobiography,
33; and egoism, 65,
113, 114, 136; and eti-
quette books, 51; and
Virginia Woolf, 153
Bloom, Lynn Z., 5, 32, 40
Boswell, James, 23, 47,
109, 120–1, 164
Botting, Cecil (White's
father). *See* White
Boussinescq, Hélène, 305,
306
Bowen, Elizabeth, 215
Bowle, John, 21–2
Boxall, Nelly, 99, 133
Breton, André, 261, 322;
"Manifesto of Surreal-
ism," 261, 322
Brittain, Vera, 239–40;
Testament of Youth,
239–40
Brodzki, Bella, 64, 148,
178, 354
Broe, Mary Lynn: and
dreams, 328; and incest
narrative, 93–4, 143,
191–2, 198, 320, 325,
333; and women's
exiles, 72–3; and
Antonia White, 168,
177
Brontës, the, 57
Brown, Ivor, 240
Browning, Elizabeth
Barrett, 57; *Sonnets
from the Portuguese*, 57
Bruss, Elizabeth W., 31
Bunkers, Suzanne, 7,
26–7, 37
Burney, Fanny, 21, 23–4,
27, 34, 45, 54, 109;
Evelina, 24
Bury, Lady Charlotte, 110
Bury, Elizabeth, 46
Buss, Helen M., 37, 67,
68
Byron, Lord, 21, 23, 26,
108

canon, literary; and

diaries, 10, 47, 68;
establishment of, 50;
and male writers, 53–4,
72, 76, 77, 160;
women's position in,
9–10, 52, 53–4,
57–8, 72, 77–8, 94–6,
160
Carlyle, Jane, 49
Carlyle, Thomas, 49
Carroll, Dr Dennis, 190,
196, 209
Cavendish, Margaret, 49
centre (position). *See*
women
Chalmers, Anne, 110
Chitty, Susan, 165–6, 169,
174, 191, 347, 350
Chodorow, Nancy, 62–3,
68, 69, 129, 148, 202
Clairouin, Denise, 338,
339
class. *See* gender
Coleman, Emily, 77, 263,
347
conduct books. *See* eti-
quette books
Conrad, Joseph, 124–5;
Heart of Darkness, 147;
"Preface" in *The Nigger
of the "Narcissus,"* 124
Culley, Margo, 50–1, 61,
82, 89

de Bezer, Benedicta, 170,
216–17, 219
Defoe, Daniel, 17, 233;
Moll Flanders, 17, 31;
Robinson Crusoe, 17,
31, 233
de Guérin, Eugénie, 305
De Man, Paul, 41, 66
DeSalvo, Louise A., 141–2
diary: as art/literature, 4,
7, 24, 36, 37, 68, 110;
and audience, 18–20,
24, 25, 26–7, 27–8;
as/vs. autobiography, 4,
13, 29–39, 41; censor-
ship in, 6; as collective
activity, 26–7;
critical/historical neglect

of (men's and/or
women's), 4, 47–8,
50–3, 98; definitions of,
14–15, 29, 43–4, 57;
and detail, 69, 81; and
editing, 35, 49–50; and
essay, 16; as female
form, 5, 45–7, 50–3, 57,
61, 67, 69–70, 77, 78,
85, 354; and
fiction/novel, 13, 17,
26, 27, 31, 38, 56,
82–4, 90–3; influences
on, 25–6; and mod-
ernism, 56, 65, 68–70,
80–4, 82–4, 88, 89,
90–6; motivations for
keeping, 52–3, 65–7;
and narrative, 30, 32,
33, 36–8, 39–40, 41,
58–60; non-professional
writers of, 37–8; origins
and development of
genre, 16–20, 46–7; and
posterity, 27; private vs.
public, 7, 18–25, 27–8;
professional writers of,
5; proper, 20, 46; and
psychoanalysis, 89–92;
publication of, 7, 20–5;
pure vs. false, 4, 22–3,
24; and role-playing,
66; and selfhood, 42–3,
91–3; and sexuality, 94;
structure of, 35, 36,
69–70, 91; as subversive
(literary) space, 6, 7, 46,
65–7, 76, 94–6; and
taboo themes, 6, 94–6;
and time, 33–4, 90–1;
tradition of, 25–7; and
truth-telling, 13, 33, 39;
women's vs. men's, 4, 6,
40, 47–52, 57; and
work ethic, 65–6. *See
also* Nin; Smart; White;
women; Woolf
Dickinson, Emily, 105,
136
Dobbs, Brian, 16, 21, 23,
50
Donne, John, 242